DEVELOPMENT FROM WITHIN

DEVELOPMENT FROM WITHIN

Toward a Neostructuralist Approach for Latin America

edited by
Osvaldo Sunkel

Lynne Rienner Publishers • Boulder & London

Published in the United States of America in 1993 by
Lynne Rienner Publishers, Inc.
1800 30th Street, Boulder, Colorado 80301

and in the United Kingdom by
Lynne Rienner Publishers, Inc.
3 Henrietta Street, Covent Garden, London WC2E 8LU

Library of Congress Cataloging-in-Publication Data
Development from within : toward a neostructuralist approach for Latin
    America / editor, Osvaldo Sunkel.
        Includes bibliographical references and index.
        ISBN 1-55587-326-X (alk. paper)
        1. Latin America—Economic policy. 2. Latin America—Economic
conditions—1945– .   . Sunkel, Osvaldo.
HC125.D488   1992
338.98—dc20   92-23922
                                                            CIP

British Cataloguing in Publication Data
A Cataloguing in Publication record for this book
is available from the British Library.

Printed and bound in the United States of America

The paper used in this publication meets the requirements
of the American National Standard for Permanence of
Paper for Printed Library Materials Z39.48-1984.

Contents

Tables and Figures

Tables

Figures

Acknowledgments

This book is the outcome of a project generously funded by the International Development Research Centre of Canada. Its undertaking owes much to the initial inspiration, patience, and constant support of Paz Buttedahl, Fernando Chaparro, and Benjamín Alvarez, officials of that institution. The Economic Commission for Latin America and the Caribbean (ECLAC) facilitated the participation of several of its economists and its coordinator, for which we are very grateful. The entire staff at the Corporación de Investigaciones para el Desarrollo (CINDE) effectively cooperated in this undertaking, particularly Ximena Moreno, who kindly and efficiently completed many secretarial and administrative tasks. Each project participant received ample comment and criticism from the others, for which we are mutually grateful.

Gustavo Zuleta deserves special mention for his efficient participation in preparing this book—commenting on, revising, and coordinating all texts and preparing the final manuscript, particularly the introduction.

To all these persons and institutions we extend our collective appreciation and my personal thanks in particular.

Osvaldo Sunkel

Introduction: In Search of Development Lost

Osvaldo Sunkel

This book is the outcome of a collective research project. Its original objective was to prepare a series of monographs on important topics on the economic development of Latin America for use as university teaching material in the respective subjects. Its aim was also to encourage curricular reforms in economics departments, to generate more appropriate and relevant research hypotheses, to review study programs, and to foster interdisciplinary activities. The underlying purpose was to revive academic interest in economic development, a discipline shelved and excluded from conventional economics departments and research in the last two decades.

Over the course of the project, and as a result of the active interchange between participants, the set of monographs became increasingly ordered and integrated around a common conceptual framework and an outline shared to a large extent by all of us. Thus, in relation to the order of presentation, each chapter begins with a review of the structuralist theories in vogue during the 1950s in the sector or subject analyzed. These theories are then compared to the actual development undergone in the 1960s and 1970s, with highlights of their successes and failures. A third section deals with the impact of the crisis of the 1980s on each of the subjects or sectors. In this context, reference is made to the renovation of structuralist thinking and its interpretation of the causes and consequences of the economic crisis. Finally, general guidelines and more specific proposals are formulated for overcoming the crisis and for reembarking upon the path of development.

Thus, the chapters gradually converged to form a coherent structure, both in background and form, and it became obvious that they should be organized into a book. The main topic is economic development in Latin America during the period 1950–1990, with a critical consideration of the strategies followed, a review of the development process and the debt crises, and the principal guidelines for a renewed development strategy from within, as compared to the previous inward-looking and current outward-looking development strategies.

This strategic option represents a Latin American attempt at formulating an alternative to neoliberalism. It is based on a critical review of the contributions of the traditional structuralism of the 1950s and 1960s and the neostructuralism of the 1980s. Thus, this book represents an effort to systematically combine structuralism and neostructuralism in an attempt to contribute to the recovery and updating of Latin American economic thinking in order to generate new options for dealing from a developmental perspective with the economic crisis that is causing such concern in all countries of the region.

The approach and proposals contained in this book are novel in some respects with regard to the prevailing neoclassical view, traditional structuralism, and early neostructuralism. It is characterized by a medium and long term historical and structural approach, seeking, however, to systematically establish the vital relation between this perspective and the short term economic situation. This contrasts with neoclassical and early neostructuralist approaches, which gave almost exclusive priority to balancing short term economic flows, markets, and prices. Likewise, it differs from the structuralist school, which tended to neglect these aspects.

On the other hand, particular importance is given to the development potential—capital, labor, natural resources, and technology—as a significant accumulation of productive resources acquired by Latin America over the postwar period. Despite all their shortcomings, they constitute a substantially broadened and enriched base for reembarking upon growth and development. Once again, the emphasis on the region's productive resources and potential differs from the unilateral concern of neoliberalism and neostructuralism with the short term equilibrium of flows and markets. But it also differs from traditional structuralism, which considered the international context as determining national policies and strategies. This new approach however, starts with a country's own potential, based on the premise that each country can and should pursue new forms of insertion into a difficult but not impenetrable international context.

It is vital to continue this task in the various directions that appear necessary in light of the work undertaken. Specifically, it is essential to carry out historical and comparative studies of Latin American development in recent decades. For the first time there is a wealth of distinctively Latin American experience. Yet very little comparative research has been done on it or learning gained from it.

A fundamental conclusion of the project is the imperative need for in-depth and unbiased research on the role of the state. This agent, which was very active and efficient in promoting development, now finds itself in a deep crisis. It is faced with sweeping restructuring and transformation to deal with the current situation of our countries and their future prospects. In particular, an in-depth examination of social policies is required. This subject was only partially dealt with in the project. Also, given the context

in which worsening social problems and extremely restricted financial resources are foreseen, the subjects of efficacy and efficiency of overall expenditures and social policies are critically raised, as is the basic issue of
tax and financial reform of the public sector.

In short, the main purpose of this book is to contribute to the rekindling of interest by economists in the subject of economic development.
This concern, predominant in the early postwar decades, has been overlooked to the point of neglect over the last twenty years. A concerned
search now emerges for answers to the generalized development crisis that
affects virtually all countries of the region to a greater or lesser extent.
However, it is not easy to improvise new development strategies and
policies.

Latin America possesses a rich tradition of autonomous and independent thinking on the subject. This must be regained, reviewed, renewed,
and applied to current issues, so as to encourage research, debate, and the
formulation of alternative strategies and policies. This is now a vital concern at all levels of intellectual activity.

Economic thinking on development was vigorous and creative during
the 1950s, particularly in our region. It was here that the concepts of center-
periphery and structural heterogeneity and the structuralist and dependence
approaches arose. But since the early 1970s, this school of thought has lost
vitality and force, undergoing severe criticism from both the Marxist and
neoliberal perspectives. The newer generations of economists have been
increasingly and overwhelmingly trained in the so-called neoclassical synthesis. This paradigm completely dominates the teaching of economics in
the United States and everywhere. This orientation, particularly in its most
ideologized version, neoliberalism, expunged the teaching of economic development and economic development research from economics departments of the most prestigious universities, causing its advancement to shift
to specialized institutes and to political science, sociology, and other social
science departments.

The foremost characteristic of the neoclassical paradigm is its focus
on the short term micro- and macroeconomic balances of the main economic agents in the various markets, assuming technology, population,
natural resources and the environment, values, cultural behavior patterns,
power structures, international relations, institutions, and social relations
to be constant. But these are precisely the principal medium and long term
variables of economic and social development. The most recent generation
of economists trained in the conventional paradigm consequently have little knowledge and interest in development theories, experiences, strategies, and policies. Our younger Latin American colleagues lack adequate
knowledge of the thinking generated in the region, by the region, and for
the region during the postwar period, except in caricatured, biased, and
one-sided versions taken out of their historical context.

However, in Latin America there is an accumulated store of knowledge, experience, and research, including outstanding contributions by many individuals and public and private institutions that have significant influence and are well known in social science circles throughout the world. This knowledge is ignored by younger economists, and represents a loss of independent, valuable, and enriching cultural heritage. This has undoubtedly contributed to the absence of adequate and creative responses on the part of these economists to the demands of Latin American society in its current crisis.

The recovery, critical review, and renovation of the intellectual tradition of the Latin American structural approach to development is clearly valuable and important today for researchers, professors, students, public officials, and politicians. This is particularly true and urgent in light of the profound economic, social, and financial crises the region is suffering from, and in light of the frequent failures, the inordinate social costs of adjustment programs, and the need for a deep restructuring and reorienting of socioeconomic processes, strategies, and policies, with a view to achieving sustainable long term development. Greater understanding is needed of the historical, institutional, and structural background and changing international context of the current crisis, its evolution, prospects, and possible solutions. In-depth knowledge of the thinking, practices, and experiences of postwar development would substantially improve economists' grasp of the true circumstances and requirements of contemporary Latin American economies and societies. It would broaden and enrich their conceptual framework, suggest new methodological approaches, facilitate interdisciplinary work that is so important, and permit placing national phenomena in their proper historical and international perspective. It would also generally increase the capacity for overcoming ideological and narrow technocratic approaches.

This book represents genuine Latin American intellectual cooperation. The authors hope to contribute to a better understanding of the problems and perspectives that set us apart, as well as to an understanding of the vast common wealth that binds us all.

1

Toward a Neostructuralist Synthesis

Joseph Ramos and Osvaldo Sunkel

Latin America has been suffering a major economic and financial crisis, its worst since the Great Depression of the 1930s. Throughout the 1980s, per capita income in the region fell well below the levels of the late 1970s, a trend that has not yet been reversed in most countries, with devastating social effects and unpredictable political consequences. Because of this bleak panorama, the 1980s have been depicted as the "lost decade" for Latin American development. The crisis, however, is not confined to economic and social issues: there is also a crisis of ideas. Both the development strategy prevailing since the 1930s—inward-oriented industrialization—and the active and prominent role of the state are undergoing sharp scrutiny.

Hence, the only coherent and comprehensive approach currently available to cope with the crisis is apparently to be found in the neoconservative adjustment and restructuring programs promoted and imposed by private and public international financial organizations, such as the International Monetary Fund (IMF), the World Bank, the transnational banking system, and the governments of developed countries. On the basis of a one-sided reading of the experience of the newly industrialized countries (NICs) of Asia, the neoconservative program dogmatically proposes a series of economic policies, the most important of which include: price liberalization and the deregulation of markets; virtual free trade and the unrestricted movement of international capital; private sector dominance with a subsidiary role for the state; an overriding emphasis on monetary policy with a virtual neglect of other short term macroeconomic policy instruments; and a disregard for the structural, institutional, and political factors that, to a large extent, are inherent to the nature and functioning of underdeveloped economies.

This neoconservative resurgence has challenged deeply rooted convictions and served as a much needed reminder of the virtues of the market, the price system, private initiative, fiscal discipline, and an outward-oriented development strategy. Nevertheless, in its eagerness to banish the structuralist approach prevailing in the region since World War II, neoconservatism has lapsed into the same dogmatic, ideological, and Manichaean temptation it criticized in structuralism, but now of opposite sign. Thus, it sees in the state the source of all our wrongs while it holds an idealized view of the market totally divorced from reality.

For did not overindebtedness reach extreme proportions precisely in those countries of the region that pursued a neoconservative strategy before the onset of the crisis, and was that overindebtedness not incurred by the very private sector supposedly incapable of economic miscalculation? Was not excessive foreign borrowing fostered precisely by the financial liberalization and deregulation proposed by neoconservatism? Were not especially severe recessions brought about in these countries by the types of adjustment programs pursued—for example, in Chile, where output fell 14 percent in 1982, by far the region's worst recession? Should this massive setback be viewed as the sign of a successful adjustment or rather as the undue costs of economic policies based on an unwarranted and prolonged faith in the merits of "automatic adjustment" with fixed exchange rates?

Furthermore, it is certainly true that inflation cannot be controlled without fiscal discipline. But is that all there is to it or is a complementary effort not needed—through price and incomes policies—to guide the expectations of private agents in order to reduce inflation without causing a major recession (as in the case of Mexico in 1988 and Costa Rica in 1982–1983), and thus prevent a drastic drop in production (as occurred in Chile in 1974–1975)? As for the Asian NICs, their growth has certainly been impressive. But to what extent is this primarily due to their outward-orientation (Hong Kong) or rather to the state's selective, but active promotion of efforts (as was the case in South Korea)?

In short, the region's crisis is serious enough without adding to it a narrow-minded and simplistic view of reality and by taking easy refuge in dogmatic stances. On the contrary, because the region faces enormous challenges and the scarcity of resources is greater than ever, an innovative and renovated approach is required. Thus, it becomes imperative again to analyze and understand the real nature and full complexity of economic issues to adequately respond to the region's crisis and reestablish the basis for solid and sustained growth for all in a democratic polity.

This book is an effort to respond to this challenge. It is based on experiences and ideas under discussion in the region for quite some time. It draws primarily, albeit not exclusively, on a school of thought that has been emerging in the past ten years—neostructuralism—and which, in turn, is rooted in the structuralist theory of the past. Initially, neostructuralism emerged as a theoretical alternative to orthodox neoconservative adjustment programs. Its aim was to stabilize and adjust with minimal recession and less regressive distributive effects, materializing in the heterodox stabilization and adjustment programs of the 1980s (Lustig 1988a). But it shared with neoconservatism a concern largely limited to the short term. However, as adjustment was prolonged and the crisis persisted, neostructuralism began to draw on the positive heritage of a more specifically Latin American approach to development: post–World War II structuralism.

Thus, neostructuralism shares the basic structuralist stance that the sources of Latin America's underdevelopment are not to be found primarily in policy-induced distortions in relative prices (of which, to be sure, there are many), but rather are rooted in endogenous structural factors. According to Rosales (1988a), tangible proof of this can be found in three crucial aspects of Latin America's economy in the late 1980s: (1) an international specialization in products lacking dynamic potential; (2) the prevalence of an uncoordinated, vulnerable, and highly heterogeneous production pattern that tends to concentrate technical progress and is incapable of fully and productively absorbing new entrants into the labor force; and (3) the persistence of a growth pattern that excludes the vast majority from the fruits of progress, evidencing the system's inability to lower poverty significantly.

Consequently, more than marginal adjustments on the transformation curve, reflecting a concern solely for the efficient allocation of resources, what is needed is to move the economy toward a full use of its production possibilities, and subsequently induce a continuing and expansive shift in those possibilities. Growth and the optimal dynamic allocation of resources requires more than free prices. The market needs as its complement the active and dynamic support of the state to provide not simply its classical functions (public goods, macroeconomic balances, equity) but also—within the limits of its administrative capacity—vigorously to: (1) promote or simulate missing markets (long term capital markets and futures markets in foreign exchange); (2) strengthen incomplete markets (the market for technology); (3) eliminate or correct structural distortions (the heterogeneity of the production structure, the concentration of property, the segmentation of the capital and labor markets); and (4) eradicate or compensate the most significant market imperfections arising from economies of scale, externalities, and learning (arising from technology or trade), among others.

Despite their close affinity, neostructuralism has also subjected key structuralist assumptions to critical examination, especially those pertaining to its excessive reliance on idealized state interventionism; its exaggerated pessimism with respect to export possibilities; and its insufficient recognition of the importance of timely and operational policies to deal with macroeconomic disequilibria, particularly its underestimation of the importance of monetary and financial aspects (Rosales 1988a). Thus, there is an explicit acknowledgment of the shortcomings in making recommendations based solely on long term considerations without paying attention to the short term effects of processes of structural change or to the problems that may arise during the transition (Lustig 1988a).

A Proposal for a Renovated Strategy: Development From Within

Such a link between short term and long term instruments has converted the recent and renovated proposal of "changing production patterns with equity" into the guiding principle for the process of recovery and consolidation of development in the region. This approach suggests concrete proposals to establish a productive structure that permits an increasingly fruitful participation of Latin America in international trade, expands the generation of productive employment, and reduces structural heterogeneity, thus improving income distribution and reducing the extreme poverty suffered by a large portion of Latin America's population (ECLAC 1990b).

This book is an effort to enrich and update this approach by focusing not only on the formulation of an overall and renovated strategy for development *from within* but also on the operational design of the essential macro-, micro-, and mezzoeconomic policies of a selective nature. Above all, in the spirit, terms, and guiding principles set forth by Prebisch in his early contributions (Prebisch 1950a; ECLA 1950), our aim is to respond to the challenge of transforming and modernizing the Latin American economies in a context of equitable and democratic growth.

In Chapter 2 ("From Inward-Looking Development to Development from Within" by Osvaldo Sunkel), this way of perceiving development essentially implies building on the process of industrialization as originally proposed by Prebisch: the creation of an endogenous mechanism of accumulation and generation of technical progress that would enable Latin America to develop its own capacity to grow dynamically and productively. Such a strategy is not oriented, a priori, in favor of import substitution, for that would eventually lead to a dead end. On the contrary, industrialization *from within* keeps open the option of orienting development toward the specific domestic and foreign markets that are considered to have priority in a long term strategy, and in which our countries already possess or may develop levels of excellence to ensure their solid insertion into the world economy.

In other words, it is not demand and markets that are critical. The heart of development lies in the supply side: quality, flexibility, the efficient combination and utilization of productive resources, the adoption of technological developments, an innovative spirit, creativity, the capacity for organization and social discipline, private and public austerity, an emphasis on savings, and the development of skills to compete internationally. In short, independent efforts undertaken *from within* to achieve self-sustained development.

Crucial for a transition to such a new strategy is funding to reform and modernize our economies, induce a recovery, and surmount the traumatic effects of the adjustment-induced recessions. In Chapter 2 Sunkel outlines a proposal for overcoming the financial obstacles. In essence, he recommends that Latin America negotiate at least a partial suspension of the enormous transfer of resources associated with debt servicing in order to raise domestic savings. Such freed resources would be channeled to a special fund for economic restructuring and social development to address the most urgent social problems and to invest in the efficient production of tradables.

Another key element in this strategy is its commitment to restore and maintain basic macroeconomic equilibria, which are a necessary though not sufficient condition for a sustained development process. Evidently, this modifies the original structuralist tolerance of inflation as the price to pay for growth—a tolerance understandable in the 1950s given the then not inordinate rates of inflation. But today's macroeconomic disequilibria exceed the limits of the tolerable, and clearly jeopardize sustainable development.

In Chapter 4 ("Macroeconomic Equilibria and Development"), Joseph Ramos argues that the magnitude of such disequilibria are due in part to inept policymaking, but above all to excess foreign borrowing and the inefficient use of such funds, both because of the failure of capital markets (international and domestic) and of the regulatory system.

Ramos believes that the reversal in the transfer of international resources and the problems in the domestic transfer between the public and the private sector are the underlying causes of the costly adjustment and stabilization processes. Hence his insistence that the restoration and maintenance of macroeconomic equilibria requires a reduction in the external transfer of resources for debt servicing. However, this measure by itself is insufficient unless it is accompanied by appropriate domestic policies. This requires retaking control of fiscal accounts, increasing fiscal revenues and not only decreasing expenditures to lower inflation, and guiding expectations via price and income policies to minimize the recessive risk of greater fiscal austerity. As for adjustment, the production of tradables, particularly that of exports, must be stimulated by especially strong "switching" policies in the initial years.

An essential goal behind this new "development agenda," is to attain equity and social justice. Nora Lustig points out in Chapter 3 ("Equity and Development") that given the restrictions imposed by the economic crisis, policies should focus on the relief and subsequent elimination of extreme poverty. Once the economy is established on a stable growth path, the longer term transformations proposed by traditional structuralist analysis to reduce inequalities can be put into effect.

In the search for social justice, Lustig suggests three areas for immediate and selective action by the state: (1) minimizing the impact of external shocks on the poorest and most vulnerable sectors of the population; (2) reducing the cost of labor relocation brought on by the structural reforms inherent to adjustment; and (3) once solid and sustained growth resumes, helping to eradicate poverty and reduce excessive concentration of income and wealth. For this it is imperative that economic policymakers reestablish fiscal control and thus regain credibility over groups whose resources are to be redistributed (including foreign entities and governments). Finally, Lustig argues the urgency of achieving a social consensus on the need to provide and allocate public resources to the fight against poverty.

The issue of a social pact and income distribution is also addressed by Víctor E. Tokman in Chapter 5 ("Labor Markets and Employment in Latin American Economic Thinking") from the perspective of the operation of labor markets and employment generation. According to Tokman, though modernization entails growing urbanization, it fails to generate sufficient industrial employment and the necessary and expected decreases in existing inequalities in productivity and income because of labor market segmentation. This results in the existence of a growing informal sector—particularly in urban areas—where employment is largely supply driven and relative immobility permits marked wage differentials.

In view of the large expansion of this sector as a result of the recent crisis and the vast concentration of the poor in this segment of the labor market, a strategy to cope with the informal sector is urgently needed. Furthermore, evidence to date suggests that few resources are required to promote activity in this sector. Still, given the external constraints on an expansive macroeconomic policy, only a selective policy to redress inequalities is financially viable. Two major approaches present themselves. Though not necessarily contradictory, they imply different emphases and policy options. The first, closer to the center-periphery model, addresses the structural factors determining the existence, persistence, and functioning of this sector. The second addresses institutional aspects and shifts the analytical focus to the prevailing legal system, thus largely inverting the causality from the structural to the juridical.

In Tokman's opinion, full and productive employment in Latin America cannot be assured by the proper operation of the labor market alone; this depends on the development process as a whole. The main task is to introduce changes and to persuade economic agents to act over and above their sectoral interests. Undoubtedly, this requires a new look toward the future because doubts as to current social pacts or consensuses cannot be settled by turning back nor by clinging to the present. The solution lies in regulating the systems through the use of adequate methods that, historically, operate above and beyond the currently prevailing institutionality.

Despite the importance of defining this strategic global framework, any attempt to give shape to a modern and relevant neostructuralist proposal must also succeed in (1) defining the agenda of truly pivotal problems and (2) drawing up operational proposals to address them. For this intellectual effort would be sterile if, instead of presenting concrete and constructive alternatives, it merely criticized orthodoxy (for example, by showing how reality departed from the assumptions of neoclassical theory and its model of perfect competition, or by exposing the limitations of its policy recommendations, as with IMF stabilization programs).

Precisely for this reason, to suggest the usefulness of the neostructuralist approach, the remaining chapters of the book are devoted to analyzing how a series of major economic problems can be profitably analyzed from the perspective of structures and institutions, not just prices, and what concrete proposals can be derived therefrom.

The Transformation and Modernization of Production

The industrialization strategy based on import substitution created a significant but underutilized industrial platform. This strategy rewarded production for the domestic market with tariffs and subsidies and penalized production oriented toward external markets with low exchange rates and artificially expensive inputs. This strategy exaggerated protection and prolonged it beyond reason. Thus, export possibilities were wasted, and the efficiency and discipline inherent to competition in foreign markets was lost. Furthermore, in countries with small domestic markets, important economies of scale were also sacrificed.

It is reasonable to presume, given the earlier bias of incentives strongly in favor of production for the domestic market, that, should incentives for generating foreign exchange via exports be equal to those for saving it via import substitution, exports would show the greatest response. Moreover, should any special additional incentives be required, these would be to penetrate external markets—the true "infant industry" of the future. Thus, the key instrument is no longer tariffs but export subsidies (or its equivalent) for pioneer firms that succeed in introducing new products and opening up new export markets. Similarly, by virtue of the process of import substitution itself, because imports consist almost entirely of intermediate inputs and capital goods, tariffs must be gradually reduced and rationalized in order to encourage exports and efficient import substitution. In addition, the production of transnational companies operating in the region must be given an outward orientation, thus taking advantage of their international marketing network; and export performance commitments must be negotiated in exchange for authorization to purchase inputs at current international prices. Therefore, a plan of selective interventions is proposed to acquire dynamic comparative advantages, for exporting is the next obvious phase for our now-existing industrial platform.

The international context is an important aspect to be considered in restructuring and modernizing production. For this reason, Winston Fritsch's contribution (Chapter 11, "The New International Setting: Challenges and Opportunities") updates structuralist analysis with respect to the elements of international dynamics that play a determining role in Latin American foreign economic policy options.

Fritsch argues that the interaction between structural factors—linked to the recent acceleration in the rate of development and nature of technological and organizational innovations in the center—and the expectations regarding institutional changes in economic blocs, coupled to the instability in international macroeconomic settings, has decisively modified the determinants of strategic decisions by governments and transnational companies. Undoubtedly, this reorganization of the international milieu has important effects—both positive and negative—in defining Latin America's role in the new international division of labor and, consequently, in an efficient redefinition of the region's long term development policies. Similarly, the explicit recognition of the region's heterogeneity, both of its productive structures and its patterns of participation in international trade flows, permit him to identify different national strategies as regards trade, industry, and foreign capital, which he characterizes as "orthodox," "selective," and "integrated."

All the chapters in this book concur in the need and desirability of restructuring production and raising exports. Indeed, these were long overdue, at least since the 1970s. Current domestic and international circumstances make the costs and efforts all the greater, as shown by the theoretical and empirical evidence on the deterioration in the terms of trade for the region included in Chapter 12 by José Antonio Ocampo ("Terms of Trade and Center-Periphery Relations"). Indeed, there is evidence that this trend might be affecting not only traditional exports but also the exporting countries themselves, thus encompassing exports of manufactured goods. Should this be the case, it will be imperative to consider a more fruitful insertion and specialization in the world economy and, consequently, to design industrial and trade policies for achieving competitiveness in the most dynamic areas of international trade.

According to Oscar Muñoz (Chapter 9, "The Process of Industrialization: Theories, Experiences, and Policies"), a new industrialization strategy is required to overcome the debt problem, stagnation, and inequality. Such a strategy must aim primarily at increasing Latin America's productivity and competitiveness so that it may become a part of the international process of modernization and productive transformation.

Muñoz holds that a neostructuralist frame of reference for industrial policy suggests the need for a better use of market signals, entrepreneurial spirit, and international competition. It is up to the state to create an institutional framework that brings out the creativity and dynamism of productive agents (entrepreneurs and workers) and induces their cooperation and coordination. The proposed institutional framework presumes complementary policies to overcome inequity, ensure macroeconomic stability, and provide the essential public goods required by productive activities (services, material and financial infrastructure, and facilities for technological mastery and development). Such a strategy would be flexible and generate specific sectoral options rather than be a simple technocratic directive imposed by the state. These options, therefore, would take full advantage of the information provided by domestic and foreign markets and of the trends in technology, institutions, and organizations.

Additionally, the new industrial strategy must overcome the false dilemma of putting off agricultural development. Adolfo Figueroa (Chapter 10, "Agricultural Development in Latin America") points out that the structural nature of the agrarian problems that confront us requires a two-pronged action by the state. Regarding macroeconomic policies, Figueroa stresses the significant role of the state in designing incentives to make full use of potential domestic demand while safeguarding macroeconomic stability. As for more sector-specific issues, in order to cope with the risks and uncertainties inherent to agriculture, Figueroa proposes farm price supports and price bands, technological research to help develop high-yield, pest-resistant crops capable of withstanding different climatic conditions, institutional innovations to establish and strengthen postharvest services, futures markets, crop insurance markets, and development of agro-industries. In addition, and still within the sectoral aspect, the author examines the possibility of the state's promoting the development of a rural financial market (a prominent example of a missing or incomplete and segmented market) in order to increase the supply of funds instead of subsidizing a privileged group of potential borrowers.

Figueroa also examines the development options available to traditional Latin American peasant agriculture. A concrete possibility has been opened up by current technological progress because the new techniques (for example, fertilizers and hybrid seeds) do not require large land holdings and, above all, are neutral with respect to scale of production. State support for such a program could take the form of providing needed finance for peasants. However, since the main constraint to the development of peasant agriculture is its lack of land, he proposes an agrarian reform for regions and countries in which rural property is still highly concentrated.

Lastly, all these proposals to restructure production and overcome the foreign exchange bottleneck must take into account the environmental impact of the reforms and on the reforms. For Nicolo Gligo (Chapter 7, "Environment and Natural Resources in Latin American Development"), this involves recognizing the structural roots of environmental problems so as to be able to design alternatives and policies suited for environmentally sustainable growth. Although natural resources are an asset for Latin American development, constant concern and public action are required to ensure the rational exploitation of the environment in order to preserve and even increase this potential for future generations. According to Gligo, this requires the involvement of the highest political spheres because the environment is a highly controversial issue that requires a profound adaptation of economic policies, both global and sectoral. In global terms the main actions must focus on policies concerning science and technology, institutional organization, and education, so as to prompt the incorporation of environmental issues into development strategies. Thus, the generation, adoption, and diffusion of technology should take into account environmental considerations aimed at reducing the ecological costs involved in the process of development.

Priority should also be given to establishing agencies to coordinate environmental actions, in sectoral and spatial aspects, while simultaneously encouraging environmentally sustainable and profitable forms of development through permanent economic activities (recycling, waste treatment, and energy-producing forests, for example). Work should also begin on developing environmental education policies to be implemented at all levels. In sectoral terms, it is necessary to promote development of the agricultural, forestry, and livestock sectors in accordance to the behavior and features of live ecosystems and the degree to which these have been built up by the human race. In this respect special attention should be given to finding a solution to the poverty afflicting peasants as, in many instances, poverty encourages overutilization of the environment.

Technology and Innovation

In the past the region followed a Keynesian growth strategy that secured demand and the market but overlooked productive efficiency. In fact, protection proved detrimental to innovation, giving rise to unproductive rent-seeking activities. What is needed, instead, is a Schumpeterian approach in which incentives encourage technological mastery and innovation and mobilize an increasing number of entrepreneurs.

According to Ennio Rodríguez (Chapter 8, "The Endogenization of Technological Change: A Development Challenge"), this requires a new approach to technological development—from within—supporting institutions devoted to development-oriented activities in science and technology. Rodríguez believes that one of the reasons why the countries of the periphery lag behind in the area of innovation may reside in an inappropriate institutional framework for technological change.

Firms must engage in a systematic and organized effort of research and development, and public policies must be designed to socialize some of the risks involved in the process. Also important in bridging the technological gap is the creation of a more sophisticated scientific and technological infrastructure, working closely with the productive sectors in long term priority areas. Success in this respect will enable the carrying out of original research and will therefore make it possible to acquire comparative advantages in strategic and dynamic export sectors.

Reinsertion into the international market with high technology products is no easy task. It requires public policies that, among other things, induce small- and medium-sized firms to participate in the process of modernization. This may be accomplished by establishing "subcontracting exchanges" and organizations to monitor quality control; by promoting innovation in the various economic sectors through technological training and the diffusion of innovations; and by providing funding for technological development in priority areas.

Lastly, Rodríguez points out that in order to obtain the maximum benefits from the third technological revolution, profound changes in the social organization of production are required. The path to development entails achieving consensus between the public and private sectors, between workers' organizations and associations of entrepreneurs, and among firms in the same sector, in order to guarantee the flexible adaptation to a new—and constantly changing—technological drive.

Capital Formation and Capacity Utilization

According to Ricardo Ffrench-Davis (Chapter 6, "Capital Formation and the Macroeconomic Framework: A Neostructuralist Approach"), a low rate of capital formation had been one of the distinctive features of Latin American economies in the 1980s. This had been compounded by a low rate of capacity utilization with the corresponding decline in ex-post productivity because both factors, and their evident interrelations, play a decisive role in the adoption of technological innovations and business decisionmaking.

It is a well-known fact that both the volume and quality of investment are affected by the prevailing macroeconomic environment. By placing the emphasis on trade balances and stabilization, Latin America has neglected specific incentives for capital formation and failed adequately to manage aggregate demand. This—together with the crisis—accounts for the significant reduction in the formation of new capital and in the under-utilization of installed capacity over the course of the decade.

Ffrench-Davis argues that in essence neostructuralism aims to harmonize capital movements, exchange rates, trade policies, and interest rates so as to generate a favorable macroeconomic framework for capital formation and the acquisition of comparative advantages, and thus make full use of—and enhance—existing opportunities for investment and innovation. Moreover, he suggests direct public policies to develop comparative advantages and complement private investment initiatives.

Drawing on the lessons from the experience of the 1980s, Ffrench-Davis concludes his chapter with a reflection on the challenge of achieving a more vigorous and sustained form of development. To this end, he lays out a series of tasks ahead, such as: restoring the macroeconomic equilibria needed for development; reducing the outward transfer of resources to increase funding for productive investment—a recurring theme in this book; and reforming the institutional and regulatory framework of the financial system. This would strengthen the long term capital market, simplify access to all forms and sizes of entrepreneurial organization, increase the availability of technology and savings, and place the financial system at the service of productive development by reducing speculation and risk, thus fostering the acquisition of new and dynamic comparative advantages in the production of exportables.

Renovating the State

The state is being subjected to an overload of demands coupled with weakened financing. At the same time, it has had serious difficulties in fulfilling some of its basic economic functions, such as safeguarding macroeconomic equilibria, promoting equity, and avoiding bottlenecks in foreign exchange, savings, and investment. José Manuel Salazar-Xirinachs (Chapter 13, "The Role of the State and the Market in Economic Development") recognizes most of these shortcomings. Pragmatism and recent experience suggest to him the virtues of formulating a more consensual proposal on the new role of the state, encompassing traditional development thinking as well as less radical neoconservative viewpoints.

In the spirit of such convergence, the essential issue is not the size of the state but rather its management capacity and its ability to concert agents. The key economic roles or functions of the state could be defined as: setting forth a strategic view of the development process; harmonizing incentives and relative prices with the objectives of that strategy; and eliciting the commitment of all social and political sectors to that strategy through dialogue and concertation. According to Salazar-Xirinachs, a state that is organized efficiently around this central function—which could be defined as a "concerting" state—corresponds to Latin America's new stage of development, marked by a democratic renewal and the need to modify development strategies.

In view of these necessary renovations and redefinitions, he points out that the state must be strengthened in its classical functions (providing public goods, maintaining macroeconomic equilibria, furthering equity); its basic functions (essential infrastructure in transport and communications, health, housing, education); and its auxiliary functions (supporting the structural competitiveness of the economy by promoting or simulating missing markets, developing scientific and technological infrastructure, eliminating or compensating for market imperfections). The state is less needed today in its entrepreneurial and productive functions. The state must put its finances in order and consolidate its revenues through tax reforms.

As for its expenditures, there is an evident need to establish priorities, organize the public investment program, and reduce subsidies, except for those with an important redistributive impact. It is also important to raise the efficiency of state-owned enterprises by limiting their objectives (to production), by enhancing their competitiveness, by granting them greater financial and management autonomy, by allowing them to apply price policies similar to those of private sector companies, by using "social" prices only in limited or exceptional situations, by subcontracting and hiring out related services, and by privatizing nonstrategic productive enterprises. Because an efficient "promotional" state is absolutely essential for development from within, it is crucial to define an optimal intervention strategy. Among the multiple aspects to be included in such a strategy, the author singles out the following four points:

1. Due to the public sector's limited administrative resources, priorities for intervention should be established. The state cannot deal with all of the economy's countless distortions and should therefore intervene only in the most pressing ones.

2. The objectives of such intervention should be clear and understandable in order for these to be evaluated. These distortions should certainly be eliminated; it is less clear that they should be "compensated"; each compensation creates a new distortion for all remaining sectors. Hence, too many compensations may make it difficult to determine whether a sector is, or is not, a net beneficiary of economic policy. Beyond this point, interventions will be excessive, jeopardizing the possibility of evaluating projects and policies from a social point of view and, therefore, rendering efficient planning impossible.

3. Decentralization and depoliticization are crucial objectives because as more conflicts are solved by the political system (as opposed to the market) or by the central government (as opposed to regional or local

governments), a greater burden of social demands is placed on the central political level, thus overloading it and hampering its capacity to act effectively. Therefore, the decentralization and depoliticization of conflicts is an indirect, but effective, method for reducing the central government's excess load and thus improving its efficacy. Obviously, this rule does not apply to imperfections and conflicts that can not be adequately handled by the market or at a decentralized level.

4. Institutional counterbalances are needed to compensate for asymmetrical pressures in favor of further intervention. Because the benefits of interventions favor only a few (who therefore exert pressure) while the benefits of reducing interventions are diluted among many (who therefore exert less pressure), interventionism works in a single direction: toward more, rather than less, intervention. In view of this asymmetry, built-in mechanisms are required to act as counterbalances. For example, without such a counterweight, a policy of differential tariffs will naturally lead to constantly increasing differentials so that not only will differentials between tariffs widen but so too will the average tariff increase. Thus, if differential tariffs are to be established, it is important that the average tariff also be agreed upon, so that each time one tariff increases, another is lowered, thus creating the institutional counterbalance to compensate the otherwise natural upward trends.

Final Comments

In short, the general features of the strategy for development from within suggested in this book are as follows:

1. It recovers, in this new phase of global transformations and profound crisis in Latin America, the original and still relevant Latin American structuralist development thought concerned with promoting modernization, structural reform, social justice, productive transformation, and the diversification of the region's exports through industrialization and the adoption of technical progress.

2. It values the often forgotten efforts in this regard undertaken in Latin America after World War II. This allowed for unprecedented economic growth, a notable modernization process, and the accumulation of multiple resources—productive, human, natural, capital, institutional, and technological—that, despite all the deficiencies and the resulting need for correction, have enriched our stock of productive capacities well beyond what existed before this process.

3. Together with acknowledging the merits of these achievements, it also recognizes the deficiencies in the structuralist development policies applied during the 1950s and the 1960s. The book likewise critically

examines the neoconservative strategy that came to the fore in the 1970s and culminated in the adjustment and restructuring programs of the 1980s.

4. Development from within considers both the neoconservative paradigm and merely updated neostructuralist stabilization experiments to be inadequate for addressing the severe problems currently afflicting Latin America. Rather, the strategy aims at recovering the positive and valuable contributions made by structuralism and neostructuralism, merging them into a renovated neostructuralist synthesis, suited to the characteristics and demands of the present without incurring the errors of the past.

This task is made easier by the existing broad consensus on the urgency of reinserting the region into the international economy and of dynamically taking rapid steps to reduce poverty and inequalities, necessary conditions for the consolidation of democracy. Although the market plays a key role in achieving these goals, its failures and insufficiencies must not be overlooked, thus the insistence on the state's role in orienting an overall and long term strategy and in exercising selectivity in economic and social policymaking. Nevertheless, the effectiveness of the state itself is in question. Its reform is therefore indispensable, including the transfer of tasks that may be handled more efficiently by social organizations or by the private sector. A lean state can thus permit a more effective, flexible, responsible, and active role for the state in the central tasks proposed by this development strategy.

It goes without saying that this book could hardly be expected to put an end to the debate. Rather, it contributes to the discussion by making a renovated proposal rooted in our intellectual tradition but open to the universal experience of the human race. The severity of the crisis makes it especially imperative for individuals and social groups to subject their interests to those of the common good. However, there are no obvious or definite solutions on how to achieve this end; only appropriate search strategies are known.

Furthermore, the challenge is immense and resources are in shorter supply than ever. Therefore, it will not be possible to do everything and—undoubtedly—not simultaneously. Nevertheless, the intention is not to compound the scarcity of resources with a paucity of ideas. In this perspective, the strategy of development from within aims to synthesize and render consistent the guiding principles underlying the manifold proposals suggested to overcome the crisis. More than a manual, this book represents an ongoing effort of exploring more adequate solutions to the region's problems, cognizant of the singularity of each country, which necessarily affects the priorities and timing of the development process in each case.

PART 1

DEVELOPMENT STRATEGY

2

From Inward-Looking Development to Development from Within

Osvaldo Sunkel

Three fundamental concerns appear to focus socioeconomic and political attention in Latin America at present. One involves the hopes and fears aroused by democracy: its establishment, its recovery, its consolidation, its deepening, its difficulties, its precariousness, its eventual failure. Closely linked to these fears are those generated by the economic and social crisis, which to a greater or lesser extent affects virtually all the region. One of its most visible and dramatic manifestations is the problem of the external debt and adjustment policies that have devastated our countries for a whole decade, with disastrous financial and social consequences. But as we shall see, this is merely one particularly acute aspect of a more serious underlying development crisis that has carried over from the 1960s. The third concern emerges from the search for answers to the other two and involves a renewed interest in development. This concern was an essential task and major effort during the postwar decades when intellectual and political initiatives in the region sought to design and implement a modernizing industrialization strategy that would respond to socioeconomic backwardness, and to the excessive external vulnerability evidenced by the Great Depression of the 1930s and the two world wars.

However, toward the late 1960s, a certain disillusionment set in with regard to the outcomes of the development policies being followed. Subsequently, the 1970s brought along more or less revolutionary experiments for in-depth sociopolitical change; then came the oil crisis and after that an extraordinary boom in international private finance, and with it a powerful upsurge in an ultraconservative version of neoliberal economic policies. This was followed by the still-ongoing external debt crisis and the collapse of real socialism in Eastern Europe and the former Soviet Union. Consequently, for nearly two decades concern for long term socioeconomic development waned in the face of dramatic political and social events and profound changes in economic doctrines.

23

But after living through these experiences, concern has reemerged for development strategies capable of achieving economically, socially, and politically sustainable progress. This calls for strategic options that can adjust to the new conditions in the international economy, provide a way out of the current crisis, and overcome the shortcomings observed in the past. Above all, they should contribute to strengthening the prospects for democracies that with such great pains have begun to be established or restored in Latin America.

This chapter attempts, first of all, to explain the beginnings and evolution of distinctive Latin American thinking on development that arose out of the *inward-looking* structuralist strategy of growth and industrialization. This strategy replaced the *outward-looking* phase of growth that prevailed up until the Great Depression of the 1930s and was the major instrument for recovery from that crisis and for subsequent postwar development. Second, it highlights certain aspects of today's critical relation between the prospects for democracy and some of the salient features of the 1980s economic crisis. Lastly, it outlines some basic guidelines for a new development approach *from within*, contributing some elements of this new strategy—and policy proposals consistent with the objective of overcoming the crisis and strengthening democracy—as an expression of the recovery and renewal of structuralist thinking.

The Historical Background of Inward-Looking Development

Classical political economy's central concern was the establishment and long term development of capitalism. This was the fundamental nature of economic thinking during the century that followed the publication of Adam Smith's *Wealth of Nations* in 1776. During the last quarter of the nineteenth century, when capitalism was expanding dynamically, and up until around 1950, when it was undergoing a serious crisis, this concern—and classical political economy itself—was displaced from mainstream economic thinking. Two dominant schools of "pure" economics emerged: neoclassical economic theory, including the theory of comparative advantage in world trade, and Keynesian macroeconomics, with its short and long term variants.

These two theoretical streams closely corresponded to the needs and characteristics of advanced capitalism: neoclassical microeconomics concentrated on the maximization of profits from enterprises and individual consumer utility in national and international markets, while Keynesian economics focused on short and long term macroeconomic policies— employment and growth, respectively—as a solution to the system's cyclical instability. For underdeveloped countries, however, policies stemming from these theoretical approaches implied drastic programs of economic, sociopolitical, and cultural transformation because very few of the underlying assumptions in neoclassical and Keynesian economics were present. To be more precise, these assumptions only applied to very partial aspects of the situation of these countries, those most closely linked to their main export sectors and major urban areas.

Virtually all underdeveloped countries at that time maintained close economic, political, and cultural ties with the major industrialized countries, to which they exported primary products and financial surpluses and from which they imported manufactures, human resources, investment, technology, institutions, and culture. Money was not a universal medium of exchange; it was only partially used in urban transactions and to a certain extent in urban-rural ones, but rarely within (or between) rural communities. Except for some important export activities and the urban sector, one could hardly speak of markets in goods and services because a large part of the population continued to be tied to agrarian communities and other primitive rural institutions, with land ownership highly concentrated in semicapitalist haciendas and plantations with their characteristic precapitalist labor relations. The few, basically foreign, modern, capitalist-type enterprises and entrepreneurs that existed were primarily in the mining or agrarian export sectors, and only a few of them were active in very incipient manufacturing sectors. Basic social capital in infrastructure (roads, energy, communications, railroads, ports) concentrated along export activities and major cities. In fact these had better and easier contact with metropolitan centers than with the interiors of their own countries. Education was limited to a small urban elite. Financial institutions, except for some foreign bank branches, were scarce and limited in scope and capacity. The state apparatus was restricted in geographic extension, and the variety of its operations, and had a very concentrated and highly unstable tax base, mostly in the external sector.

Empirical studies of Latin America's past development show that many of these structural and institutional characteristics were also present in all our economies, emphasizing similarities regarding the absence of integrated and homogeneous national markets of goods and services and the extreme dependence on the primary export sector, resulting in great external vulnerability. At the same time, these studies also recognize the diversity of Latin American countries regarding size, natural resources, location, social structure, and cultural conditions.[1] Efforts to develop suitable theoretical interpretations on this factual basis were at the origin of the Economic Commission for Latin America's (ECLA) economic school of thought, primarily from the extraordinary figure of Raúl Prebisch (Prebisch 1950a, 1950b; ECLA 1950).[2]

The incapacity of neoclassical theory and its market logic to adequately explain the operation of economies so alien to its assumptions, and the interest in understanding the dynamics of its past formation and its prospects for modernization and evolution within the context of the expansion of industrial capitalism, led to the retrieval of the main body of classical political economy, mainly as expressed and passed on by Baran (1957). This view stressed that the essence of capitalist development lay in the accumulation of capital and the increase in labor productivity. The increase in labor productivity was basically due to the incorporation of technological innovations and to growing specialization, both closely related to capital accumulation. This allowed for an increase in income and, based on this, the possibility of an increase in savings and investment. Insofar as it was possible to expand the accumulation process, incorporate technical progress, and utilize its benefits for new processes of this type, a cumulative, dynamic, and expansive process would be achieved according to the essence of the development of capitalism.

Nevertheless, the conditions existing in Latin America during the 1940s and early 1950s were clearly in contradiction with the many centuries during which this capitalist accumulation process had been in force, especially since its increased intensity during the latter part of the nineteenth and early part of the twentieth centuries. Although dynamic and surplus-generating export sectors of high and growing productivity had been long in existence, the resulting economies were structured in a very different way from those resulting from the processes that had taken place during the Industrial Revolution in the central countries. The region showed an overexpansion of the export sector and scant or virtually nonexistent development of other sectors, particularly the industrial one. Only Argentina, Brazil, Chile, Colombia, and Mexico had achieved a modest degree of industrialization. Modernization in general was limited to geographic areas tied to the main export sectors, while primitive productive and social conditions and colonial institutions continued to prevail in extensive areas and sectors in the remainder of the countries. In short, profound structural heterogeneity was the predominant situation (Pinto 1965).

What had happened in these countries to the process of accumulation and expansion of surplus and the distribution of its benefits? A large part of the surplus generated by capital accumulation and the incorporation of technological innovations had reverted back to the central countries rather than toward the interiors of these peripheral countries. In other words, surplus was generated, but for a number of domestic and external reasons— among these, foreign property, overexploitation of labor, the absence of domestic infrastructure, a weak national entrepreneurial sector, the lack of decisive participation and state control, the long term deterioration of the terms of trade for primary products, and the inelasticity of international demand for these types of products—a large part of the surplus generated in the export sector was transferred back to the central countries instead of being reinvested and spread into the rest of the economy.[3] It was therefore necessary to recognize the historical specificity of these economies, which Prebisch called "peripheral" countries. This represented a direct challenge to the doctrine of static comparative advantage underlying free trade and international development ideology. Consequently, Prebisch suggested that the economic development of these peripheral countries demanded structural and institutional reforms, particularly industrialization and technological innovation, in order to succeed in transferring to them their own capacity for generating and disseminating technical progress with its attendant increases in productivity and the retention, absorption, and local reinvestment of its benefits.

In the 1950s, in the aftermath of World War II, when the need for special action for the development of underdeveloped countries began to be recognized, a whole series of theories of underdevelopment appeared, theories associated with Singer (1949, 1950), Rosenstein-Rodan (1943, 1944), Hirschman (1958), Lewis (1954, 1955), Nurkse (1953a, 1953b), Meier and Seers (1984), and others. In hindsight, it is apparent that their essential argument was that there was ample idle productive capacity in these countries because they did not adequately or fully utilize their available resources and that, consequently, only deliberate action by the state could change the situation.[4]

Lewis's (1954) contribution on "growth with unlimited supplies of labor" and that of Singer (1950), who pointed out the possibilities of industrialization by transferring surplus labor from agriculture to industry, are representative of a trend that emphasized ample and underutilized labor resources. This element is also present in Prebisch's work (1950a) and in ECLA (1950), as well as in contributions by Mandelbaum (1945), Rosenstein-Rodan (1944, 1945), and Nurkse (1953b), who proposed, in a similar vein, that the absence of a domestic market resulted from idleness of available productive resources. Capital was a scarce resource, but it could be generated in Keynesian fashion by employing idle factors; in addition, there was an export sector with substantial surplus accumulation capacity. What had to be done was to tap this sector's resources via state intervention and to promote an extensive investment program: a "big push" as Rosenstein-Rodan (1957) defined it, "balanced growth" as Nurkse (1953b) described it, or "unbalanced growth" as Hirschman (1958) characteristically put it.

Basically, what was being said was that an underdeveloped country possessed quite distinctive features (very different from the supposed well-functioning markets and full employment of factors of production of neoclassical economics), where there was ample availability of factors (particularly human and natural) but insufficient capital. Capital is used here in the sense of a stock of accumulated economic infrastructure (productive capacity, transportation, energy, communications) that would enable the mobilization of those resources, and capital in the sense of a flow of savings and investment that could be added to them. This latter form of capital could be obtained from two sources: from the better utilization of the surplus generated by the export sector and from direct foreign investment or external financial contributions.

Such ideas brought about the emergence in practice of a development strategy that Prebisch and ECLA rationalized and streamlined. Many Latin American countries, faced in the 1930s and 1940s with the international crisis originated by the Great Depression and World War II, had in fact already begun to apply these policies: they protected their economies, tapped resources from the export sector, and reinvested them through state action in creating infrastructure, promoting industrial development, modernizing agriculture, and even in providing some limited basic social services such as education, health, and housing. This experience was taken up later by other countries in the region and by many other countries in the rest of the world, giving rise to a development strategy and policy that proved highly successful in the 1950s and 1960s (Sunkel and Paz 1970; Rodríguez 1980; Gurrieri 1980; Kay 1989).

Nevertheless, toward the late 1960s this strategy and development policy came under growing, ever-sharper, and well-aimed criticism. The process, which came to be known as import substitution industrialization, had proven quite successful for more than two decades but began to show some rather serious flaws. Protected industrial development and diversification, which took place thanks to the expansion of the domestic market and in the case of Central America through regional integration as an extension of the domestic market, became increasingly dependent on foreign capital in its production, technology, and ownership patterns. Thus, although an industrial sector developed and agriculture was partially modernized, it failed to generate a modern and competitive national entrepreneurial class and to meet the basic objectives of dynamizing and diversifying exports. To a large extent, exports continued to be commodities subject to terms of trade deterioration, fluctuations, instability, and vulnerability (see Chapter 12).

The assumption had been that industrialization would start off with the domestic market, but that it would eventually generate an expansion of industrial exports, which was after all the fundamental original reason for this strategy. But ultimately, although policies in that direction were implemented as of the late 1960s, this objective was only very partially achieved. In this respect, we should bear in mind that ECLA (1961) gave early warnings as to the essential problems of the industrialization process undertaken in the region.

> The industrialization process has three basic flaws that have undermined its contribution to improving living standards, namely: a) virtually all industrializing action is aimed at the domestic market, b) industries have

been chosen on the basis of circumstance rather than on financial viability, and c) industrialization has not corrected the external vulnerability of Latin American countries. . . . The excessive orientation of industry towards the domestic market results from the development policy implemented in Latin American countries and from the lack of international incentives for industrial exports. Development policy has been discriminatory in terms of exports. Indeed, industrial production for domestic consumption has been subsidized through tariffs and other restrictions, but that which could be destined for export has not. Thus, many industrial goods have been produced that are costlier than international ones, when they could have been obtained at much lower costs in exchange for exports of other industrial goods that could have been produced to better advantage. The same could be said of the new lines of primary exports and even of traditional lines within relatively narrow limits. . . . Thus a suitable division of labor could have been developed in industry, very different from the traditional scheme of exchanging commodities for industrial products. Until recently, no weighty efforts were made to establish this division of industrial labor among Latin American countries.

Another major flaw appeared in the labor market. The industrialization process opened up new jobs with relatively high productivity, but it also gradually shifted a sizable part of the rapidly growing rural underemployed population toward urban underemployment sectors, generating the phenomenon of marginality of the informal sector (see Chapter 5). An over-supplied and segmented labor market contributed to worsening the historical problem of inequitable income distribution. Because many people were unemployed, underemployed, and working in low productivity jobs, the deplorable income distribution prevalent in our countries—deriving essentially from basic conditions of unfair distribution and unequal access to property and education—was not corrected. It was unsuccessful also in the overriding need to substantially raise savings and investment rates to much higher levels, except on the part of the state and later the external contribution.

In the face of these and other failings, toward the late 1960s criticism from both the left and the right grew more severe. Criticism from the left essentially focused on external dependence and social polarization. It denounced the existence of a new element of dependence, which added to the specialization of the primary export sector. The new industrial sector merely reproduced consumption and technological patterns from the center, through foreign investment and the penetration of transnational corporations, without generating additional capital accumulation and technological capabilities or expanding and diversifying exports. Instead, a situation had emerged in which a large part of the industrial expansion, modernization, and growth had been, so to speak, co-opted by an increasingly dependent and transnationalized sector (Sunkel 1969, 1973; Cardoso and Faletto 1979; Palma 1978; Blomström and Hettne 1984).

To this interpretation from the left came a corresponding criticism from the right—a neoliberal, neoclassical criticism that coincided to a large extent with the above diagnoses related to the flaws of the development strategy, but which was based on neoclassical arguments. According to this criticism, the state was intervening too much. This was stifling private initiative; market prices were distorted by planning and state controls; wages were too high; agricultural prices were overly controlled and too low; the exchange rate was overvalued; and there was excessive protection—all of which meant inefficiencies and an irrational allocation of productive resources (Balassa 1977; Krueger 1978b).

In the early 1970s, as a result of historical realities and these serious doctrinal divergences, thinking about development took three different lines: a radical criticism from the left and from the right and a revised structuralist position that favored some changes in the prevailing developmental approach. In reply to the evolving development crisis, three corresponding attempts were made in practice to modify the strategy. The leftist option involved greater socialization, an even more active, interventionist, and definitely wider role of the state. This was the case of experiences such as the Unidad Popular in Chile, the Velasco Alvarado government in Peru, and brief similar experiences in Bolivia and Argentina, all of which were rather short lived, mainly for political but also for economic reasons.

The right-wing option—neoliberal and monetarist—replaced these socialist or socializing experiments and had great influence in Latin America, reaching its most extreme expression in Uruguay, Argentina, and Chile. These experiences, which developed primarily during the latter half of the 1970s and up until the crisis of the 1980s, had generally quite negative effects: stagnation of the basic productive sectors and particularly of the industrial sector, syphoning off of savings and investment to speculative activities and capital flight, worsening social problems and unemployment, heavy concentration of income and wealth, colossal external and domestic indebtedness, and extreme external dependence.

The third option, structuralist developmentalism, continued to be applied with substantial corrections, particularly in the external sector, in Brazil, Mexico, and Venezuela. This allowed these countries to continue growing, despite the already described problems of dependence and social polarization, which had arisen toward the end of the 1960s.

At present, and with the clarity of hindsight from having lived through these experiences, there would seem to be agreement that the structuralist development strategy was very biased toward industrialization via import substitution. However, despite the fact that this critical judgment appears to be basically correct, it draws attention away from the essential to the ancillary. What seems more important is that the past industrialization and development strategy focused mostly on exploiting the domestic market

and promoting domestic production of previously imported industrial consumer goods. This preference for consumption and the existing domestic
market—middle and upper sector demands—is what permeated and biased
the industrialization strategy and resulted in a foreign trade policy characterized by excessive protectionism, a consumption-promoting policy
through subsidies, controlled prices and consumer credits, and an investment policy preferentially aimed at expanding the imitative consumer
durables market, to the detriment of, for example, agricultural or manufacturing production for popular consumption and exports, and of an increased savings and investment effort.

Therefore, it is not so much a matter of criticizing such partial and instrumental aspects of economic policy as tariffs, exchange rates, or price
controls. The problem is much more fundamental. It has to do with a generalized national syndrome arising from a populist-consumist-industrialist
national strategy that emerged in response to the pressure of past experiences and unfavorable contemporary external circumstances—not from the
express will of economic authorities—and which subsequently persisted
because it yielded good dividends for quite some time. Prominent among
these past experiences are the already-mentioned and well-known devastating effects of the Great Depression of the 1930s and the serious economic difficulties brought about by World War II.

Most importantly, critics of the import substitution process also over-
look the adverse external conditions that prevailed at least until the end of
the 1950s. First of all, inflation and the devaluations that took place in industrialized countries abruptly devalued the abundant international reserves that Latin American countries had accumulated during World War
II. In addition, in the postwar period the United States opposed the industrialization of Latin America and channeled its resources into the reconstruction of Europe and the containment of the Soviet Union. International
private financial markets and direct private investment had all but disappeared since their collapse during the Great Depression. International public financing was very limited and conditioned. European economies were
beginning their reconstruction with strict import limitations and severe exchange control systems, due to the prevailing "dollar shortage." Last but
certainly not least, the United States and the European countries continued
to carry on their own import substitution policies through the still-ongoing
massive agricultural support programs started in the 1930s. Moreover, the
foreign trade boom that began in the late 1950s was essentially attributable
to the reestablishment of trade between the United States and the European
economies and between the latter and their former colonies, within the
framework of the reconstitution of the Atlantic and colonial economies,
while discriminating against Latin American exports.

In the late 1960s these adverse external conditions changed, and
the import substitution industrialization strategy began to show signs of

exhaustion. However, it was difficult to reorient it because, more than a simple liberalization of markets, it was necessary to undertake an in-depth reformulation: nothing short of a global shift in development strategy based on the opening up to world markets, with all the complex implications this meant for our countries. At a domestic level, this involved considerable demands in terms of creating competitiveness, innovation capacity, and technological adaptation; reallocating investment; channeling credit from the promotion of internal consumption to the promotion of exports; and, with very serious consequences regarding intersectoral linkages, channeling productivity, competitiveness, and patterns of production, consumption, and employment, aside from the more obvious policy aspects related to exchange rates, tariffs, and other instruments. Many of these recommendations for overcoming the shortcomings of import substitution industrialization are present in the structuralist literature from the 1960s, and point to domestic and external markets as vitalizing sources of growth. They suggest distributive reforms as mechanisms for domestic market expansion (see Lustig 1981, 1988a, and Chapter 3 in this book) and emphasize the critical importance of growth and diversification of exports for the very survival of a dynamic development strategy (Sunkel 1969).

Subsequently, the international financial permissiveness that began to prevail in the late 1960s and increased in the 1970s made it possible to evade most of the emerging problems. During those years—characterized by easy access to abundant external financing—concern for development theory, strategies, and medium and long term concerns and policies waned; everything seemed solvable through external financing. As growth seemed assured—economies had grown and continued to grow during the 1970s—fundamental concerns thus centered on stability and efficiency. Short term neoclassical views became overwhelming and any notion of the need for a long term strategy that would allow for the rational planning of the unexpectedly abundant external savings simply evaporated.

Thus, despite the early warnings afforded by the first oil crisis of 1973, Latin American economies continued to expand quite vigorously in the years that followed, even though most of them were net oil importers. Instead of immediately adopting adjustment and restructuring policies required by the energy crisis, the extremely serious recession that was affecting the world economy, and the looming development problems, Latin American countries persisted in their expansionist policies. Only Brazil began a serious economic restructuring program, emphasizing the export of manufactures and alternative sources of energy. Otherwise, it was even claimed that continued growth demonstrated these economies' degree of development, the vigor of their accumulation capacity, and the strength of their productive forces and industrial development.

However, what was really occurring was that heavy external indebtedness made it possible to compensate this new external imbalance. It is for this reason that I have been arguing for a long time that the real "lost decade" for Latin America was the 1970s. Instead of using easily available external financing to correct the structural problems generated previously and to adjust in some degree to the new international economic conditions and to the new energy prices, most countries continued to expand in an absurdly irresponsible manner, confident that they could continue to increase their indebtedness indefinitely. This is a tragic, practical demonstration of the degree to which neoliberal conceptions led to losing sight of the need for a long term growth strategy, replacing it with the mistaken signals of the short term financial market with its negative real interest rates that invited excessive indebtedness and the eventual unleashing of a major financial crisis as soon as conditions changed. (See Sunkel 1984; Griffith-Jones and Sunkel 1986; and Chapter 6).

This is precisely what occurred between 1979 and 1982 when the second oil shock and changes in the economic policy of the United States led to another world recession, skyrocketing interest rates, the contraction of international trade, the sharp deterioration of Latin American terms of trade, and the outbreak of the external debt crisis and its dramatic aftermath in the latter part of 1982.

Prospects for Democracy and the Development Crisis of the 1980s

Notwithstanding the diversity of national situations that prevail in Latin America, two generalized sets of trends can be clearly discerned, corresponding to two profound and long term processes that are unfortunately contradictory and on a collision course. On the one hand, there is the demand for democratization and citizen participation that has been inexorably mounting, based on the profound socioeconomic and cultural changes—both domestic and external—that have taken place in recent decades. On the other hand, there is a development crisis of major proportions and already lengthy duration as a result of the external debt crisis and the adjustment and restructuring policies that have been implemented since then.

While the first process leads to demands and hopes that involve the need for allocating greater financial and economic resources to ever-wider popular sectors, the second works in the other direction, restricting, denying, and even severely cutting back resources. This results in serious concern regarding the prospects for democracy both in recently established democracies and in those of longer standing. The challenge facing the institutionality, parties, corporate actors, and other political elements of each country's political regime is dramatic: How should the intense and growing conflict between contained social aspirations, which are expressed with greater freedom and insistence within the new democratic framework, be processed and politically directed vis-à-vis the restrictions, sacrifices, and postponements peremptorily demanded by the economic crisis? The political and technical capacity of each country in overcoming this crisis without exceeding the tolerable limits of democratic operation and the economic process will be crucial for the prospects of consolidating democracy and development.

There is broad consensus as to the growing democratic demands that have been increasingly manifested in various countries in the past decades and, particularly, in more recent ones. By democratic demands, we understand the aspirations and demands for greater participation in the economic (income, consumption, work), social (education, mobility, organization), political (elections, decisions, participation), and cultural (information, access to cultural goods and services, communications media) spheres.

The elements underlying this great expansion of democratic demand include long term and short term, as well as domestic and external, factors. Among the domestic factors are the major social changes experienced in our countries in the recent past: rapid urbanization and industrialization, the partial modernization of agriculture, the expansion of education systems, the veritable revolution in information and mass media, and the constitution and diffusion of a great variety and diversity of social, political, and cultural organizations at all levels, strata, and sectors of society. (Tables 2.1 to 2.5 illustrate some of these phenomena.)

Among the most recent and prominent factors with the greatest impact is the collapse of the dictatorships that predominated in many Latin American countries in the mid-1970s. From 1978 on, military dictatorships have been forced to abandon government in virtually all Latin American countries with the sole exception of Cuba and recently Haiti, and civil governments and democratic regimes have been established or reestablished.[5] Although the extent of this change in terms of real political power and effective social participation remains to be seen, and has been very diverse in the various countries, it was everywhere a powerful boost to setting free democratic demands that had been incubating in the structural changes indicated above, but which had remained relatively contained by military regimes.

Another relatively recent domestic factor of great importance in several countries is the process of maturation, moderation, renovation, and unification of the major left-wing political streams, movements, parties, and trends, inspired by a new sense of realism and pragmatism, forming more or less unified conglomerates that value the democratic game.[6] This was undoubtedly affected by the defeat of previous left-wing governments, the difficulties of surviving under military regimes, the hard experience of life in exile, and the experiences of European social democratic and socialist parties. They were also limited in their political and policy options by the economic crisis and the rapidly growing degree of internationalization of their economies and societies.

Table 2.1. Latin America: Urbanization
           (percentage of total population)

	Population in localities with 20,000 inhabitants or more				Population in localities with 100,000 inhabitants or more			
	1950	1960	1970	1980	1950	1960	1970	1980
Argentina	49.9	59.0	66.3	70.6	41.7	50.6	55.6	57.9
Bolivia	19.4	22.9	37.2	32.0	9.9	15.3	20.9	26.4
Brazil	20.3	28.1	39.5	52.2	13.3	18.8	27.8	42.0
Chile	42.6	50.6	60.6	68.6	28.5	32.9	41.7	56.0
Colombia	23.0	36.6	46.2	55.1	15.4	27.5	35.7	46.2
Costa Rica	17.7	24.4	27.0	33.6	17.7	18.4	19.2	25.1
Dominican Rep.	11.1	18.7	30.2	41.9	8.5	12.1	20.7	28.2
Ecuador	17.8	27.9	35.3	42.9	14.6	19.3	23.4	33.2
El Salvador	13.0	17.7	20.5	—	8.7	10.2	9.5	—
Guatemala	11.2	15.5	16.1	22.6	10.2	13.4	13.5	19.9
Haiti	5.1	7.5	12.7	22.6	4.3	6.6	10.4	14.3
Honduras	6.8	11.5	20.2	—	—	7.1	15.8	—
Mexico	23.6	28.9	35.2	51.4	15.2	18.4	23.3	43.4
Nicaragua	15.2	23.0	31.0	—	10.3	15.3	20.8	—
Panama	22.4	33.1	39.4	43.0	15.9	25.4	30.3	33.3
Paraguay	15.2	15.9	21.5	29.3	15.2	15.9	16.7	23.3
Peru	18.1	28.5	40.3	49.6	13.8	19.3	30.0	40.4
Uruguay	53.1	61.4	64.7	70.5	40.4	44.7	44.5	49.5
Venezuela	31.0	47.0	59.4	70.3	16.6	25.5	40.4	59.5

Source: ECLAC, *Statistical Yearbook*, 1980 (for 1950 to 1970) and 1989 (for 1980).

Table 2.2. Latin America: Industry Share in GDP
           (percentage of GDP at constant 1980 prices)

	1960[a]	1970	1980	1989
Argentina	26.3	27.5	25.0	22.6
Bolivia	11.4	13.4	14.6	13.0
Brazil	25.8	32.2	33.1	29.4
Chile	24.9	24.5	21.4	21.7
Colombia	16.4	22.1	23.3	21.1
Costa Rica	11.1	15.5	18.6	18.9
Dominican Rep.	14.7	15.5	15.3	13.6
Ecuador	15.1	8.6	8.8	7.4
El Salvador	13.8	15.2	15.0	15.4
Guatemala	11.7	13.5	13.6	13.0
Haiti	8.8	12.5	17.6	14.1
Honduras	11.6	14.2	15.7	17.1
Mexico	19.2	21.2	22.1	22.3
Nicaragua	12.6	20.9	25.6	20.2
Panama	11.6	11.8	10.0	8.5
Paraguay	14.1	17.1	16.5	15.0
Peru	18.7	21.4	20.2	18.4
Uruguay	22.8	28.0	28.7	25.8
Venezuela	12.9	13.6	16.2	17.4

Source: ECLAC, *Statistical Yearbook*, 1980 and 1990.
Note: a. Percent of GDP at constant 1970 prices.

Development Strategy

Table 2.3. Latin America: Agricultural Mechanization
            (hectares of arable lands per tractor)

	1961–1965	1970	1980	1988
Argentina	202	197	211	170
Bolivia	6,832	—	843	739
Brazil	326	205	130	116
Chile	200	241	161	117
Colombia	210	181	183	154
Costa Rica	112	97	85	83
Dominican Rep.	369	230	660	639
Ecuador	1,491	824	397	319
El Salvador	364	249	220	215
Guatemala	641	490	438	448
Haiti	2,590	—	5,086	4,209
Honduras	4,529	912	541	522
Mexico	346	238	213	150
Nicaragua	5,430	1,830	566	507
Panama	710	226	144	92
Paraguay	568	430	255	211
Peru	305	256	248	233
Uruguay	75	69	44	38
Venezuela	399	275	99	83

Source: ECLAC, *Statistical Yearbook,* 1980 and 1990.

Besides, the turbulent international milieu of the last decade experienced interesting and positive changes from the perspective of Latin American democratization. The cases of Spain, Portugal, and even Greece provided important stimuli and background from the Mediterranean, which exerts significant cultural and political influence in Latin America. The international policy for the defense of human rights inaugurated by President Carter in the United States and continued under subsequent administrations, specifically including support for the establishment of democratic regimes in various cases—notwithstanding its ambiguities and contradictions—meant an important positive change with respect to the traditionally prodictatorial attitude of our influential neighbor to the north. European social democratic parties have acted similarly by reaffirming their will to express themselves through European international policy, particularly with respect to Latin America. Lastly, and most importantly, another international influence that has gained great prominence has been the terminal crisis and transformation of communist thinking, parties, and regimes, which was first and timidly expressed within European communism and more recently in the epochal changes, unsuspected in scope, that have occurred in the communist regimes of Europe and the former Soviet Union.

However, all these domestic and international social and political trends that favor the implanting and consolidation of democratic regimes in Latin America come up against major obstacles. One of these is the persistence of antidemocratic cultures characterized by intolerance, paternalism,

Table 2.4. Latin America and the Caribbean: Estimates of School Enrollment and Enrollment Ratios (in thousands and percentages)

Educational Level	1960	1970	1980	1985	1986	1988	Annual average growth rate				
							1960–70	1970–80	1980–85	1985–88	1980–88
Pre-school education											
Attendance	983	1,728	4,739	8,264	8,619	9,491	5.8	10.6	11.8	4.7	9.1
Attendance ratio[b]	2.4	3.3	7.9	12.8	15.0	14.0					
Primary education											
Number of students	26,653	43,983	64,795	69,646	71,419	72,741	5.1	4.0	1.5	1.5	1.5
Net enrollment ratio, population age 6–11	57.7	71.0	82.4	85.2	85.0	87.6[a]					
Gross enrollment ratio	72.7	90.7	104.8	106.4	107.3	109.3[a]					
Secondary education											
Number of students	4,085	10,662	17,595	21,318	22,054	23,434	10.1	5.1	3.9	3.2	3.6
Net enrollment ratio, population age 12–17	36.3	49.8	62.6	66.2	—	71.6[a]					
Gross enrollment ratio	14.6	25.5	44.9	50.7	51.6	57.6[a]					
Higher education											
Number of students	573	1,460	4,872	6,363	6,784	6,978	11.1	11.5	5.5	3.1	4.6
Net enrollment ratio, population age 18–23	5.7	11.6	23.6	23.8	—	27.2[a]					
Gross enrollment ratio	3.0	6.3	13.5	15.9	16.8	18.7[a]					

Source: UNESCO, *Statistical Yearbook*, 1978–1979, 1978–1985, 1978–1988, 1978–1990.
Notes: a. For the year 1990.
b. Figures calculated using population age 0–5 from CELADE, Demographic Bulletin 38, July 1986.
Net enrollment ratio: number of students in an age group (regardless of grade of grade in school) divided by population of same age group.
Gross enrollment ratio: total enrollment in grade (regardless of age) divided by population of age group corresponding to that grade.

Table 2.5.   Latin America: Television Sets
             (per 1,000 inhabitants)

	1960	1970	1980
Argentina	21	147	182
Bolivia	—	—	54
Brazil	18	64	124
Chile	—	53	110
Colombia	11	39	87
Costa Rica	3	58	71
Dominican Rep.	6	22	68
Ecuador	1	25	62
El Salvador	8	26	66
Guatemala	8	13	25
Haiti	1	2	3
Honduras	1	8	13
Mexico	19	58	108
Nicaragua	3	28	63
Panama	10	97	113
Paraguay	—	15	22
Peru	3	29	49
Uruguay	9	92	125
Venezuela	37	72	114

Source: ECLAC, *Statistical Yearbook,* 1980 and 1987.

patronage, authoritarianism, and extremism. In addition, the persistence or resurgence of guerilla activity, as well as the dramatic and increasingly deep-rooted problem of drug trafficking—which has already extended in one way or another to many countries, gaining undertones of an out-and-out war—all lead to a counterpoint of multipolar violence and militarization characterizing the countries in which these problems occur in a particularly virulent manner. Such obstacles reinforce negative trends that lead to the formation of democratic regimes that are restricted in scope, elitist, oligarchic, exclusionary, and increasingly supported and infiltrated by the armed forces. Table 2.6 shows some figures on defense expenditures and arms strength that indicate the importance of the military in Latin America.

A worrisome contributing element is the generalized contemporary phenomenon of the internationalization and transnationalization of the region's economies and societies. There is an ever closer link between middle- and upper-class segments of the local bourgeoisie and technocracies with transnational economic, financial, military, technological, and mass media power structures, which conform a highly homogeneous and integrated nucleus sharing a similar life-style and strong political, social, and cultural affinities. This process implies a dangerous tendency toward the disintegration and exclusion of a large part of the remainder of society, confining it to a national complement of activities, regions, and social groups that are subordinate, marginal, backward, and isolated (Sunkel

Table 2.6.   Latin America: Military Expenditures and Arms Imports

	Military Expenditures (1984 billion US$)	Armed Forces (thous)	Arms Imports (1984 billion US$)	Military Expenditures/ Gross Domestic Product	Military Expenditures/ Fiscal Expenditures	Armed Forces/ 1,000 inhab	Arms Imports/ Total Imports
1975	8.6	1,297	—	1.6	7.3	4.1	—
1976	9.8	1,328	—	1.7	8.0	4.1	—
1977	10.5	1,438	2.287	1.8	8.0	4.3	2.5
1978	10.2	1,478	2.967	1.7	7.4	4.3	3.1
1979	10.1	1,491	2.884	1.6	7.2	4.2	2.6
1980	10.8	1,361	2.445	1.6	6.9	4.3	1.8
1981	11.0	1,617	4.022	1.6	6.1	4.4	3.1
1982	13.7	1,687	4.011	2.1	7.0	4.5	4.0
1983	12.3	1,746	3.451	1.9	6.5	4.5	4.6
1984	12.7	1,798	4.145	1.9	7.0	4.6	5.6
1985	12.5	1,814	3.348	1.8	7.5	4.5	4.7

Source: Arms Control and Disarmament Agency, *World Military Expenditures and Arms Transfers,* Washington, D.C., May 1985. Reproduced with amendments in "Militares y Armas en América Latina," Augusto Varas (1988), pages 99, 101.

1973, 1979). This increases the resistance to making the economic and political concessions needed for a fairer distribution of the dire consequences of the economic crisis and of the adjustment and restructuring policies.

In many countries the debt crisis and the ensuing adjustment and restructuring policies have brought to light this violent contradiction in a particularly acute manner. The ruling classes have let the adjustment burden fall, to a large extent, upon the popular sectors and segments of the middle class, preserving at any price the privileges and interests of transnationalized sectors, the upper middle class, and international business.[7]

In political terms these sectors rely on the staunch defense of right-wing ideological tendencies and forces that swing between incorporation into the democratic game and the temptation of resorting again to anti-democratic practices in order to guarantee system continuity. In contrast, the working and marginal classes, which have been hit severely by the economic crisis and the adjustment and restructuring policies, for the most part until now have been interpreted by left-wing ideologies and political movements. In most cases, and by virtue of the political change and renovation referred to, these have so far moderated their social demands and confined them within democratic channels. All countries are facing this serious contradiction, which will become more or less acute depending, among other factors, on the outcome of the economic crisis.

The conservation of democracy and the restoration of economic growth and development depend crucially on whether the right, upper, middle, and entrepreneurial classes recognize the need to accept some restrictions in their extravagant consumption levels and life-styles and give their support to policies that will ease poverty and stimulate growth. It also depends on whether the Left and their social basis remain predisposed to continue to accept sacrifices and the postponement of their demands in the hope that the rules of the democratic game will eventually reward them with greater political participation and economic and social benefits. If such a political consensus is not reached, economic adjustment and reform policies, which are inevitable, will be imposed, as has been the case in several countries, regardless of economic and political costs, and may well lead to prolonged sociopolitical and economic instability and even to the breakdown of democracy.

During the postwar decades, a model of economic growth and partial modernization was articulated in many of our countries that was very dynamic and profoundly changed our societies, giving rise to the demands for democratization. To a greater or lesser extent, depending on the case, that model's sociopolitical and economic axis was the developmental state, which became more extended and took on new and various functions, such as employment generation, capital accumulation, creation of public enterprises, provision of social services (health care, housing, education, social welfare), and support for the private sector through subsidies, protection, and financing. In this way populist social and political pluralistic class coalitions were articulated in which entrepreneurs, middle classes, and organized working classes participated, and in which some support was even given to the informal urban sectors.

This was initially feasible, thanks to the tapping by the state of the surplus generated in the traditional specialized agricultural and mining export sectors, which was then channeled toward the multiple uses and sectors indicated (ECLA 1956).[8] But over time this major source of public income became relatively less important. The contribution of foreign financing and investment was very modest during the 1950s and 1960s, and there was strong resistance to the creation, expansion, and modernization of an efficient taxation system. As a consequence, inflationary financing of the fiscal gap became increasingly prevalent. Thus, based on all these elements and others indicated in the relevant literature, the structural conditioning factors of the inflationary phenomenon were activated through cumulative propagating mechanisms leading to spiraling inflation.[9] Later, in the mid-1970s, when the increasing scarcity of foreign exchange, the oil crisis, runaway inflation, and the previously mentioned development problems called for urgent adjustments of the development strategy, the extraordinary boom in the international private financial market provided an abundance of easy credits under very favorable initial terms. In these circumstances, most countries preferred to evade the necessary, inevitable, and long overdue restructuring and adjustment of their economies. Instead, most embarked on a path of heavy and increasing external indebtedness until the early 1980s.

In spite of this structurally flawed situation, it was thus possible to maintain an expanding economy and continue to distribute an apparently ever-greater surplus through the state apparatus. In this way, although in different and unfair proportions, major social sectors managed to improve their living standards during the whole postwar period until the 1980s. This last supporting basis that had allowed the state to continue to perform simultaneously its accumulation and redistribution functions collapsed suddenly and unexpectedly in 1982. The external debt crisis not only eliminated that growing source of external financing, but in fact reversed it, forcing an enormous drain of surplus to the exterior (see Table 2.7 and Figure 2.1).

In the face of the need to turn around an external situation that until 1982 had been characterized by a large excess of imports over exports and of external financing over foreign remittances, it became imperative to drastically reduce imports and to increase considerably the financial payments abroad. This reorientation in the flow of trade and finance demanded, as a logical domestic counterpart, a considerable surplus in domestic savings accounts.

Table 2.7. Latin America: Net Capital Inflow and Transfer of Resources (billions of dollars and percentages)

Year	1. Net Capital Inflow	2. Net Payments of Profit and Interest	3. Transfer of Resources (1-2)	4. Goods and Services Exports	5. Transfer of Resources/ Goods and Services Exports (3/4) (%)
1973	7.9	4.2	3.7	28.9	12.8
1974	11.4	5.0	6.4	43.6	14.7
1975	14.3	5.6	8.7	41.1	21.2
1976	17.9	6.8	11.1	47.3	23.5
1977	17.2	8.2	9.0	55.9	16.1
1978	26.2	10.2	16.0	61.3	26.1
1979	29.1	13.6	15.5	82.0	18.9
1980	32.0	18.9	13.1	104.9	12.5
1981	39.8	28.5	11.3	113.2	10.0
1982	20.1	38.8	-18.7	103.0	-18.2
1983	2.9	34.5	-31.6	102.4	-30.9
1984	10.4	37.3	-26.9	113.8	-23.6
1985	3.0	35.3	-32.3	109.0	-29.6
1986	9.9	32.7	-22.8	94.7	-24.9
1987	15.1	31.4	-16.3	108.1	-15.1
1988	5.5	34.3	-28.8	122.8	-23.5
1989	10.1	37.4	-27.3	136.4	-20.0
1990[a]	17.9	36.8	-18.9	147.1	-12.8

Sources: 1973–1988: ECLAC based on data provided by IMF.
1990: ECLAC based on official figures.
Note: a. Preliminary estimations subject to review.

Figure 2.1. Latin America: Net Capital Inflow and Net Transfer of Resources (billions of dollars)

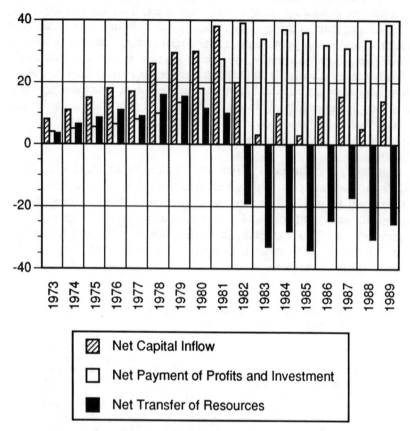

Net Capital Inflow

Net Payment of Profits and Investment

Net Transfer of Resources

Source: ECLAC based on data provided by IMF.

To bring about this mammoth national saving effort within the canons set by international financial agencies and foreign banks and governments, a series of economic adjustment and restructuring policies were implemented. On the one hand, the private sector was forced to reduce its consumption and investment through a major cutback in private incomes. On the other hand, a strict conditionality was imposed on public sector management, which, as it was forced to guarantee external commitments, had to shoulder the great cost of the adjustment. Thus the attempt was made to stymie the state in its multiple roles by reducing the number of public officials and their wages, cutting back on spending in social services, eliminating subsidies, reducing public investment, privatizing state activities and enterprises, and by attempting to quickly raise revenues through tax reforms that assigned greater priority to indirect over direct taxation.

In both private and public fronts, actions were undertaken with the objective of reducing expenditures and generating the domestic saving surplus needed to compensate payments abroad. But the recessive nature of all these measures made it very difficult to achieve an increase in savings, and consequently, the greater part of the adjustment resulted in a reduction in investment, jeopardizing future growth (see Table 2.8). It is also evident that this set of policies was implemented with a severely regressive bias, placing almost all the burden of adjustment and restructuring on the middle sectors and popular classes, who have witnessed an increase in unemployment and underemployment (and therefore of the informal sector); a reduction in their incomes and wages; an increase in their tax burden; cutbacks, impoverishment, and a rise in the cost of education, health care, housing, and social welfare services; and generally a lessening of opportunities and the frustration of the hopes for economic and social improvement that had been kindled by a return to democracy.

Table 2.8. Latin America: Effect of Debt Burden on Investment, Wages, and Product (percentages)

	Debt/GDP		Investment/GDP		Accumulated Variation in Real Wages		Accumulated Variation in Per Capita Product	
	1982–87	(70–81)	1982–87	(70–81)	1982–87	(70–81)	1982–87	(70–81)
Latin America	56	(38)	16.6	(22.6)	—		-3.3	(32.9)
Argentina	73	(40)	12.7	(20.8)	16	(-7)	-14.5	(9.5)
Brazil	45	(32)	16.3	(23.3)	3	(56)	3.9	(81.5)
Chile	90	(60)	12.0	(16.7)	-13	(-3)	-5.7	(12.9)
Colombia	25	(20)	18.3	(18.4)	18	(-1)	9.0	(36.7)
Costa Rica	110	(82)	18.2	(22.5)	-2	(32)	-9.7	(29.2)
Ecuador	61	(35)	17.8	(24.2)	—		-10.5	(87.3)
Mexico	65	(35)	17.8	(23.2)	-30	(15)	-14.4	(49.2)
Peru	61	(42)	21.2	(23.4)	3	(-14)	-5.7	(13.5)
Uruguay	88	(41)	9.7	(12.3)	-8	(-35)	-9.7	(35.8)
Venezuela	58	(40)	19.0	(25.9)	—		-13.1	(5.7)

Source: ECLAC (1988a: 13).
Notes: Debt = Total external debt disbursements; Investment = Gross domestic investment.
    Data in parentheses refers to the precrisis period and other data to the crisis period.
    Since the crisis did not begin simultaneously in all countries, accumulated changes for the most suitable periods were included for each country in order to reflect the effect of adjustment over real wages. Therefore, figures for the last two columns refer to changes registered between 1981 and 1987 in Argentina, Brazil, Costa Rica, and Ecuador, and between 1982 and 1987 for the remaining countries.

In these conditions, the prospects for consolidating existing and newly established democratic regimes are evidently not good in many countries. It is not merely a matter of overcoming the external debt problem. What is at stake is an in-depth reorganization of the state and its relations with civil society in order to rearticulate a dynamic sociopolitical and economic model of capital accumulation, growth, and development and to replace the one that had come into being in the postwar period, was eroding in the late 1960s, and collapsed in 1982.

The only proposal currently available for facing the economic crisis—strongly encouraged by international agencies responsible for implementing adjustment and restructuring policies, by the governments of industrialized countries, by transnational banks, and by the transnationalized sectors of Latin American society—is the neoliberal program with its well-known social and dynamic limitations. The surprising economic policy reversals in recent years by such presidential candidates as Carlos Andres Pérez, Fernando Collor de Melo, Alberto Fujimori, and Carlos Saúl Menem after populist electoral campaigns, as well as the relative continuity of the economic policies of the new Chilean democratic government, are based on these new historical realities rather than on profound ideological conversions. Some of the elements included in the neoliberal program are unquestionably necessary in any renewed development process: new dynamic forms of export growth; the raising of productivity, efficiency, and competitiveness; the increase in savings and investment; the reduction, rationalization, flexibilization, and greater efficiency of the state apparatus; the achievement and maintenance of a reasonable degree of macroeconomic balances; and expansion in the role of the market and private economic agents.

This latter emphasis, and the attempt to reduce the debt burden through debt-for-equity swaps, has led to a massive and indiscriminate wave of privatization. In this, as in other policies, it would be wise to differentiate between those processes inspired in an authentic rationalizing and modernizing project, and others marked by ideological dogmatism and for whom liberalization, deregulation, and privatization are ends in themselves. The former involves the pursuit of a more competitive and dynamic economy that contributes a long term solution to the chronic fiscal and external deficit, imposing the need to adjust an oversized state when in fact there is a more appropriate private alternative. The latter primarily pursues an ideological end of reducing the role of the state to a minimum or easing short term financial pressures on the public sector without taking into account the ultimate spinoffs on overall economic and social efficiency.[10]

Even while accepting the general relevance of conventional recommendations, with the reservation just expressed, democratization processes face the enormous challenge of: reconciling these reforms with an improved standard of living in at least those sectors most deprived in recent decades and most negatively affected by recent policies; reaffirming the critical role of the state in guiding long term economic and social development; ensuring that the search for international competitiveness be achieved by increasing productivity and not by reducing wages; and guaranteeing that the decentralization and privatization of activities and public enterprises will strengthen civil society, increase social and political participation, and strengthen medium, small, and cooperative private enterprises, and will not simply serve as a pretext to abandon basic public functions or leave them to the market and thus allow uncontrollable national and foreign private monopolies in public services and business.

In short, the policy restrictions imposed by the economy demand creative political and economic answers in terms of the external debt, state reform, social policies, international reinsertion, productive restructuring, capital accumulation, and technical progress in order to sustain the democratization process, which appears so threatened. Both domestic and external economic conditions constitute a limiting framework, but the breadth or narrowness of this framework depends on the efficacy, creativity, and responsibility of political, intellectual, and technical actors leading the political process. The challenge is enormous, but so are the opportunities for reorganizing our economies and societies in order to achieve a new stage of stable and consolidated democratic development.

Toward Development From Within: Bases for a Proposal

It is well known that it has become customary in the literature on Latin American development to distinguish between the outward-looking development prior to the 1930s and the inward-looking development through import substitution industrialization from the 1930s onwards. However, as pointed out in the initial section of this chapter, the actual course followed by past development responded more to pressures from adverse external circumstances than to a preconceived purpose on the part of economic or intellectual authorities at the time.

The following quotation from one of the pioneering works of Raúl Prebisch provides a faithful account of the true meaning that the ECLA school of thought gave the industrialization process in its origins.

> The economic development of the peripheral countries is one more stage in the world-wide spread of the new forms of productive technique. . . .
> A few early signs of this new stage had already appeared in the primary producer countries before the First World War. But it was the war, with the consequent difficulties of maintaining imports, which revealed the industrial possibilities of those countries, while the great economic depression of the 1930s strengthened the conviction that those possibilities had to be used in order to offset, by means of internal development,[11] the manifest failure of the external incentive which until then had stimulated Latin-American economy; this conviction was confirmed during the Second World War, when Latin-American industry, with all its improvisations and difficulties, nevertheless became a source of employment

and of consumption for a large and increasing part of the population (ECLA 1950).

It is thus clear that Prebisch's original proposal distinguished both stages in terms of compensating the dynamic stimulus of the propagation of modern techniques that came *from without*, and which had become insufficient, by developing stimulus *from within*. The change of wording suggests a fundamental distinction. Prebisch was thinking of a domestic industrialization process capable of creating an endogenous mechanism of capital accumulation and generation of technical progress and improvements in productivity, as constituted in the central countries since the Industrial Revolution.

Thus, Prebisch describes Japan's incorporation into the "universal propagation of technical progress," pointing out that incorporation occurred when Japan "set out to rapidly assimilate western production modes." The latter expression is particularly revealing, since it refers to *assimilating* and not transferring, copying, or reproducing technical progress, and places express emphasis on production modes, in other words, on the supply side of the economy.

In contrast, inward-looking development places the emphasis on demand, on the expansion of the domestic market, and on replacing previously imported goods with locally produced goods, instead of placing the emphasis on accumulation, technical progress, and productivity. This led to a strategy based on the expansion of domestic consumption and the local reproduction of consumption, industrial production, and technological patterns of central countries, primarily through import substitution guided by a narrow and biased domestic demand shaped by a very unequal pattern of domestic income distribution (Sunkel 1987a).

The strategy of industrial development from within has very different implications. In short, in the words of Fajnzylber (1983), it involves a "creative domestic effort to shape a productive structure that is functional to the specific national deficiencies and potentials." Responding to this logic, one begins by establishing those industries considered to be the essential pillars for creating what we would call today a basic endogenous nucleus for industrialization, accumulation, the generation and diffusion of technical progress, and the increase of productivity. This initial creative impulse gives rise to industries such as iron and steel, electrical machinery and engineering, and basic chemistry and petrochemicals and to the infrastructure for energy, transportation, and communications, based on the use of hitherto idle natural resources and from the articulation and integration of the national territory and market.

According to Fajnzylber, once this foundational stage has passed, the reinforcement of domestic creativity demands greater participation and closer interrelation between different agents and motivations: large industrial plants tied to medium and small business, scientific, and technological infrastructure (technological and basic sciences research institutions and the like); the training of skilled human resources; mass communications media; and public agencies defining strategy, policies, and standards. Once the communication, interaction, and fluidity of the articulation between these actors, agencies, and levels of decisionmaking are consolidated as a national practice, an "endogenous nucleus of technological dynamism" will have been formed. Only then will it be possible to generate articulated systems capable of reaching international levels of excellence in every link of the productive specialization chain (see Chapter 9).

Such a strategy is not directed, a priori, toward meeting the final consumption demands of medium- and upper-income sectors, nor does it start out prejudging in favor of an import substitution process that would eventually lead down a blind alley. It leaves open the options to orient this industrialization from within toward strategic domestic, regional, and world markets, based on activities in which our countries possess or can acquire relative levels of excellence that guarantee them a solid and dynamic insertion into the world economy. Dynamic linkages do not occur, as in import substitution industrialization, from final demand backwards toward inputs and capital goods and technology, but rather from the latter elements toward the selective tapping of domestic and external demands considered to be essential for a long term strategy. A veritable and solid national and regional development will have to be based primarily on the transformation of the natural resources Latin America possesses in relative abundance; the extensive and efficient utilization of the considerable accumulated productive infrastructure of the region; a determined savings and investment effort; the effective contribution of the entire population— in particular those that have remained in the informal sector; and the adoption of life and consumption styles and productive techniques and organizational forms that are in line with the enormous tasks ahead.

The traumatic experiences of the recent past are compounded by the somber international prospects for the near future. Table 2.9 compares the rather positive trends of the 1950–1970 period with the much less favorable contemporary situation. In these conditions the main issues affecting Latin America in the current critical historic moment are debt, crisis, the appalling social cost of adjustment and restructuring, and the need to overcome them as soon as possible. Transition strategies and policies are required that will reestablish and affirm democracy and be sustainable over the medium and long terms. The success of this transition obviously involves overcoming both the past inward-looking stage of development and the present, rather one-sided experiences of renewed outward-looking growth. The alternative is to embark upon a development and industrialization strategy from within, which brings with it dynamic accumulation, innovation, and increased productivity. Given the current scenario of

Table 2.9.   Long Term Trends in the International Economy
             Before and After the 1970s

	Between 1950 and 1970	After 1980
World economy	Exceptionally rapid and sustained growth	Slow and unstable growth
International trade	Great expansion	Slow growth, instability
Terms of trade	Relatively low and stable (in relation to early 1950s)	Severe deterioration (in relation to 1980)
Public international financing	Rapid and sustained increase	Limited expansion
Direct foreign investment	Rapid and sustained expansion	Very scarce
Private financing	Exceptional expansion since mid-1960s	Scarce, decreasing, and substantial negative net flow (debt servicing)
Interest rates	Very low	Very high
Protectionism	Decreasing	Strong increase
International cooperation	Very favorable attitude	Very negative attitude
External conditionality in economic policy matters	Short term IMF	Short term: IMF, international banks, U.S. government Long term: World Bank, U.S. government

Source: Osvaldo Sunkel (1987) "El futuro del desarrollo latinoamericano: algunos temas de reflexion," in *Neoliberalismo y politicas economicas alternativas*, Cordes, Quito, Ecuador.

depressed investment, one should particularly stress that the efficient allocation of resources—and, consequently, increased productivity—is a necessary but insufficient condition for achieving the objective of growth with greater equity.

An additional challenge is the increased internal and external financing required to implement the new strategy, particularly at a time when Latin America is experiencing severe fiscal problems and chronic scarcity of foreign exchange due to the heavy burden of servicing the foreign debt. An immediate alternative is imperative and at hand: at least a partial suspension of transfers of domestic savings abroad in order to recover investment levels. As Ramos points out in Chapter 4, an adjustment program will be efficient only if it helps to correct the permanent imbalances in the external accounts, not only the transitory imbalances. On the basic premise, optimum conditionality should ensure external financing as a counterpart to an equivalent permanent domestic adjustment effort. It should be emphasized again that what is involved is a suspension of transfers abroad, but not suspension of the corresponding domestic savings effort.

This measure, which should be negotiated and agreed upon with the creditors, would make available a considerable volume of foreign exchange. The exact amount would depend on the debt servicing burden of each country, on the proportion of the payment it is agreed to suspend, and, as has been stressed, on the premise that the increased foreign exchange availability is not used to finance an expansionary process based on increases in consumption. If it were possible to ensure that by means of these actions one could effectively dispose of a significant portion of this potential volume of foreign exchange, a good part of the strategy's initial financing needs would be ensured within an encouraging context of economic recovery that would facilitate its consolidation at higher levels of domestic investment and saving.

A domestic effort of such magnitude and economic and social seriousness should elicit the cooperation of the international community not directly affected by the partial suspension of debt servicing, which would be the large majority, and which could exert positive influence on industrialized countries and international agencies. In some industrialized countries, the United States in particular, there are important voices and sectors that have expressed dissatisfaction with official policy. Latin America should support and strengthen those sectors with concrete and sound technical and political arguments. This debate and the ensuing internal political pressures in industrialized countries are critical in changing official positions. The world economy is in a negative-sum-game situation in which all, or virtually all, lose or at least do not win. Debtor countries are the most affected, particularly their popular classes, but creditor countries also lose or do not win. The lower levels of economic activity, employment, trade, investments, and international financial flows constitute a recessive influence on the world economy and a factor of instability and uncertainty.

However, any success achieved in suspending external debt servicing should in no way mean a suspension of the corresponding domestic saving effort. This is the main difference with populist proposals for suspending external debt servicing. Rather, this effort should be formalized by means of an institutional framework, such as a National Fund for Economic Restructuring and Social Development. Moreover, as a means of simultaneously promoting social and political consensus and support, all social sectors should be democratically represented in this fund. Initially, at least, priority should be given to applying its resources to the most pressing social problems and to raising the efficient production of tradables (Sunkel 1989).[12]

In order to deal more generally with the fundamental problem of linking the short term with the long term and linking the structural factors with those of the current functioning of the economy, as well as with the social, cultural, and political aspects of a renewed development strategy from within, it is imperative to overcome the prevailing conventional economic approaches. One way to attempt this complex articulation task, at least conceptually, is to distinguish clearly between annual short term flows, which are what conventional economics deals with almost exclusively, and the national wealth, assets, or stocks acquired and accumulated over the long term, which are usually neglected. The nature and characteristics of annual flows condition and shape national assets in the long term; these assets in turn constitute the structural factors that largely condition short term flows.

Three kinds of stock may be distinguished: social and cultural assets (population and its demographic characteristics, traditions, values, educational levels, scientific and technological capacity, institutional organization, ideologies and political systems, and regimes); natural endowments (the territory, its ecosystemic characteristics, and the current and potential availability of renewable and nonrenewable natural resources); and fixed capital assets (productive capacity and installed and accumulated infrastructure, or the built environment). These are obviously merely extended political economy versions of the three classical productive resources: labor, land, and capital. Although it is basically an economic approach, it has the advantage of suggesting linkages between the social, cultural, and political aspects of development and the spatial and environmental aspects, as well as with accumulated productive capacity—in other words, the relationship of the assets among themselves and with the system of flows, and, therefore, the relationship between the medium and long term trends and the annual flows. These refer essentially to short term macroeconomic balances and focus on fiscal, monetary, external, employment, and income balances and their implications and sociopolitical conditioning factors.

Thus, for example, the serious negative external imbalance in income flows and foreign exchange outlays severely curtails imports, causing considerable underutilization of the accumulated sociocultural, human, natural, and productive potential. This means that a considerable amount of resources (cultural, organizational, and material) could be mobilized with a modest availability of imported inputs. This reveals in turn the structurally dependent nature of the former development pattern, and with it the critical link between the domestic and the external, both at the macroeconomic policy level of short term flows and in view of the longer term development strategy and policies regarding the utilization of the endowment of productive assets.

This conceptualization also helps to shed light on the issue of the passage from a conventional recessive adjustment to an expansionary adjustment, and to the transition toward development from within. Recessive adjustment essentially consists of manipulating short term economic policy instruments aimed at limiting global demand, cutting back on public expenditure, reducing investment, lowering income, curbing monetary expansion, and devaluating the currency, all of this for the purpose of reducing imports and achieving external balance, but with serious effects on capital accumulation, production, wages, and employment. Expansive adjustment, rather than placing the accent unilaterally on, or giving priority to, curbing demand and imports, would combine a policy of selective restriction of demand with a policy of selective expansion of supply. The aim would be to change the composition of both to achieve their reciprocal adjustment and balance. A simultaneous effort would also be undertaken to utilize the idle and available sociocultural, natural, and capital productive potentials in the short term, while shaping an investment policy and institutional and sociocultural changes aimed at modifying in the longer term the dependent, heterogeneous, disconnected, and polarized structure of those sociocultural, natural, and capital assets.

While the ultimate goal of the recessive route is payment of the external debt, the selective recovery alternative has as a ruling horizon the payment of the "social debt."[13] In the latter approach, primary importance is given both to short term actions, aimed at reducing the extent and degree of poverty, and to long term policies that seek to overcome extreme poverty levels through necessary distributive changes in order to reach a socially acceptable equity level. Moreover, recessive demand policy relies on the market to impose its selectiveness, with well-known regressive effects given the income and power concentration and the heterogeneity of the productive structure, whereas a combined policy of selective restriction of demand and selective expansion of supply would have to make intelligent use of the mobilizing, guiding, and coordinating capacity of the state.

In the light of these considerations and appealing to the wealth of sociocultural and political experience of the last decade, it is advisable to reexamine the role of each social agent in the political and economic tasks of a transition toward self-sustained and equitable development. Bearing this in mind, the much-maligned use of state intervention should be analyzed using a more pragmatic criterion, recognizing the vital role of the state in making up for market failures and for negative trends in the distribution of the benefits of growth, as well as its role in guiding long term development and its unavoidable commitment as guarantor of democratic institutionality (see Chapter 13).

For their part, the private sector, workers, and entrepreneurs have the legitimate right to demand respect for the rules of the game and for individual freedom and creativity. However, they should also assume the responsibility of responding with their utmost productive potential to the demands of efficient economic development and to moderate their socioeconomic demands as an effective way of contributing to political stability.

As Rosenthal (1989) suggests, the legitimacy of the state should not be established at the expense of the private sector, but at the same time, the legitimacy of the private sector cannot be founded at the expense of the state and, in particular, of the most vulnerable strata of society. Both agents should be important actors in the economic domain and only through their reciprocal support, by means of consensus-building processes, will a space of democratic political convergence be achieved in which an efficient and modern state can function without restricting the initiative and freedom of private agents.

With regard to the preceding considerations, it is important to point out that in Latin American countries there is a wealth of macroeconomic and sociopolitical experience, in addition to more detailed sectoral, regional, and specific practical knowledge of grass-roots social organizations. This should also serve as a basis to attempt the formulation of concrete proposals for development actions aimed at mutually supporting and adequately handling accumulated assets. Proposals should focus both at the microeconomic and local as well as the mezzoeconomic, regional, and macroeconomic policy levels. All of these dimensions are important and complementary given the structurally heterogeneous nature of the poverty conditions in which a large part of the Latin American population remains. (See Tables 2.10 and 2.11 for background information on the region's serious poverty problem.) Efforts at efficient social assistance will have greater impact and lower costs in the short term, and in turn, a correct macroeconomic deployment could contribute to eliminating the structural conditioning factors of extreme poverty (PREALC-ILO 1988b).

Assistance or direct policies can focus their redistributive efforts in three areas: social expenditure policies, contingency employment programs, and policies directed at the informal sector and small and medium business. First, social expenditure should focus on the neediest groups in urban and rural areas, favoring their access to social programs involving nutrition, health care, education, housing, and social security. It would be advisable to insist on specific measures aimed at improving nutritional programs directed at the child and maternal sector, without detriment to continuing this assistance to the rest of the population; introducing legislative reforms on health care to include the unemployed and reduce the contributions of lower income taxpayers; universalizing basic general education; overcoming the enormous housing deficit; and increasing retirement pensions and the coverage of the poorest groups in the social security system.

In terms of the second set of policies, we can point to massive labor employment programs for construction and reconstruction of housing, sanitation works, infrastructure, and community improvements in popular settlements; construction, reconstruction, and maintenance of road infrastructure, public works, and human settlements in general; protection against floods and other disasters caused by natural forces; forestation and terrace formation in erosion-prone areas; clean-up and protection of rivers and canals, drainage works, and irrigation; incorporation of new lands; repair and maintenance of public buildings, machinery, and equipment; and other such labor intensive productive activities.

Table 2.10. Evolution of Poverty in Latin America, 1960–1985

	1960	1970	1977	1980	1985
Total population (in millions)	216	283	339	361	405
Number of poor (in millions)	110	113	112	119	158
Extension of poverty (%)	51	40	33	33	39
Poverty gap (over GDP) (%)	9.1[a]	4.5	2.7	—	—

Sources: PREALC (Working Document No. 318).
CELADE (Demographic Bulletins, January 1985 and July 1987).
Reproduced with amendments by PREALC-ILO (1988a: 12 and 38).
Note: a. Estimated.

Table 2.11. Latin America: Conjectural Evolution of Poverty, 1980–1985

	1980			1985		
	Urban	Rural	Total	Urban	Rural	Total
Population (in millions)	228.9	132.4	361.3	267.3	137.4	404.7
Poor	47.3	71.9	119.2	77.3	80.5	157.8
Not poor	181.6	60.5	242.1	190.0	56.9	246.9
Poverty coverage[a]	20.7	54.3	33.0	28.9	54.6	39.0
Localization of poverty[b]	39.7	60.3	100.0	49.0	51.0	100.0

Sources: PREALC (Working Document No. 318).
CELADE (Demographic Bulletins, January 1985 and July 1987).
Reproduced with amendments by PREALC-ILO (1988a: 12 and 38).
Notes: a. Percentage of the population under the poverty line over urban, rural, and total populations, respectively.
b. Percentage of population under urban and rural poverty line over total poor population.

In many cases and countries, there are also ample possibilities for taking advantage of accumulated resource potential through social reforms and structural, legal, institutional, and technological innovations that facilitate access by vast social sectors to underutilized or neglected natural resources, and that improve their management. It is imperative to include in the agenda structural and institutional reforms and social organization innovations at all levels. Many of these reforms can be seen as being the necessary support that small and medium-sized business and the informal sectors should receive, to cut the noose that is choking full expression of their productive potential.

A large part of the income of the most impoverished social groups comes from the labor market, for which reason the array of selective measures and programs evaluated at the macro level should underscore the increase in investment and its reorientation toward activities that maximize the generation of productive employment. Ensuring the permanence of this salutary effect requires that investment be allocated to tradable sectors, particularly exportables and basic consumption, with the greatest employment linkage.

Remuneration policy that pursues the preceding objective must focus on the recovery of depressed real wage levels and on scheduling rates of increase according to productive performance. Targeting its effect on the poorest strata also requires an active minimum wage policy aimed at improving the remuneration levels of these workers. To prevent inflationary breakouts and provide workers incentives, part of the real wage paid over and above productivity could take the form of an investment wage, increasing worker participation in company equity and becoming an adequate mechanism for permanently altering the distributive structure.

Nevertheless, it must be recognized that the debt crisis has imposed a temporary structural impediment to the challenge of substantially reversing regressive income distribution in the short term. The immediate need to generate external surplus demands the maintenance of a high real exchange rate, and, consequently, this demands moderation in wage claims. Only over the medium and long term, and to the extent that productivity is increased, can greater and fairer wage aspirations be addressed in order to render them compatible with the necessary incentives to the tradable sector.

At another overall development strategy level, it is necessary to recognize the need for coordinated natural resource and environmental management that allows for the sustainable exploitation of the immense potential available and the generation and development of "new" productive resources (Sunkel 1980, 1987b). The rational transformation of the natural environment through scientific and technological research permits the utilization of opportunities and implies appropriate management of the environmental supply. Natural resources are not a static geographic datum, but are created by society to the extent that society decides and knows how to seek them and utilize them.

Biased by its dependent and imitative development, the region has been unimaginative both in terms of avoiding waste and in optimizing the utilization of its resources. Scientific and technological research has not been aimed primarily at protecting environmental resources or promoting their adequate management. Our countries have not devoted efforts to identifying unrecognized or neglected resources, improving technical efficiency in the use of raw materials and energy, nor improving energy conservation, much less the utilization of waste and residues. Consequently, this enormous latent potential could eventually be transformed through adequate science and technology policy into a concrete and important contribution to future development.

In addition, it is possible to improve the utilization of accumulated productive assets by seeking a more systematic, interconnected, and comprehensive utilization of the external economies created by capital invested in a given sector for its utilization in other sectors. This situation arises frequently in the case of large projects, for example, hydroelectric dams, roads, ports and harbors, urban infrastructure, and social services. The prevalence of the sectoral approach, the customary classification of the economy into sectors—industry, agriculture, mining, energy, transportation, construction, housing, health, education—pervades economic policy and planning, public administration, and professional disciplines and credit institutions. This gives rise to the duplication of activities and the waste of obvious opportunities for mutual support and complementation in the utilization of the multiple positive external economies that arise when a sectoral approach is replaced by a spatial-regional one.

Adequate regional or spatial management also allows a series of positive interconnected benefits to be obtained. Thus, for example, when the need is pointed out for protection of upper river basin forests, not only is the supply of timber and firewood and the preservation of wild flora and fauna ensured, but soil loss and river and dam silting is also prevented, the useful life of dams and irrigation schemes is lengthened, the risk of flooding is reduced, and the development of aquaculture and tourism is supported. When explicit consideration of the regional environment is put forward at the project preparation stage of major infrastructure works, the purpose is not only to protect the ecosystemic base of those very works and therefore their long term durability and profitability, but also to bring out the development potential and rational utilization of a series of resources and external economies that are generated by those works, and which could have a highly positive impact on the quality of life of regional and local communities. The same applies to national development programs, plans, and policies.

On the other hand, the wealth of local development alternatives proposed and experimented with over the last decades—such as integrated productive systems, combined technologies, and ecodevelopment—should be considered. They are directly aimed at production to meet basic needs through the utilization of local knowledge, labor, natural resources, wastes, and residues. Combined with appropriate technical, credit, management, and marketing support, they could make a considerable contribution at the community level.

They have been resorted to in the current economic crisis situation but should be upgraded to help overcome the structural heterogeneity that characterizes our economies and societies. They revalue the work process aimed at meeting essential needs and at organizing labor and underutilized skills and other potentialities, making less use of scarce factors, such as capital and foreign exchange, and taking advantage of specific geographic contexts, daily experience, local knowledge, and cultural traditions.

Such possibilities do not come about automatically. Instead, these activities tend to be generated strictly within a contingency framework. It is crucial, then, to take advantage of the crisis period to identify and promote those activities that promise to become self-sustaining and commercially viable. In other cases these activities involve collective consumption or productive infrastructures that are not likely to develop into profitable private activities, either because these investments are of a long term nature, yield very low profits, and favor lower income sectors and therefore have scarce effective demand, or because they involve attempts to create external economies or to avoid external diseconomies whose surplus cannot be tapped by the private investor. Consequently, these are all activities that need to be supported and nurtured by the public sector through a whole variety of policies.

Another main characteristic of these activities and projects is their local geographic specificity in concrete locations and sites. Therefore, they involve an area of public activity that lends itself particularly to decentralization and community participation, issues of special interest and priority in the search for democratic planning and decisionmaking systems. Although the circumstances of the crisis have served as a catalyst to start movements of this type, the fact that they involve basic needs that are systematically unmet, even in an expanding economy, suggests the need to create permanent programs and activities that are adequately institutionalized and financed.

Moving to the other extreme of the income structure, given the severe scarcity of resources and the enormous savings and investment efforts required—not to mention considerations of equity and sociopolitical viability—it will be imperative to limit consumption in general and conspicuous consumption in particular, especially consumption that directly or indirectly implies a high import component. We must encourage, on the one hand, efficient replacement with goods and services, technologies and designs that are based on the use of national and local material and human resources and, on the other hand, encourage an extraordinary effort to increase exports of goods and services.

A development strategy from within, based on national effort and the exploitation of our own resources, demands that we come down from exaggerated levels of abstraction to the concrete consideration of the specific availability of human resources and technology, the characteristics of size and location of each country, the relation between population and natural resources, the environmental and energy situation, and the degree and characteristics of urbanization. This means that development policies will have to differ for countries exhibiting marked differences in these aspects; it also means that policies, applied to each country in particular, will have to give priority to consideration of differentiated regional and spatial aspects (including the urban-rural issue). All of this is in contrast to the homogenizing trends that have tried to be imposed in many different areas: economic policies, consumption patterns, technology, architectural designs, environmental standards, and the like.

The international crisis has once again brought to the fore the importance of Latin American regional integration and cooperation. This integration process, which was initially conceived as a regional extension of the domestic market to favor import substitution, must now be rethought in terms of its contribution to the launching of a strong export drive and an efficient import substitution strategy. Likewise, the utilization of the extensive shared potential resources of Latin America should be a very important avenue for reviving regional cooperation. Joint and coordinated sustainable utilization of areas such as the River Plate basin, the Amazon basin, the Caribbean, Pacific, and Atlantic marine and coastal areas, and Patagonia constitutes an enormous potential in agriculture, forestry, energy, mining, and river and sea transportation for the region.

An additional comment has to do with the distinction between short and long term policies. This is of great importance when dealing with both the recession and the structural crisis. Long term policies—such as those that have an impact on natural resource conservation, population, education, science and technology, international relations, regional cooperation, and social organization—would seem not to have any bearing on short term problems. But as we have attempted to show, they provide ample opportunities to contribute to resolving some of them, such as employment generation, the meeting of basic needs, and the development of new exports and opportunities for import substitution. Conversely, short term economic policies, particularly special employment programs, formulated in reaction to the recession could be designed so as to contribute to preserving and improving the existing social infrastructure, productive capital, natural resources, and the environment. Therefore, the close collaboration between those responsible for short term macroeconomic balances (ministries of finance, central banks) and those concerned with development over the medium and longer term (planning offices, sectoral ministries, regional agencies, public enterprises) could make a positive and fruitful contribution to the objective of achieving sustainable development.

In the final analysis, all the preceding thoughts lead to the conclusion that an enormous and complex task is implicit in the renewed challenge of achieving democratically and environmentally sustainable and sustained socioeconomic development from within. In economic terms, it requires an adequate level of capital accumulation, competitiveness, and creativity to penetrate and satisfy critical markets, whether these be domestic or foreign. In the social sphere, it urgently requires the alleviation of poverty and the achievement of a reasonable level of social justice, as well as sufficient labor and educational opportunities and substantially wider access to a decent standard of living. At the international level, it requires a domestic performance that allows our countries to participate individually and collectively as respected actors in the community of nations with mutually balanced and satisfactory international relations. In the cultural field, it requires the attainment of a sufficient level of national identity to represent in a pluralistic way the best values and traditions that shape and distinguish our nations, while incorporating selectively and with creativity what world culture has to offer. In the political arena, it requires the achievement and maintenance of an acceptable degree of legitimacy, representation, efficiency, responsibility, and renovation of authorities, and ample participation by the people in national, regional, and local government institutions. Regarding human rights, a fundamental component of democracy, the necessary respect must be ensured for the fundamental rights of the individual, the family, and basic social organizations. Last, but certainly not least, actions must be taken in the environmental sphere to ensure that the natural endowment inherited from the past be passed down to future generations in the best possible conditions to ensure an improved material base for their future well-being.

Notes

The author wishes to thank Gustavo Zuleta for his collaboration in preparing this chapter.

1. See ECLA (1950), which includes case studies of Argentina, Brazil, Chile, and Mexico; ECLA (1954) on Ecuador; and the series of studies published by ECLA under the general title *Analysis and Projections of Economic Development*, including separate volumes on case studies of Brazil (1956), Colombia (1957), Bolivia (1958), Argentina (1959), Peru (1959), Panama (1959), El Salvador (1959), Honduras (1960), and Nicaragua (1966). There also was a study on Costa Rica, published by the University of Costa Rica, and unpublished studies of Chile and Mexico.

2. Although the latter work was not published under his name, Prebisch inspired it and wrote the general introductory sections.

3. To explain the differential impact of the export sector on the internal economy, the concept of the "capacity for diversification" of export sector growth, and a historically based typology of the countries of the region, was developed (Sunkel and Paz 1970: part 4, especially p. 317).

4. This idea, undoubtedly Keynesian in inspiration, was also based on the welfare state and New Deal experiences, and on the economic planning systems adopted by the socialist, fascist, and war economies.

5. The democratizing wave in Latin America began with the fall of dictator Somoza in Nicaragua (1978) and continued in Ecuador (1979), Peru (1980),

Honduras and Bolivia (1982), Argentina (1983), El Salvador (1984), Uruguay and Brazil (1985), Guatemala (1986), Paraguay (1989), and Chile (1990).

6. An in-depth analysis of the political reality of various countries of the region that provides background information on this process of democratic renovation of large parts of the Latin American Left is contained in several articles published in *Pensamiento Iberoamericano: Revista de Economía Política* (1988). .

7. The enormous public financial transfers to private national and foreign banks following the debt crisis are clear evidence of the privilege granted these sectors and the unfair conditionality that the transnationalized sector imposes on our economies: benefits are privatized but losses are socialized.

8. Herrera and Vignolo (1981) present a documented review of the series of mechanisms used by the Chilean state in tapping surplus from the large-scale copper mining sector. They point to the progressive increases in direct and indirect taxation on that sector, the imposition of an overvalued peso exchange rate on export proceeds, the subsequent "Chileanization" of the large copper enterprises, which meant majority participation by the state, and finally their nationalization in 1971. Similar itineraries were followed by most of the region's countries although obviously with variations, particularly in the case of countries with nationally owned agricultural export sectors.

9. For a recent survey of inflation in Latin America, see *Pensamiento Iberoamericano: Revista de Economía Política* (1986). See also Sunkel (1960) and Chapter 4.

10. Marcel (1988) in particular evaluates the recent and radical privatization process in Chile, drawing two important conclusions. One establishes that whenever privatized enterprises were economically viable prior to their sale, the effect on public finance will most probably be negative over the long term. The other indicates that, compared to alternative sources of fiscal financing, privatizations will have a greater crowding out effect on private investment, given that they attract resources that could have been destined for new investment. In the light of this research, the greater efficiency argument with which the privatizing zeal tends to be justified is questionable.

11. The original Spanish text of this crucial phrase reads "mediante el desarrollo desde dentro," which I have found more appropriate to translate as "development from within" (Sunkel 1990).

12. The proposal was first put forward by Sunkel (1985).

13. The concept of "social debt" refers to a domestic commitment to recover the deterioration in the standard of living of the most vulnerable sectors of the population, which is in fact the other side of the recessive adjustment policies adopted to meet the external debt commitment (PREALC-ILO 1988a).

3

Equity and Development

Nora Lustig

This chapter deals with the relation between equity and growth, both in terms of currents of thought and in Latin America's recent history.[1] Throughout history, Latin American countries have been characterized by a relative inequity. From its inception at the end of the 1940s, structuralist thought has tried to explain this phenomenon and suggest ways to encourage a more egalitarian society.

The chapter is organized as follows. The first section presents a summary of the evolution of structuralist ideas with respect to growth and equity between, approximately, the 1950s and late 1970s. The second section summarizes available information on the evolution of income distribution, poverty levels, and living conditions in Latin America during approximately the same period. It also presents empirical evidence in relation to some of the structuralist ideas regarding the relation between income distribution and growth. The third section describes how the equity indicators were affected by the crisis of the 1980s. The evolution of neostructuralist thinking in recent years is presented in the fourth section. The last section analyzes the restrictions and possibilities involved in the search for greater equity at present.

Structuralism and the Relation Between Growth and Equity

The Impact of Economic Growth on Income Distribution and Poverty

Both classical and Marxist theories, either due to Malthusian-type processes or to the displacement of labor resulting from technological change, predict that poverty and income distribution worsen with economic growth. The outlook of the simpler version of neoclassical theory, however, is that income distribution and living standards improve with economic growth because the accumulation of capital results in a modification of the relative scarcity of factors and therefore increases the productivity of labor and its retribution.

The relation between economic growth and income distribution has been widely dealt with in economic development literature.[2] One of the pioneers in this matter was Kuznets,[3] who, on the basis of his observations on time series in developed countries, proposed the theory that income distribution worsens during the initial stages of economic development, improving thereafter. This is known as the "Kuznets curve." The author explains this behavior on the basis that urbanization and the concentration of savings contribute to inequality. Kuznets's hypothesis has given rise to a great number of empirical studies based on time series and cross-sectional data, some of which validate the hypothesis while others disprove it.[4]

In Latin America the relation between income distribution and economic growth has been studied within the framework of the global conception of the development process set forth by the Economic Commission for Latin America (ECLAC). ECLAC's first contributions in this area in the late 1940s and early 1950s, which can be attributed primarily to Raúl Prebisch, then its executive secretary, consisted in developing the *center-peripheral* concept and the theory on the deterioration of the terms of trade.[5] These ideas marked the beginning of structuralist thought in Latin America.

According to the center-periphery concept, during the first half of this century the global development of the capitalist system resulted in an asymmetric spreading of technological progress in the centers and in the periphery.[6] As part of this process, the structure of the periphery acquired two fundamental characteristics. On the one hand, peripheral economies became specialized, inasmuch as development took place almost exclusively in the primary-goods export sector whereas demand for industrial goods was met, to a large extent, with imports. On the other hand, the peripheral structure is heterogeneous, as it includes sectors that use advanced technology imported from the centers, and in which there is a comparable level of labor productivity, as well as sectors in which obsolete and outdated techniques are used, thus leading to much lower productivity levels than those in analogous activities in central economies.

However, perhaps the most important aspect of the center-periphery concept is the idea that these characteristics of the peripheral productive structure, far from disappearing as capitalism makes progress, tend to perpetuate and reinforce themselves. This is due fundamentally to the fact that technological change is far more pronounced in the industrial sector than in the primary sector. The former leads to an increase in the productivity and income gap between the center and the periphery. This polarization tends to increase given the degree of organization of the working class and the oligopolist power of the private business sector in central economies in comparison to the more competitive and nonunionized peripheral structures.

According to this view, inequality, poverty, and lack of development in the periphery therefore result from the specialization pattern determined by the international division of labor. In order to break this trend, the periphery needs to change the historical pattern of specialization based on exploiting static comparative advantages and, instead, promote industrial development through import substitution and furnishing the necessary protection to infant industries. Industrialization is considered "a means to prevent productivity increases from being transferred abroad through a fall in the terms of trade, thus negatively affecting wages" (Rodríguez 1980: 280) in the periphery.[7]

Structuralism found fertile ground for its ideas in favor of industrialization via import substitution in postwar Latin American economies. During the 1930s and 1940s, the combination of controls on international trade, restrictions on foreign exchange, and expansive demand policies in Latin American economies resulted in a speedy economic recovery after the Great Depression, recovery that was headed by the industrial sector.[8]

The economic policy recommended by structuralism was also congruent with modernization in its broadest sense: it implied encouraging the growth of an urban labor sector and strengthening the position of industrial businesses vis-à-vis the oligarchical agro-export sector. It was assumed that industrialization through import substitution would lead the peripheral economies to a more independent, democratic, and egalitarian growth path than that based on primary goods exports. However, the increasing external imbalance in the late 1950s indicated that the expectations created by industrialization through import substitution did not necessarily come true as anticipated.

This perception of the favorable effect of "deliberate industrialization" on income distribution is not shared by other authors interested in studying the features that characterize development in dual economies. Arthur Lewis, for example, considers that income distribution is more concentrated in the case of a growth path oriented toward the modern (industrial) sector because it involves higher profits than in the traditional sector.[9]

In actual practice, industrialization through import substitution did not bring about the much-desired financial independence, nor the expected reduction of poverty and inequity.[10] For some authors this outcome was the consequence of the concentration of income that characterized the kind of import substitution implemented during the "difficult" stage (development of consumer durables and capital goods), which generated a demand for goods manufactured with capital-intensive techniques and encouraged the industrial sector to become monopolistic and inefficient.[11]

During this period, structuralists believed that the inward-looking development strategy had intensified the contrast between the privileges held by the wealthier sectors and by those who had not been absorbed by the modern sector of the economy. As we shall see, in addition to restating the income concentration tendency, structuralists in the 1960s and early 1970s believed that concentration of income and social inequality prevented any advance in the process of accumulation and growth.

> In contrast with the optimistic view held during the 1950s with respect to the sustainability of industrialization and its renovating role, it is suggested that in order to overcome the structural obstacles that hamper its performance and prevent the transformation of the entire socioeconomic system, it is necessary to promote and implement structural changes deliberately, from without the system (Rodríguez 1980: 296).

The view of a need to foster change from outside the system was shared by a wide variety of people, ranging from revolutionaries who called for delinking from world economy and implementing socialism,[12] to reformists who believed it possible to make improvements within the political and social limits set by the system,[13] and for whom the reforms could contemplate a redistribution of assets, albeit a "voluntary" one.

The idea that growth based on import substitution increased inequality and impoverishment was formally presented by Bacha and Taylor (1973) in their renowned article on Belindia. In general, the authors who developed these conceptions did so by deriving the implications of an economy with strong technological and organizational rigidities (resulting from advanced technology imported from the developed world) that allowed greater flexibility to some sectors (owners and workers of the modern sector) than to others (traditional sector workers and the excluded sectors).

The negative view on the distribution effects of industrialization via import substitution is also held by other authors who do not share the outlook of Latin American structuralist thought. They believe that a great part of the distribution problem is due to distorted relative prices caused by the protectionism applied during the import substitution process, which implied that capital became artificially relatively cheaper, thus giving rise to the use of capital-intensive technology in countries with an abundance of labor force.[14]

In clear contrast, the structuralist line of thought is that price distortion is less significant vis-à-vis structural factors such as the oligopolistic nature of the market, the segmentation of labor markets, and the concentration of wealth. Inequity does not arise from the distortion of prices generated by state intervention per se, but rather from a poorly managed intervention.[15]

The Effects of Income Distribution on Economic Growth

The analysis of the effects of income distribution on growth has focused on two types of mechanisms: the relation between income distribution and savings and the relation between income distribution and the magnitude and structure of internal demand and growth. The argument concerning the issue of savings is fairly well known: greater concentration of income may generate a higher marginal propensity to save and, therefore, result in a higher rate of growth. The underlying assumption is that the wealthier sectors have a higher marginal propensity toward saving than the poorer sectors.

Theoretically, the relation between income distribution, the demand structure, and growth takes place through the following mechanisms. As demand elasticities may vary according to income level, each distributive profile has a specific demand structure and, therefore, produces a specific supply structure. The supply structure may affect growth if the various productive sectors have different import requirements, economies of scale, or intensity of factors. It is also contended that some sectors are able to generate stronger dynamic linkages than others, or that they have more possibilities of creating or assimilating technological changes and, therefore, of encouraging further increases in productivity and growth.[16]

During the 1960s and early 1970s, a majority of the Latin American structuralist writers focused on this type of connection. Some of these authors enhanced the negative relation between concentration of income and growth.[17] Furtado, for example, tried to explain the decreasing rate of growth experienced by several Latin American countries in the late 1950s and early 1960s as a consequence of the characteristics of the import substitution process. Furtado considered Latin American countries to be the victims of a "vicious spiral" triggered by the interaction between growth and income distribution.[18] The prevalent growth model generated a high concentration of income, which in turn implied a demand structure (oriented toward durable consumer goods) that induced the productive structure to lean toward sectors with greater capital intensity (a greater capital-output relation) and higher import requirements, thus hindering the possibility of sustaining a certain growth rate.[19]

Furtado's pessimism with respect to the possibilities of continued growth was not shared by other structuralists,[20] partly because the rekindling of economic growth somewhat diminished the validity of the "stagnation" theories. According to Pinto and Vuskovic, for example, although the growth obstacles resulting from the productive structure's orientation toward durable or modern consumer goods were surmountable, these areas were characterized by a higher capital-output ratio and a lower labor coefficient than traditional sectors, while participation rates for transnational companies were higher. Under these assumptions, a relative expansion of the durable consumer goods sector is associated with relatively *lower* output and employment growth rates—rather than stagnation—and to higher inflow of foreign capital. Within this framework, a more equal distribution of income would be accompanied by increased output and employment growth rates and by a higher degree of national control over the productive apparatus.

Other Latin American authors, however, believed that the durable consumer goods sector played a role exactly opposite to that suggested by the authors mentioned previously.[21] According to Serra and Tavares, for example, the accumulation of capital during the industrialization process was stimulated by the expansion of the modern sector, owing to the magnitude of its dynamic linkages and the external economies it produced. For these authors accumulation could only continue if they solved the so-called realization problems in the modern or durable consumer goods sector, as it was perceived to be the leading sector of the economy in the Shumpeterian sense of the word.

In other words, the decreased growth rate during the difficult stage of import substitution was the result of the so-called realization crisis in the leading sector, brought about by an underconsumption of the goods produced in that sector. This underconsumption was due to the distributive profile, which induced a saturation of the demand for these goods. In order to overcome this problem, higher income concentration in the middle groups was required.[22]

For these authors the durable consumer goods sector was the leader of the economy, and therefore, income concentration was necessary to guarantee an adequate market. In contrast, redistributionists considered that the durable goods sector was exactly the one that should not expand, as it had the greatest import requirements and capital-labor ratio. However, in both conceptions, growth based on the expansion of the modern or durable consumer goods sector meant that the growth path would remain underdeveloped in nature, expressed in the exclusion of vast sectors of the population and in foreign dependency.

Evidence Regarding the Relation Between Economic Growth and Equity

The Validity of the Kuznets Curve

A considerable number of empirical studies, using cross-sectional data as well as time series, have tried to confirm the applicability of Kuznets's hypothesis on the inverted U-curve relation between income distribution and per capita income level. Bacha presents a summary of the best-known empirical estimates of this relation.[23] Apparently, many of the cross-sectional studies have found that the relation proposed by Kuznets is valid.

In contrast, a recent study by Papanek and Kyn (1986) found that although there is evidence validating Kuznets's hypothesis, such evidence is not very solid and, furthermore, may be diminishing over time (the so-called flattening of the Kuznets curve). Perhaps the most outstanding finding of this study is that there is no trade-off between growth rate and equity and that a higher rate of growth implies a much quicker reduction of poverty.[24]

Economic Growth and Income Distribution in Latin America

In Latin America the empirical analysis of Kuznets's hypothesis, of the structuralist hypotheses, or, indeed, of any other hypothesis on the relation between growth, income distribution, and the incidence of poverty in given countries is complicated because of the limitations of the data. Altimir expresses this quite well when he refers to the comparison of income distribution over time or between countries in Latin America.

> The main problems one must face in trying to attain this purpose are: the differences in coverage and the fact that most of the studies are not at a national level, the various concepts of income according to the way it was measured, the use of different reference periods, and, in general, the great variety of research methodologies for income applied by the different surveys, the difference in the quality of the data obtained and, therefore, the extent to which each survey underestimates households incomes, at least in relation to the framework established by the national accounts (Altimir 1981: 88).

Studies that have tried to analyze the relation between growth and income distribution in Latin America show that the results are not uniform for the countries analyzed.[25] That is to say, in some cases rapid growth was accompanied by a more unequal income distribution and in other cases this was not so. According to Altimir (1981: 88–91), the comparability of the surveys is adequate enough to make it possible to analyze the evolution of income distribution over time in three countries: Brazil, Colombia, and Mexico. In Brazil evidence showed a worsening in the distribution of income between 1960 and 1970; Colombia showed a slight improvement between 1964 and 1971; and in Mexico income distribution remained relatively constant between 1963 and 1968, slightly ameliorating between 1968 and 1977.

According to Iglesias, in seven combined Latin American countries inequality intensified between 1960 and 1975. Participation by the sector comprising the poorest 20 percent of the population decreased from 2.8 percent to 2.3 percent, while that of the wealthiest 10 percent increased from 46.6 percent to 47.3 percent. In absolute terms, it was estimated that "during this period, the average income of the poorest 40 percent of the population experienced an increase of less that 130 dollars (in dollars of 1970), while for the wealthiest 10 percent, the average income increased by approximately 4,400 dollars" (Iglesias 1981: 12).

Although it is difficult to generalize about the course of the evolution of income distribution over time in Latin America, the fact is that in the

1970s the countries in the region had a high concentration of income. Table 3.1 shows the distribution of income by decile for various years in the 1970s. Leaving aside the comparability issue raised above, countries may be classified into three groups: countries with high concentration, defined as those in which the share in the top decile was greater than 40 percent (Brazil, Colombia, and Mexico); those with intermediate concentration, where the share in the top decile was between 30 and 40 percent (Costa Rica, Chile, and Venezuela); and countries with low concentration, where the share in the top decile was less than 30 percent.

Economic Growth and Poverty in Latin America

Structuralist writers also estimated that the development of capitalism in the periphery would lead to increasing marginalization and poverty. Marginalization and poverty are not the same. The concept of exclusion includes poverty but encompasses more than just the economic dimension. Marginalization implies, in addition to insufficient satisfaction of material needs, exclusion from the political, social, and cultural spheres. Exclusion also has an intertemporal implication; among the marginal sectors, the next generation's probability of being better off is very low.

Table 3.1.   Income Distribution in Some Latin American Countries (in the 1970s)

Decile	1	2	3	4	5	6	7	8	9	10
Argentina (1972)	2.2	4.1	5.4	6.6	7.7	8.9	10.1	12.0	15.3	27.7
Brazil (1972)	0.6	1.4	2.1	2.9	4.0	5.4	7.1	9.9	16.0	50.6
Chile (1971)	1.5	2.8	3.9	4.9	6.1	7.4	9.2	11.9	16.5	35.8
Colombia (1972)	1.5	2.5	3.3	4.0	5.1	6.3	8.0	10.7	16.4	42.2
Costa Rica (1971)	2.0	3.0	3.9	4.8	5.9	7.0	8.6	11.2	15.8	37.8
Mexico (1977)	1.1	2.1	3.1	4.1	5.2	6.5	8.3	11.6	17.9	40.1
Venezuela (1977)	1.6	2.9	4.1	5.3	6.5	8.0	9.7	12.7	17.3	32.1

Source: ECLAC, *Serie distribución del ingreso,* various years; Argentina, Table 5.1; Brazil, Table 5.1; Chile, Table 5.1; Colombia, Table 5; Costa Rica, Table 5.1; Mexico, Table 5; Venezuela, Table 5.

In Latin America available indicators show no evidence of an increasing incidence of poverty in the 1960s. On the contrary, all cases with enough information to carry out the analysis showed a decrease in poverty; that is to say, there was a decrease of the proportion of households below the poverty line. For example, a study by Piñera (1979) indicates that the proportion of the population in Latin America living in poverty decreased from 66 percent to 43 percent, according to a comparison of data corresponding to 1963 and to 1974. In Costa Rica it diminished from 51 percent to 20 percent between 1961 and 1971; in Mexico, from 36 percent to 27 percent between 1963 and 1968; in Brazil, from 52 percent to 44 percent between 1960 and 1970; and in Peru, from 58 percent to 52 percent between 1961 and 1971.[26]

The problem with these figures is that in some cases data sources in the different periods of time are not comparable (Altimir 1981: 82). Nevertheless, even with comparable and adjusted data the tendency remains the same, although its magnitude does not. A study by Altimir (1981: 83–84), which uses surveys that are comparable, indicates that the proportion of households below the poverty line decreased from 46 percent to 35 percent in Mexico between 1963 and 1968; from 61 percent to 55 percent in Brazil between 1960 and 1970; and from 55 percent to 52 percent in Colombia between 1964 and 1971. Even when adjustments were made so that the poverty line would move upward with the increment in the average income,[27] results indicate that the proportion of the poor decreased between 1960 and 1970 (Altimir 1981: 84–85). Perhaps it should be underscored that although the proportion of poor households and individuals seemingly declined, this is not the case in absolute terms. Due to a high population growth, in many Latin American countries the relative reduction of poverty may have been accompanied by an increase in the total number of people living in poverty.[28]

Although during the 1960s relative poverty decreased in a significant number of Latin American countries, its incidence was still considerable. Table 3.2 shows an estimate of the incidence of poverty in Latin America in approximately 1970. As may be seen, there are great differences between the countries under consideration.[29] The combined data of Tables 3.1 and 3.2 show that Argentina had a more equitable income distribution and a very low poverty index according to Latin American standards. Brazil's case was exactly the opposite: high income concentration and high incidence of poverty. Mexico had high income concentration, but the incidence of poverty was lower than average in Latin America.

Besides income, there are other important indicators that show the evolution of the population's living conditions. Table 3.3 shows indicators of life expectancy, infant mortality, and illiteracy rates. Once again, significant differences may be observed from one country to another. Notwithstanding, in all cases there was an improvement in those indicators during the periods 1960–1965 and 1970–1975. Another article that presents data on schooling and nutrition also shows they have improved. For example, the average literacy rate for Latin American children ages 6–11

Table 3.2.   Percentage of Households Below the Poverty Line in Latin America
             (approximately 1970)

	Urban	Rural	National
Argentina	5	19	8
Brazil	35	73	49
Colombia	38	54	45
Costa Rica	15	30	24
Chile	12	25	17
Honduras	40	75	65
Mexico	20	49	34
Peru	28	68	50
Uruguay	10	—	—
Venezuela	20	36	25
Latin America	26	62	40

Source: Altimir (1981: 77, Table 2).

increased from 57.3 percent in 1960 to 82.3 percent in 1980. Likewise, the average caloric intake as a percentage of the minimum required intake increased from 104.8 percent in 1961–1963 to 110.9 percent in 1975–1977.[30]

The Impact of Income Distribution on Growth

With respect to the distributive effects on growth, there are a series of studies that present simulation exercises intended to study the potential impact of distribution changes on the growth rate.[31] These studies indicate that income redistribution would have a negative effect on growth (due to the negative effect on savings), but that it would be a minor effect. However, this kind of study cannot be used as the basis to analyze the actual effects that a redistributive process would have in practice, simply because these processes do not operate in the margin (as simulations models do) in the real world.

Irrespective of what the simulation exercises might show, historical experience suggests that the impact of redistribution on growth must be analyzed within a political economy framework. That is, one must "model" the reaction of the various actors that are affected by redistribution, both negatively and positively, and analyze how the reaction differs depending on the policies used. For example, redistribution via tax-financed public expenditures in education and health care might be more acceptable than redistribution through changes in property rights.[32]

In practice, redistributive processes fostered by the state have tried to modify the distribution of assets, the primary distribution, and/or the secondary distribution. The first type of modification includes agrarian reforms and the nationalization of enterprises. The second includes all the

Table 3.3.   Recent Evolution of Some Basic Social Indicators

Country	Life expectancy (years)		Child Mortality 0–1 year-olds (per thousand)		Illiteracy (% of the population age 15 and over)	
	1960–65	1970–75	1960–65	1970–75	1960–65	1970–75
Argentina	66.0	68.4	54	44	8.6	7.4
Bolivia	43.5	46.7	225	157	61.2	37.3
Brazil	55.9	59.8	112	95	39.0	33.8
Chile	57.6	64.2	107	72	16.4	11.9
Colombia	56.2	60.4	85	67	27.1	19.2
Costa Rica	63.0	68.1	80	50	16.0	11.6
Cuba	65.1	70.9				
Dominican Rep.	52.6	57.9	110	83	35.5	32.8
Ecuador	51.9	57.1	132	100	32.5	25.8
El Salvador	52.3	59.1	123	92	51.0	42.9
Guatemala	48.2	54.6	128	104	62.1	53.9
Haiti	43.6	48.5	171	135	85.5	76.7
Honduras	47.9	54.1	137	110	55.0	43.1
Mexico	59.2	62.7	86	69	34.6	25.8
Nicaragua	47.9	52.9	137	109	50.4	42.5
Panama	63.2	67.4	67	47	26.7	21.7
Paraguay	56.6	63.1	81	53	25.4	19.9
Peru	48.8	55.0	161	122	38.9	27.6
Uruguay	68.3	68.6	49	47	9.6	6.1
Venezuela	58.9	64.5	77	53	36.7	23.5

Source: Altimir (1981: 87, Table 5).

measures that alter labor and capital incomes and, therefore, encompasses both legal and institutional processes (for example, the government's role in establishing wages for the private sector), as well as the entire range of macroeconomic and sectorial policies that affect relative prices (for example, trade, exchange rate, credit, and fiscal policies). Modification of the secondary distribution is mainly carried out by measures that determine the distribution of taxes and public services.

During the course of the 1950s, 1960s, and 1970s, several Latin American governments attempted to foster redistributive processes and improve living conditions through some or all of the mechanisms mentioned above. Some of those governments, such as the Christian Democrats in Chile, tried to achieve this through reforms based on some sort of social consensus. Others attempted more radical processes of asset redistribution and socialization, as was the case in Chile during Allende's government. Others tried to achieve these goals by some sort of state populism characterized by a large variety of subsidies and government-provided services, such as in the case of Velasco and Garcia in Peru and Echeverria and Lopez-Portillo in Mexico. The degree of effectiveness in fulfilling the redistributive objectives has varied, but in general certain problems have recurred.[33] The two most common ones have been, on the one hand, the inflationary and balance of payments crisis derived from unsustainable public deficits and, on the other hand, the supply constraints that resulted either from economic response to a bad set of incentives or from political reaction against the redistributive policies per se.[34]

As for the relation between income distribution and demand patterns, on the one hand, and productive structure characteristics, on the other,[35] it is interesting to note that contrary to some of the structuralists' writings, the empirical studies show that there are no systematic patterns.[36] First, the relation between alternative income distributions and the rise of the demand for durable or modern consumer goods is different for different kinds of durables. The demand for cars increases with greater concentration of income, but the demand for home appliances benefits from redistribution away from the top. Second, there was no inherent characteristic in the modern sector that could make its expansion either more growth enhancing or growth restricting. Some modern industries have higher investment and import requirements than the traditional ones, and vice versa. Similarly, the employment coefficient in some traditional industries is higher, and in others it is lower than in some modern industries. In other words, the generalizations proposed by structuralist writers on the characteristics of the modern sector, or on the relation between distributive profile and consumption patterns, could not be empirically verified.[37]

The Crisis of the 1980s, Adjustment, and Equity

The combination of growing domestic macroeconomic imbalances coupled with the fall in commodities prices in the late 1970s, the recession experienced in developed countries, higher world interest, and the sudden unavailability of external financing (especially from private sources) resulted in severe crises followed by economic downturns in most Latin American countries during the 1980s. For practically every country in the region, the accumulated growth rate in the per capita gross domestic product was either negative or close to zero between 1982 and 1989.[38] Since 1982, very much in contrast with the historical trend, Latin America produced a large net transfer of resources to the outside world. That is, Latin America became a capital-exporting area. This drastic change in the availability of external savings, coupled with a situation of domestic macroeconomic disorder, has forced most countries to go through drastic adjustment and profound economic restructuring.

In most countries the adjustment process has resulted in a drop in real average incomes, a reduction of subsidies for basic foodstuffs, and a reduction in public expenditure in the social sectors. It should be expected then that the crisis and subsequent adjustment have resulted in rising poverty and deteriorating social indicators.[39] Once again, the possibility of an empirical evaluation of these changes is limited by the information available. Nevertheless, it is possible to identify some trends that indicate the kinds of transformation and impact that have taken place.[40]

Indicators estimated by the Regional Employment Program for Latin America and the Caribbean (PREALC) on the evolution of functional or factorial income distribution in Latin America indicate an average drop in wage participation in labor from 41.5 percent in 1980 to 37.9 percent in 1985 (PREALC-ILO 1988a: 10, table 3).[41] However, given that in Latin America a large part of the low incomes come from nonwage sources, it is not feasible to make inferences as to the effect on the size distribution of income.

In general, the urban unemployment rate experienced an upward trend in many Latin American countries. However, there were notable exceptions, such as Mexico and Brazil, where the unemployment rate actually decreased slightly.[42] The minimum wage level, in real terms, was lower in 1988 than in 1980 in practically all the countries, with the exception of Colombia, Costa Rica, and Paraguay. In countries for which information is available, average wages also dropped or remained frozen, with the exception of Colombia (ECLAC 1989a: 32 and 33, tables 24 and 25).

According to recent estimations by PREALC, the conjectural evolution of poverty in Latin America points to a worsening. The percentage of the population below the poverty line increased from 33 percent in 1980 to 39 percent in 1985. This implies a return to the poverty situation existing in 1970, as well as an increase in the absolute number of the poor from 120 to 160 million. Also, poverty has become more urbanized. In 1980 the urban population classified as poor included almost 40 percent of the total population living in poverty, while in 1985 this proportion increased to 49 percent. The incidence of poverty, however, is still higher in rural areas (PREALC-ILO 1988a: 6, table 1).[43] Similar results are found in a more recent study published by ECLAC (1990a).

PREALC-ILO (1988a) also states that approximately 60 percent of the increase in the incidence of poverty was concentrated in the group of the unemployed, and 39 percent in the families of informal workers. In fact, the informal sector served as a cushion for those who did not find employment in the formal sector and resorted to activities that provide some remuneration, albeit a very meager one.

Besides the drop in the monetary income, the poor may have also suffered from the fact that during the crisis governments had to reduce social expenditures. In relative terms, the proportion of central government public expenditures destined for education and health care has fallen in most Latin American countries, particularly as a result of the rising proportion of public expenditures allocated to debt servicing.[44] To a great extent, this has meant a reduction in per capita expenditures. In relative terms it was

found that in Latin America expenditures destined for health care were
protected more than those destined for education.[45] However, there is no
automatic correlation between this drop in expenditures and the availability of physical resources in the education and health care services. In fact,
the drop in expenditures to a greater extent reflects the contraction of
workers' wages and of investment in social sectors rather than an actual
drop in physical inputs such as teachers or schools per student, or doctors
and hospital beds per capita.[46]

In general, the average social indicators did not pick up negative
changes during the crisis itself. For example, infant mortality rates continued to drop and average schooling continued to rise. However, perhaps
neither of these two adequately reflected the effects of the crisis. Ideally,
the evolution of these indicators for the most vulnerable groups should be
available. Furthermore, it is advisable to examine the trends shown by
other indicators that are more sensitive to changes in income and in living
conditions. For example, in the case of Mexico[47] it was possible to identify an increase in the proportion of deaths or illnesses caused by nutritional deficiencies, a relative decrease in the number of children enrolled
in primary school, and a relative decrease in the proportion that went on to
secondary school, which indicated a postponement of the educational pursuit or the decision to abandon it altogether (Lustig 1988b, 1989b).

Equity Issues in the Neostructuralist Conception

From approximately the second half of the 1970s until now, Latin American structuralist thinking has been gradually shifting its subject matter.
Analysis has increasingly focused on short term problems and policies,
while the issue of development strategies has lost impetus. The development of an alternative line of thought concerned with short term problems
may be

> a natural reaction to the "orthodox" stabilization packages applied in
> Southern Cone countries during the 1970s under the patronage of military
> regimes. It may also be a reply to the difficulties involved in the style of
> structural change recommended by the "redistributionists," as the Chilean
> case—in particular—exemplified. An alternative school of thought could
> not remain totally passive vis-à-vis rampant inflationary processes, sim-
> ply because the solution it offered was not feasible through long term
> changes (by eliminating bottle-necks in supply, for example). Such atti-
> tude could only lead to intellectual atony and to policy irrelevance
> (Lustig 1988a: 47).

One of the significant differences between structuralism and neostructuralism is the recognition that recommendations cannot stem from an
exclusively long term perspective, without taking into consideration the

possible consequences of any structural change process and without having already set up ways to face the problems originated during the transition. "In fact, in clear contrast with structuralism, it could well be said that neostructuralism presents—perhaps—the opposite deficiency: too much emphasis has been placed on short term analysis and relatively little on the long term (Lustig 1988a: 48).[48]

This is evident if we review the recent bibliography. A large part of what could be denominated neostructuralist thinking and, particularly, its theoretical and methodological contributions, has focused on analyzing inflationary processes and in proposing ways to combat them in the short term. In fact, neostructuralist proposals have tried to create an alternative to the orthodox stabilization plans that is less recessive and less regressive in distributive matters. A fundamental difference between structuralist thinking and orthodox analysis rests on the emphasis placed by the former on the inertial characteristics of inflation and on the ineffectiveness of the orthodox plans to combat it.[49]

In practice, the neostructuralist conception of the inflationary process was incorporated into the so-called heterodox shocks applied in the Austral Plan in Argentina, in the Cruzado Plan in Brazil, and in the Economic Solidarity Pact in Mexico.[50] Although quite successful in their early stages, the outcomes of the Austral and Cruzado plans were rather unfortunate. The Economic Solidarity Pact, however, may be a good example of a successful application of the recommendations derived from the neostructuralist analysis regarding the ways to fight inflation's inertial component.[51]

The remarkable emphasis placed by recent neostructuralist literature on the analysis of short term problems reflects, on the one hand, the compelling characteristics of these problems, such as uncontrolled inflationary processes and the severe external restrictions since the debt crisis, and, on the other hand, the desire to find less costly and disruptive ways of promoting stabilization and adjustment than those used by the orthodox programs.

> It may also result from the fact that the appropriate long term strategies are less clear. The negative consequences of the recommendations stemming from what we might call the most naive version of structuralism, regarding the efficiency of the private and public productive apparatus, has resulted in an increased skepticism with respect to the use of direct or indirect state control in regulating resource allocation. Many countries have experienced a revival of democratic regimes, and the desire to maintain them leads to a more cautious attitude in relation to economic policy proposals. The years of dictatorship and repression are evidence of the political brittleness of many societies and their sensitivity vis-à-vis unpopular or highly conflicting measures. Neostructuralist thinking is quite aware that solutions have to be arrived at by consensus (Lustig 1988a: 48).

The latter perhaps also explains another change that has taken place in the literature on development prevailing in Latin America.[52] During the 1960s and 1970s, the main concern of structuralist authors focused on the economic concentration and marginalization that accompanied growth, and on seeking more virtuous alternatives. In contrast, in the past few years Latin American authors have been looking for ways to diminish the social cost—in terms of increasing poverty—of the stabilization and adjustment programs established after the debt crisis during the 1980s.[53]

Reflections on the Desire for a Better Future and How to Achieve It

Latin America's recent history has made an important impact in the region's economic thinking. The complexity involved in the management of the economy, the magnitude of the costs associated with policy mistakes, and the obvious vulnerability of the countries vis-à-vis external shocks have introduced a considerable amount of realism among policymakers, politicians, and intellectuals. Proposals have increasingly lost the theoretical and political naivete that sometimes characterized them. At present, it is fully recognized that voluntaristic proposals regarding the modification of income distribution or the improvement of living standards can produce unwanted but serious disruptions. Some of the experiences in Latin America proved that, in practice, redistributive processes—or the attempts to promote them—may give rise to severe economic, political, and social imbalances.

In the economic sphere, for example, imbalances at both macro and sectoral levels may be generated, with negative consequences on the balance of payments and price stability. Among other reasons, this happens because *nonmarginal* redistribution of income implies an increase in demand, while at the same time there might be a contraction in supply.[54] Furthermore, when redistributive processes are part of a socializing or socialist platform, external mistrust and pressures are added to the internal pressures set forth by the propertied classes. The final result may be a continuous worsening of economic disequilibria, an intensification of price instability, and, in many cases, the breaking up of the institutional order.

The difficulties and failures encountered in the past by redistributive attempts, however, should not lead to forsaking the objectives. Since its inception, structuralist thought has been committed to social justice as a primary objective of the development process. Nevertheless, the margin to achieve this objective is currently even narrower than in the past. The debt crisis has left most Latin American countries without access to external financing, and in practically every Latin American country, the state had to relinquish policy instruments and command over resources.

Financing of higher levels of public expenditure is difficult, and a large part of noninflationary current outlays is committed to external and internal debt servicing. The possibility of taxing the private sector and the power to foster institutional changes in some countries are deteriorated. At the same time, the possibility of the social groups themselves promoting and demanding distributive changes in their benefit is restricted by the limited resources available for redistribution in stagnant economies.

Under the current circumstances, equity goals are perhaps the most difficult to pursue because the state and the rest of the social forces are in a weakened condition. Accumulated experience and the awareness of current restrictions recommend a period of reflection to discover new ways, perhaps more unpretentious but enduring, of achieving greater social justice in Latin America.

Adjustment, either voluntary or involuntary, orderly or disorderly, implies a reduction in product growth due to the restrictions imposed by external shocks.[55] An adjustment is successful if it concludes with the recovery of growth. An essential component to achieve successful adjustment is the increase in resource productivity. Although there is consensus on this point, differences arise with respect to the way such increase should be promoted. In particular, the debate focuses on the role of the state versus market forces in the process.[56]

However, beyond general discussion, the central problem consists in defining the specific forms of intervention that will allow maximization of the dynamic comparative advantages and promote technical progress. Recent theoretical literature has made some progress on these matters in the abstract field.[57] The challenge consists in translating these proposals into concrete measures to achieve the much-desired "effective selectivity" in state intervention (Fajnzylber 1989b: 47).

In the field of equity, there are three central ways in which effective selectivity should be promoted: (1) finding ways to minimize the impact of external shocks on the poorest sectors, (2) compensating for displacement costs caused by economic reforms on the structurally poor and also on the new poor, and (3) facilitating the elimination of poverty once growth has been recovered. One of the central elements that make it difficult to protect low-income groups from external shocks and from adjustment costs is that higher-income sectors can protect themselves from the costs, for example, by transferring their wealth (or part of it) abroad. This process, on the one hand, increases the adjustment costs for those who have no wealth and whose income derives from the employment of their labor and human capital. On the other hand, it erodes even further the government's ability to generate the necessary resources to protect the low-income sectors.

Recovery of credibility and the faculty to exert fiscal authority vis-à-vis population sectors that must contribute the necessary resources (including foreign organizations and governments) are, then, priority tasks for governments. The other great task is working to achieve social consensus concerning the need to provide and destine public resources to fight poverty.[58] In other words, to promote society's "aversion to poverty." Perhaps both objectives can be encouraged simultaneously. Programs that identify clearly and transparently the benefits and the recipients of the resources may prove useful.[59]

The period in which the external shock and the adjustment took place was characterized, among other things, by the need to reduce the fiscal deficit. This in itself hinders fulfilling the objective of diminishing the impact of the external shock, or of the adjustment, on the poorest and the impoverished sectors. However, there is margin for this. For example, reductions in expenditures and subsidies may be done in such a way to ensure that low-income sectors are more protected.[60] Similarly, an attempt might be made to increase public revenue, making the tax base broader and the burden more progressive.[61]

It should be noted that not enough attention has been given to the matter of differentiating the origin of resources in order to mitigate adjustment costs for the poor. Oftentimes it seems that if these resources come from the nonpoor, this is no longer a matter of concern. However, there is evidence that the crisis and the adjustment process have had significant costs for the so-called middle sectors in Latin America, which include the urban poor and the middle classes. The contribution to a country's development by the middle class is manyfold. It provides most of the skilled labor. It constitutes an example of the potential for social mobility by means of material and intellectual efforts. Perhaps an effort should be made to try to prevent the middle class from being the major supplier of resources.

With respect to the longer term measures geared to foster equity following a successful adjustment process—once product growth has been recovered and productivity is on the upswing—the existing options are well known. In particular, the most mentioned in the literature are increasing physical assets and their productivity and expanding the skills of the poor.[62] Additionally, although it tends to be rejected in many circles, promoting a reduction in the fertility rate may, in many cases, contribute to reducing the incidence of poverty.[63] Earlier in the chapter, I mentioned the difficulties that may arise during processes involving redistribution of assets or income without the existence of some amount of social consensus about their implementation, and without a coherent macroeconomic policy. Some Latin American countries are presently in the happy situation of no longer having to think about adjustments but rather about equity, within the framework of an economy experiencing moderate growth.[64] Hopefully, both the governments and the people will achieve this consensus and find ways to promote equity without falling into self-defeating processes.

Notes

1. In this chapter, the concept of equity refers to the characteristics of income distribution, poverty level, and general living conditions.

2. See, for example, the references mentioned in Cline's article (1975) and in Todaro's book (1989). See also Field (1979) and the other papers presented in Muñoz (1979).

3. See Kuznets (1955).

4. See the abstracts presented in Cline (1975) and Bacha (1979).

5. The most significant ideas set forth by ECLAC at the start of its activities may be found in ECLA (1950) and Prebisch (1950a and 1950b). An excellent extract of ECLA's ideas may be found in Rodríguez (1980).

6. The discussion in this and the following paragraph may be found in Lustig (1988a).

7. Similar arguments are presented by Ocampo in Chapter 12.

8. See Fishlow (1985).

9. See Lewis (1954) and Cline (1975: 370). However, this tendency toward income concentration may be somewhat counteracted by a smaller wage gap between workers in the traditional sector and those in the modern sector.

10. One of the first manifestations about the "failure" of the import substitution process may be found in Hirschman (1968); for a more recent analysis, see Fajnzylber (1983).

11. See, for example, the ideas set forth by Furtado (1966, 1969a), Pinto (1970, 1974), Sunkel and Paz (1970), Tavares (1973), Vuskovic (1974), and Serra and Tavares (1974). See also Di Filippo (1981).

12. See, for example, Gunder Frank (1969), as well as many of the "dependency" authors.

13. See Vuskovic (1974) and Pinto (1970, 1974).

14. See, for example, Frank and Webb (1977) and Bruton (1977), among others.

15. See the comparison shown in Fajnzylber (1989b).

16. The formal presentation of the structuralist notions about the relation between growth and income distribution may be found in Taylor (1983). Hirschman (1958) was the first author to set forth the role played by linkages.

17. Lustig (1981) summarizes structuralist ideas at that time with respect to the relation between income distribution and growth.

18. See Furtado (1966).

19. See Furtado (1969a).

20. See, for example, Sunkel and Paz (1970), Pinto (1970, 1974), and Vuskovic (1974).

21. See, for example, Tavares (1973) and Serra and Tavares (1974).

22. Serra and Tavares (1974) developed this theory in reply to Furtado's (1966, 1969a) "stagnation" outlook.

23. See Bacha (1979).

24. It might be interesting to note that in this study the authors find that the proportion of manufactured exports is *not* correlated to any specific distributive pattern. On the other hand, what the authors call a dual socio-political structure is highly correlated with inequality. Participation of public investment in overall investment shows no significant relation with income distribution, while education is positively correlated.

25. See, for example, the articles by Fishlow (1972), Langoni (1973), and Pfeffermann and Webb (1979) on Brazil; Webb (1972) on Peru; Weisskopf (1970)

on Argentina, Mexico, and Puerto Rico; Navarrete (1960), Felix (1977), Bergsman (1982), and a large number of recent studies cited in Lustig (1984) and García-Rocha (1986) on Mexico; Berry and Urrutia (1976) on Colombia; Altimir (1975, 1981, 1982) on several countries; Altimir (1986) on Argentina; and the series of documents recently published by ECLAC that summarize the available statistical data on income distribution for Argentina, Brazil, Colombia, Costa Rica, Chile, Mexico, and Venezuela. In view of the difficulties already mentioned, in the author's opinion it is not convenient to summarize the findings of the empirical studies, as each one of them has, as it were, its own story about adjustments and possibilities of comparison. Perhaps it might be better for the reader to peruse the findings for the cases that interest him/her.

26. It should be noted that this form of measuring the incidence of poverty, i.e., calculating the proportion of families under the line of poverty, is not the best way, from a methodological point of view, to make comparisons over time or between countries. See the analysis made by Foster (1984) of the different methods to measure poverty and their properties.

27. That is to say, to base the social definition of the poverty line in relation to the population mean, instead of considering it a certain level that remains constant over time.

28. This might partly explain the impressionist idea that poverty has grown. Another phenomenon that might have taken place is that the increase in the number of poor people became more evident as it occurred in densely populated areas, thus giving rise to the creation and/or expansion of the famous poverty belts, *favelas* and *villas miseria.*

29. See Altimir (1981: 77). The incidence of poverty in urban zones was also calculated by Couriel (1984).

30. See Iglesias (1981).

31. For example, see the summary of results presented by Cline (1975).

32. See the article by Ffrench-Davis (1974) and several of the papers included in Foxley (1974).

33. See Ascher's (1984) analysis of Argentina, Chile, and Peru.

34. See the articles by Sachs (1989a) and Dornbusch and Edwards (1989a). Unfortunately, there are very few studies in Latin America that analyze the redistributive impact of government tax and expenditure schemes. Obviously, there are studies analyzing, for example, the impact of state action in specific countries. See, for example, Foxley, Aninat, and Arellano (1980) and Reyes-Heroles (1976).

35. Shown, for example, by Vuskovic (1974) and by Serra and Tavares (1974).

36. See, for example, Lustig (1981).

37. With respect to the relation between income distribution and consumption structure, an aspect that, as mentioned earlier, was dealt with in considerable detail by structuralist authors during the late 1960s and early 1970s, income concentration was not necessarily favorable for the consumption expansion of durable consumer goods such as household appliances, nor was there any evidence found of saturation of the consumption of durable goods in the upper distributive bracket. That is to say, income redistribution does not necessarily produce a consumption pattern less oriented to durables; the exception to this result was clearly shown in the case of cars (Lustig 1981).

38. See ECLAC (1989a: 23, table 1).

39. A very difficult question to answer is which part of the income deterioration can be attributed to the crisis and which to the types of policies applied.

40. Several articles analyze the effects in specific countries. See, for example, Ffrench-Davis and Raczynski (1987) for the case of Chile; Lustig (1988b, 1989b)

and Samaniego (1986) for Mexico; and Macedo (1987) for Brazil. In the course of the past few years, the World Bank and the International Monetary Fund have also analyzed the effects on distribution and on living conditions in countries that applied adjustment programs and in those that adjusted chaotically.

41. Some countries showed much sharper decreases than the average; for example, in Mexico labor participation dropped by 10 percent (Lustig 1988b, 1989b).

42. See ECLAC (1989a: 24, table 2).

43. Similar results may be found in Altimir (1984).

44. See ECLAC (1989b: 35, 37, tables 27 and 29). See also the estimations in Pinto de la Piedra (1988).

45. This refers to the comparison between the evolution of expenditures in the specific sector with total expenditures. See Pinstrup-Andersen (1987: 97, tables 3 and 4).

46. This phenomenon was proven in the case of Mexico, where the reduction in health and education expenditures did not reflect similar drops in the availability of hospital beds, physicians, schools, or teachers per capita (Lustig 1988b).

47. In Mexico real wages dropped by almost 50 percent between 1981 and 1988, and the average product growth was close to zero.

48. In any case, it should be noted that the main objective of this book is to recover the long term perspective of the development process, while not ignoring the crucial importance of short term economic balances and the continuity of such process (see Chapters 2 and 4).

49. See, among others, the contributions by Alberro and Ibarra (1987), Arida and Lara-Resende (1985), Bacha (1987), Frenkel and Fanelli (1987), Heymann (1986), Lopes (1984), Modiano (1987), Ocampo (1987), and Ros (1988). See also articles included in *Colección de Estudios CIEPLAN* (1988) and Chapter 4.

50. The Austral Plan began in 1985, the Cruzado Plan in 1986, and the Economic Solidarity Pact in 1988. The latter has recently been renamed, but in essence continues to have the same characteristics. A comparison between the plans implemented in Argentina, Brazil, Mexico, and Peru during the 1980s, and their impact on the activity level, inflation rate, real wages, and the employment rate, may be found in Lustig (1989a).

51. However, the relative success of the pact was partly possible thanks to the considerable reserves available at the beginning, which gave credibility to the exchange policy and made it possible to finance the liberalization of foreign trade. Please note that the program also included, aside from the agreed price and wage controls, the application of measures that are typically characteristic of heterodox programs, such as the reduction of public deficits and fiscal austerity.

52. I refer not only to the economic literature available, but also to that of the social sciences in general.

53. See, for example, ECLAC (1988b), PREALC-ILO (1988a), and, from ECLAC's Social Development Division, the article "El desarrollo social en los años noventa: principales opciones" (1988).

54. This contraction may be caused by the same conflict and might be a deliberate decision by the group affected by redistribution; or it might be a decision free from political contention, simply a consequence of the uncertainty and imbalance linked to the redistributive process.

55. Bourguignon (1989) makes an interesting analytical presentation of the impact of adjustment on growth.

56. See the comparison between various transformation patterns in Latin America in the 1990s, presented by Fajnzylber (1989b). This debate is also dealt with in the rest of the chapters in this book.

57. See, for example, the article on subsidies and tariffs by Grossman and Helpman (1989).

58. As Sheahan (1989) indicates, social consensus is a prerequisite to implement measures involving the transfer of resources from one group of the population to another.

59. The Social Emergency Fund, applied in Bolivia since December 1986, seems to be an example of this (Romero 1988).

60. In the case of subsidies, for example, by protecting subsidies applied to popular consumption foodstuffs rather than to goods consumed mainly by higher-income groups, such as gasoline.

61. It is difficult to weigh the consequences on equity of deciding whether public expenditure cuts should involve a reduction of jobs or wages.

62. See Bourguignon's (1989) presentation of the distributive alternatives and their impact within an analytical framework.

63. Thus eliminating a factor that effectively diminishes the incomes of agricultural workers and urban wage earners, particularly of the informal sector. In many countries a lower rate of population growth would ease the pressure on public resources and enable replacing quantity with quality in the services rendered.

64. This, for example, is the case of Chile.

4

Macroeconomic Equilibria and Development

Joseph Ramos

The 1980s were a "lost decade" for Latin American development. Not only was growth slowed by the macroeconomic excesses that occurred, but the various attempts to restore basic balances were also usually recessive. In fact, if there is one lesson to be read from the Latin American experience of the 1980s, it is that, in practice, solid and sustained growth is impossible unless macroeconomic imbalances are kept within tolerable limits.

To be sure, how much of an imbalance is tolerable is a question open to debate. Nevertheless, it is clear that triple digit inflation, unemployment rates that double historical levels, or current account deficits amounting to 4 percent of the GDP and more, such as were experienced in the region in the last few years, are imbalances that well exceed tolerable economic and social limits. They weaken, and may even render impossible, all rational economic calculations or evaluations and, as a result, jeopardize investment and growth. Therefore, no one questions the necessity of keeping macroeconomic imbalances within prudent limits. To do so is simply to recognize that there are objective restrictions of a fundamental accounting nature, which transcend theoretical or ideological differences, and which every economy must respect.

For example, if a country systematically attempts to spend more foreign exchange than it is capable of generating, it falls into external imbalance. Likewise, if a country tries to spend more than it is capable of producing, and does not have the foreign exchange to cover the difference, it will set off an inflationary spiral (internal imbalance) that becomes intolerable to the extent that it seriously affects the distribution of income, efficiency, and investment levels. Finally, if the level of production and capacity utilization falls below "normal," an internal imbalance occurs that, although sustainable, is economically and socially undesirable, insofar as it seriously affects not only current levels of output and distribution, but also future investment and growth.

Thus, within certain limits, what level of imbalance is tolerable is an issue open to debate, and was so especially in the 1950s. However, since from all accounts tolerable limits clearly were exceeded in the 1980s, current debate no longer centers on defining these limits, but rather on determining how to restore such balances without seriously aggravating the others.[1] More concretely, how can unsustainable deficits in the balance of payments be reduced without aggravating inflation and without giving rise to a recession (in other words, how to carry out an adjustment that is neither recessive nor inflationary)? And how can inflation be reduced, especially high inflation, without provoking a recession (in other words, how to carry out a nonrecessive stabilization program)?[2] Hence, rather than analyzing the causes of such imbalances, this chapter centers on how better to eliminate them. For neostructuralism differs from the orthodox approach in that it not only emphasizes the structural causes of the crisis, but also attempts to offer alternative *operational* solutions to restore macroeconomic balances without provoking recession.

The chapter is divided into four sections. The first compares the relation between macroeconomic disequilibria and growth in the 1950s and at present. It concludes that: (1) Both the magnitude and the nature of the imbalances are radically different; thus, the debate in the 1950s centered on the tolerable limits of imbalance, whereas today, because these limits have clearly been exceeded, debate focuses on finding alternatives to restore equilibrium at the least possible cost in recession. (2) Current macroeconomic excesses do not respond so much to ineptitude in policymaking (which has undoubtedly existed), as to economic policy's limited degrees of freedom vis-à-vis the strong reversal in the external transfer of resources. (3) It is necessary to distinguish between adjustment programs (to an external imbalance) and stabilization (anti-inflationary) programs, because they differ in nature, costs, and instruments. For this reason it may be preferable to deal with these imbalances sequentially rather than simultaneously.

The second section explains why adjustment was so costly and how it can be tackled without prompting a recession. It concludes that: (1) Adjustment has overemphasized demand control policies, which rapidly contract production, instead of switching policies, which expand production, albeit slowly. Moreover, because efficient adjustment requires a reallocation of resources and the transformation of production, a shock-type adjustment cannot be efficient. (2) Thus, heterodox adjustment would require, on the one hand, a new role for the IMF to provide adequate financing for a gradual adjustment and, on the other hand, outward-oriented domestic adjustment policies, as suggested by the orthodox approach, together with active policies that rapidly and selectively promote exports and efficient import substitutes and selectively control demand.

The third section analyzes inflation and the possibility of designing a nonrecessive stabilization program. It concludes that, in general, all inflation has two components—an inertial component that keeps it going and a disequilibrium component that explains accelerations (or decelerations). Policies that control demand and correct relative prices are needed for the latter, while price and income policies are appropriate for the former. The need to combine both policies constitutes a basic premise of a heterodox or neostructuralist stabilization program. The final section compares neostructuralist approaches, both with orthodoxy and with the structuralist school of thinking from which it derives.

The Debate and Its Context

In the 1950s, debate between the orthodox and heterodox approaches with respect to stabilization focused on three issues: (1) The causes of inflation—was it essentially due to the issuing of money and to the fiscal deficit, or were there structural factors that fueled the increase in the money supply? (2) The instruments of stabilization programs—was it sufficient to concentrate on controlling demand, fiscal deficits, and money supply, or was such an approach recessive in its neglect of supply factors and investment and their structural determinants? (3) What degree of imbalance was tolerable? Insofar as growth is compatible with some degree of inflation, would it not be preferable to tolerate inflation, rather than embark on stabilization programs that risk serious recessions?

In order to understand that debate, as well as the current one, it is important to examine the context in which it took place. (See Table 4.1.) Indeed, two periods can be clearly differentiated, 1950–1970 and 1982–1988, with an intermediary transitional period. Between 1950 and 1970, Latin America experienced a period of solid and sustained growth (2.5 percent per capita per year). The only obvious imbalance was inflation, which was moderate, on the order of 20 percent per year, with no serious external imbalances (the current account deficit amounted to less than 1 percent of the GDP). In the transition period, the early 1970s to 1981, growth continued, albeit at declining rates; inflation doubled; and the current account deficit grew, reaching 4.5 percent of GDP, which was covered by massive foreign borrowing. Finally, the crisis broke out in 1982 with the collapse in capital inflows, giving rise to the third period. This period was characterized by adjustment policies aimed at reducing the foreign deficit but at the cost of a prolonged recession and an inflationary explosion.

From the Limits of the Tolerable (1950s) to
How to Restore Balances (1980s)

There are essential differences in the economic situation in the two periods (see Table 4.1) that explain the course of the debate: from establishing the

Table 4.1.   Latin America: Inflation, External Imbalance, and Growth, 1950–1988
              (annual averages in percentages)

	1950–54	1955–59	1960–64	1965–69	1970–74	1975–79	1980–81	1982–88
Annual rate of growth GDP/per capita	2.0	1.9	2.8	2.7	4.3	3.1	1.0	-0.8
Annual rate of inflation	13.0	17.0	25.0	19.0	23.0	50.0	57.0	240.0
Current account deficit/ GDP	0.3	0.7	0.6	0.8	1.5	3.2	4.6	1.2[b]
Net capital inflows/ GDP	0.4	0.7	0.5	1.0	2.3	4.4	4.5	1.4
Net transfer of resources/GDP[a]	-0.3	-0.1	-0.2	-0.3	+0.3	+1.4	+1.5	-4.0

Source: ECLAC, Department of Economic Development, based on official data.
Notes: a. + : transfer to Latin America; - : transfer abroad.
     b. 1983–88, since a large part of the adjustment was not complete in 1982 and it was still being financed by reserves.

tolerable limits of imbalances (the 1950s) to restoring basic balances at the lowest possible recessive cost (the central topic of the 1980s). First, as has already been pointed out, there is the fifteenfold difference in inflation rates. With an average inflation of 15 percent, it is understandable that many people in the 1950s were prepared to risk a moderate acceleration in prices, if by this means a definite savings increase could be obtained to finance industrialization and break the structural inertia that blocked development possibilities. In contrast, triple-digit inflation rates, like the current ones, can hardly be reconciled with growth. For the same reason, one can understand that, in the 1950s, the search for price stability was not considered worth the risk of slowing down a satisfactory growth rate of 5 percent, while the economic stagnation of the 1980s, in large part brought on by the burst in inflation, made it imperative to bring down inflation.

Second, the imbalance of the 1950s was largely limited to inflation; external imbalances were relatively insignificant. Although many inflationary increases in the 1950s were set in motion by balance of payments crises, those crises were due to losses in the terms of trade, which tended to be either cyclical or relatively slight (less than 1 percent of gross domestic product [GDP] in the whole of the 1950s).[3] Hence, stabilization efforts usually centered on lowering inflation by offsetting cyclical downturns in the terms of trade with foreign loans rather than by adjustment programs. Moreover, insofar as the need for external adjustment was perceived as slight or temporary, the use of real exchange rate devaluations was viewed with skepticism (all the more so since elasticities were presumed to be low); hence tariffs or direct instruments were considered preferable. However, in the 1980s rising inflation was fueled by an unprecedented external imbalance, as evidenced in the sustained reversal in the transfer of resources abroad, equivalent to almost 6 percent of GDP as of 1982.

Third, in the 1950s annual inflation never reached 100 percent, and such outbursts were but occasional, abrupt accelerations, which did not continue at elevated rates. However, in the 1980s average inflation not only was exorbitant, but has also persisted at such high rates for several years. As we shall see, this persistence indicates the existence of inertial mechanisms that institutionalize high inflation, making it tolerable to live with but making it much more difficult and costly to reduce.

Fourth, the structuralist distinction between factors explaining inflationary outbursts and factors explaining its continuation is still valid. However, the latter-day conclusion is the opposite of the earlier one: attempts to reduce relatively moderate inflation, like in the 1950s, may fail or be short-lived if only propagation mechanisms are controlled and structural rigidities are not dealt with. In contrast, it is obvious that for triple-digit inflation rates, such as current ones, the control of originating factors is of much less significance, and for that reason, effort has to be expended precisely on braking the price and wage spiral.

Therefore, since today's excesses are beyond any reasonable notion of what is tolerable, debate no longer focuses on determining, as in the 1950s, whether it is possible to grow while having imbalances, but rather on how to restore basic macroeconomic equilibria via a nonrecessive adjustment or stabilization program. Shifting the debate has required important developments in heterodox thinking (the central theme of the following sections). Indeed, although structuralist criticism of the orthodox programs of the 1950s was fierce—they were considered recessive—one would have to admit that the alternatives proposed were hardly practical. Structuralists were skeptical of the instruments in the hands of the authorities (monetary, fiscal, and exchange policies), while proposing profound changes that were largely out of reach or that yielded results only in the long run, well beyond the urgency of the imbalances.[4] It is hardly surprising, then, that Fishlow (1985: 141) described structuralism as "a long-term theory of Latin American development. Incidentally, structuralism was also a short-term macroeconomic theory which denied the efficacy of orthodox monetary, fiscal and exchange policies for fighting inflation."

The Causes of the Crisis:
The Ineptitude of Economic Policy or the Transfer Problem

Debate on the causes of imbalances in the 1950s centered principally on whether monetary expansion and fiscal excesses were due to ineptitude, or whether they responded to more fundamental pressures, such as food supply inelasticities, a persistent deterioration of the terms of trade, the inflexibility or inelasticity of taxation, and the like. The debate is different now because the causes are multiple, and definitely more complex. Nevertheless, orthodox thinking continues to emphasize errors in the design of economic policy, while neostructuralism, in addition to recognizing those errors, concentrates on the limited degrees of freedom left to economic policy, after the crisis had broken out, because of the reversal in the transfer of resources required by the problem of foreign overindebtedness.

Indeed, because of the crisis, the region ceased to be a net importer of financial resources (on the order of 1.5 percent of GDP before the crisis)— as is natural for developing countries—and became a net exporter (at 4 percent of GDP).[5] This reversal in the transfer of resources is, in the neostructuralist view, the central—although obviously not the only—factor that explains both the economic stagnation and the inflationary outbursts in Latin America in the period after 1982.

Needless to say, this transfer problem would hardly have existed at all if precrisis borrowing had been invested in export or import substitution activities.[6] However, as the bulk was either used to finance consumption or fed capital flight, and what was invested largely went into projects with low rates of return, current transfers are a deadweight, resembling the payment of war reparations (indeed, in relative terms, they exceed the transfers imposed on Germany after World War I).

From the moment the region decided to service its foreign debt, it was forced to generate an equivalent trade surplus. To achieve this, the ideal would have been an increase in exports, with a contraction only in nonessential imports, substituting, as far as possible, essential imports (capital goods and intermediate inputs). However, it was virtually impossible to produce a 6 percent change in GDP in scarcely two years on the basis of this ideal scheme, given the weak trade situation of the region at the beginning of the crisis.

First, past development strategies had left our economies with relatively low export (or import) coefficients (barely 15 percent of the regional GDP compared to 40 percent in South Korea and Taiwan, at the other extreme). Second, 75 percent of our imports were primary products that, because of their relatively low short term supply and demand elasticity, were difficult to place in international markets. Therefore, the bulk of expansion in exports could only come in nontraditional areas that, in spite of the progress of the 1970s, accounted for little more than 4 percent of GDP at the beginning of the crisis. Thus, the reversal in transfers required an unfeasible (in the short term) increase of nontraditional exports (92 percent) (see Table 4.2). This contrasted with the situation of South Korea and Taiwan, where almost 90 percent of exports (and 35 to 40 percent of the GDP) corresponded to manufactured goods, with a much greater price and income elasticity. Third, due to the advanced stage of import substitution carried out in the past, at the beginning of the crisis less than 15 percent of imports (or 2 percent of the GDP) were consumer goods, the compression of which would not affect production; the rest were intermediate inputs that were vital for production, or capital goods, indispensable for restructuring and future growth.

Latin America's weak commercial position was no chance occurrence. It was partly due to the region's rich endowment of natural resources; but above all, it reflected the decision to pursue a development strategy during most of the postwar period oriented almost exclusively to the domestic market, favoring the substitution of imports at almost any cost, but at the clear expense of exports, in particular nontraditional exports. Because, as percentages of the GDP, nontraditional exports and nonessential imports were not significant, there was little room for nonrecessive adjustment, even less than the 6 percent required for the transfer. Accordingly, it is not surprising that most of the adjustment came from the compression (and not substitution) of importation of essential intermediate inputs and machinery (the volume of which fell by around 40 percent), thus generating not only a recessive adjustment (per capita production is still 7 percent below its 1980 figure), but also jeopardizing future growth.

This reversal in the transfer of resources not only obstructed growth, but also contributed to the inflationary explosion that the region experienced in the 1980s.[7] Apart from the costs of obtaining foreign exchange and increasing the trade surplus, the financing of the external transfer of resources required a second transfer—this one internal—from the private to the public sector. Indeed, as the bulk of foreign debt was public or had a public guarantee (70 percent before the crisis, over 80 percent at present), most of the transfer of resources carried out after 1982 came from the public sector.

Insofar as domestic capital markets were not highly developed, or could hardly absorb—and then only with soaring interest rates—the additional noninflationary financing, which represented 4 percent of the GDP (the part of the reversal in transfers corresponding to the public sector), funding had to come from equivalent increases in public revenues or reductions in its expenditures. Given that the revenues or expenditures of central government are a modest fraction of GDP (around 10–15 percent), in the majority of our countries the reversal in the transfer of resources amounting to 4 percent of GDP on the part of the government would have meant increasing revenues or reducing expenditures by substantial percentages. In view of the difficulties involved in such a significant real fiscal adjustment, it is no wonder that most countries resorted to money issues and to the "inflation tax" in order to mobilize private sector resources and finance the required foreign transfer.[8] It is estimated that the sums collected under this tax were equivalent to 3 or 4 percent of the GDP of the region in the period of the crisis (Selowsky 1989).

Table 4.2. The Macroeconomic Burden of the Transfer of
            Resources Abroad, 1982–1988[a]
            (percentages)

	$\dfrac{I_b}{PIB}$	$\dfrac{TR}{PIB}$	$\dfrac{TR}{I_b}$	$\dfrac{TR}{X}$	$\dfrac{TR}{X_{nt}}$	$\dfrac{TR}{X_i}$	$\dfrac{TR}{M_c}$	$\dfrac{TR}{I}$
Latin America	6.1	4.1	67	26	92	115	331	24
Argentina	6.6	4.0	60	31	147	121	1,100	31
Brazil	4.5	3.3	74	29	61	60	700	20
Chile	10.0	3.8	38	13	45	58	71	30
Colombia	3.3	1.2	36	5	18	40	97	5
Costa Rica	8.2	-0.7	-8	-2	-7	-10	-15	-4
Ecuador	8.3	4.4	53	15	170	165	265	25
Mexico	6.4	6.7	110	41	251	335	1,144	27
Peru	5.7	0.5	8	2	11	23	25	2
Uruguay	6.7	4.4	65	15	34	50	280	45
Venezuela	8.5	10.6	129	31	417	714	290	56

Source: ECLAC, Department of Economic Development, based on official data.
Note: a. 1988: Preliminary figures.
Symbols:
I_b: Gross interest paid.
TR: Net Transfer of resources. Equivalent to the net payments of profit and interest less the net capital inflow.
X: Exports of goods and services.
X_{nt}: Exports of nontraditional goods.
X_i: Exports of industrial goods.
M_c: Imports of consumer goods.
I: Gross domestic investment.

Because, as a result of the traditionally high inflation that characterizes the region, the monetary base was already low before the crisis (5–10 percent of the GDP), a monetary expansion equivalent to several points of GDP caused a rapid acceleration in inflation. And because inflation was previously high, the outcome was unheard of rates of inflation and even hyperinflation.[9]

The region's poor economic performance since 1982 is due, then, not so much to the ineptness of economic policy, but to the sharp imbalances associated with the double transfer, both internal and external, that arose from foreign overindebtedness.

External and Internal Imbalances and the Need to Distinguish Adjustment Programs from Stabilization Programs

When disequilibria were minor or cyclical, as in the 1950s, stabilization programs could center basically on the problem of inflation. However, in the 1980s external imbalances became as significant as high inflation, if not more so, requiring the design of both adjustment (to external imbalance) and price stabilization programs without recession (restoration of internal balance). Thus, before entering fully into a discussion of our central theme—how to restore balance without recession—it would be useful to distinguish between external and internal imbalances, and between the respective natures of adjustment and stabilization programs. Although many analyses treat them as being the same—partly because in recent years external and internal imbalances have tended to be tackled simultaneously—the adjustment process differs significantly from the stabilization process, both in nature and instruments.

First, a stabilization policy (aimed at reducing inflation) does not have an unavoidable cost; insofar as inflation is only "too much money after too few goods," producing fewer goods (recession) could even make that task more difficult. On the contrary, as "only" changes in the nominal values of the critical variables (exchange rate, wages, prices, money supply) are needed, stabilization requires no significant (systematic) modification of production. Therefore, a recession is an avoidable (although perhaps frequent) cost of stabilization. An adjustment program, on the other hand, carries an inevitable cost: it must transfer resources abroad (or at least endure a reduction in the transfer of resources into the country), which requires a reduction in the availability of goods and services for the domestic market (or deceleration in its growth). However, although domestic expenditure (or absorption) must inevitably decrease in relation to the product, production itself does not have to fall. Rather, its composition has to change: increasing the production of tradables (exports and import substitutes) and reducing the production of nontradables.

Second, insofar as it is possible to tolerate high inflation by means of indexing and expectations, a stabilization program can be put off indefinitely (at least until hyperinflation sets in). However, this is not the case with an external imbalance. Once reserves and access to foreign credit are exhausted, the balance of payments places an inevitable restriction, similar to a budgetary limit, which automatically brings on adjustment.

Third, since a stabilization program "merely" requires the deceleration of nominal values, it may be of a shock type and yet be efficient (nonrecessive); moreover, triple- or quadruple-digit inflation could hardly be dealt with gradually. However, since an adjustment program requires real changes in the area of production (increased production of tradables and reduced production of nontradables), gradualism is essential if the program is going to be carried out efficiently (without recession). The production of nontradables can be reduced as quickly as desired, but increase in the production of tradables takes time because it requires reallocating investment. Thus, gradualism is essential for an adjustment to external imbalances to be efficient (nonrecessive). In the light of this conclusion, it is striking that IMF recommendations tend to go in the other direction: they are usually too quick regarding adjustment (perhaps because it is considered an immediate need), but more gradual than necessary regarding price stabilization.

Fourth, while some components of an adjustment program serve both to reduce external imbalance and inflation (for example, reduction in expenditures), others (devaluation, increases in public tariffs) improve the external imbalance at the cost of raising price levels, at least in the short term. This implies that it would be better, if possible, to tackle the two imbalances separately and sequentially, rather than simultaneously. The preferred sequence will depend on the circumstances. If the greatest restriction is an external imbalance (the usual situation, except in hyperinflation), it would seem reasonable to adjust first, as Brazil did in the period 1983–1985, even at the expense of higher inflation, and to try to reduce inflation afterwards. However, in other situations, and certainly under hyperinflation, it would be preferable to tackle inflation first, without making an external adjustment and at the expense of debt servicing, as Bolivia did in 1985, in order to gradually carry out an adjustment and debt servicing compatible with balance and growth, once control of the economy is reestablished.

External Imbalance and Adjustment Policies

Since 1981 Latin America has suffered the worst economic crisis since the Great Depression. Thirty-five years of solid regional economic growth in the postwar period came to an end in the early 1980s when the foreign debt crisis broke out with the Mexican moratorium in August 1982. The subsequent abrupt and virtually total withdrawal of what had been, until then, abundant foreign credit forced the countries to correct a current account deficit of 40 billion dollars (equivalent to around 35 percent of their exports and 6 percent of their product) in just two years.

The Theory and Practice of Adjustment:
Why was Adjustment so Costly in Latin America?

As has already been pointed out, the central reason for the costs of adjustment was the sharp reversal in the external transfer of resources, in a short time span and from a reduced initial commercial base. Moreover, misguided economic policies often worsened the recession.

From the national accounting identities, it is known that GDP is equal to domestic expenditure (E) plus the trade surplus (that is, GDP = E + (X-M). Thus, the reversal in the transfer of resources, Δ (X-M), is inevitably offset by a reduction in the relation between expenditures and product, Δ (GDP-E) = Δ (X-M). This equation gives rise to two types of policies: (1) switching policies (devaluation or its equivalent) to encourage an increase in exports and the substitution of imports, and (2) expenditure policies to reduce the ratio of expenditures to production.[10] In general terms, the region pursued both types of policies during the crisis. Exchange rates were dramatically increased and trade policies were modified to stimulate exports and import substitution, while an attempt was made to reduce expenditures, by cutting real wages and fiscal expenditures and increasing interest rates.

Even so, the crisis was worsened by the instability of the exchange and trade policies. Indeed, movements in the exchange rate have usually been very abrupt, with marked cycles of excessive devaluations followed by periods of lagging exchange rates. This made it difficult for potential exporters to determine whether there was, in fact, any advantage in exporting (apart from purely temporary advantages) and discouraged them from incurring costs that are necessary for the penetration and development of foreign markets. Mexican exchange policy was for some time one of the most remarkable examples of this lack of continuity. The real effective exchange rate doubled between late 1981 and the beginning of 1983; after that it dropped steadily until the middle of 1985, when it dropped almost to its 1981 level. Then it rose almost 60 percent in the following 18 months, before starting to drop again (especially if the sharp reduction in tariffs in 1988 is taken into account). Such volatility in the exchange rate robbed it of any value as a useful indicator for exporters.

The frequency of changes in exchange rate systems in Chile in 1982 also intensified the severe recession of that year (-14 percent). The year started off with a fixed exchange rate; according to the authorities, adjustment would have to take place via absolute drops in domestic prices. However, by mid-year this policy was amended; the exchange rate was increased by 18 percent, and it was announced in advance that there would be a monthly nominal devaluation of 0.8 percent. Two months later, a third system was established: a floating rate (so as not to lose any more international reserves). After one month this was changed to a dirty float (again using reserves to control the exchange rate), and in addition, a preferential exchange rate was created to service foreign debt. One month later, and after a new maxi devaluation, a controlled system of mini devaluations was reestablished. Thus, in less than six months five markedly different exchange systems were experimented with.

As for expenditure policies, if it were sufficient to reduce and reallocate expenditures to the equivalent of 6 percent of the GDP in order to improve the trade surplus by the same amount, the cost would have been high but tolerable. However, if in the attempt to reduce and reallocate expenditures, output also falls, an even greater reduction in expenditures is needed to achieve the required trade surplus. Indeed, a reduction in total expenditures (lower wages, fewer public subsidies, higher taxes, less public investment) usually falls not only on tradables (around 40 percent of GDP) but also on nontradables (including tradables that are not in fact traded, as is the case with a good part of domestic manufactures). Therefore, if a recession is to be avoided, reductions in expenditures should be selective, centered on tradables, because the reduction of expenditures on nontradables supports adjustment only slightly (to the extent that the production of nontradables uses tradable inputs) but at a high cost in terms of output.[11]

Latin American practice was the reverse: not only were reductions in expenditures not limited to tradables, but they actually tended to center on nontradables. Thus, because the fiscal sector is primarily a producer of nontradables, the reduction in fiscal expenditures was implicitly biased against nontradables, and was therefore unnecessarily recessive. Likewise, insofar as food and energy subsidies (for the entire population)—both tradables—were not reduced, adjustment mainly affected nontradables, making it unnecessarily recessive. Venezuela is perhaps the most conspicuous example of this (closely followed by Ecuador, among the oil exporting countries); gasoline was sold there at less than five cents a liter, retail, until 1985, while the international price at the same time was five times higher. Peru, for its part, maintained food subsidies for the entire population, which implied buying basic foodstuffs at a fifth of their international value (and this until mid-1988).

Expenditure policies have been neither stable nor neutral. In fact, wages have been subject to erratic fluctuations, although with a downward tendency. For example, real wages in Argentina fell by 20 percent between 1980 and 1982, grew by 59 percent in the two subsequent years, and fell again, by 15 percent, in 1985. Because employers tend to hire personnel on the basis of expected labor costs, employment becomes inelastic with regard to current wage variations, except when variations are very severe. Wages thus cease to play a role in the allocation of resources, which in turn reinforces the confrontational (zero sum) perspective on the subject, which prevails in many countries where only the distributive role of wages is considered and efficiency considerations are left aside.

With respect to its neutrality, expenditure reduction has often been excessively centered on the labor factor. Noteworthy in this regard were the respective drops of 30 percent and 40 percent in real wages in Mexico (1982–1985) and Peru (1987–1988). These drops were far greater than the improvement required or achieved in the trade surplus. Rather, they suggest that when macroeconomic imbalances become severe, authorities make use of available instruments, regardless of their neutrality.

Just as it is important to center the reduction in expenditures on tradables, it is also important to determine where to cut expenditures: in consumption or investment, in physical capital or social expenditures (human capital). Although all these reductions can improve the balance of trade similarly, a reduction in investment implies sacrificing both future growth and future improvement of the balance of trade; a reduction in human capital (social expenditures) deteriorates the distribution of income and lowers growth. Indeed, the pace at which production is oriented toward exports and efficient import substitution depends to a large extent on the amount of investment available for that purpose.

Once again, actual experience in the region has been the reverse. Reductions in expenditures have fallen especially on investment—both physical and social. During the crisis, per capita investment dropped by 40 percent; therefore, its share in the product dropped from 22 to 16 percent of the GDP. This implies that the 6 percent reversal in external transfers was virtually achieved at the cost of investment.

Even so, it is only fair to admit that there have also been economic policy successes. For example, thanks to its proverbial prudence, Colombia resisted overindebtedness in the 1970s, and therefore did not suffer a serious external imbalance, thus becoming the only country in the region whose output never stopped growing during the 1980s. Similarly, Brazil's external adjustment has been impressive (although this is not true of the internal adjustment). On the one hand, using the loans of the 1970s, Brazil made major investments in energy and intermediate input industries, so that during the adjustment of the 1980s it was able to substitute and not simply cut back these imports, which are particularly vital for growth. On the other hand, its policy involving strong and selective credit and tax (and not just exchange) incentives for exports meant that its industrial exports more than doubled between 1982 and 1988, currently exceeding 24 billion dollars and representing more than 70 percent of its total exports.

Finally, the Chilean economy, after a disastrous "automatic" adjustment in 1982, which brought on a sharp contraction of 13 percent in GDP and the abandonment of its fixed exchange rate policy, has since grown at an average rate of 5 percent a year, with moderate inflation (on the order of 20 percent). This was due, externally, to (1) the abandonment of a fixed (and lagging) exchange rate and its replacement with a high and stable real effective exchange rate, with special incentives to small exporters, thus raising nontraditional exports by 1.2 billion dollars—almost doubling, between 1982 and 1988; and (2) minimum price supports for basic agricultural products, so that over 500 million dollars in food imports were substituted by national production. Internally, it was due to (1) the strong control of fiscal spending; (2) the possibility of being able to make use of the well-developed domestic capital market to finance the fiscal deficit instead of increasing the money supply; and (3) as the state owns the large copper mining industry, the steep rise in the price of copper since 1982 (as well as the real devaluation required by the adjustment), which directly improved both the foreign accounts and public revenue.

Heterodox Alternatives for a Non-Recessive Adjustment:
Criteria for a More Efficient and Symmetrical Conditionality

In brief, three main reasons explain why adjustment in Latin America from 1982 onward was so recessive: (1) the severity of adjustment, (2) its speed (from 1982 onward, once it had become unpostponable), and (3) poor macroeconomic management of the adjustment. A nonrecessive adjustment will depend on overcoming these problems.

The role of the IMF: adequate financing for a gradual adjustment. First, adjustment becomes necessary when it is no longer possible to finance the current account deficit. In general, a country should adjust by an amount equal to that part of the deterioration in its foreign accounts that is permanent, while financing the temporary component of the deficit using reserves or increased borrowing. In practice, it is not easy to determine what part of the deterioration is temporary and what part is permanent. For example, if higher interest payments due to a real international rate of more than 2 percent a year (historical rate) are considered temporary, then the current account deficit in the region would have been 7 billion dollars less (the current account deficit would have been half of what it actually was as of 1982). Similarly, prices of basic export products in the nonoil exporting countries in the period 1981–1988 were 15 percent lower (in real terms) than their historical values (1950–1970), which meant an average loss of almost 10 billion dollars. Part of this decline may have been permanent; nevertheless, it would be extreme to suppose that none of it was temporary. Yet, in effect, because of the lack of financing, the region was forced to eliminate the bulk of its current account deficit as if all of it were permanent. The point is not unimportant. Indeed, if interest rates and unit prices for exports (apart from oil) had remained at their historical levels, or had rapidly returned to them, the necessary adjustment would have been relatively moderate and the region would have achieved a current account surplus as of 1983 (thus, in theory, it would have been possible to reduce its debt as of 1983).

The region was forced to eliminate all of its current account deficit, and not just its permanent component, because the possibility of financing the temporary part depended on the disposition of creditors. Yet capital inflow contracted just when it was needed most (1982), increasing the required adjustment. Indeed, much as the procyclical inflow of capital led to overindebtedness before 1982, it brought an overadjustment after 1982. Thus, rather than alleviating external imbalances, capital movements became yet another variable to which countries had to adjust.

Second, gradualism is vital because, more than expenditure reductions—which can be as rapid as required—adjustment also needs shifts in the very structure of production, from nontradables to tradables. Indeed, the fact that it could be gradual is one reason that the non–oil exporting countries in Latin America were able to make an adjustment (1974–1977), without triggering a recession, after the first increase in oil prices in 1973.

Therefore, the possibility of making a nonrecessive adjustment would have required a very different policy on the part of commercial banking and, especially, the IMF, an organization responsible for assuring stable commercial flows and foreign financing.[12] Instead of determining the magnitude of the permanent imbalance to which countries had to adjust and requiring bank financing for the rest, the IMF basically obliged countries to adjust to the new level of financing that the commercial banking system was prepared to put up, and offered its relatively meager resources on the condition of an internal adjustment. This meant that adjustments had to be carried out as if the entire imbalance was permanent, without adequate financing so that it might have been carried out more efficiently, but gradually, on the basis of restructuring production. Let us be clear. The problem did not lie in the demand for conditionality in itself (more on this subject below), but in the fact that the IMF did not also press to assure adequate bank financing.

For example, it could have given its endorsement to a reasonable adjustment program and, if the banks had not offered sufficient financing, made IMF resources conditional on their not being used to pay interest, thus in effect backing partial moratoria. This reordering of priorities would have allowed a less recessive adjustment, with lower and more symmetrical costs between creditors and debtors, and would have returned the IMF to its role of safeguarding the primary interests of greater trade flows, instead of subordinating these concerns to the specific interests of creditors. An optimal adjustment, then, corrects *permanent* external imbalances; and it is done gradually, on the basis of the reallocation of investment, not just expenditures, to transfer resources from nontradable to tradable activities.

Domestic policies: a new conditionality. However, what should be done if the borrowing of previous years was not used to invest well and sufficiently in anticipation of an external crisis such as the current one? What should be done if financing is not available for adjustment based on the reallocation of investment? Under these circumstances, there are still possibilities for minimizing the recessive cost of adjustment, basing it on an at least temporary reduction of transfers (in a nonconfrontational manner, but unilaterally if necessary), and adjusting, to start with, on the basis of the reallocation and greater use of installed capacity.[13]

Two major faults in the macroeconomic management of adjustment were evidenced by the region (Bianchi, Devlin, and Ramos 1987). The programs were recessive, in the first place, because they were excessively centered on instruments that tended to contract spending and production. Reductions in spending and the correction of relative prices were both

contractive. Because of the limited time available to correct external imbalances, the main initial impact of the devaluations was to reduce domestic expenditures still further. In other words, the income effect (reduction
of demand) took precedence over the price effect (which encouraged the
replacement of foreign production with domestic production and domestic
expenditures with foreign expenditures), and, since adequate steps were
not taken to compensate for this asymmetry, it led to exaggerated reductions in production.

In the second place, expenditure cuts in adjustment programs tended
to be defined in unnecessarily aggregate terms without sufficiently distinguishing whether the measures were cutting expenditures on tradables (desirable, because foreign exchange may thus be saved without affecting
production) or on nontradables (clearly recessive); or if it reduced consumer expenditures (desirable) or spending on investment (as was too
often the case). A more adequate conditionality has to correct these two
great faults so that the adjustment's macroeconomic management is less
recessive. Three economic policy guidelines arise from this analysis:[14]

1. The cost of saving or generating foreign exchange by means of
switching policies (reallocation) must be balanced with expenditure-
reducing policies (absorption). Precisely because it is possible to predict
that expenditure-reducing policies (demand) will work faster than produc-
tion-reallocation policies, it will be justifiable to use temporary super-
switching policies to compensate for this effect. Indeed, the region pursued
both reallocation and expenditure policies in its adjustment. However, because of the limited time available to correct the current accounts, the
main impact, including reallocation policies such as devaluation, was to
reduce expenditures; that is, the income effect (reducing demand yet further) had precedence over the price effect (replacing foreign with domestic production and domestic demand with foreign demand). Very roughly,
we estimate that in order to improve the trade balance by 100 billion dollars in three years, the region sacrificed around 250 billion dollars in output loss;[15] that is, $2^1/_2$ dollars of domestic production were sacrificed for 1
dollar of foreign exchange that was saved. This implies that any combination of tariff surcharges and/or special subsidies to exports would have
been preferable to the adjustment policy that was followed, if it had saved
or generated a dollar at a cost lower than the loss of $2^1/_2$ dollars in production. Certainly, devaluations of this magnitude should not be attempted;
because it is a temporary problem, efforts should be made to speed positive switching effects to avoid negative income effects focusing incentives
on those products with a greater short term price elasticity. Extraordinary
incentives to reallocate would be temporary, for although reallocation
through generalized devaluation works more slowly than reduction of
demand, it yields results in the long term. Once its effects have made

themselves fully felt, extraordinary incentives to reallocate would be unnecessary.

2. A less recessive adjustment requires incentives for investment in, and increased production of, tradable goods—which implies reaching and maintaining a high and stable real effective exchange rate—and also equalizing the incentives for saving foreign exchange through the efficient substitution of imports with those for generating foreign exchange by export promotion. In view of the current incentive structure in the region— high tariffs combined with few special export incentives—there exists a strong presumption that additional policies to encourage exports would be more productive (in terms of foreign exchange) than those that promote import substitution even further.

Before equalizing export incentives with those to substitute for imports, it would be necessary to revise the policy on tariffs. This "policy" has actually resulted from the principle of offering "each activity the protection it needs"—in other words, protection at any social cost—rather than from any studied attempt to eliminate differences between social and private costs associated, for example, with infant industries, technological externalities, or distortions in the labor market. This does not imply that tariffs need to be totally eliminated but rather that they should be reduced to levels proportional to social (rather than private) necessity, and rationalized in a way that would permit equalizing effective protection for different activities.

For this reason, to the extent that intervention is called for socially to protect a particular sector, equivalent incentives should be offered for all that sector's production, whether it is destined for domestic or foreign markets. In other words, unlike what happened in the past, when incentives were only granted to production destined for domestic markets (at the expense of exports and, above all, nontraditional exports), in the future such incentives should be provided for production destined for international markets, especially to take advantage of economies of scale.[16]

In essence, the idea would be to start exporting many tradables that are in fact not traded internationally (the bulk consists of import substitution industries), equalizing incentives for export production (which are few at present) with the considerable current incentives for the domestic market (at the cost, of course, of nontradables). Thus, growth would not only be more outward oriented—which is necessary to overcome the weak current commercial position of the majority of the countries in the region— but would also be based on a larger number of nontraditional exports, especially manufactured goods. This would take advantage of the extensive industrial platform created by the previous import substitution strategy.

3. The above-mentioned reduction in expenditures should use instruments that allow selective cuts. Hence, reductions should focus on consumer spending rather than on physical or social investment; and cuts in

consumption should be applied primarily to tradables (for example energy subsidies, while food subsidies should be limited only to the neediest). In addition, since investment in machinery usually involves imported equipment, this investment should be reduced in the short term, replacing it with more investment in public works, especially in works that facilitate productive activity.

Indeed, we must accept that it is not advisable to reduce the production of nontradables before expanding the production of tradables. However, the traditional (recessive) adjustment policy suggests that the reduction of the former almost automatically ensures the expansion of the latter. In fact, the production of nontradables usually drops easily and rapidly, while the expansion of the production of tradables is neither quick nor certain. For example, in the first two years of adjustment, the production of nontradables plummeted—construction fell by 30 percent—and resources thus freed were not automatically transferred to expand production of tradable goods. In fact, the production of tradable goods dropped by more than 10 percent. Hence, unlike in traditional adjustment programs, it would not appear advisable to cut back construction or production of other nontradable goods, except when these resources are necessary for the production of tradables. For to do so would save foreign exchange at an exaggerated cost, roughly the reciprocal of the marginal propensity to import (in other words, at an approximate cost, in terms of sacrificed production, four times higher than the exchange rate per dollar saved).

Even so, and following these three criteria, the recessive cost of the typical adjustment carried out in the region may be reduced, but not eliminated. This is due to the fact that efficient adjustment will be based, above all, on the reallocation of investment, which requires time; and, in addition, it will be efficient only if it is limited to correcting the permanent imbalance in the foreign accounts and not if it also attempts to correct temporary imbalances in these accounts, as it did, with negative results, in these last few years. Optimal conditionality will guarantee this financing as a compensation to the region's effort in adjusting. In its absence, the efficiency of national adjustment policies—even the best designed—will, in part, be determined by the success in reducing the transfer of resources abroad because both the pace of adjustment and the effort it demands will depend on the availability of external resources.

Thus, heterodox adjustment incorporates orthodox components and links them to the structuralist tradition. It recognizes that an outward orientation is necessary to take advantage of the industrial base created by import substitution, and thus will overcome the region's structurally weak commercial situation that has made it vulnerable to external shocks. It agrees with the structuralist school of thought of earlier times in that the penetration of external markets has to be actively promoted. It acknowledges that just as tariffs were a suitable instrument for import substitution, a high and stable exchange rate, in addition to selective credit and tax incentives, are now the instruments most suited to promoting exports. For neostructuralism does not trust the market's supposed capacity to automatically reestablish full employment in the face of significant shocks away from equilibrium. Therefore, in such situations, it advocates a resolutely active and selective macroeconomic policy.

Internal Disequilibria and Stabilization Policies

During the crisis, average inflation in the region climbed from under 60 percent in 1981 to almost 300 percent in 1985. Although inflation was strongly reduced in 1986—due to strong decelerations in Argentina (Austral Plan), Bolivia, Brazil (Cruzado Plan), and Peru (Inti Plan)—with the notable exception of Bolivia, the rest of the achievements proved temporary, and average inflation in the region took off again, exceeding 700 percent in 1988. Thus in the course of the 1980s, seven countries—Argentina, Bolivia, Brazil, Ecuador, Mexico, Nicaragua, and Peru—experienced triple-digit inflation, or greater, and three—Argentina, Bolivia, and Nicaragua—suffered hyperinflation.

The inflationary phenomenon is impressive, not only in magnitude but also in scope. Before 1970, inflation was basically restricted to the Southern Cone countries, Bolivia, and Brazil; in the remaining countries the average annual increase in prices was below 10 percent. Now only Haiti, Honduras, and Panama have inflation below this figure, while countries like Costa Rica, Ecuador, Mexico, the Dominican Republic, and Venezuela, which previously enjoyed stability, have experienced inflation rates of over 50 percent during the decade of the 1980s. In others—El Salvador, Guatemala, and Paraguay—although the rate is lower, 15–30 percent, the problem is no longer temporary but has become endemic.

The Avoidable Costs of Stabilization

The causes of this inflationary explosion were examined in a previous section. At this point we wish to examine the programs designed to combat it. The inflationary explosion of the last ten to fifteen years has given rise to innumerable stabilization programs, with a rich variety of approaches—shock and gradual—of orthodox and heterodox designs. However, before examining these experiences it is important to have a clear idea of the costs that these programs need incur, if any, in order to have a point of reference from which to make an evaluation.

If reducing inflation would necessarily bring on a recession—as has tended to be the case when traditional stabilization programs have been applied—lowering inflation from such high levels would require an un-precedented depression. Fortunately, there are well-founded, theoretical reasons for arguing that a stabilization program does not have to produce a recession. Indeed, from an analytical point of view, reducing inflation "merely" requires the smoothest possible deceleration in the growth of the nominal values of the principal economic variables, such as the exchange rate, the interest rate, and wages. It requires no systematic changes in real variables and, in particular, in output or employment; nor does it involve systematic income redistribution. The latter is not merely a theoretical issue. Although there are ample examples of failures, there have also been stabilization programs that were not recessive. Such was the case, for example, in the abrupt halt of some hyperinflations after World War I (Sargent 1981); or in more recent times of Indonesia, which cut its inflation from 1,000 percent to 10 percent between 1965 and 1970 without sacrificing its growth process (Papanek 1981); or in Latin America itself, when Bolivia reduced inflation from 63 percent in 1974 to 11 percent in 1975, while growing 6 percent, and Uruguay reduced an inflation rate of 125 percent to 20 percent between 1968 and 1969 without falling into recession.

On the other hand, we must recall that just as many stabilization programs failed in that they reduced inflation but at a significant recessive cost. In addition, other programs failed in a more fundamental sense: they did not reduce inflation at all, or only managed to do so temporarily, for which reason a new stabilization program had to be implemented shortly thereafter. A succession of stabilization programs has the additional negative effect that each failure reduces the next program's credibility, so that every new attempt has to be even sharper and is thus more likely to produce recession (for example, Argentina and Peru between 1987 and 1989, after the failures of the Austral and Inti plans).

The Conceptualization of Inflation

If an anti-inflationary policy does not necessarily have to bring about a recession, then why is this the usual outcome of stabilization programs? There appear to be two main reasons for these failures: on the one hand, errors of interpretation or conceptualization (tackling the wrong cause); and, on the other hand, errors in implementation, because however well conceived a program may be, the instruments adopted may not be the most suitable for executing it, or it may, in fact, be implemented in a partial or inadequate manner.

Inflation theories.[17] From the quantitative identity and the separation of the different factors that have an effect on costs, and therefore on prices, the principal theories with respect to the causes of inflation may be easily classified. From the quantitative identity, we know that national income

(Y) is equal to the price level (P) multiplied by the volume of production (Q), which is, by definition, equal to the quantity of money (M) multiplied by its velocity of circulation (V). In its dynamic version this implies that:

(1) $$m + v = y = p + q$$

where lowercase letters refer to the rates of growth of the variable.

In the same way, prices may be broken down into unit costs of wages (S), of imported inputs that are affected by the exchange rate (E), and of capital or margins (K), each one multiplied by the quantity of each factor per unit of production, α, β, Γ, respectively. In dynamic terms:

(2) $$p = \alpha s + \beta e + \Gamma k - \mu$$

where μ is the growth in productivity (which is assumed to be independent of the other factors).

Substituting (2) in (1) gives us:

(3) $$m + v = \alpha s + \beta e + \Gamma k - \mu + q = p + q \text{ or}$$

(4) $$\alpha s + \beta e + \Gamma k - \mu = p$$
or
the variation of costs = p.

Because it can, in fact, be assumed that only monetary expansion and costs are subject to important variations—virtually without limit[18]—most theories explain inflation in terms of variations in the money supply or costs or in any factor that affects both. Demand-pull (or monetarist) theories of inflation emphasize the left-hand side of equation 3. An increase in the money supply—whether due to a growing fiscal deficit or to improper expansion of credit to the private sector[19]—increases prices and costs. In contrast, cost-push theories of inflation (or distributive conflicts)[20] emphasize the increase of one or the other of the cost components in the right-hand side of equations 2 and 3 as the initial trigger, which forces the central bank to pursue a monetary policy confirming this level of costs and prices, or risk recession.

It is notable that both theories recognize the close relationship between M and P—a tendency that, moreover, has been thoroughly confirmed in the region, at least in the long run.[21] Where they do differ is in the direction of causality. According to demand theories, this is unmistakably from M to P. Cost theories, on the other hand, argue that causality can also go from increases in costs to prices and then to a monetary expansion to validate it.

Linked to cost inflation are structuralist approaches, which point to low price elasticity, particularly of traditional exports and agricultural produce, as the relevant rigidity. Hence, declines in the terms of trade or in agricultural production lead to jumps in the exchange rate or agricultural prices, generating strong upward pressures on costs. Whether these rigidities are due to the economic structure (segmented markets, concentration of income and property, lack of entrepreneurial initiative, lack of competition) or are the result of incorrect policies (protective tariffs with an anti-export bias, control of agricultural prices for distributive purposes, negative interest rates) is what distinguishes heterodox structuralists (ECLA 1962; Seers 1964; Sunkel 1960; among others), who support market intervention, from orthodox or neoconservative structuralists (Balassa 1982b; Krueger 1981; McKinnon 1973; among others), who support market liberalization.

Finally, inertial or equilibrium inflation may emerge if, as inflation persists over time, expectations arise about its continuity, and these come to be institutionalized in ever-widening indexation mechanisms. These mechanisms propagate inflation from one period to the next in such a way that even though the factors that caused the initial outbreak of inflation may have disappeared, inflation continues of its own accord in an inertial form. There would be inflation, then—and certainly monetary expansion, fiscal deficit, and an increase in costs—because in the long term inflation cannot occur if the medium of payments and living standards do not rise; but these factors would not be the cause of the inflation. The cause would be inflationary expectations and the indexation mechanisms to which they give rise. Indeed, at this level of inflation, although it may seem paradoxical, there would be no excess demand or cost pressures; it would be an equilibrium inflation. Certainly, propagating factors do not initiate the inflation or its acceleration, but once it has been triggered they keep it going.

To sum up, experience generally suggests that all inflation has two components: a disequilibrium component that is unexpected, which explains the inflationary outbreak; and an expected or equilibrium component, which causes it to persist. Demand, cost pressure, and structuralist theories all explain the origin of inflation, but not its persistence. Instead, this is explained by propagation factors, such as inflationary expectations and indexation mechanisms. The key analytic distinction, then, does not lie in whether or not inflation exists, but in the relative importance of the unexpected component (the outbreak) and the expected, inertial component.

In fact, in the region discussion on inflation long centered on the basic causes (the disequilibrium component), giving rise to the famous debate between monetarists and structuralists (see, for example, Noyola 1956; Hirschman 1961; Pinto 1961; ECLA 1962; Baer and Kerstenetzky 1964). Although in the 1950s and 1960s the distinction had already been made between basic pressures and propagation mechanisms, the emphasis continued to be on the former, given that average inflation in the region amounted to "only" 15 percent annually. However, the debate was overtaken by facts, as average inflation in the region rose rapidly, reaching triple digits in the 1980s. At such levels, basic pressures were swamped by propagation mechanisms.

The costs of inflation. The unfortunate wealth of inflationary experience in the region reveals a spectrum of inflation much greater than that conceived of in traditional theory, with different implications for costs and policy. In this sense, it is useful to distinguish three types of inflation: occasional inflation (which is typical but not exclusive to the countries of Central America and the Caribbean); high and persistent inflation (which can vary from 20–200 percent annually without necessarily becoming socially and economically intolerable); and acute inflation in the process of becoming hyperinflation.

More than the rate, what distinguishes occasional inflation from persistent inflation is that in the case of the former, there is no general expectation that inflation will continue, while with persistent inflation this belief is so widespread that indexation mechanisms arise that tend to perpetuate inflation. Once wages, exchange rates, and interest rates are adjusted, decreases in wages, balance of payments deficits, and a fall in savings, which are normally associated with inflation, are avoided. Indeed, these evils, classically attributed to inflation itself, really arise only with occasional inflation; for, strictly speaking, these costs are proportional to the difference between expected inflation (low or zero) and actual inflation (higher). Thus, as long as the economy is fully indexed, the costs of high and persistent but relatively stable inflation will be less than those of occasional inflation, since the difference between expected (indexed) inflation and actual inflation is minimal. Hence, as demonstrated by the experience of various countries in the region, high and persistent inflation, even at rates of 100 percent, may be compatible with satisfactory economic growth and external balance, and be tolerable in that sense.

However, these costs rise and become intolerable if inflation reaches such a level that it shortens contract periods.[22] Once the frequency of adjustments increases in this way from annually to semiannually or even monthly, economic calculation becomes all but impossible. The process moves toward hyperinflation, where planning becomes impossible. Moreover, the process becomes extremely sensitive to exogenous disturbances, because with such frequent indexing, changes in relative prices can only be accommodated with marked accelerations in inflation. Finally, hyperinflation gives rise to sharp reductions in the demand for money, generating a flight to goods or foreign exchange, leading to a breakdown of the economy and the reemergence of barter.

For the reasons described, the costs of inflation usually have a sinusoidal form, depending on whether there is occasional, persistent, or hyperinflation.

Stabilization Programs

Stabilization programs have failed for two types of reasons: either they turn out to be recessive or, more fundamentally, they are not effective in definitively reducing inflation.

From the above analysis it is clear that to reduce inflation, the growth of nominal aggregate demand should normally be decelerated (which, as we have seen, does not mean that this is the basic cause of inflation). Indeed, as every type of inflationary process, especially acute inflation, is usually accompanied by a monetary expansion (whether exogenous or endogenous), control of aggregate demand, monetary expansion, and the public deficit—which is typically, at least in recent years, the basic cause —is generally a necessary condition for the reduction of inflation.

This deficit can obviously be lowered by increasing income or cutting expenditures.[23] The increase in government revenues does not only consist of higher public tariffs or increased tax rates, but also increased tax collection, whether by an increase in the tax base, indexation of taxes paid in arrears, reduction of multiple tax exemptions, or a reduction in evasion. Similarly, the reduction of expenditures does not only refer to lower wages or investment levels (both of which are currently already depressed) or less public employment, but also reductions in (and targeting of) subsidies and the financial costs of the debt, both internal and external (whether through a lower interest rate or through writing off the debt). The counterpart of this reduction in the deficit is a deceleration in monetary expansion, which indeed serves as one of the "nominal anchors" of the program.

Although such measures have a similar impact on nominal aggregate demand, they differ in their degree of recessive risk and in their distributive consequences.[24] In fact, there is a presumption in favor of eliminating the deficit on the basis of increasing revenues because taxation usually affects the bulk of the economy, whereas cuts in expenditures are usually concentrated on a fraction of the economy (the 20 percent of GDP in the public sector and construction); therefore, expenditure reduction is more likely to give rise to undesirable adjustments in quantity (recession) and not just in prices. This presumption is reinforced when it is considered that inflation is a form of tax. It would seem more reasonable then, and certainly less discriminatory, to eliminate the deficit by means of higher taxation—which replaces the implicit inflation tax by an explicit one, while maintaining the effective taxation level—rather than by means of a reduction in spending (as long as the initial inflationary acceleration was not due to the increase of nonfinancial expenditures in output).

All in all, stabilization programs have failed in controlling demand because the deceleration in nominal aggregate demand has often provoked recession, and not just a reduction in inflation. The central problem to be resolved in macroeconomic theory and policy is to determine why such decelerations in nominal aggregate demand sometimes affect prices exclusively, without a recessive cost, and sometimes also affect production.

The Risk of Recession in Stabilization Programs:
Theory and Practice

Persistent inflation. When dealing with persistent inflation, a key factor that hinders rapid price adjustment arises from a very particular rigidity—the formation of inflationary expectations—which, due to their amorphous nature, do not lend themselves to easy or direct modification. Indeed, if the inflationary target implicit in macroeconomic policy is less than the public's inflationary expectations, part of the deceleration in nominal aggregate demand will affect production, thus triggering recession. If so, the government will be faced with the dilemma of foregoing its inflationary program and stimulating demand in order to avoid a recession, or persisting with its program but at the cost of generating recession.[25] Hence, a stabilization program that only controls aggregate demand—by means of a restrictive monetary and fiscal policy (the traditional orthodoxy)—will tend to provoke recession, at least in the case of persistent inflation.[26]

On the other hand, there is a credibility problem. Although the government may present a solid, coherent, and comprehensive stabilization program, there is no guarantee that the authorities will persist with its execution no matter what. This means that the private sector will assume that inflation will decelerate by less than the target (provoking recession). Thus a vicious circle is created: prices do not drop, in spite of aggregate demand being controlled, because everyone first wants to see the results before decelerating their own prices. With everybody following this pattern, the program will tend to fail.

Finally, there is a problem of lack of coordination (of the "prisoners dilemma" type). Although all agents may believe in the coherence of the program and its continuance, they will not decelerate their prices according to the inflationary target if they are not sure that others—above all, their suppliers—will do the same. Indeed, they risk large losses if they decelerate their prices according to the inflationary target and their suppliers reduce their prices at a slower pace. Faced with such uncertainty regarding the behavior of other agents, the prudent policy is to decelerate prices, but not as much as the inflationary target. When the same reasoning is used by everyone, it is predictable that average prices will remain above those of equilibrium, inducing an economic contraction because nominal aggregate demand will be insufficient to maintain real sales and production at this (inflated) price level.

Hence, programs to stabilize persistent inflation should include some type of policy to influence expectations, precisely to avoid a recession caused by problems of credibility, indexation, expectations, and coordination. In addition to slowing down aggregated demand, the typically orthodox version of incorporating expectations into stabilization programs concentrates its efforts on controlling expectations in the labor market. Indeed, the "backward" indexation mechanisms in labor contracts—which maintain purchasing power if inflation persists—increase the real cost of labor if inflation decelerates, thus provoking ever worse unemployment and recession the larger the desired price deceleration. In order to avoid such unemployment (neoclassical because it is caused by increases in real wages), these stabilization policies index wages at a lower rate than previous inflation.

However, even these programs have failed when the inflationary expectations of producers were based not only on their labor costs, but also on the movement of other key prices (for example, the exchange rate, the price of public tariffs, financial costs), or when producers doubted the soundness and credibility of the program or the firm commitment to the established goal. In these cases producers will adjust their prices at higher rates than the target inflation incorporated in the adjustment of wages. This problem will be even more serious if attempts are made to correct key relative prices at the same time as reducing inflation, as was the case of the neoconservative stabilization programs in Chile (1973–1975) and Argentina (1976–1978). Strong devaluations (above the inflationary target), recovery of important lags in public tariffs or in the prices of controlled products, or large increases in the interest rate led producers (especially producers of nonperishable goods in those two countries) to raise their prices above the inflationary target. Because this price level (or inflation rate) was greater than that compatible with the stabilization program, at that price (or inflation level) demand was insufficient to buy all the goods that the economy was capable of producing, which provoked a decline in sales, production, and employment. Thus, in spite of the fact that real wages dropped by 30 percent, unemployment went up. For, in market disequilibrium when companies cannot sell all that they are capable of producing at current prices, the demand for work ceases to be a function of the cost of labor and becomes, basically, a function of sales (Patinkin 1956; Barro and Grossman 1971; Leijonhufvud 1968). Hence, recession and unemployment in these two cases were of a Keynesian type, because of excessively high prices, not wages (ECLA 1984).

Similarly, on other occasions the attempt to influence expectations was focused on the exchange market. Partly due to the importance of imported inputs in costs, variations in the exchange rate (or expectations of variations) have frequently been used by economic agents as the best indicator of future inflation. Hence, some stabilization programs for persistent inflation have complemented the deceleration in aggregate demand with control of the exchange rate, to move expectations toward the inflationary target and thus decelerate inflation. In other words, instead of regular devaluations based on past inflation, devaluation is carried out according to the inflationary target implicit in the planned decrease in the fiscal deficit.

The success of this kind of program depends both on effectively harmonizing the deceleration of aggregate demand and exchange policy, and on how fast the "law of one price" does or does not manage to move domestic prices and their variations to international prices and variations. The harmonization of domestic and international inflation by means of the exchange rate may be obstructed by a policy of backward wage indexation, leading to greater increases in real wages (and thus exerting pressure on costs) the greater the attempted deceleration of inflation (as was partly the case in Argentina in 1978–1980 and in Chile in 1978–1981; see Corbo 1985). However, even if backward indexation does not take place (Uruguay 1978–1981), domestic inflation may not match international inflation plus devaluation for a long time if, for different reasons, inflationary expectations remain above the inflationary target (since the law of one price only operates in the long run), consequently giving rise to real exchange rate revaluations where imported products are sold at inflated domestic prices instead of at their international prices.[27] Such a real exchange rate revaluation will naturally decelerate inflation, but at the cost of a growing deficit in the balance of trade, financed by unsustainable levels of external borrowing. This may ultimately make a sharp devaluation necessary, with the consequent failure of the stabilization program (inflationary acceleration and a drop in output), as was in fact the case in the Southern Cone (1978–1982) and in Chile (1959–1962).

Past stabilization programs thus also failed because they were not always sufficient to control inflationary expectations in one market (the labor or exchange market) in order to influence expectations in other markets. Prices in uncontrolled markets often behaved in a manner incompatible with the stabilization program—even in cases such as Chile and Uruguay, where the fiscal deficit had been cleared—thus provoking recession or a growing deficit in the balance of payments.

In order to avoid this problem, heterodox stabilization programs,[28] together with trying to control demand, include a transitional price and income policy to influence the movement of the nominal values of critical variables—wages, exchange rates, interest rates, prices (at least of key products)—so that they will all decelerate simultaneously and evenly, according to the inflationary target implicit in the planned monetary and fiscal program. However, contrary to traditional price controls, this is done not to repress inflation, but to speed, as soon as possible, the magnitudes of key variables to their final equilibrium positions. Hence, in heterodox stabilization programs price controls are a complement to, but not a substitute for, control of aggregate demand. Indeed, the basic objective of this policy should be, as far as possible, to assure every economic agent that if they adjust their prices according to the inflationary target, they will not suffer a systematic relative loss, given that all other agents will also be induced to adjust their prices according to the same target. Thus the idea is to coordinate expectations among agents and to make them compatible with the inflationary target implicit in monetary and fiscal policy. For this reason, an abrupt liberalization of prices and interest rates (as is usually done in orthodox stabilization policies) is not advisable at the start of a stabilization program, since its success is sensitive to the behavior of inflationary expectations.

At the same time, there are limits to the inflationary deceleration that can be aimed for. The target must be compatible with the monetary and fiscal control that can be realistically obtained. If it is not credible that this degree of control will be obtained, the program will lack coherence, giving rise to expectations that prices will actually rise more than planned in the program. For example, if the monetary base is equivalent to 10 percent of GDP, and the projected fiscal deficit is equivalent to 5 percent of GDP, and if the deficit can only be financed by means of central bank credits, the monetary base would have to grow by 50 percent just to cover the public sector's imbalance. Thus, unless there is a considerable increase in the demand for money or a very marked growth in economic activity, it would not be possible to reduce inflation by much more than 50 percent per annum. A deceleration in key prices greater than that would not be consistent with the monetary and fiscal program and would therefore end in failure.

Apparently, this lack of control of aggregate demand would explain the eventual failure of the Cruzado, Austral, and Inti plans (Kiguel and Liviatan 1988; Ocampo 1987; Machinea and Fanelli 1988; Canavese and Di Tella 1988; Simonsen 1988). Indeed, the operational deficit was not sufficiently reduced (Argentina) or it was kept high or even increased, stimulating demand (Brazil and Peru).[29] The incompatibility between the inflationary target (zero or low) and the insufficient control of demand meant that inflationary achievements were transitory, for which reason inflation subsequently accelerated again. Thus, the three countries eventually ended up with higher inflation than that existing before they launched the stabilization programs.

This explanation is confirmed by the success achieved by analogous programs in Mexico and Israel in which a freeze (and correction of relative prices) was accompanied (Israel) by measures to reduce the deficit (mainly reductions in subsidies) or was even preceded by such reductions (Mexico).[30] In fact, in the latter case, the freeze was only implemented once the fiscal sector's operational accounts were in surplus.

To sum up, what all of these experiences demonstrate is the importance, and difficulty, of influencing expectations in cases of persistent inflation. Indeed, the same expectations and indexing that make high, but persistent and relatively expected inflation tolerable make it more difficult to reduce inflation, because they induce a rigidity in the response of the system to decelerations in aggregate demand, leading to undesired declines in output instead of the targeted deceleration of prices. Hence, one understands the importance of managing inflationary expectations so that, together with an adequate control of demand, expectations and indexation may be in harmony with the inflationary target (and not with past inflation), thus avoiding recession.

Occasional inflation. In contrast, the risk of recession is lower with occasional inflation. Precisely because there is no previous experience of prolonged inflation, indexation mechanisms do not exist, and most economic agents act on the premise that the normal situation is stability and not continuous increases in the level of prices. In this case an orthodox stabilization program centered on control of aggregate demand has a greater chance of success.[31]

Nevertheless, even in such situations, with no expectational problems, recessions have, on occasion, been triggered for two sets of reasons. First, inflationary pressure has sometimes come from the supply side, rather than the demand side. Any attempt at stabilization on the basis of controlling demand alone will provoke a recession in such a situation. This would be the case, for example, if, in order to reduce the inflationary impact of a devaluation (which was necessary because of a deterioration in the terms of trade, for example), demand was restricted when, in the short term, such a devaluation was contractive (a J curve). Indeed, in such situations devaluation should not be accompanied by a restriction in demand, but by a temporary expansion, so as to compensate for the initial contractive effect on the sector comprising nontradables and tradables that are not traded (Taylor 1981).[32]

Second, a cut in demand has often given rise to adjustments not just in prices, but also in production because it was directly concentrated on a few activities, for example, public works (hence making it difficult for the adjustment to be absorbed by prices alone), or because effort was concentrated on instruments such as credit, which particularly affects labor-intensive activities (housing construction, agriculture, trade, small and medium business).[33] Hence, it may be prudent for stabilization programs addressed to occasional inflation to also include complementary components to control aggregate demand, if the risk of recession originating from factors such as those indicated above is to be avoided. For example, the Costa Rican stabilization program of 1982–1983 not only reduced the fiscal deficit of 11 percent in 1982 to 3 percent in 1983, but also implemented a price and income policy (based on costs), which prevented the deceleration in nominal aggregate demand from being translated into higher margins, lower sales, and recession. It was thus able to reduce inflation from over 80 percent in 1982 to almost 10 percent in 1983, and with an expansion in production.[34]

Hyperinflation. Experience also suggests that ending hyperinflation may risk less of a recession than stabilizing a lower but persistent inflation. This is for two reasons. First, although inflationary expectations certainly will exist, they are less rigid; in other words, they are not consolidated at these extreme levels because the public understands that the situation is so intolerable that it cannot last, and that when it ends, it will end abruptly, not gradually. In fact, hardly any hyperinflation has lasted more than two years.[35]

Second, because under hyperinflation prices have to be set daily, adjustments are increasingly based on the currency's price in the free market as this is the only parameter that has an important impact on prices, which change daily or hourly and are universally known. Consequently, if the exchange rate can be stabilized, all other prices will tend rapidly to come into line automatically and in a synchronized form. Therefore, stabilization of the exchange rate during hyperinflation is equivalent to a synchronized and general price and income policy. Additional price controls become redundant. In effect, under hyperinflation the heterodox and orthodox approaches become equivalent.

To be sure, the exchange rate cannot be fixed arbitrarily;[36] nor will it be possible to maintain it, unless it is accompanied by effective control of aggregate demand. For example, the Bolivian success (Morales 1988) in lowering inflation of 20,000 percent per annum to less than 2 percent per month, in less than six months—and at a cost of, at most, a 3 percent drop in GDP[37]—was due to its drastic reduction of the fiscal deficit, and consequent control of aggregate demand, together with a free float (real devaluation) and the subsequent stabilization of the exchange rate. Because the Bolivian public sector was running a foreign exchange surplus, the devaluation itself increased government revenues by 5 percent of GDP; another increase of 2.5 percent of GDP was due to the increase in the domestic price of gasoline to international levels (and subsequently beyond those). Therefore, a single instrument favored both external and internal balance.[38] Moreover, most reductions in the deficit were achieved on the basis of increasing government revenues, which is usually a less recessive way to proceed because most sectors are affected more or less equally (which compensates, on the other hand, for the "loss" to the national treasury of the imposed inflation tax, which benefits all sectors more or less equally). Finally, the fact that when the program was initiated, M2 money supply scarcely amounted to 100 million dollars at the free exchange rate (more or less equal to the amount of gross international reserves) meant that a speculative attack against the exchange rate could be endured.

Synthesis: The Relative Costs of Inflation Versus the Risks of Recession in Stabilization Programs

For the reasons mentioned above, the costs of inflation usually have a sinusoidal form (see Figure 4.1): proportional to inflation in the first phase, when inflation is recent and unexpected; relatively low in the second phase, since persistent inflation comes to be expected and indexation is widely extended; and high and growing in the third phase, once inflation passes a critical threshold, which leads to a continual shortening of the duration of contracts and price and wage adjustments, a flight from the currency, and a slide into hyperinflation.

The risk of recession is lower with occasional inflation precisely because there is no previous experience of prolonged inflation, indexation mechanisms do not exist, and most economic agents act on the premise

Figure 4.1. Relative Costs of Inflation and Risks Involved in Stabilization Programs

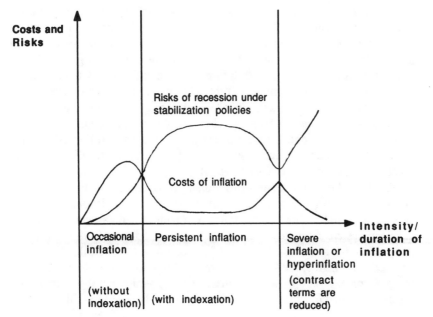

that the normal situation is stability and not continuous increases in the level of prices. Similarly, the ending of hyperinflation also runs a relatively lower risk of recession because inflationary expectations are still not consolidated at the new rates (nor can they be, given their intrinsic instability at these extreme rates), nor are significant reductions in aggregate demand required because, if it is credible, the inflationary deceleration itself will give rise to a sharp increase in the demand for money. Hence, the least recessive stabilization programs have usually been associated with cases of hyperinflation (Bolivia 1985) and occasional inflation (Costa Rica 1982). On the other hand, the stabilization of persistent inflation runs a greater risk of recession because the same expectations and indexation that make persistent inflation tolerable usually make price movements more rigid in the face of decelerations in aggregate demand (see the cases of recessive stabilization in Argentina and Chile in the mid-1970s). Hence, the risks of recession under a stabilization program tend to take the form of an inverted U, as shown in Figure 4.1.

The preceding analysis has clear implications for economic policy. Because the costs of occasional inflation are high and are proportional to the intensity of the inflationary outbreak, and the risk of a stabilization program provoking a fall in economic activity is lower, the decision to tackle occasional inflation should be taken quickly (the monetarist position in the 1950s), thus preventing it from becoming persistent, giving rise to indexation mechanisms and inflationary expectations that later make it much more costly to eliminate. On the other hand, if the risk of a recession seems high (as in the structuralists' view), it may be decided to live with inflation, indexing most variables. This sharply lowers the distributive and allocative costs associated with occasional inflation, but the risks of recession are considerably increased for any later attempt at stabilization because inflation now becomes persistent.

On the other hand, an anti-inflationary program is less urgent and stabilization programs tend to be put off when inflation, although high and persistent, is stable. For the existence of a widespread and generalized indexation system markedly reduces the negative effects of inflation, while it significantly increases the risks of recession in case stabilization is attempted. In practice, these two factors tend to reduce both the pressure on the government to apply an anti-inflationary program and the support that the best organized social groups are effectively disposed to deliver.

Additional Considerations for a Non-Recessive Stabilization Program

In addition to the lessons noted in the analysis above, others must also be highlighted.

1. Every inflationary process has a disequilibrium component (the limit is zero), which explains the outburst, and an inertial component,

which explains its persistence. Three policies, which are normally included in all stabilization programs, will be combined according to the relative importance of each of these components: the control of aggregate demand, the correction of relative prices to correct the disequilibrium component, and the management of expectations—the possible control of prices and incomes—to combat the inertial or equilibrium component.

2. The greater the inertial component, the greater the importance of tackling the factors of propagation; the lower the inertial factor, the greater the need to tackle the fundamental causal factors. In any case, the program must include both sets of policies, or risk being recessive if it only tackles the fundamental factors or ephemeral if it only controls prices. It is worth noting, in the latter case, that experience shows that the failure of a stabilization attempt (because of its short-lived success) makes future stabilization programs less credible and therefore more costly.

3. In general, stabilization will not last if programs do not succeed in controlling aggregate demand. This does not mean that all inflation is basically caused by an autonomous increase in aggregate demand. It simply affirms that a monetary-fiscal expansion (whether autonomous or induced) usually accompanies every inflationary process; therefore force stabilization requires the control of nominal aggregate demand.

4. In order to avoid recession, especially in the case of persistent inflation, the transitional control of key prices and incomes may be useful to convince the different economic agents that other agents, especially suppliers, will also decelerate their prices in accordance with the inflationary target announced. However, unlike traditional price controls, which concentrate on food prices because of their great impact on the cost of living, in this approach the purpose of price controls is to influence those prices in which inflationary expectations play a major role: industrial rather than agricultural prices (because producers have greater freedom to set their prices), wages, public tariffs, and exchange rates.

5. By contributing to the rapid reduction of inflation, price controls set off a "virtuous circle." Their initially satisfactory results provide needed confidence and credibility, thus reducing the speculative demand for goods and foreign exchange, increasing the demand for money, and raising real fiscal revenues. However, for analogous reasons, the process may revert and set off a vicious circle if such controls are not complemented with policies that control demand and correct relative prices, which in the last analysis determine the feasibility of restoring macroeconomic equilibria.

6. Because in most inflationary processes the increase in prices is not even, a lasting and efficient stabilization program must usually correct relative prices. Unfortunately, there is a conflict between moving prices to equilibrium—running the risk that the public does not believe that they can be maintained, causing the program to fail—and overshooting equilibrium levels for some key prices to gain credibility—at the risk of recession because overblown prices reduce aggregate demand below equilibrium levels.

7. The prudent policy apparently would be to overshoot equilibrium at the beginning in two, fast-adjusting key prices—exchange rates and interest rates—thus discouraging a flight from domestic currency to the dollar or to goods. Once inflation drops, and the program gains credibility, it will be possible to ease up, reducing (revaluing) the real exchange rate to its longer term equilibrium; at the same time, it will be possible to expand the money supply pari passu with the demand for money in order to lower real interest rates and thus provide the system with the necessary liquidity. In theory it is easy to reconcile this problem; the difficulty—the art—lies in identifying the key moments for action and the magnitudes by which equilibrium values have to be momentarily exceeded. Nevertheless, the nature of the choice between credibility and equilibrium is as described, and it has to be continuously reconciled at the risk of having the stabilization attempt fail or producing a costly and prolonged recession.

8. Finally, not only does the deficit have to be reduced, but institutional reforms have to be implemented in the public sector to encourage the structural equilibrium of public sector finances and make them less liable to excesses. Two reforms are particularly important in this regard. First, the possibility of approving expenditures without the need to simultaneously assure financing makes the budgetary process liable to almost limitless pressure. Indeed, if decided separately, greater benefits, lower taxes, and a smaller deficit are things that everybody favors. But it is not possible to have the three things simultaneously. Hence, the budgetary process must approve expenditures and financing, simultaneously and as a whole, as a means of introducing counterbalances and discipline in public sector finances. Second, central government adjustments can be neutralized by deficits in other public sector organizations—regional governments, state companies, state and provincial banks—which usually have their deficits absorbed ex post facto by the central government. As long as the spending autonomy of these organizations is not accompanied by a corresponding autonomy in financial responsibility, there will arise a serious asymmetry in which decentralized deficits are transmitted to the center, while surpluses will tend to stay where they arise.

Conclusion

The macroeconomic excesses of the 1980s and the attempts to correct them have been extremely costly for the region. Although there have been variations in the exact situation of each country since the beginning of the crisis, the region as a whole has been unable simultaneously to achieve economic growth, external balance, and price stability. On the contrary, the search for each of these basic macroeconomic equilibria, sequentially, has favored the achievement of one at the expense of another, rendering advances inconsistent or passing. Thus, inflation (accelerated by large devaluations) or stagnation (due to the compression of imports) has often been the price of correcting external imbalances; recession and a worsening of income distribution (produced by policies that excessively cut demand), the price of reducing inflation; and balance of payments deficits (because of the excessive expansion of aggregate demand), the price of recovery. The cumulative effect of these swings in policy has been to accentuate the region's economic cycles, rendering even more difficult the attainment of solid and persistent growth.

Such instability does not so much reflect deficiencies in economic policies as it does the limited degree of freedom available to policymakers as a result of the foreign exchange bottleneck arising from the sharp reversal in the transfer of resources. Hence, the need to redress priorities: subordinating debt-servicing to the achievement of an acceptable, stable, and equitable rate of economic growth, rather than sacrificing the achievement of minimum domestic goals, as has been the case until now, in pursuit of external balance at almost any cost. Thus, the transfer of resources would come to be an adjustment variable, instead of being the dominant restriction to which all other goals are subordinated. And precisely because of the heavy burden that the transfer of resources represents to exports, investment, and public expenditure, a significant reduction in that transfer (2–3 percent of GDP perhaps) would provide the leeway to permit the simultaneous achievement of growth, stabilization, and equity.

This approach requires that all the principal players—private creditor banks, debtors, national and international public financial institutions, and the governments of the developing countries and the Organization for Economic Cooperation and Development (OECD)—recognize that the debt problem is a systemic problem and not just a particular problem of individual creditors and debtors. This is what the region means when it talks of a political solution to the debt problem.

Of course, this strategy, which aims to solve the debt problem through growth, requires, as its counterpart, domestic structural adjustment. If not, the greater leeway that comes from a reduction in the transfer of resources will vanish rapidly (consider Peru after 1985). Hence, a significant reduction in the outward transfer of resources is a necessary, but not sufficient, condition for reinitiating a sustained, stable, and equitable process of development. The counterpart to the reduction in the transfer of resources is a domestic adjustment and stabilization program, following the (neostructural) guidelines described, to restore internal and external balances at a minimal recessive cost (consider Costa Rica after 1982).[39]

This program draws on structuralist thinking because of its emphasis on real and not just financial variables; because of its concerns for recession and the concentration of income, and not simply instability; because it points to a profound (although not unique) cause of the crisis—the problem of the transfer of resources, both internally and externally—rather than just attributing it to the ineptitude of economic policy; because it favors supply (and investment) policies and not just demand policies; because of its more disaggregated approach, using more selective instruments; and because of its skepticism with regard to the market's ability to adjust efficiently and automatically to major disequilibria, above all, in the short term and, therefore, because of its vindication of an active macroeconomic role for the state.

Neostructuralism not only draws on structural thinking, but also takes in important orthodox emphases. For example, it affirms the importance of an outward orientation, but combined with structural emphases in favor of industrialization (now outward oriented) and the use of active instruments for the selective promotion of exports (and not just a reduction in tariffs) together with a high and stable real exchange rate. Finally, neostructuralism does not simply criticize macroeconomic orthodoxy, but it offers an alternative approach to stabilization and adjustment that is constructive and operational, respectful and not complacent, toward short term financial restrictions.[40]

Needless to say, rather than implementing these adjustment and stabilization programs—however neostructural they may be—it would be better to avoid their need altogether. In short, because experience demonstrates that the cost of restoring macroeconomic equilibria can be quite high—normally higher than the potential benefit from risking disequilibria—a central objective of steady state macroeconomic policy should be to avoid such excesses.

Notes

1. For example, it is always possible to increase employment, at least temporarily, if pressure on the balance of payments or the risk of higher inflation is accepted. The challenge is to increase employment permanently, on the basis of a sustained flow of foreign exchange, without dangerously accelerating inflation.

2. I do not include the third possible formulation, which relates to recovery, because I presume that any existing unused capacity is due to a recessive adjustment or stabilization program. That is to say, if recovery is possible, it is because overadjustment took place. In that case, it would be necessary to return to the principles of efficient, nonrecessive adjustment or stabilization, recommended in the following sections.

3. A complete review of the theoretical and empirical literature on the behavior of the terms of trade for the region is to be found in Chapter 12.

4. See Lustig (1988a) and Rosales (1988a) for criticisms in this vein from the structuralist stance, which confirm Lewis's intuition (1964) almost twenty-five years in advance.

5. To simplify, the transfer of resources is here defined and measured as the difference between net capital inflow (including direct investment) and payments due to interest and capital remittances. By virtue of balance of payments identities, this transfer of resources is equal to the trade surplus.

6. It is worth noting that only Brazil and Colombia were able to improve their balance of trade, basically by means of increasing exports and substituting (rather than compressing) imports, due to the major investments they made in these activities from as early as the mid-1970s.

7. Obviously, there are other explanatory factors, but in general, these are attributable to increases in the public deficit (deriving from domestic wars, higher subsidies, and the like), which contributed to the inflationary escalation. This is particularly true in Central American and Caribbean countries—in which the transfer of resources is still inward, toward the country, although it is less so than in earlier times—and in Peru because interest payments have been unilaterally stopped since 1985.

8. However, not all did. Some countries with relatively high interest payments and, therefore, important outward transfers (Chile) have been capable of carrying out an internal transfer without significant inflationary financing; other countries with no transfers abroad (Peru is, perhaps, the most striking example in this sense) have experienced soaring inflation anyway. In other words, transfers abroad tend to generate inflationary pressures, but do not totally eliminate economic policy's freedom to control them. Therefore, the reduction of the transfer is not sufficient a condition for reducing inflation.

9. Note that this phase of financing or transfer of resources to the public sector is more difficult in countries where the public sector normally runs a foreign exchange deficit (Argentina, Brazil, Central America, Uruguay) because the very devaluation required by the external adjustment worsens the fiscal deficit (in domestic currency). Hence, if increasing inflationary pressure is to be avoided, devaluations in these countries should be accompanied by additional measures to control demand, since devaluation tends to boost the income of the private sector, while accentuating the public deficit.

This difference may help to explain why the greatest achievements in the area of stabilization in this decade have been recorded in countries such as Bolivia, Chile, and Mexico where the public sector owns the principal source of foreign exchange generation, and therefore usually has a foreign exchange surplus. In such countries devaluation reduces both external imbalances and the fiscal deficit. Yet even this does not assure success; note the failure in Venezuela and, above all, in Peru, countries where the public sector also has a foreign exchange surplus.

10. Of course, if it were possible to raise output above its trend, this would be preferable to reducing expenditures. However, because indebtedness was not used to raise (or improve) investment, this was an option no longer available in 1982. Therefore, in 1982 there was no other choice but to cut expenditures.

11. This is easy to demonstrate. GDP is broken down into the production of tradables (Qt) and nontradables (Qn). In addition, the gross value of production ($Qt + Qn$) less imported inputs for their production ($MtQt + MnQn$) is equal to GDP; and total expenditure is equal to expenditure on tradables (Dt) plus expenditure on nontradables (Dn). Then, the trade surplus, $B = GDP - E$, can be expressed as $B = Qt + Qn - MtQt - MnQn - Dt - Dn$. If inflexibility of prices is assumed, the production of tradables is determined by demand of nontradables, $Qn = Dn$. Therefore, $\Delta B = \Delta Qt (1 - Mt) - Dt - MnQn$. Thus, assuming that the m's are constant in the short term, an improvement in the trade surplus leads to: $\Delta B = \Delta Qt (1 - Mt) + \nabla Dt + \nabla Qn$. That is, the trade surplus improves (1) if the production of tradables increases Qt (increases in exports and import substitution), (2) if the demand for tradables falls, or (3) if the demand for nontradables falls. The first is optimal—the route followed by the Asian NICs—because it increases output without reducing the standard of living (national expenditure). The second, a reduction in expenditure on tradables, does not reduce output but reduces the standard of living (Brazil followed this route in conjunction with the first option). The third

option is the most costly. It not only reduces the standard of living in direct proportion to the reduction in expenditure on nontradables, but it also reduces output, and by much more than it improves the trade surplus, because the latter only improves in proportion to the portion of imported inputs involved in the expenditure on nontradables. This gives rise to a recessive adjustment (Arellano 1986).

12. See, for example, Devlin (1985), Feinberg and Ffrench-Davis (1988), Griffith-Jones and Sunkel (1986), and Sachs (1989b).

13. A similar, more detailed, proposal is analyzed in Chapter 2.

14. As this chapter focuses on the short term, long term considerations that require deeper transformations—such as those dealt with in the rest of the book— have been left aside. For this reason the macroeconomic management suggested would have to be incorporated into a long-range development strategy.

15. The accumulated improvement in the trade balance between 1981 and 1984 amounted to 100 million dollars. In this same period the accumulated loss in output amounted to 6 percent. If we add the fact that production would have grown by perhaps 5 percent per year, the accumulated loss reaches 36 percent of the region's GDP, approximately 250 billion dollars.

16. It would not be sufficient to eliminate all tariffs and incentives to exports and replace them with higher exchange rates. In fact, this would be the correct approach if all sectors merited the same level of protection and similar incentives to export. But this would be an extreme case. There will probably be important divergences between social and private beneficiaries only in some sectors, and such divergences will vary in magnitude and over time. Thus, at any given moment, some activities may be basically taking advantage of tariff protection, while mature activities in import substitution will increasingly have access only to export incentives and fully mature activities will receive no special incentive.

17. This section is based on Ramos (1986a).

18. Velocity of circulation varies, but predictably or steadily; moreover, its variation (except in hyperinflation) is not unlimited.

19. Although the fiscal deficit has often been the principal source of monetary expansion, money issues may also arise from an undue expansion of credit to the private sector—for example, in Argentina (1976–1979), where domestic credit to the private sector rose thirty-threefold, accounting for 80 percent of total domestic credit, while the fiscal deficit was reduced from 10.3 percent to 2.7 percent of GDP; or Uruguay (1975–1979), where domestic credit to the private sector rose twelve times, accounting for 90 percent of the total increase in domestic credit, while the fiscal deficit was reduced from 4.3 percent of GDP to zero; and Ecuador (1980–1983), where credit to the private sector almost tripled (increasing prices by 95 percent), while the government created a surplus (as a result of oil revenues). To be sure, cases abound where the public deficit is the prime source of money issue: Chile (1971–1974), where 85 percent of the hundredfold increase in domestic credit went to the public sector; Mexico (1980–1983), where domestic credit was almost quintupled and 75 percent went to the public sector; and Costa Rica (1978–1980), where two-thirds of the 80 percent increase in domestic credit went to the public sector. The point is that the fiscal deficit is not always the principal source. Therefore, it is not sufficient to merely control the fiscal deficit to reduce inflation, if the monetary expansion originated in a disproportionate increase of credit to the private sector.

20. Because these factors that pressure costs—wages, exchange rates, margins—influence income distribution, they are also known as theories of distributive conflict.

21. With data for ten Latin American countries over the last twenty-five years, an application of equation 1, using $v = o$ to simplify, that is to say, $p = a + bm - cy$,

demonstrates that inflation, p, is strongly and positively correlated to monetary expansion, m, with b equal to 1, and strongly but inversely correlated with variations in the product, with c = 1. R^2 was of the order of 90 percent for the region as a whole and above 75 percent for the majority of countries taken separately. However, this proposition, which is clear and strong in the long term, is not so in the short term, thus giving rise to the various theories of inflation, suggesting the need, as regards stabilization policy, to use other instruments in addition to monetary and fiscal instruments.

22. Pazos (1969) was a pioneer in the analysis of this phenomenon.

23. The relevant deficit is what is known as the operational deficit, in other words, that which *excludes* the inflationary component incorporated in interest rates. Indeed, the higher the inflation, the higher the nominal interest rate and the higher the deficit. In other words, inflation increases the deficit and not vice versa. This apparent paradox is due to the fact that an important component of the interest rate compensates for the loss of real value of the principal; in other words, higher inflation pays the debt more rapidly. Indeed, payments made under the heading of the inflationary component of the interest rate correspond to the loss of the public debt's real value, and can therefore normally be financed with higher nominal indebtedness (without increasing the real debt). For which reason, they generally do not require an increase in debt (real) issues, and there is therefore no reason why they should accelerate prices.

24. For example, it is obvious that the cost for the country will be lower as it becomes more feasible to make the fiscal adjustment on the basis of cuts in interest payments on the foreign debt. Therefore, and perhaps only in adjustment's early stages, reducing the transfer of resources abroad may be fundamental to gain time while the other fiscal measures (many of which may be slow in yielding results) have the desired effects. In this respect, it is interesting to note that the successful stabilization programs applied in Bolivia (1985), Israel (1986), and Germany (1923) were carried out with the suspension of debt servicing or with strong foreign financial support.

25. The Chilean stabilization program of 1965–1967 illustrates the problem of not considering expectations. After two years of apparent success in reducing inflation, the government strongly contracted demand in 1967 to achieve its goal of 10 percent inflation (versus 18 percent the previous year). Nevertheless, because demand dropped within a framework of increasing, not decreasing, inflationary expectations (in fact, wages went up by 37 percent, double the inflation of 1966 and almost four times the target inflation), instead of falling, inflation accelerated and per capita output dropped. Hence, the recession (or stagnation) was of a neoclassical variety, rather than Keynesian, because it was produced by an increase in real wages (15 percent).

26. Of course, a recession will eventually modify expectations or render them inoperative, but the point is to avoid this rather costly method of modification.

27. This may happen when small importers try to maximize their short term earnings; or when most imports are brought in by large domestic producers who therefore set a price that maximizes their income in both operations (production and import); or when imports are, to a large extent, centered on products that differ more in quality than price, taking market shares from domestic producers but leaving prices largely unaffected, because this area of the market is relatively insensitive to price and more sensitive to quality or differentiation.

28. These were the Argentine Austral Plan, in 1985; the Peruvian Inti Plan, in 1985; the Brazilian Cruzado Plan, in 1986; and the Mexican Economic Solidarity Pact, in 1987–1988. Although outside the region, the Israeli stabilization plan of 1985 was also inspired by this heterodox approach. See Bruno et al. (1988).

29. Further, an important part of the reduction in the deficit was also transitory. That is, when inflation decreased, the loss in the real value of taxation decreased, but due to the inevitable time lag in collection, the fiscal deficit was reduced. However, once inflation accelerated again, the reverse happened, increasing the deficit. See Olivera (1972) and Tanzi (1977). The partial suspension of interest payments on its foreign debt gave Peru additional room for the stimulation of demand. Nevertheless, because demand was overstimulated, at the end of two years, the increase in imports had used up this room, turning it into a simple populist program, which stimulated demand through price controls. See Dornbusch and Edwards (1989b).

30. For Israel, see Bruno and Piterman (1988) and Cukierman (1988) and, for Mexico, see Dornbusch (1988).

31. Thus, for example, Bolivia reduced an inflation rate of 63 percent in 1974 to 11 percent in 1975 with a severe deceleration in the money supply (from 43 percent to 12 percent); in the same way, Ecuador reduced its inflation from 53 percent to 19 percent between 1983 and 1984 with an accompanying reduction in its fiscal deficit (from 2.5 percent to 1.9 percent of GDP); and Costa Rica reduced its inflation rate of 82 percent in 1982 to 11 percent in 1983 by decelerating its money supply from 68 percent to 36 percent—together with less orthodox price and income control policies—within a framework of ample external financing. Production did not drop in any of these three cases. In fact, together with the deceleration of prices, production grew over 6 percent in Bolivia and rose 3 percent and 2.3 percent in Ecuador and Costa Rica, respectively.

32. This is because, if the price elasticity for imports and exports is low, devaluation will reduce the trade deficit expressed in foreign currency, but may increase it in terms of domestic currency. Hence, for the same nominal aggregate demand, there would remain insufficient nominal demand to buy domestic production at the previous price level. If there was insufficient downward flexibility in these prices (which is probable, given that there has been a devaluation), production would fall. A similar, although perhaps less severe, case has occurred when, together with control of demand, prices that were previously subsidized and controlled (for example, oil, basic foodstuffs, public tariffs) have been liberalized in order to slow inflation. See, for example, Chu and Feltenstein (1978) and World Bank (1983).

33. For these reasons, the Venezuelan stabilization program from 1979 onward, for example, managed to spark a recession in spite of the doubling of oil prices. This was because credit to the private sector, which had been growing at an annual rate of over 20 percent since 1973, was suddenly decreased to 5 percent in 1979, and government expenditures were reduced, even in nominal terms, hitting especially investment and construction. The negative experience of Venezuela contrasts with that of Bolivia in 1974–1975 and Ecuador in 1983–1984. The deceleration in aggregate demand in these two countries did not center on the construction industry; on the contrary, this sector grew strongly in Bolivia (13 percent) during its 1975 stabilization and rose slightly (1 percent) together with investment (8 percent) in Ecuador in 1984. This certainly does not mean that investment and construction are sacrosanct activities, but that when deceleration in demand is concentrated on a few activities, such as these, there is a risk of quantity adjustments and not just in prices.

34. Note that this program, in contrast with the vast majority in the region, had strong external support, therefore the transfer of resources toward the country never ceased to be positive. Incidentally, this demonstrates the importance of reducing the outward transfers of resources for the success of a nonrecessive

stabilization program, when it is accompanied by internal adjustment measures (Parot, Rodríguez, and Schydlowsky 1988).

35. I was made aware of this fact thanks to Daniel Heymann. See his essay on hyperinflation in ECLAC (1986).

36. However, if it is correctly set, it does not have to produce a real exchange rate revaluation, as in the Southern Cone examples. Under high but persistent inflation—the case of the Southern Cone—the exchange rate is only one of various factors that influence expectations. In contrast, because under hyperinflation all prices tend to be fixed in terms of the exchange rate, once it is stabilized, the rest will automatically slow down.

37. Moreover, an important part of this drop was due not to the effects of the stabilization program, but to the abrupt collapse of the international tin market.

38. This contrasts with the situation of Argentina and Brazil, where the public sectors suffer from a chronic foreign exchange deficit. Therefore, every time they need to devalue in order to improve their external position, the fiscal deficit, in pesos, worsens, so that additional restrictive demand policies are required in order to transfer resources from the private to the public sector.

39. It is worth noting, once again, that an "expansive" adjustment to the external problem is in line with the longer term strategy of development from within suggested by Osvaldo Sunkel in Chapter 2.

40. For more detailed works on neostructuralist macroeconomics, see, for example, Cortázar (1986), Arida (1986), and Taylor (1987).

PART 2

PRODUCTIVE RESOURCES

5

Labor Markets and Employment in Latin American Economic Thinking

Víctor E. Tokman

This chapter deals with the topic of labor force absorption in Latin America from the perspective of accumulation, in other words, in relation to the expansion of the productive system and, particularly, to economic growth. This structural perspective also entails an interpretation on the operation of the labor market. Section one intends to answer questions such as: Which interpretations underlie Latin American thinking in this field? and, What has been the response based on the interpretation of conditions existing in the region, which is characterized by weak labor absorption?

Section two goes from interpreting to analyzing action, exploring economic and growth policy responses and their effect on employment. The objective is not to evaluate the policies implemented but rather to analyze the research available in terms of its usefulness, both before and after the fact, in validating the conceptual frameworks that underlie the decisions adopted. The chapter concludes with a look at the future based on the current crisis. It examines the options for creating employment and labor market policies associated with the debate on structural adjustment.

Throughout the chapter an aggregate and historical perspective has been adopted. The periphery refers to Latin America as a whole and the center to one country, the United States. This is an oversimplification, but at the same time it helps to identify the more general causes and trends without attempting to explain specific national conditions. The period analyzed extends from the postwar period to the present, since the search— from a structural perspective—requires extended periods that make it possible to differentiate the more permanent factors from the short term ones.

Theoretical Approaches on Employment Creation and Labor Market Operation

The Implicit Normal Model

Interpretations available at the beginning of the period under analysis allow us to define the behavior of labor force absorption during the process of modernization. These interpretations postulate three basic trends associated with growth. The first is the migration of population from rural to urban areas. The second is that secondary sectors (particularly manufacturing) turn into the most dynamic sector regarding labor absorption. The third is the increasing degree of homogenization that results from reducing intersectoral differences in productivity.

The most influential theoretical article is by Lewis (1954). He provides an analytical framework in which the main factor is the initial existence of an unlimited labor supply and its gradual depletion as modernization advances. This occurs within a context of increasing urbanization due to labor force migration from the countryside to the cities. This excess of labor allows destination sectors to generate surpluses with low and stable wages without affecting the productivity of the sector of origin (agriculture). During the course of this process, it undergoes changes as excess labor is depleted in the face of expanded demand. Thus, the labor supply changes from a horizontal to a positive slope, and new hirings can only occur at higher wages. Fei and Ranis (1961) pinpoint the key moments of this transfer of labor between sectors.

Other works analyze the historical validity of the normal model, among them Clark (1951) and Kuznets (1957). Both, and particularly the latter, analyze the changes in the sectoral distribution of output and employment and the differences in productivity. For that purpose, information available on numerous countries was reviewed and comparisons were made between countries in a given year (around 1947), as well as the changes recorded within the same country over time (from the mid-nineteenth century to around 1950). This analysis allows one to empirically establish the validity of two expected trends. Indeed, there is a clear association between growth and the shift in labor toward nonagricultural sectors. Also, differences in productivity tend to decline as countries develop, which occurs both in the comparisons between countries and over time. However, the role played by secondary sectors in the absorption of labor over time is not so clear. The analysis between countries reaffirms the normal model, since countries record a growing absorption of labor in nonagricultural activities and within them, primarily in secondary activities. On the other hand, the analysis over time indicates that tertiary sectors absorb the greatest proportion of labor moving from agricultural activities, while secondary sectors show an asystematic performance, with expansion in some countries and contraction in others, but generally with lower rates of employment growth than tertiary sectors.

Kuznets (1955) links the preceding analysis to changes in income distribution. His main thesis is that greater inequality will unavoidably occur during the early transition phases from preindustrial to industrial economies. This behavior is the outcome of the higher degree of inequality and the greater per capita income prevalent in the points of destination for migrants from rural areas. Kuznets estimates that inequality should increase until the share of the nonagricultural sector reaches between 60 and 70 percent of the total labor force. Ahluwalia (1976) and Lydall (1977) confirm the results anticipated by Kuznets from information between countries. Inequality is lower in poor countries; it reaches a maximum at higher per capita income levels and then declines. Ahluwalia shows that the 40 percent share of the lowest incomes declines as per capita income increases, reaching its minimum at 468 dollars (at 1971 prices). Lydall observes, in turn, that the minimum reached by the lowest 20 percent occurs at 500 dollars per capita. Bacha (1979), using a somewhat different methodology, confirms the expected trend, but with a cutoff point at 900 dollars.

This structural analytical framework that establishes an association between modernization and growth with labor absorption and homogenization has its theoretical underpinnings in the Keynesian approach. This approach also provides the backing for economic policymaking and, furthermore, for organizing society around an implicit consensus where stability, growth, and increasing equity are combined. The association between employment and effective demand and the role assigned to the government in ensuring adequate expansion levels, in fact, allows the pursuit of an expansion path with full employment and without inflation. The homogenization of the labor force can only progress so far as it does not imply violating the two basic requirements of the labor process (Reich, Gordon, and Edwards 1975), which are maintaining the initiative that affords increases in productivity and exercising labor discipline to avoid exaggerated increases in costs. The implicit social pact is ensured through acceptance, by the workers, of a certain degree of subordination to decisions adopted by those at the top in exchange for certain benefits, particularly full, stable, and protected employment with increasing real wages. Benefits are partly generated by the normal functioning of the economic system, but the state becomes the guarantor for this to occur by sanctioning adequate labor legislation and assuming a welfare role that ensures care of the neediest. Essentially, until the recent crisis, this was the Keynesian consensus in force.

The Center-Periphery Model[1]

Prebisch believed that employment trends in Latin America, which, in his opinion, were noted for inadequate growth tied to the peripheral nature of the Latin American economy, had to be analyzed in the context of accumulation. Investment was inadequate because the surplus generated did not reach its productive destination—it was transferred abroad through the deterioration in terms of trade or the remittance of profits by transnational corporations—or because it was consumed by the imitative behavior among the middle and upper levels of the population in their constant attempts to reproduce the consumption patterns of developed countries. In the latter case, the surplus was not only consumed; in addition, an important part of consumption was also reflected in further demands for foreign exchange.

The surplus for investment was thus lower than necessary and had to be used to acquire technologies produced according to the needs of central countries, which implied greater capital costs and inadequate use of available productive resources. As a result, job openings were insufficient to absorb the burgeoning labor force, particularly the high number of immigrants flowing from rural areas to major cities. Thus, numerous low-productive jobs were generated in what Prebisch referred to as the inferior technical strata, which has subsequently been called the "informal sector." This is what Prebisch called the social inefficiency of the peripheral capitalist model, which is incapable of gainfully incorporating the entire population (see Prebisch 1970, 1976, 1981).

The inadequate growth of Latin American economies should be understood in terms related to the growth of the urban population and their aspirations (Tokman 1982, 1987). In the thirty years prior to the crisis, the region was characterized by high economic dynamism, stemming from a high investment ratio. Between 1950 and 1980, the investment ratio in Latin America was over 20 percent, similar to that recorded in the United States between 1870 and 1905 (see Table 5.1).[2] This high growth of investment resulted in a growth of output of over 5.5 percent per annum during the period analyzed, which is slightly higher than that recorded by the US economy during the period under comparison.

From the standpoint of accumulation, the high economic growth rate denotes a relation of dependency, in the absence of a national class of entrepreneurs capable of making the process autonomous. Investment is marked by a high participation of foreign capital, whether through direct investment or external financing. In domestic terms, the public sector is responsible for a major part of investment (Tokman 1985).[3] The disruption of foreign investment that occurred in the 1980s and the need to reduce public expenditures because of adjustment policies implied a contraction in investment in view of the nonexistent autonomous national investment capacity. In line with the favorable records in investment and growth, employment absorption in modern nonagricultural sectors also expanded rapidly. Between 1950 and 1980 growth was 4.1 percent per annum while manufacturing reached 3.5 percent per annum. Both figures compare favorably to the experience of the United States during the period analyzed (see Table 5.1).

The foregoing suggests that despite its peripheral weakness, Latin America achieved economic records similar to those of the most dynamic experiences in worldwide capitalist development. However, there are major

Table 5.1.　Accumulation and Employment in Latin America

	Latin America[a]	United States[a]		
	1950–1980	1870–1910	1930	1970
A. *Accumulation and Growth*				
Investment[b]	20.8	18.9		
Gross Domestic Product[c]	5.5	4.8		
B. *Employment Growth*				
Working Population (WP)[c]	2.5	2.7		
1. Urbanization and Modernization				
Nonagricultural WP[c]	4.0	3.7		
Employment in nonagricultural modern sectors[c]	4.1	4.4		
Participation of nonagricultural labor in total labor forces	44/67	45/65		
Participation of informal sector in nonagricultural labor forces	31/29	34/20[d]		15
2. Proletarization				
Participation of urban wage earners[e]	65/67	63/78[d]	77	90
Participation of employment in secondary sectors[e]	42/39	50/48	40	37
Participation of manual wage earners in secondary sectors[e]	46/39	57/55[d]	50	38
Participation of self-employment in manufacturing	22/21	7/3[d]		
3. Occupational Heterogeneity				
Ratio nonagricultural nonmanual wage earners to secondary manual wage earners	75/97	49/62	74[d]	128
Ratio nonagricultural technicians and supervisors to secondary manual wage earners		28/30[d]	36	60
4. Productivity and Wage Earning				
Ratio of agricultural to nonagricultural productivity	0.20/0.24	0.26/0.46		
Ratio agricultural to manufacturing productivity	0.24/0.24	0.48/0.65		
Ratio manufacturing to services	0.75/0.96	0.37/0.56		
Ratio manufacturing wages to construction wages	1.76/1.92	0.82/0.89[d]	0.98	0.88
Ratio manufacturing wages to unskilled services wages	2.13/2.28	1.48/1.63[d]	1.28	1.57

Source: Tokman (1987).
Notes: a. When two figures are incorporated the first refers to the initial year and the second to the end year.
　b. Investment–gross domestic product.
　c. Annual cumulative rate.
　d. Refers to 1900–1920.
　e. In relation to nonagricultural force.

differences involved in the relatively inadequate growth identified by Prebisch and supplemented later by other Latin American authors. The differences can be related to the characteristics expected in the normal model discussed in the preceding section. Of the three basic characteristics, only one (urbanization) is fully recorded in Latin America, while the other two (industrialization and homogenization) are affected by factors inherent to the region. This makes it possible to identify three major differences with the normal model. First, in worldwide experience, particularly in the United States, the shift in labor from the countryside to the city effectively occurs, but the growth rate of the supply of workers is greater still. Although growth of the total labor force is similar, nonagricultural labor increased by 4 percent per annum between 1950 and 1980 compared to the 3.7 percent per annum recorded in the United States during the period under comparison.

The second difference is Latin America's late industrialization, a fact that implies access to technology with at least half a century of difference. This means resorting to more capital-intensive technologies, which respond to the needs of central countries but are inadequate for the resource base of the region. The effect is a lower return on investment in terms of job creation, as well as lower labor absorption in secondary sectors. Between 1950 and 1980 employment in the secondary sector in Latin America declined from 42 percent to 39 percent of the nonagricultural labor force. Between 1870 and 1900 secondary employment in the United States dropped from 50 percent to 48 percent. This means that the decline of secondary employment, as well as the sharpness of this drop, is not peculiar to Latin America, as believed in the past (ECLA 1966). But relative participation clearly shows that available technology allowed the United States to incorporate a much higher percentage of the labor force into sectors that produce manufactured goods than the one reached more recently in Latin America.

The third difference between Latin America and the normal model is that technical progress takes place in a different structural context as a result of greater population growth and a more concentrated distribution of wealth. Consequently, there are major differences in productivity and, therefore, in income. Besides, these disparities do not decline but, rather, make up what Pinto (1970) has referred to as a situation of structural heterogeneity. Technical advances in Latin America are concentrated in given sectors and their dissemination is restricted. The result is that differences in productivity—both between sectors and between enterprises within a given sector—are more pronounced than what they were historically in the United States where, in addition, they declined rapidly. In the region, on the other hand, differences in productivity do not show a declining trend. This situation is also reflected in greater differences and different trends in relation to wages (see Table 5.1).

The Neo-ECLAC Model: The PREALC Approach on Informality

Based on the ECLAC interpretation, and inspired in part by the international discussion begun by ILO (International Labor Office) on Kenya (1972) in the 1970s, PREALC (Regional Employment Program for Latin America and the Caribbean) delved deeper into the analysis of the operation and assessment of income for the lower technical strata, as Prebisch referred to it, or the informal sector, as it was subsequently termed. This line of analysis starts out by verifying that unemployment is a "luxury" that poor families (particularly heads of households) can ill afford in developing countries and that, therefore, the alternative to stable and well-paid employment in modern sectors is to produce and trade goods and services that allow them to obtain the necessary income for survival. This is how the concept of "working poor" arises. It favors forms of production as a unit of analysis, shifting the emphasis placed on population in Latin America to the marginality approach. The analysis, however, stays within the boundaries of a historical and structural perspective.

In conceptual terms, the origin of the informal sector is due to the relative inadequacy of labor absorption analyzed by Prebisch (1981) within the framework of the center-periphery model. Inequality in international relations and subordination in light of technical progress are key factors regarding the employment creation rate (Pinto 1965; Sunkel 1973). The different structural context, marked by a rapidly expanding population and a high concentration of assets (Tokman 1982), in turn leads to a high percentage of the labor force being employed in low productivity activities and to differences in productivity and income that are greater than at the center (Pinto 1970).[4]

In empirical terms, the comparison of changes in the employment structure in Latin America with those in the United States (Tokman 1982) allows one to confirm not only a high participation of informal employment in the labor force, but, what is more important, that informal employment does not show a significant declining trend, despite the high growth rate in modern sectors prior to the crisis. For example, in the United States in about 1930, the percentage of self-employed individuals only amounted to 3 percent, while in Latin America it remained constant at around 20 percent between 1950 and 1980.

Given that individuals who form the surplus labor force generally lack both physical and human capital, the type of economic activities available to them are those of easy entry. This requirement is, in turn, associated with the organization of production and the insertion of these activities into the market. The organization of production requires low capital and few skills and lacks a clear division of labor or of ownership of the means of production. In terms of market type, they operate in competitive markets or are based on concentrated markets because these are the ones that afford easy entry and where average income is the adjustment variable. Therefore, the larger the labor supply surplus, the lower the income received by each worker in the informal sector (PREALC 1978).

Research studies undertaken by PREALC attempted to answer the question of whether the permanence of a significant informal sector—despite high economic growth—could be accompanied by growing income or whether, on the contrary, the expansion of informal employment over the long term would show declining incomes. This led to an analysis of the nature of the relation between the informal sector and the rest of the economy (Tokman 1978). Some authors (Webb 1974) emphasized the existence of a benign relation that would allow an evolutionary growth to be expected. Others (Quijano 1974; Bromley 1979) pointed to the existing relations of exploitation, both in the labor market, through the provision of cheap labor, and in the commodities market, through the provision of low-cost wage goods.

The study by PREALC (Tokman 1978, 1989) takes into account the existing heterogeneity in the informal sector. On this basis, the expected long term trend is differentiated from a reduction in the sector's participation in employment and output; the structural changes expected to occur will be due to the future expansion of some informal activities (primarily in business and services), while others facing greater competition (for example, manufacturing) will possibly reduce their market participation. If adequate policies are followed, an evolutionary growth of the informal sector can be expected (at least during a period of transition), until more productive employment is generated in modern sectors. We refer to this approach as "heterogeneous subordination," because the informal sector as a whole is subordinate and as such should present an inverse relation between size and economic growth. But the evolution of the informal sector would be accompanied by changes in its structure, as a consequence of the heterogeneous functional relations that prevail in it.

Labor Market, Income Distribution, and Social Pacts

The contrast between available theories and reality provides the bases for the conceptual development formulated in the region. Modernization, the mandatory path for development, brings rising urbanization but not an increase in jobs in industry, nor a greater decrease in inequalities in productivity and income. Sectoral analysis is not adequate to understand the alterations in the employment structure because the adoption of technical advances creates differences both between sectors and within them. The informal sector thus emerges as a key element for conceptualizing the labor market, the changes in income distribution, and the implicit or explicit social pacts that allow the system as a whole to function.

In relation to the labor market, the existence of different standards to determine employment and income in the informal sector involves recognizing that the latter is segmented. Contrary to what is assumed by conventional theory, various interrelated segments coexist, but they lack sufficient mobility to ensure a single income of balance. Essentially, segmentation results from differences in the type of employment generated, which are associated in turn with capital stock and access to capital and to how the productive unit is organized. In fact, individuals who share the same characteristics (sex, age, education, and experience) show significant differences in income according to the position they hold, whether they are in the informal sector or elsewhere (Souza and Tokman 1978).[5]

The existence of a large and permanent informal sector affects income distribution trends. The hypothesis developed by Kuznets (1955) presupposes a two-sector model where the destination sector shows higher per capita income than incomes in the sector of origin, and that the difference in income does not change during the shift of the labor force from agriculture to the other sector. The segmentation that exists in nonagricultural sectors makes it necessary to observe the behavior of two differences in income and their evolution. One is between agriculture and the informal sector and the other is between the informal and the modern sector. Furthermore, the degree of inequality prevalent in each sector must be taken into account. Both the theoretical conceptualization and the empirical evidence allow one to argue that inequality is greater in modern sectors than in the informal sector, and that the inequality in the latter is greater than inequality in the agricultural sector; that the income differential between agriculture and the informal sector declines during the first phase of migration and then remains constant, while the differential between the informal and the modern sector increases at the outset and then declines; and lastly, that the participation of the informal sector in nonagricultural employment initially declines and subsequently remains constant.

Bearing in mind the preceding factors, the hypothesis proposed by Kuznets is still valid, but the distinctive performance of the labor force affects it in three fundamental ways. First, the point of greatest inequality is reached at a higher per capita income level than expected. Second, the cutoff point occurs at a greater level of inequality, owing to the increase in intersectoral income differentials. Third, the transition from agriculture to urban activities is, in terms of inequality, less costly than expected, because migrants enter the urban labor force through the informal sector (Tokman 1982).

The implicit Keynesian pact that exists in more developed countries is only met imperfectly in Latin America. Full employment is only achieved if one forgoes productivity levels because, in fact, informal employment cannot be equated with full employment. Likewise, real wages increase only in those key sectors where increases in productivity are very rapid. In turn, the state intervenes formally to guarantee the implicit pact, but its actual capacity to implement it is limited. Labor laws are only in effect in the more organized segments of the labor market, and even there only partially. The welfare state only extends partial protection and shows its great deficiencies in attempting to cover the many who are excluded and to base its financing on levying taxes on the incorporated group.[6]

Therefore, the system operates with great instability, either because the state validates the claims of each social group through its macroeconomic policy or because the system is structurally imbalanced. The economic result is the lack of sustained growth and recurrent crises in the balance of payments and inflation. In social terms, tensions exist between the main actors working in the modern sectors, which in many cases lead to the collapse of the democratic regime but in most cases do not go beyond a partial legitimization of one social group over another. Meanwhile, excluded individuals, who are in the informal sector, do not participate nor exert systematic pressure on the system; resignation is the attitude that follows frustration. Their actions are not directed primarily at economic claims, but rather at obtaining intangible goods that are generally traded in the "political market" through bargaining and compromise (Tironi 1989). Violence as a response is associated more with groups whose exclusion is temporary (the recently unemployed) or who are waiting to become part of the modern sectors (young people).

The Conceptualization of Action for Employment Creation

Specific policies to ensure the greatest possible level of employment have up to now played a limited role. Confidence in the model of growth with incorporation, backed by high growth rates and even by job creation in modern sectors, concealed the fact that despite this growth, underemployment levels decreased at a very slow rate. The only exceptions were interventions in the labor market aimed, on the one hand, at supporting the Keynesian consensus of protecting and ensuring minimum wages to incorporated workers and, on the other hand, at correcting the imbalances that may have arisen between supply and demand of labor either as a result of a mismatch of skills or of lack of information between suppliers and demanders. Professional training institutions expanded their programs, while labor exchanges were gradually included in the ministries of labor of the region. Their effects, although positive, were limited, since they responded to an inadequate assessment of the prevailing situation, where employment problems were due primarily to the lack of productive employment rather than to a mismatch of skills or between vacant positions and unemployed workers.

Foreign Trade and Employment Strategies

Responsibility for job creation was shifted to the orientation given to growth and to the macroeconomic policies implemented (Tokman 1988). From this perspective the subject that received the most attention was trade strategies that guide the development model. Historically, the largest countries in the region followed an industrialization strategy based on import substitution, whereas from the 1970s on, there were increasing attempts to demonstrate the superiority of diversification and the promotion of exports.

Strictly speaking, many Latin American countries adopted a strategy of industrialization through import substitution because this was the only option available, given the prevailing international economic environment in the 1930s.[7] The key instrument for this policy was high protection assured through different means, ranging from tariffs to import quotas. The policy was successful both for helping the region emerge more rapidly from the Great Depression (Díaz-Alejandro 1981) and for giving the region a broad industrial base. Industry was the engine of growth, and directly and indirectly created a large part of productive employment in the postwar period (García and Marfán 1981). Employment in manufacturing grew at 3.5 percent per annum between 1950 and 1980, a rate similar to that of other developed countries during periods of expansion. Real wages increased and the profile of skills improved, while labor unions strengthened their bargaining power during the period.

Despite these achievements, the strategy depleted itself after the substitution of consumer goods. Progress increasingly came up against restrictions in foreign exchange because substitution primarily meant changing the structure of imports (rather than decreasing them), and the bias introduced into economic policy by high tariffs and undervalued exchange rates conspired against an increase in exports. This is the scenario within which various policy proposals were explored. Some authors (Fajnzylber 1983) underscored the need to reach a higher degree of integration and greater industrial specialization, favoring the protection of capital goods— as a way to decrease imports—thus generating more productive employment and increasing the possibilities of endogenous technological changes. Others (Krueger 1978b; Balassa 1977) stressed the need to open up economies to ensure the expansion of exports, faster growth, and employment creation.

This was the same policy prescription proposed at world level, especially encouraged by the success experienced in countries in Southeast Asia. Research followed two basic lines. The first—on a macroeconomic level—was devoted to comparing the results of different trade regimes (such as the Krueger-Bhagwati [National Bureau of Economic Research] project) or, more specifically, comparing the results of Asian countries with Latin American ones. In both cases the conclusion favored opening the economy as a method to ensure greater growth and therefore higher employment levels.[8]

A second line of research was to estimate the differential effect on employment of import substitution and the promotion of exports. This was done for Brazil, Chile, Colombia, and Uruguay (Krueger 1981) by using input-output models. The general conclusion was that the basket of exports is more labor intensive, whereas the structure tends to be dominated by processed raw materials where countries possess absolute comparative advantages.

The conclusions of available research point to the need for outward-oriented strategies that make better use of trade instruments, particularly lower tariffs and higher exchange rates. This could be accompanied by incentives for a selective increase in the degree of industrial integration. At this stage of development, the dilemma between import substitution and the promotion of exports is false. Most Latin American countries already possess an industrial base, which can be improved upon, but which already and increasingly provides exports. The issue is still, as Prebisch put it almost forty years ago, how to make industrialization capable of autonomously generating technical progress and improvements in productivity that ensure its international competitiveness and its function as a source of employment and consumption for the population. As Sunkel reminds us in Chapter 2, this must involve development from within more than the inauguration of new stages of outward-looking or inward-looking growth.

Despite the fact that a change in strategy was started in the 1960s, the latter part of the 1970s witnessed more profound changes. In economic terms, this refers to a degree of openness within a neoliberal context and, in political terms, it refers to military regimes, particularly in the Latin American countries of the Southern Cone. Research carried out allows one to identify errors committed in economic policy management that led to more regressive income distribution, lower employment levels, and wage reductions (Foxley 1982; Cortazar, Foxley, and Tokman 1984; Canitrot 1983; Prebisch 1982). These studies analyze the first impact of neoliberal policies that resulted in deindustrialization, due to the excessive openness of the economy, combining low tariffs and undervalued and fixed exchange rates. Competition from imports plus high capital costs brought about a large number of bankruptcies and a deterioration in the financial situation of enterprises, which in many cases still persists. High interest rates distorted resource allocation toward the short term and speculation.

Wage policies were very restrictive, since it was assumed that in a neoclassical macroeconomic regime, real wages are inversely proportional to employment, and that with an undervalued exchange rate wages should remain low in order to increase international competitiveness (Cortazar 1984; Canitrot 1981). The effect on employment was a reduction in employment levels in modern sectors, with resulting increases in unemployment

(Chile and Uruguay), underemployment by means of expansion of the informal sector (Argentina), or a combination of both (Costa Rica).[9] The employment structure changed to the detriment of industry and, in some cases, of public employment. Some positive changes also came about, primarily as a result of the diversification of exports. This led to new, productive jobs, particularly in modern agriculture and connected industries. In the industrial sector some branches reacted positively to the external shock, becoming technologically updated and achieving significant increases in productivity.

Income Distribution, Domestic Market, and Employment

A second trend of analyses and policies is related to the orientation of domestic demand because, in the Keynesian macroeconomic scheme, the inadequacy of domestic demand is associated with lower employment creation. Existing assessments and interpretations made it possible to identify the ties between the concentration of income and demand, the latter being restricted in terms of volume, but extremely diversified in terms of product type. From this arose a strategy—particularly in the early 1970s when the political forces were more favorable to income redistribution—that transformed redistribution from an objective into an instrument. Redistribution in favor of lower income groups would create a virtuous circle of employment creation, saving of foreign exchange, and growth (ILO 1970).

The main argument is that the basket of consumer goods for lower income groups is more labor intensive and demands less foreign exchange than that of higher income groups. The production of food, clothing, and footwear is more labor intensive per unit of capital and requires fewer imports than consumer durables generally manufactured through the assembly of imported components. The various analyses carried out (ILO 1975; Foxley 1974; Cline 1972; Figueroa 1972; Tokman 1975) make it possible to conclude that the strategy proposed would be a more job-generating strategy, primarily because of its impact on the balance of payments, while the changes in the consumption structure would also favor employment. This latter effect would, however, be small because the net impact on industrial employment is limited, owing to the high capital intensity of food and beverage production, and because the greater demand for agricultural products is partly compensated by a reduction in the demand for services.

Technology is also an important factor. Specifically, the size of establishments supplying the goods generated by increased demand and the capacity to respond shown by the different strata have a significant impact on the employment level (Tokman 1975). Likewise, indirect effects are important, given that the production of wage goods is generally more integrated than that of consumer durables (García 1984; García and Marfán 1981).

Given the existing context of inadequate effective demand, expansive wage policies were the key instruments to accomplish the redistribution sought. Also, this was favored by the existence of idle capacity in many industrial branches, particularly those that had to provide wage goods. These policies were applied in differing degrees of intensity in various countries. Their duration, however, was only temporary due to an underestimation of macroeconomic imbalances (lack of supply and inflation) and radical changes in the international economic situation due to the oil crisis. More important still was the political instability in some countries, caused by altering the balance of power between social groups, that accompanied this strategy.

Informal Sector and Employment

The conceptual advances made in the 1970s made it possible to identify the informal sector—and its association with underemployment and poverty—as a key factor in interpreting the problem of employment and labor market operation in Latin America. The analysis of the labor market's characteristics and the nature of its interrelations allows one to understand the role it played in labor force absorption. The challenge that concerns us today—perhaps more than before—is thus one of dealing with the analysis of options for action in light of the latter.

The need for a strategy regarding the informal sector is growing, given its expansion as a result of the recent crisis. To this is added the inadequate capacity to reduce the informal sector, despite rapid economic growth over the long term. Interest in the informal sector is also growing due to the high concentration of poor people in the informal sector and growing evidence that few resources are needed to develop a policy aimed at promoting it. Political and ideological factors contribute to increasing the political timeliness for such decisions (Tokman 1989). Future economic prospects indicate that should external debt problems persist, growth will be scant and therefore the possibilities for job creation in modern sectors will also be limited. Thus, the natural valve allowing the informal sector to decline will be shut. Likewise, the dominant external restriction introduces barriers to expansive macroeconomic policies, which forces a greater selectiveness in policies, so that they may help to reestablish the recently worsened distributive imbalances and be economically feasible at the same time.

There are two major analytical trends on this subject, which are not necessarily contradictory, but which nevertheless lead to differences in emphases and proposals. The first is closer to the neo–center-periphery model and stresses structural factors that determine the existence, permanence, and operation of the sector (PREALC 1978; Tokman 1989). The second deals with institutional aspects and shifts the analysis to the existing legal system, reversing the causality somewhat from the structural to the legal (De Soto 1986).

According to the PREALC approach, the informal sector can help make compatible the need for income redistribution with the framework of current macroeconomic restrictions. This can be done by two main routes. The first, because it would permit the generation of virtuous circles of expansion of demand and productive response, takes advantage of the existing segmentation that makes the informal sector an important source to supply the demand of the poorest groups and wage earners. Antipoverty measures and wage increases would widen markets for informal production, with the attendant effect on employment and income of those employed therein. This argument is similar to the one developed in the preceding section, although it is more selective by combining a segment of (informal) supply with a stratum of demand. The second path consists in broadening productive interrelations through subcontracting or other forms of relation that would allow the informal units to have access to markets represented by modern enterprises, whether by supplying inputs and parts or by providing services. This would afford insertion into more dynamic markets and the transfer of technology, which would serve to improve productivity and product quality and design. The counterpart to this path is that it involves the risk of having greater integration being associated with a greater instability of demand, since demand shifts are one of the most important incentives for subcontracting enterprises. It could also result in greater exploitation of the labor force, a subject we shall return to in the next section.

Both paths described above constitute ways to ease demand restrictions. They must be complemented by the widening of access to productive resources, particularly to capital. According to the structural interpretation, the origin of the informal sector is linked to the characteristics of the process of technology adoption in peripheral economies. Technological options for Latin American countries are dependent on the availability of imported technologies, which are concentrated in extremes in terms of capital requirements, either because, at one extreme, use of capital is scarce or, at the other extreme, minimal initial amounts required exceed the possibilities of the greater part of the labor force. Other options between these extremes are scarce. Given that the members of the surplus labor force possess little capital and that their access to credit is limited, they are forced to operate at low technological levels, which is reflected in low capital requirements per unit of labor. Given the discontinuity of the aggregate production function and the limited accumulation capacity of informal units, the latter tend to be concentrated at the bottom end, whereas modern enterprises are concentrated at the top (Carbonnetto and Kritz 1983; Carbonnetto and Chavez 1984; Mezzera and Carbonnetto 1983; Mezzera 1984; Tokman 1981). Access to credit and the possibilities of continuously introducing technological improvements thus constitute necessary responses to allow supply from the informal sector to react to changes in demand.

The second approach to the informal sector highlights the need to modify or repeal legislation in force, particularly in the trade and fiscal areas, which is seen as the main barrier to productive development in this sector (De Soto 1986). The argument is made in causal terms and also in terms of restrictions, since the origin of the informal sector is attributed to the need to operate outside the prevailing institutionality, which in turn limits its possibilities for growth, given that illegality leads to exclusion from the usual trade mechanisms (contracts, credits, and the like). A procedural argument is also added, since legislation is seen not only as inadequate, but also as needlessly complex, which, together with an inefficient bureaucracy, transforms the process of legalization into an unsurmountable barrier. This interpretation adds the legal and procedural element to the informal sector, thus enriching it. However, it could lead to the oversimplification of assuming that the solution to the informal sector's situation—and therefore to underemployment and poverty—can be resolved merely at a legal level, without affecting its structural causes. It is a fact that some structural rigidities are legitimized under current legislation—primarily in relation to ownership—but from that to supposing that amending these laws is enough to generate structural changes is going too far, and reverses the order of causality.

The Crisis of the 1980s as an Opportunity

It is generally accepted that crises also provide opportunities for change. The 1980s have left a clear mark on Latin America in terms of the costs and legacy for the future. The beginning of the 1990s finds a region burdened by this legacy, with major social imbalances worsened by the adjustment to the crisis, and disoriented and even confused as to where it is heading. Progress has been made in many fields from a short term perspective. But the enigmas regarding the future still persist.

The crisis is not only an external debt crisis, nor did it commence in August 1982. These are merely symptoms of deeper changes that occurred previously in the world economy and that, upon reaching the region, acquired distinctive features. Already by the early 1970s, central countries were in crisis, partly because of the rise in oil prices, but undoubtedly, in the case of the United States, due to lags in productivity increases. The deterioration in investment rates led to a search for answers in production organization and the labor process. Increasingly, the response consisted of decentralizing the productive process in an attempt to obtain greater flexibility both in production and in the use of labor. In older, established sectors organized on the basis of subcontracting relations—as in the case of textiles and clothing—the reintroduction of these forms of organization became valid once more to deal with fluctuations in demand and to shift the associated risks onto subcontractors.

Possibilities of decentralizing leading sectors, where technological change is concentrated, also emerged, since the transformation in this field showed considerable progress owing to the introduction of new technologies. Thus it was that in the most dynamic sectors in the United States and Europe, one observed a decentralized productive organization based on small units, which was not an obstacle for these units to undergo an intense process of technological change, which in turn led to technical progress in other sectors (Piore and Sabel 1984; Sabel 1982). Adaptation in the face of the crisis led to microeconomic adjustments in an attempt to lower labor costs, which also led to a reviewing of the protection that the state afforded workers through public protection mechanisms. The feasibility of the welfare state came under increasing questioning, and in many cases its dismantling was called for.

As a consequence of the processes described above, in the United States in particular and in central countries in general, today there is a more diversified productive structure and a less organized and more fragmented labor force. Consequently, the capacity of the labor force to dispute the secondary distribution of income has been undermined, although paradoxically its access to primary distribution could be strengthened through more autonomous forms of organization. This leads to a downgrading in working conditions, protection mechanisms for workers, and job stability. In exchange, greater independence is acquired and possibly higher incomes than those received under dependent wage-earning conditions. A growing informal sector emerges in the center, and as it operates outside state regulations, informality apparently becomes more universal. We will return to this subject further on.

The international crisis was almost a decade late in reaching Latin America. The great international liquidity that was channeled toward the region was the mechanism that allowed the arrival of the crisis to be delayed, but it was also the detonator that heightened its effects and gave it greater permanence over time (Griffith-Jones and Sunkel 1986). In fact, despite the fact that central countries and most Asian countries recovered as of 1984, Latin America continues to fluctuate between recession and stagnation. An analysis of the crisis is beyond the scope of this chapter. It is enough to point out very briefly the effects on employment and income distribution (PREALC-ILO 1988a).

For most Latin American countries, the crisis meant the emergence of high and sustained unemployment levels. Economic contraction produced a contraction in new job openings, while labor supply continued to grow. The result was greater open unemployment, given that the recovery of

1985 was insufficient to produce a significant decline in unemployment. A change also came about in the employment structure as a result of the triple process of informalization, tertiarization, and statization. The first two are tightly interrelated, since the burgeoning of informal jobs occurred essentially within the service industry while the process of deindustrialization, which began in the mid-1970s, had worsened, with a decline in industrial employment in absolute terms. The public sector, in turn, increased its participation in nonagricultural employment, not so much due to its dynamism, but essentially because of the reduction in employment recorded in larger private enterprises. Lastly, real labor income decreased, both in wages and in income in the informal sector. Likewise, there was a drop in per capita social expenditures.

The cost of adjustment is not equitably distributed, thus giving rise to what PREALC-ILO (1988a) has referred to as the "social debt." This results in a regressive income distribution by sector, since the percentage of poor people increases; and the same occurs in functional distribution, since one witnesses a reduction in the participation of labor income in national income. The poverty levels and inequality prevailing toward the end of the decade were greater than those prevalent in the past, which significantly conditions future development policies.[10] Social imbalances are not just unfair, they affect the capacity to grow. Unemployment and low-productivity jobs not only lead to low income but also to frustration, loss of skills, and negative working attitudes. Low incomes mean fewer incentives, when what is required is a collective effort to overcome the crisis. Reductions in public expenditures in education, health care, nutrition, and housing decrease the quality of human resources available, particularly among the young, and thus production capacity is lost (ILO 1989).

The implicit pact that organized the operation of the system in general and that of the labor market in particular—and which could only be met imperfectly prior to the crisis—underwent new tensions. The effects noted render the expectations, on which the minimal consensus reached had been based, less realizable. Social actors, primarily labor unions, become weaker as they lose power for making claims, given high unemployment rates and growing informal employment. To the tensions emerging from domestic changes are added the questioning of the Keynesian consensus that comes from the North. High unemployment rates and the difficulty in reducing them, particularly in Western Europe, cast doubts on the very bases of consensus, in some cases leading the government to explicitly abandon its responsibility to ensure full employment.[11] In this case in the history of the periphery, as in many others, the instability associated with the imperfect adaptation of schemes devised in the North was worsened by the change in orientation undergone by the schemes in the countries of origin in response to their own needs.

The change in this aspect goes beyond the negation of full employment as a government goal. Acceptance of the existence of a "natural" unemployment rate is leading to a reevaluation of the role of macroeconomic policies such as those that affect the labor market in particular. The major macroeconomic change involves taking away from the state its previous role of ensuring full employment and assigning to the state tasks that were previously the domain of microeconomic policies, specifically, keeping inflation under control. Responsibility for employment levels has been shifted to the operation of the labor market, which, in turn, reflects institutional mechanisms, the behavior and expectations of entrepreneurs, labor unions, and workers.

On the basis of the new role assigned to labor market policies, high unemployment rates are interpreted as the existence of rigidities or lack of incentives in adapting to changes in the international economy. Flexibility is the goal, and deregulation is the conventional prescription in this supply-side approach. The factors questioned now include various variables. Wages are above their equilibrium price and therefore affect employment levels, while the reduction of differentials restrains mobility and the incentives to acquire new skills. Lower mobility produced by the lack of incentives and legal restrictions prevents structural adjustment, raises labor costs, and reduces labor efficiency. Lastly, the regulations adopted to protect workers' stability and income are also viewed as rigid elements because they raise costs and establish reserve wages below which there are no incentives to accept employment. According to this interpretation, the presence of powerful labor unions—particularly those noted for centralized bargaining systems—poses hindrances or delays to structural adaptation. It is argued that this trend in labor market policies accounts for the "success" of the United States in creating jobs in the 1980s, while "Eurosclerosis" is attributed to overregulation.

Debate on these subjects has just begun in the North (Standing 1986, 1988). Critical arguments range from different interpretations of labor market trends to the lack of evidence supporting prescriptions, passing through accusations on the theoretical inconsistency of such propositions. There is, however, a basic agreement: labor market flexibility is a requirement for structural adaptation, and it is in fact occurring with or without reforms to policies that regulate the labor market.

There is evidence that temporary, occasional, and part-time jobs are increasing. In fact, in developed countries only slightly over a third of the adult population (16 or older) are employed in full-time jobs. The number of persons in special programs is growing. Policies are implemented to reduce labor supply (such as early retirement). Precarious forms of underemployment are increasing, and new forms of subcontracting are emerging. All of this gives rise to a progressive informalization of the employment structure.[12] There are also changes in payment systems, and differentiated wages are now being introduced that encourage decentralization and fragmentation. Flexibility is also expressed in changes in job positions and in hierarchies. Protective regulations are traded in some cases for higher wages, while in others, wage reductions are accepted in exchange for better job security.

Labor relations are also becoming more flexible because the trend toward bargaining at the company level is growing, which in light of the current wave of decentralization implies less bargaining power for labor unions and provides an additional incentive for large companies to decentralize their production. At the company level, technological change leads to contradictory trends with regard to the power of labor unions. The elimination of hierarchies increases the homogeneity of less-skilled workers, but at a cost of greater segmentation that detaches them from decision-making centers. Likewise, new positions require greater versatility and less specialization, which introduces greater competitiveness among workers already employed and makes them more vulnerable to competition from potential company workers.

The debate—and particularly the prescriptions—reach the periphery and are changed into new policy approaches. Wage policies "must now" be contractionary and inclined to broaden differentials. Labor market regulations "must now" be reviewed, and protection systems, particularly social security, "must be reformed." These new approaches should be examined in light of current conditions in Latin America. Some are justified, perhaps for reasons other than those in central countries, but other approaches do not provide any responses, but rather encumber problem-solving. The most important historical trait of the region is that full employment is only apparent, since underemployment persists in hardly perceptible forms. This makes the labor market flexible, particularly at present, when the crisis has meant an overexpansion of the informal market, high unemployment, and lower real incomes. Nor can one argue that wages conspire against job creation when they have plummeted in real terms and employment has not increased, or argue that regulations prevent layoffs when the unemployment rate rises substantially or when informal activity plays an important economic role.

In Latin America the creation of productive employment cannot be left to the operation of the labor market because this task is inherent to development. Macroeconomic policy cannot stay on the sidelines, but rather, within the existing restrictions (a lesson learned from the recent past), must ensure the greatest expansion possible. This is even more important if one accepts the fact that the current situation requires a greater degree of distributive equality. Selectivity in macro policy becomes an important element for analysis. Wage policies cannot continue to be contractionary because minimums have reached such levels of inefficiency that in addition to being inadequate for survival, they do not provide the necessary incentives for increasing productivity. The market has ensured wage differentials for its operation that far from proving a hindrance to mobility have meant the growing fragmentation of the labor force.

It would also be necessary to review the systems of labor protection and regulation, not so much because of their inflexibility, but rather because of their inefficiency in fulfilling the appropriate roles. A social security system that fails to provide care for its own affiliates must be reviewed, not only due to changes in the labor market, but because of the system's poor operation. Regulations that no longer apply to new forms of work lose their raison d'être. However, this field cannot be dealt with in abstract terms, since labor market institutions reflect the current social order to a certain extent. The microeconomy of adjustment must understand the policy of reform, which must be compatible with current economic challenges. Labor cannot be left unprotected and have its wages reduced while at the same time workers are expected to take an active part in development tasks, nor can profits be eliminated and greater private investment be expected at the same time.

The main task is to make the necessary changes and manage to have social agents look beyond their sectoral interests. This requires a new look at the future; doubts in connection with agreements or consensus in force cannot be solved by looking back nor by hanging on to the present. Paradoxically, the questioning of Keynesian consensus in the center has brought Northern countries closer to the conditions in the periphery, where imperfection has been a historical constant. The challenge involves finding adequate forms to regulate systems that operate historically, in the case of Latin America, or more recently in the center, beyond the institutionality in force.

Notes

1. A full review of the literature on the subject is found in Chapter 12.

2. For a definition of comparable historical periods, see Tokman (1982). We should remember that the economic period selected in the United States showed the highest rates of investment of the past 150 years, and that the United States showed the highest investment rates of the world, both for the period between the mid-nineteenth century and World War I, and from the end of the nineteenth century roughly until 1960.

3. Direct investment prevailed in the 1950s, while external financing became crucial between 1970 and 1980. Public investment accounted for about 29 percent of total investment in Latin America compared to 9 percent in the United States. In some countries, such as Chile, public investment was close to 50 percent of total investment between 1950 and 1980.

4. These factors do not operate independently and in a linear manner; they interact, at times compensating for each other. Thus, although the more rapid growth

of the total or urban population contributes to a larger and dynamic informal sector, this definitely depends on the way in which other variables behave. Costa Rica and Venezuela, for example, are countries with the highest population growth between 1950 and 1980. However, the size of the informal sector is the lowest for Latin America, and its expansion was the slowest. On the other hand, countries such as Ecuador, Peru, and Bolivia, with population growth rates similar to the regional average, are those with the highest levels and greatest expansion of the informal sector. Chile, Argentina, and Uruguay, which are mature countries from a demographic standpoint, have witnessed the growth of their informal sectors in the 1970s owing to the effects of economic policies implemented (Tokman and García 1981).

5. At the same time, progress is underway in the United States in analyzing labor market segmentation. Unlike the Latin American discussion, emphases in preliminary analyses focus on race or sex discrimination (Vietoritz and Harrison 1973; Doringer and Piore 1971; Reich, Gordon, and Edwards 1975).

6. The situation varies between countries. In some, like Argentina, Chile, Costa Rica, and Uruguay, the existence of a broad, organized sector is added to the role historically played by the state in the area of labor protection and social security so that, for a period at least, the implicit social agreement will be respected. Even in these countries, from the mid-1970s on, the system's incapacity to ensure fulfillment of these agreements becomes apparent. In other places, as in the relatively less developed countries in the region, the virtual nonexistence of organized sectors, and the limited tradition of the state as an institutional guarantor, allows rules of subordination to be imposed on labor without compensatory considerations being necessary.

7. On this subject, see section one in Chapter 2.

8. As a matter of fact, the conclusions are not free from controversy, as indicated by the need of NBER project coordinators to write two separate books (1978) and the more refined analysis subsequently carried out by Ranis (1983).

9. There are various factors that explain why the adjustment of the labor market occurs differently between countries. Worthy of note are: the growth rate of labor supply, the degree of saturation of the informal sector (primarily its size and income level), the expectations related to modern employment (wages expected and unemployment rate level), and the severity of the adjustment, as well as its distribution over time (shock versus gradual).

10. See Chapter 3.

11. The chancellor of the exchequer of the United Kingdom, Nigel Lawson, stated in March 1984 that "it has not been clearly understood that it is simply not within Government's power to determine the unemployment level" (quoted in Standing 1986).

12. Arguments on behalf of the universality of the informal sector are made by Portes and Sassen-Koob (1987), among others. The similarities are, however, more apparent than real, due to three interrelated reasons (Tokman 1985). The first is that informal activities in developed countries are induced by a decentralization of the productive process, while in developing countries they are largely due to the need for survival. The second is that growth of the informal sector takes place in a different structural context, particularly in terms of whether or not there is a labor surplus. The third is that there is an institutional difference given the fact that developed countries have a high-coverage protection system that guarantees a minimum income below which there are no incentives to work. The result is, therefore, different: while in Latin America informality generates low income and scant accumulation, in developed countries the income received in subcontracting

enterprises exceeds wages paid in the modern sector, even at the expense of loss of work protection and job security. The definition of the informal sector should therefore refer not only to the organization of production at microeconomic level, but also to the structural context in which it occurs, which varies according to the level of development.

6

Capital Formation and the Macroeconomic Framework: A Neostructuralist Approach

Ricardo Ffrench-Davis

One of the most characteristic features of Latin American economies during the 1980s was the low rate of capital formation. In addition, the rate of utilization of the available productive capacity exhibited a steep decline, carrying with it a drop in actual average productivity. These factors, which in fact bolster each other, account for the noticeable contrast between the slack economic growth in the 1980s and the dynamism exhibited by Latin American countries (LACs) in the three previous decades. Between 1950 and 1980, Latin America sustained significant economic growth, with a 5.5 percent rise per annum in GDP. On the average, Latin America maintained rising investment rates and a relatively high utilization of installed capacity.

This situation underwent a sudden reversal in the early 1980s. During the decade, there was a sharp decline in capital formation ratios throughout Latin America. This was associated with the long adjustment period experienced by the region during the 1980s. The nature of the adjustment was predominantly recessive, due both to the conditions prevailing in the world economy and to the types of domestic policies adopted. Most LACs suffered severe financial shocks due to highly negative net transfers abroad coupled with a deterioration in the terms of trade. Generally, domestic demand-reducing policies were the main ones implemented in response to the external shocks, thus strengthening the recessive bias of the adjustment process. This was accompanied by a drop of public investment and the liberalization of financial markets.

The effects varied between countries and between productive sectors according to the nature of the external changes, the kind of adjustment policies adopted, and the specific characteristics of each sector or country. Irrespective of the national responses, however, the most significant consequences were reductions in per capita output, capacity utilization rates, and capital formation, with a worsened income distribution.

This chapter will focus mainly on the analysis of the variables determining capital formation and capacity utilization. Both factors and their interrelations play a pivotal role in economic growth, owing both to their direct impact and to the fact that they constitute channels for the incorporation of technological innovations and improved systematic productivity. Section one examines the conceptual aspects that denote the most significant differences between the neoliberal and neostructural approaches. Section two summarizes the more relevant features concerning capital formation in Latin America, particularly during the 1970s and 1980s. Section three focuses on the examination of the most suitable conditions required to generate a macroeconomic ambiance favorable to capital formation; it also includes a discussion on the regulation of prices that have macroeconomic implications. Section four moves ahead in analyzing the components of a policy intended to foster the acquisition of comparative advantages. Lastly, some recommendations on economic policy are set forth, aimed at promoting capital formation and rising productivity.

Conceptual Approaches

The neoliberal approach rests on the liberalization of markets as the catalyst for savings, investment, and productivity. The liberalization of financial markets plays a crucial role. It is not easy to characterize an alternative approach to this orthodox view.[1] It is relatively simple and precise, its characterization made even easier by the changes that occurred in the 1970s. The prevalence of the monetary approach to the balance of payments simplified it, and therefore, its conclusions and recommendations on economic policy became even more extreme. With the occurrence of the debt crisis in the early 1980s, the orthodox approach, partly responsible for that crisis, appeared to lose ground.[2] However, such reversal was short-lived, since neoliberal approaches, both theoretical and applied, have had a dominant role in the management of the debt crisis and in adjustment processes started thereafter.

In spite of serious flaws, Latin America was able to sustain successful development for three decades, between 1950 and 1980 (Ffrench-Davis, Muñoz, and Palma 1991). In the 1980s, however, the results showed a noticeable downswing. Today, it is a continent searching for a new development strategy, better suited to its semi-industrialized status, inserted in an international economic setting anticipated to be less dynamic and more unstable during the 1990s than in the previous decades. In this framework, the development of neostructural proposals may prove to be very useful in the definition of coherent and efficient strategies.

No theoretical approach starts from scratch. All are founded on predominant contemporary approaches, either as an extension or as their antithesis. This was the case in classical, Marxist, and Keynesian thinking. Different approaches rise and fall under the influence of social and economic phenomena and changes in the balance of political forces. Occasionally, some of them are reborn, often with very similar views to historically distant forerunners. This is the case of the monetary approach to the balance of payments, similar to the gold standard and automatic adjustment processes of the nineteenth century. Creation, positive or negative, consists in a new way of combining several well-known elements, adding some new ones or some that had been forgotten. However, despite having common elements with a previous approach, the new package can lead to radically different conclusions and recommendations.

Most clearly our discussion is placed within a market economy. It is not a matter of accepting or rejecting the market. Actually, it is assigned ample space in most approaches. The relevant question is how much space is it granted and what are the adjuncts and compensatory mechanisms that go with it.

Structuralism, which emerged and developed vigorously in the interpretation of Latin America's problems, was significantly influenced by Keynesianism and post-Keynesianism. At the same time, neostructuralism has benefited from the structuralist tradition. But it goes further, in the sense that it is definitely policy oriented. That is, its analytic development is markedly oriented to the design and implementation of economic strategies and policies. Undoubtedly, many contributions inherited from the evolvement of structuralist thinking in the 1950s and thereafter are still relevant.

Significant contributions were made in relation to capital formation. Structuralist thinking assigned capital formation a pivotal position as a determinant of growth (Cardoso 1977; Hirschman 1971; Prebisch 1963). It advocated the increase of financing sources by channeling domestic savings to development banks through long term loans, and encouraged foreign investment as an additional way to accelerate capital formation and technical progress (Prebisch 1951). Public investment in infrastructure and strategic industries was also seen as stimulus to private investment, national integration, and regional and sectoral linkages.

Both structuralists and those whom Cardoso (1977) referred to as heterodox liberals contributed with their discussions on the "big push," dynamic externalities and productive linkages in the investment process (Rosenstein-Rodan 1943; Chenery 1961; Hirschman 1958), both in the balanced and unbalanced growth variants. The abundant literature on the two or three gap model, lead by Chenery, was also a valuable contribution to the study of economic development in situations of imbalance and to the role of external funding and domestic reforms.

From the onset, the issue of savings and imitative consumption also held an important place. Contributions by Duesenberry, Furtado, Kaldor, Nurkse, and Sunkel had great influence in Latin America.[3] ECLAC included it in its proposals on fiscal reform and public savings.

Furthermore, as mentioned before, in the financial sphere the shortcomings of the existing capital market were acknowledged in relation to long term financing, and this resulted in advocating the creation of development banks geared to productive investment. Rather than merely considering its capacity to encourage savings, the main emphasis was placed on its effects in channeling existing savings toward long term investment, thus discouraging speculative investment and the financing of conspicuous consumption.

At a more general level, significant analytical studies have been undertaken on the structural heterogeneity of the domestic and world economies; the simultaneous presence of multiple imbalances; the fundamental role played by institutional variables; the implications of the instability and deterioration in the terms of trade that affect inflexible economies; and the asymmetric distribution of the benefits of technological change. Furthermore, prominent structuralist authors forewarned about the forthcoming end of the easy period of import substitution, stressing the role of economies of scale and the need to promote exports (Prebisch 1961; Sunkel 1969; see Rodríguez 1980 for an account). In this context, the role of transnational corporations was also reconsidered. In view of the growing importance granted to exports of manufactured goods in the 1960s, it was pointed out that these corporations should be induced to export rather than to restrict their operations to protected domestic markets (Sunkel 1969). Increasing exports to other regions or to the rest of the world was envisaged as a means for taking fuller advantage of economies of scale and installed capacity, thus raising global productivity.

Structuralism, however, suffered from two deficiencies at the implementation level. One was the limited concern for the management of short term, macroeconomic variables: structuralist thinking gave a secondary priority to analyses related to fiscal and monetary policies and regulation of the balance of payments. There was no systematic transition from the diagnosis of what originated imbalances to the design of policies suited to face them.

The other limitation was an insufficient consideration of medium term strategies that could have linked short term policies with domestic development objectives and planning. In this context, there was also an incomplete examination of the determinants of investment. These shortcomings, however, are in favorable contrast with the notorious absence of medium term issues in neoliberal proposals, except in their liberalizing generalities and the assumed virtuous behavior of full free markets.

The concentration of neoclassical thought on examining extreme positions, such as arbitrary protectionism versus total free trade, or the excessive segmentation between the "short run" and the "long run" and between "real" and "financial" aspects, contributed to this inadequacy of structuralism. This discouraged the search within structuralism for constructive and co-optable contributions from the orthodox world, thus losing the opportunity to profit from the many rich venues of neoclassical thought.

Foreign trade regulation criteria, the definition of public enterprise objectives and regulations, the examination of alternative mechanisms for encouraging investment, productive employment generation, foreign investment regulation, and financial system organization, all generally took second place in the development of structuralist thinking. Undoubtedly, structuralism contributed to the progress made in public policy implementation in these areas and was sound in fostering comparative analysis and in combining the abstract analysis and the historical perspective (as mentioned by Sunkel and Paz 1970). However, a systematic effort at the design of economic policy was lacking in structuralist diagnosis. Progress in this area was not a main concern.

After the analytic setback experienced under global monetarism first and then with straight neoliberalism, a renewed look into the structuralist tradition is in order, incorporating a systematic concern for economic policy design. Among other major, relevant aspects, these should involve macroeconomic balances, coordination of the short and the long run, concertation between public and private sectors, construction of more egalitarian productive and management structures, and consideration of strategies and policies that allow for a delicate balance between the active insertion in international markets and greater national autonomy. This then can be called "neostructuralism." Its most outstanding feature would involve selective policies to provide an alternative to theoretically neutral neoliberal policies,[4] arbitrary interventionism, and the imbalances and short-run bias of what is commonly referred to as populism.

The major analytic difference between the neoliberal and neostructuralist approaches may be summarized in their specific assumptions on the degree of market integration or segmentation, and on the homogeneity or heterogeneity of products and factors. The differences in the assumptions underlying each approach lead to divergent policies, within a common market economy, with significant implications with respect to income distribution dynamics and to the allocation and generation of productive resources. In short, the neoliberal approach advocates the use of "neutral" policies versus the use by neostructuralism of a mix of neutral and selective policies.

The neoliberal approach assumes that in the absence of governmental obstacles, markets are homogeneous and integrated. Therefore, market signals flow easily, transparently, and with high elasticity of prices between markets and between generations.[5] In doing so, structural imbalances are not recognized, except those generated by state interventions. These assumptions lead to an underestimation of the negative effects on capital formation and the utilization rate that orthodox adjustment processes could generate in the face of external shocks or severe inflationary phenomena.

Paradoxically, the microeconomic theory of price optimization on which neoliberalism is based jumps to policy recommendations based on the maximization of liberalization. It does not recognize the existence of intermediate positions between the extremes of indiscriminate liberalization and arbitrary interventionism. Syntheses of the neoliberal approach are, for example: (1) the set of theoretical and policy propositions that make up the monetary approach to the balance of payments, and (2) proposals for "financial deepening or liberalization"; the latter confuses the need to reform and broaden financial markets in a manner consistent with productive capacity development with rash across-the-board liberalization.

These policy proposals gave analytic support to the financial reforms implemented in the 1970s by the countries of the Latin American Southern Cone and other nations. They had negative effects on economic stability and on capital formation (Ffrench-Davis 1983).

It is clear that many neoclassical specialists in the northern academic world do not share many of the traits that are commonly attributed to the neoliberal position.[6] The latter has been based on positions occupying a hegemonic role in the recommendations and on pressures exercised over the developing world in recent years, rather than on the "traditional" neoclassical position. It is also representative of the interpretations and policies implemented in the Southern Cone in the 1970s and in several other Latin American nations in the 1980s; the most distinctive case is Chile (Ffrench-Davis and Muñoz 1990; Ramos 1986b).

Table 6.1.   **Gross Fixed Investment Ratios**
(as percentages of GDP in 1980 US dollars)

	1950–1959	1960–1972	1973–1981	1982–1990
Argentina	15.1	19.0	20.8	11.7
Brazil	21.9	19.6	23.6	17.2
Chile	20.6	18.5	14.9	15.7
Mexico	16.7	18.8	22.7	17.8
Latin America	18.4	17.9	22.2	16.7

Source: Data from ECLAC, Division of Statistics and Projections. Includes nineteen countries.

A neostructuralist approach, on the other hand, assigns a paramount role to the various dimensions of structural heterogeneity: among others, external market heterogeneity, heterogeneity between stages of the business cycle (different market responses during upswings and downswings); variety in the response to incentives among regions and among market segments (big and small business, rural and urban enterprises, infant and mature firms); and the effect of the adjustment process on the feasibility of attaining different sets of objectives (histeresis), which implies that there is no single equilibrium, but rather multiple ones. In short, the degree of resource mobility and price flexibility are very important, as are the eventually perverse dynamics of macroeconomic adjustment processes, depending on the intensity of the response from various sectors and markets, and depending on the perceptions or expectations of economic agents.

The latter is illustrated by the buildup in the 1970s of the current debt crisis: (1) most leading agents did not realize that, by the end of the decade, the international private capital market for developing countries was maturing (Ffrench-Davis 1983), and consequently that net capital flows, which were very high during its formation, could be abruptly reduced upon their approaching maturity (upon their reaching "equilibrium" stocks); (2) the liberalization of capital movements, amidst a plentiful supply, caused an adjustment of production structures and domestic expenditures to unsustainable high flows of external funds; (3) a perverse adjustment of the exchange rate occurred in response to financial forces as opposed to real variables (exchange rate revaluations despite growing current account deficits); and (4) there was a leakage of external credit toward consumption, where shortsighted economic agents assumed, without major analysis, that the flow of funds and flexible interest rates would remain at levels favorable to debtors over long periods.

Hence there arose the neostructuralist recommendation of regulating capital movements, exchange rates, and trade policy, and of applying a deliberate productive development policy of channeling resources toward investment and promoting the acquisition of comparative advantages as a means to generate and make greater use of investment and innovation opportunities. At this level, the neostructuralist option of commanding a development process from within (see Chapter 2) occupies a central role. This is the constructive option, in contrast to inward-looking development options in the simpler approaches of import substitution, or outward-looking ones in the approaches based on the integration into world markets via abrupt and indiscriminate import liberalization and the fading out of the sense of nation. The option from within is consistent with a vigorous expansion of exports, as is proposed further on.

Latin America's adjustment after the debt shock is another example of the divergent paths taken by the two approaches. The adjustment has been based primarily on policies geared to reduce demand, while policies fostering reallocation in the structure of supply and of expenditure structure have played a minor role, as the sharp decline of economic activity in Latin America proved (see Table 6.2). The neoliberal approach focuses on reducing aggregate demand wherever there is a current account deficit, regardless of whether production falls and investment contracts, and demand must subsequently, again, be immediately reduced to follow production in its downward course. The neostructural emphasis relies on a better mix of aggregate demand regulation and switching (reallocating) policies, which implies readjusting production and expenditure structures to capital flows in amounts sustainable over time, in other words, lower than those prior to 1982.

What was needed in the early 1980s was to adjust the excess demand over domestic output, a gap that had been covered in the preceding decade by an unsustainable volume of net transfers from abroad. In the adjustment process, a sizable drop in domestic output implies heavy inefficiency and reduces the output achievable over time. In fact, it curtails effective productivity in the short run, and this in turn drives investment down, discouraged by the underutilization of the installed capacity and by a recessive macroeconomic environment. Hence, neostructuralists recommend selective policies on public expenditures, taxation, credit, and trade, which, together with an active exchange rate policy help to:

1. Localize the reduction of aggregate demand where it is desired, on expenditures in tradables, maintaining (as far as possible) effective demand at levels consistent with existing productive capacity; and
2. Strengthen instead of weaken capital formation. Since aggregate demand must be reduced, it is then inevitable to reduce its other component, which is consumption. Two courses of action emerge once again: placing the burden either on the curtailment of wages and/or employment or putting greater emphasis on the reduction of nonessential consumption; the blend can be influenced strongly by the policy mix to be chosen.

The debate has great bearing for the future. Neoliberalism has unlimited faith in the efficiency of the traditional private sector and extremely mistrusts the public sector. Neostructuralism, on the other hand, requires a dynamic and modern private sector together with an active and efficient state.[7] Since, in a framework of structural heterogeneity, it is not easy to achieve an efficient state, it is also necessary to be selective in dealing only with that quantity and quality of actions that the state is capable of undertaking with social efficiency, and focusing efforts where they will have the greatest macroeconomic impact. What is required is the building up of a state with muscles instead of fat.

The Recent Experience of Latin America

Between 1950 and 1980 the economic growth of Latin America reached an average rate of 5.5 percent per annum (see Ffrench-Davis, Muñoz, and Palma 1991). This rate exceeded the prevailing trend in other developing regions (with the exception of the East Asian countries) and was well above the average for the industrialized nations (4.2 percent). The gross domestic product (GDP) of Latin America in 1980 was five times that of 1950. This growth was associated with moderately high investment rates of around 20 percent, increased capacity utilization rates, and the expansion of sectors intensive in improved technology.

In the early 1950s Latin America faced bottlenecks linked to the scarcity of external financing, due to the financial and real problems inherited from the Great Depression, as well as to the limited access to export markets and the supply of imported goods during the 1930s and 1940s. The region's access to international capital and goods markets improved over the following two decades. Its agricultural frontier of arable and irrigated lands also expanded, and new crops, seeds, and fertilizers were introduced. However, the leading sector was that of manufactured goods, which underwent a very rapid growth that reached 7 percent annually in the 1960s, coupled to a significant increase in the incorporation of new technology. The 1960s was the decade when Latin America enjoyed the greatest domestic and external stability of the postwar period, with rather minor crises in the balance of payments, and rising global productivity.

Nevertheless, there was growing dissatisfaction with respect to economic performance, and many authors attempted various explanations for the "failure" of the development strategies adopted in the region.[8] In fact, as easy import substitution gradually came to an end, it generated increasing difficulties, involving limited investment opportunities for the domestic market and restricted utilization of the installed capacity. Producing only for domestic markets prevented an increasing number of manufacturing activities to take full advantage of economies of scale. In response to this, the region started to foster its manufactured exports. Countries such as Brazil, Colombia, and Chile began to implement crawling-peg exchange rate policies (Williamson 1981) and established other incentives to exports. In the second half of the 1960s, total manufactured exports increased, in real terms, 12 percent per annum, and the growth of intraregional exports reached 16 percent annually (Ffrench-Davis, Muñoz, and Palma 1991: table 4).

In addition to implementing export-promoting reforms, some countries put into effect financial reforms, most of which involved establishing adjustment mechanisms to protect savings from inflation and prevent negative real interest rates. At the same time, the expansion of long term loans by the World Bank and the creation of the Inter-American Development Bank helped finance public investment.

Beginning in the mid-1960s, the capital formation rate began to rise steadily, accelerating further during the 1970s. This rise was associated with changes in external funding opportunities and the manner in which the countries in the region reacted to these options in the 1970s (see

Ffrench-Davis 1983). The section begins by examining that decade, then analyzes the adjustment processes during the 1980s, placing particular emphasis on the effects on capital formation and the capacity utilization rate.

Expansive Adjustment in the 1970s

Two events had a determinant impact on Latin American economies during the 1970s: the indebtedness with creditor banks and the oil shocks. As a net oil exporter, the region reaped significant benefits, whereby its oil account increased its positive balance from US$3 billion in 1973 to US$23 billion in 1981. Oil-producing countries expanded their external borrowing instead of decreasing it. This was fostered by the improved creditworthiness of LACs, which encouraged lenders to exert stronger pressures on these countries in order for them to liberalize capital movements and thus take on larger loans. The prevalence of both free access to the local foreign exchange market and appreciating exchange rates prompted a significant capital flight in several debtor countries. Nonetheless, domestic investment increased vigorously in Ecuador, Mexico, and Venezuela.

Oil-importing countries faced the 1973–1974 external shock in various ways. Those countries with better access to bank loans and a declared preference for growth borrowed heavily. This was true in the case of Brazil, which, in spite of the negative impact on its oil account, increased its capital formation and experienced continued economic growth. At the other end of the spectrum, Chile, which additionally faced a sharp fall in the price of copper, reduced its economic activity and curtailed investment sharply in 1975–1976.

During the second half of the decade, however, most of the countries contracted heavy debts with creditor banks, to the point that on average the respective debt stock increased around 30 percent per annum and by 1981 represented over 80 percent of the region's total debt. In the latter year, the current account deficit rose to 5.6 percent of GDP and net positive transfers reached 2 percent. The result was that most LACs, between the mid-1970s and early 1980s, made adjustments to accommodate a large transfer of funds from abroad, which induced a growing deficit in the trade balance of the region. The large supply of foreign funds fostered a revaluation of real exchange rates in many of the nations. The diversity of the reactions by the different countries could also be seen in this area, with Brazil and Colombia being able to maintain more stable real rates. As a whole, however, the region exhibited an exchange rate appreciation vis-à-vis the rest of the world. In addition, import liberalization was put into effect in order to encourage the adjustment of domestic economies to the growing availability of foreign funds. The process was particularly intense in Chile and somewhat so in other countries, like Argentina, that implemented monetarist experiments, as well as in new oil-exporting countries, like Mexico, that made adjustments to accommodate both the increase in foreign loans and its remarkable expansion in oil exports.

Notwithstanding real exchange rate revaluations, Latin America achieved a significant increase in the volume of exports until 1981. This trend was due to domestic incentives and to the continued development of international markets for manufactured exports of industrializing countries. In other words, these countries had access to an international market in a vigorous process of development for this segment of products. This compensated for the declining trend shown by the expansion of overall international trade, which decreased from an annual growth rate of 8.2 percent in the 1960s to 5.4 percent in 1970–1981 (UN 1984). In the meantime, the non–oil-exporting LACs raised their export volume by 6.6 percent annually in the 1970–1981 period, notwithstanding high domestic demand and appreciating exchange rates in several nations.

Investment rates rose significantly during the increasing indebtedness period in the 1970s, which leads one to conclude that external resources contributed to the development of productive capacity of the region as a whole. During the period 1974–1981, the gross fixed capital formation ratio exceeded by 4 points the coefficient achieved in 1960–1973. Nonetheless, the response of economic growth was proportionately lower. This was due to the fact that the copious amount of external funds promoted capital-intensive investment with long term maturity periods, particularly in oil-producing countries. In some countries it also involved less rigorous (or a lack of) evaluations of investment projects, a trend spurred by the permissiveness of bank loans and the prevalence, during several years, of low or negative real interest rates in international markets.

There were significant differences in performance between countries. For example, countries that liberalized across-the-board capital inflows, domestic financial markets, and imports tended to show a lower investment volume and reduced domestic savings. That is to say, external funds were directed at consumption, as in the case of Chile, and to capital flight, as in Argentina. On the other hand, a better performance was obtained by countries, such as Brazil and Colombia, that implemented selective and moderate reforms in their trade and financial policies in the 1960s and 1970s, and encouraged use of the external debt to expand public and private investment.[9] Thus, it is clear that the greater capital formation in those countries was not a spontaneous phenomenon but, rather, a deliberate one.

In this way, many Latin American economies were able to sustain significant economic growth until the beginning of the 1980s. Their heavy indebtedness was partly used to finance vigorous investment. This was the outcome of national policies that deliberately channeled external funds toward productive investment. Thus the region's fixed capital formation ratio rose to 22 percent in the latter part of the 1970s and early 1980s.

High effective demand and buoyant international commodities markets were macroeconomic factors that completed a virtuous circle. However, a huge external debt was accumulated and a growing current account deficit was incubated, while the abundance of funds led some countries to postpone necessary reforms in their domestic policies; they could not, therefore, update them to the new world reality and to the progress made in their productive and social development.

Recessive Adjustment in the 1980s

In the 1980s Latin America faced a deep crisis arising from the large debt accumulated in the 1970s and a deterioration in the international capital and goods markets in which it operates. The abrupt reduction of external bank loans, together with a deterioration in the terms of trade, brought about an acute shortage of foreign exchange, causing a severe recession in the domestic economies of the region. At the same time, the adjustment policies implemented, based primarily on restricting aggregate demand and weak on switching policies, discouraged investment. The setback in the region's output meant an underutilization of its installed capacity. Labor, land, and accumulated investment were utilized to a sizably lesser extent than in 1980–1981. Capital formation underwent a similar experience, both as a result of the recessive domestic situation and the drying up of external financing.

It is very enlightening to examine in greater detail the adjustment process undertaken by Latin America as a whole in the 1980s.[10] This can be extremely relevant when designing an alternative approach because, in order to get back to the development path, the region needs to carry out a sharp effort in terms of savings, investment, and efficient utilization of its productive resources.

For the purpose of quantifying the adjustment recorded in the main macroeconomic variables, the 1980–1981 biennium was used as a base in Table 6.2.[11] This biennium marks the peak in per capita production, capacity utilization, and investment in most countries of the region. All variables are in 1980 prices, expressed as a percentage of GDP in that biennium and are adjusted by a population index, so that all series are measured in per capita terms. Table 6.2 describes the annual values of the main domestic macroeconomic variables that refer to GDP, aggregate demand (domestic expenditures), capital formation, exports and imports, and sources of external shocks: capital movements, financial services (mainly interest remittances), and terms of trade effect (measured as the direct impact on the real purchasing power of GDP).

At a domestic level, the average over the eight-year period (1983–1990) shows the disappearance of the vigorous growth recorded by Latin America and the systematic reduction in investment. The adjustment

Table 6.2. Per Capita Production, Consumption, Investment, and External Shocks in Latin America, 1979–1990 (percentages of per capita average GDP in 1980/81)

	1979	1980	1981	1982	1983	1984	1985	1986	1987	1988	1989	1990	Average 1980–81	Average 1983–90
1. GDP	97.6	101.0	99.0	95.5	90.8	91.8	92.9	94.4	95.3	94.2	93.5	91.8	100.0	93.3
2. Domestic absorption	98.0	102.8	100.1	93.1	84.3	84.7	85.8	88.1	88.2	86.9	85.6	84.4	101.4	86.2
3. Consumption	75.1	77.8	76.3	73.6	69.9	70.1	70.0	72.0	71.6	70.6	70.7	69.9	77.0	70.7
4. Gross fixed capital formation	22.4	23.4	22.7	19.3	15.2	14.7	15.0	15.9	15.9	15.5	14.8	14.4	23.0	15.3
5. Domestic saving[a]	22.5	23.2	22.7	21.9	20.9	21.7	22.9	22.3	23.7	23.6	22.8	21.9	23.0	22.6
6. Nonfinancial current account[b]	(0.4)	(1.6)	(1.1)	2.4	6.6	7.1	7.0	6.3	7.1	7.3	7.8	7.5	(1.4)	7.0
a) Exports of goods and services	15.0	15.2	15.8	15.9	16.7	17.5	17.2	17.0	18.1	19.0	19.6	20.1	15.5	17.9
b) Imports of goods and services	(15.4)	(16.8)	(16.9)	(13.5)	(10.1)	(10.4)	(10.2)	(10.7)	(11.0)	(11.7)	(11.8)	(12.6)	(16.9)	(10.9)
7. Net transfers of funds (c-d)	1.1	1.8	1.9	0.2	(3.8)	(4.8)	(4.1)	(1.9)	(2.4)	(2.4)	(3.0)	(2.5)	1.8	(3.2)
a) Capital movements[b]	5.1	4.8	5.3	2.6	0.3	1.4	0.5	1.5	2.1	0.8	1.4	2.5	5.0	1.2
b) Net profit and interest payments	(2.4)	(2.8)	(3.8)	(5.1)	(4.7)	(5.0)	(4.7)	(4.4)	(3.9)	(3.9)	(4.1)	(3.5)	(3.3)	(4.4)
c) Subtotal	2.7	2.0	1.5	2.5	4.4	3.6	4.2	2.9	1.8	3.1	2.7	1.0	1.7	3.2
d) Change in international reserves	1.6	0.2	(0.4)	(2.7)	(0.6)	1.2	(0.1)	1.0	0.6	(0.7)	0.3	1.5	(0.1)	0.0
8. Terms of trade effect	(0.7)	0.0	(0.8)	(2.6)	(2.7)	(2.3)	(3.0)	(4.4)	(4.7)	(4.9)	(4.9)	(4.9)	(0.4)	(3.9)

Source: Calculations based on CEPAL, Statistics Division, covering nineteen countries.
Notes: a. Calculated as the difference between GDP and expenditure on consumption.
b. Unilateral net transfers are included in capital movements.

process was put into motion by the external shocks measured in lines 7 and 8. During this period, and notwithstanding the low gross investment rate recorded during the adjustment, it is estimated that per capita production capacity remained approximately constant. On the contrary, effective per capita production was, on average, 7 percent lower than in 1980–1981. This is an output-reducing effect that emerged as a result of excessively restrictive demand policies and weak switching policies.

In an ideal adjustment process, excess aggregate demand is eliminated without a decline in production (or more precisely, in the growth rate). In a totally flexible economy, the drop in production, if it occurs, should be negligible. On the other hand, in an economy that is underutilizing its output capacity of tradables, an adjustment with a suitable mix of reallocation policies can increase GDP. Lastly, in the typical Keynesian setting of an economy with price inflexibility and imperfect mobility of factors, "neutral" demand-reducing policies can generate a significant drop in production because they diminish demand for both tradables and nontradables.

In the real world, in downward adjustment processes, there is usually a drop in production. This gives rise to a lower utilization rate of installed capacity and a decrease in the capital formation ratio. Selective policies, with reallocating effects on the composition of output and expenditures, could mitigate the negative effects on economic activity and aggregate demand. A good combination of expenditure-reducing and switching policies should allow a result closer to the production frontier, that is, closer to a constant rate of utilization of potential GDP (see Ffrench-Davis and Marfán 1988).

Line 3 in Table 6.2 shows the plummeting of per capita consumption. But the greatest impact was absorbed by capital formation. During this adjustment process, investment and imports of capital goods fell substantially below precrisis levels. Per capita fixed capital formation declined by one-third between 1980–1981 and 1983–1990, with the resulting negative effect on productive capacity and employment generation. The decline between both periods was not associated with a lower domestic savings effort (line 5). On the contrary, domestic savings exhibited a slight rise as a share of GDP.[12] External shocks were responsible for the decline in available financing for capital formation.

Both public and private sectors were forced to channel a considerable part of their savings to interest payments to foreign creditors.[13] In fact, the shock of the net transfer of funds abroad amounted to between one-half and two-thirds of the net capital formation recorded during 1983–1990.[14] In addition, the terms of trade deteriorated, which also reduced the availability of funds for investment.

External, financial, and commercial shocks are presented in lines 7 and 8 and can be measured by comparing their averages in both periods under study. Foreign capital inflows declined to one-fourth their level during the biennium used as a base, while interest and profit payments rose nearly by one-third. The deterioration in the net transfer of funds (5.1 points) accounts for almost 60 percent of the decline in resources caused by external shocks (8.6 points) during the eight-year period 1983–1990, as compared to precrisis years. This item describes the extent of the financial shock and its prolonged duration. The remaining 40 percent was a result of a marked deterioration in terms of trade (the terms-of-trade shock of 3.5 points).[15]

The combination of these external shocks meant that a given volume of domestic production became consistent with domestic expenditures notably lower than the precedent level. As Table 6.2 shows, per capita output (GDP) decreased by 7 percent between both periods; and domestic expenditures dropped 15 points. Both coefficients also indicate a notable break in the trend of the 1970s, which had involved an annual growth in production (5.6 percent), consumption (6.1 percent), and investment (7.3 percent) vis-à-vis an annual increase of 2.7 percent in population.

In short, both the recessive domestic framework and the marked uncertainty and restrictions that hampered the management and investment capacity of the public and private sectors contributed to a decline in the demand for investment funds. Repression of effective demand led to a major underutilization of installed capacity, which naturally also depressed demand for investment. In this external and domestic framework, debtor countries had difficulties in designing development strategies consistent with domestic structural adjustment and restrictions imposed by the world economy. This situation undermines self-identity and the ability to design domestic development programs and achieve consensus around them; it also undermines the capacity of governments in debtor countries to think of the future. The continuous transfer of funds abroad represents a significant additional limitation on the investment capacity of debtor nations.

Macroeconomic Environment and Productive Investment

Both the volume and productivity (quality) of investment are affected by the macroeconomic environment that prevails in the domestic economy. A comparative analysis of the various experiences of countries with very dissimilar economic strategies and political regimes brings to light some constants in the economic performance of semi-industrialized countries.

Comparatively speaking, in a historical sense, the postwar period was one of high effective demand, which involved a macroeconomic framework that encouraged investment and the use of installed capacity. This was associated with rates of output growth that were notably higher between 1950 and 1980 compared to those recorded in the past. Undoubtedly, the strength of post-Keynesian compensatory approaches, rather than the neutral or automatic adjustment gold standard, is an important explanatory factor.

However, while in the industrialized world a high capital formation process was combined with finely tuned macroeconomic policies, major macroeconomic imbalances were observed in the developing world. This was a reflection of the insufficient analytical and political concern for a macroeconomic policy design and implementation that would safeguard basic balances. As a result of this, inflationary processes and/or balance of payments crises arose.

The 1980s witnessed an inversion in policy objectives. The weight assigned to trade surpluses and debt service was emphasized, while capital formation and the regulation of activity levels were neglected. This was a serious deficiency that helped explain the notable reduction in capital formation and capacity utilization during this decade.

Adjustment of Aggregate Demand

The global macroeconomic framework in which specific productive development policies are implemented has a decisive impact on investment and savings levels (Fischer 1992), the rate of utilization of resources, consumption structure, and the attitude and skills that are promoted within a country. If an instrument is given excessive priority, at the expense of the rest, this can result in the reallocation of a resource stock that fails to grow, probably ending up with high rates of underutilization. Then, policies that may appear to be very efficient in a microeconomic sense (for example in enterprises that survive a given adjustment process) turn out to be inefficient at a macroeconomic or global level (which takes into account the effective productivity of all available resources).

Anti-inflationary and adjustment policies designed to deal with external shocks have an impact on the macroeconomic setting and the rate of utilization of available resources.[16] In turn, the latter affects the rate of return and the formation of new productive capital. Cyclical markets, in contrast to more stable ones, have negative effects on the variables mentioned. Orthodox anti-inflationary and adjustment approaches tend to give rise to procyclical performance. The essential feature of the approach in discussion is the use of one variable to deal with each problem, and its application in a uniform rather than a selective manner.

Conventional price stabilization policies are based either upon the deliberate restriction of overall demand (in its closed economy, monetarist variant, à la Friedman) or in freezing the exchange rate and passive monetary policy tied to the availability of international reserves (in the so-called monetary approach to the balance of payments). As it is known, this mechanism is equivalent to the automatic adjustment of the gold standard. The mechanism is intended to act in such a way that the evolution of domestic aggregate demand and/or the external prices of tradable products determine the domestic performance of price levels. They may in effect do so, but with significant lags. Hence, substantial rates of underutilization of available resources result, on the average, from automatic adjustment processes.

Diverse varieties of post-Keynesian approaches prevailed for almost three postwar decades. Compensatory public policies, the simultaneous utilization of a set of variables that are regulated coordinately, and the concertation between representatives of social actors contributed to a prolonged period of productive expansion in the world economy. The increased relative stability provided an incentive to capital formation: a more favorable environment for improvements in productivity rather than speculative operations, greater emphasis on increased capacity instead of expansion of economic groups through purchases and mergers, and greater social productivity thanks to a larger rate of utilization of the existing capacity of capital and labor. All of this contributed to creating a virtuous circle that encouraged capital formation and increases in productivity.

The existence of prolonged, external, recessive shocks—as in the current debt crisis—obviously cannot be ignored, but how to deal with them is an entirely different matter. The automatic adjustment approach has been characterized, in the past, by amplifying the effects of the external recession at a domestic level. In other words, given the drop in national income originated in the deterioration of the terms of trade and the lower access to real and financial markets, the automatic adjustment adds a further deterioration by lowering domestic output. The automatic adjustment is undoubtedly very effective in reducing the external gap but seriously inefficient at the overall macroeconomic level.

Rather than automatic adjustment, preventing this destructive multiplication of external shocks requires active monetary, credit, fiscal, and foreign exchange policies, as well as a productive development policy. This essentially involves coordinating the development program and short-run policies in order to promote a change in the structure of expenditures and output, so as to maintain a greater rate of utilization of domestic productive capacity. Therein lies room for direct and indirect public policies that may regulate overall aggregate demand and affect the composition of expenditures and production with selective reallocative instruments.

Productive Forces and Financierism

Another distinctive feature of macroeconomic management in developed nations and in the most successful newly industrialized (or semi-industrialized) countries (NICs) is the predominance of productive over financial dimensions. Development is led by the "real" side, with financial aspects at its disposal. It is a policy correlation contrary to the monetary approach and the standard thesis of financial liberalization and deepening (McKinnon 1979b; 1988).

The phenomenon of "financierism" was particularly strong in some Latin American countries by the 1970s. At that time, monetary approaches to the balance of payments and financial liberalization experienced a strong boost. Some economics scholars achieved great influence in the United States and in various countries of the region preaching that monetary approach. A dogmatic surge occurred with notable force in "orthodox practice," as Bacha and Díaz-Alejandro (1983) referred to it, advocating intense domestic financial liberalization as well as deregulation of capital movements.[17] Implementation of these proposals was characterized in that decade by the open supremacy of financial activity over productive activity.

The predominance of financierism was mainly associated with the presence of two main factors: on the one hand, the nature of financial reforms being implemented in many countries, primarily in the Southern Cone; and, on the other hand, the nature of the specialization of the economic agents that became more influential. The reform consisted in the extensive liberalization of interest rates, maturity terms, and credit allocation (Arellano 1985; Sarmiento 1985) and the relaxation of regulations on financial institutions. There was widespread disregard for the risk of generating speculative bubbles, adverse selection, and moral hazard (Díaz-Alejandro 1985). It is interesting to note that financierist orthodoxy assigned a strategic role to the sector's liberalization, without considering the characteristics of the product in question, which could lead to a quite different performance of this market as compared to that of current goods markets that operate in cash.

The strength of the new proposals was partly reinforced by policies already in force. The deepening of inflationary trends, fueled by the 1973 oil crisis, worsened the negative effects of the "financial repression," which was reflected in frozen nominal interest rates whose real value rapidly became negative. The increased demand for loans widened the gap with the available supply of funds. These negative factors encouraged naive orthodoxy to speed up across-the-board financial liberalization, regardless of the economic conditions prevailing in each country.[18]

The reforms undertaken, primarily in the Southern Cone, led to the establishment of banks that did not duly guarantee their trustworthiness, excessive self-loans to owners of financial companies, very short term maturities, and unstable interest rates, with substantial spreads between active (loan) and passive (deposit) rates. This resulted in short term factors bearing more weight than long term ones, which increased domestic instability, causing a negative effect on output and a boom in credit for consumption (and for imported consumer goods in those countries that had liberalized imports). Thus, the naive financial reform served to greatly increase consumer goods imports, but it also weakened the domestic productive apparatus and the net financing of investment (Arellano 1985; Sarmiento 1985). The growing link with the international financial system facilitated the disassociation with domestic productive system needs and sparked a capital flight in times of domestic trouble. For instance, in Chile average capital formation was lower after the reform as compared with the 1960s, but capital flight was limited while imports boomed; on the contrary, in Argentina and Venezuela capital flight was notably large.

The second factor was that economic agents linked to the financial sphere gained greater overall influence in public and private enterprises, as well as in ministries and other governmental departments. This situation imposed the predominance at these levels of a short term bias over concerns for productivity and additions to productive capacity. In speculative markets, as Arrow (1979) points out, a considerable part of the efforts of economic agents focuses on acquiring information for personal benefit and leads to a zero sum or negative sum redistribution, owing to the use of real resources for these purposes. At a distributive level, indiscriminate deregulation also concentrates opportunities in favor of sectors with greater access to the financial system.

The nature of the new relations established with foreign creditor banks after the 1982 debt crisis also favored the financial dimension. When one examines the agreements signed with banks, a clear reinforcement of financial elements over productive ones can be observed. This includes debt-equity swaps, which tended to encourage transfers of existing firms rather than the expansion of productive capacity. In addition, at the fiscal level the financial element once again prevailed: the nature of the fiscal deficit showed by many countries of the region was no longer generated primarily by excessive expenditures on consumption and investment over tax revenue, but by interest payments deriving from domestic and external indebtedness. Domestically, financing required by the public treasury became very expensive, with excessively high real rates. At the external level, in addition to the greater cost, a major statization of the external debt occurred in various countries. This phenomenon was greater in the Southern Cone, since in the 1970s these countries had, to a great extent, privatized capital inflows.

The financial system should doubtless play an essential role in the attraction and allocation of savings. In this respect, financial reforms usually were needed. The main issue is how to achieve this objective so as to contribute to productive development and macroeconomic stability, rather than the reverse. Indiscriminate liberalization has proven inefficient on both counts, particularly during the adjustment process (Arellano 1985; Díaz-Alejandro 1985; Ffrench-Davis 1983; Massad and Zahler 1988; Ramos 1986b; Sarmiento 1985). It is important to take care that financial reforms do not represent a diversion of savings toward consumption, speculation, and the concentration of wealth, rather than toward investment.

The reorganization of the financial system should aim at harnessing resources toward savings and investment, in direct connection with the productive apparatus. This is a very important role that, paradoxically, has been undermined in recent years owing to naive monetarist reforms. A new approach should adequately respond to the need to link the financial system to the domestic investment process rather than the external financial economy, to contribute to greater economic stability (which implies regulating interest rates so as to avoid very abrupt fluctuations, or negative or exorbitantly high real interest rates), and to deconcentrate economic power.

These objectives require a more complete capital market than the standard outcome of neoliberal reforms. What is needed is an institutionality that encompasses a vigorous, long term segment, in order to finance productive investment. Greater access is also needed by sectors with low- and medium-income levels, which typically suffer the social segmentation of the capital market. They need this market to deal with contingencies, invest in training, and promote the development of productive activities and their modernization. Specialized credit entities and guarantee mechanisms are required in order to do what the market has been unable to do spontaneously. The priority in this field should not be to subsidize the cost of credit, but to favor access to financing at normal rates, as well as access to the remaining resources that these low- and medium-income sectors do not possess: technology, some inputs and services, marketing channels, and infrastructure.

The relation between domestic and external capital markets would require a chapter of its own. In short, total openness to the international market can disarticulate any comprehensive effort at domestic stabilization and encourage capital flight (Dornbusch 1991). In fact, it could imply integration into more speculative segments of developed world markets. In contrast, insertion into world economy should be aimed at promoting long term capital inflows, accompanied by access to technology and export markets. With regard to short term capital movements, what is clearly needed is the expeditious availability of trade credit.

Adequate Regulation of Key Prices

There are prices that, owing to their impact on the economy as a whole, perform as macrovariables. Among these are exchange rates, interest rates, and trade policy.[19]

Foreign exchange policy. Foreign currency constitutes a strategic resource, whose availability and rate of exchange have a decisive impact on domestic economic performance. This involves the level of economic activity, the degree of optimal autonomy vis-à-vis the international markets, the structure of production, and domestic price stability. However, due to its nature, foreign currency lends itself to bubbles and speculative operations more than other items, since it serves as an instrument for capital flight and a medium of exchange and hoarding.[20] Consequently, the working of the foreign exchange market (access to foreign exchange and the exchange rate adjustment) has significant macroeconomic effects, unlike many other goods or assets with purely micro implications.

The set of conditions reflecting the reality of most LACs in recent years—variable and structural inflation, fluctuating terms of trade, inflexible productive structure, the need to transform this structure, and abrupt changes in external financing terms—render the two traditional extreme formulas of free and fixed nominal exchange rates inconvenient.[21] The alternative vis-à-vis the problems that arise from these two options consists of a crawling-peg exchange rate policy regulated by the Central Bank, within a system of controlled access to the foreign exchange market, in accordance with recommendations resulting from medium term projections of the external sector (Ffrench-Davis 1979: chapter VI; and survey in Williamson 1981).

External market instability and unexpected fluctuations in domestic activities tied to the balance of payments pose two of the main problems that an efficient foreign exchange policy must deal with. Two of the most common sources of instability in LACs are inflation and the variability of export prices. Both discontinuous and massive adjustments of the nominal exchange rate, particularly within an inflationary setting, and continuous modifications that follow fluctuations in export proceeds cause irregular variations in the real exchange rate, which generate instability in price relations between foreign and domestic goods, with corresponding uncertainty for the domestic economy.[22]

Exchange rate instability tends to reduce the capacity to identify comparative advantages, a trend that undermines capital formation. It often has a negative and stronger impact on new exports, those undertaken by companies with less diversified markets, and those with more limited access to capital markets. Consequently, exchange rate instability, although affecting all exports, is biased against nontraditional products. The bias also affects nationally owned enterprises as compared to transnational companies. The latter, due to the diversity of markets of goods and finance in which they operate, are in a position to better protect themselves from exchange rate risks.

The existence of instability, given imperfect capital markets and external binding restrictions, also involves a relation between foreign exchange policy and the average level of effective demand. Instability tends to reduce the average rate of use of resources. A higher exchange rate (depreciated) allows for a sustainable higher average level of effective demand and economic activity.[23] Therefore, it tends to allow for a greater utilization of capacity and to encourage investment; this could even take

place in the production of nontradables, as long as the income effect
(owing to the greater rate of utilization and capital formation) exceeds the
price effect (higher relative price of tradables). A depreciated exchange
rate (or a good substitute for it) also allows for reduced involvement of
scarce governmental human resources in the management of critical balance of payments situations.

In short, it is convenient, on the one hand, for the exchange rate to be
modified continuously and simultaneously with the foreseen or programmed evolution of net inflation; on the other hand, it should be guided
by the trend shown by balance of payments projections (at full employment) that seek to attenuate the transmission of short term fluctuations of
the terms of trade or capital movements into the domestic economy.[24] Regulation of access to the market is crucial to moderate destabilizing capital
movements. The cases of Brazil, Colombia, Japan, and South Korea during the 1960s and 1970s are illustrative of the advantages of regulated
market access, while Argentina and Mexico are illustrative of the risks of
fully free access.

Interest rate. The interest rate is another variable of macroeconomic importance. The orthodox proposal is to leave it free and allow it to be indirectly regulated by changes in liquidity. According to this approach, in
"small countries" the liberalization of interest rates would imply the parity
with the international rate. Actually, this latter does not happen even between most developed countries, for instance between the United States
and the former West Germany during the 1980s. Liberalization experiences have shown that external and domestic rates do not converge rapidly
to a unique level, that domestic interest rates are unstable and much higher
than international ones, and that spreads (commissions) are markedly
higher (Arellano 1985; Frenkel 1983; Ramos 1986b; Sarmiento 1985;
Zahler 1988). The predominant trend, for example in the Southern Cone
countries, appears to have been a deterioration of the support given by the
financial system to productive development. Investment was faced with
notably fluctuating and high interest rates and short maturities. In Chile,
for example, a thirty-day term was the overwhelmingly larger segment of
the market, which operated for seven years, between 1975 and 1982, with
a very unstable interest rate, exhibiting an average real value approaching
40 percent yearly. Consequently, the resulting framework lent itself to
speculative activities. This result was reinforced in countries where capital
movements were also liberalized (Bacha 1983, 1986).

Proposals for financial liberalization were encouraged by the unsatis-
factory experience with increasingly interventionist policies and heavily
subsidized interest rates. The latter occurred particularly in countries with
high inflation and low nominal interest rates. In response to this, some of
the countries that succeeded in increasing investment during the 1970s

undertook financial reforms, but these were heterodox in nature: capital movements and domestic loans were controlled, orienting them toward investment; positive and active but moderate real interest rates were established and long term financing channels were created. Brazil and Colombia followed this approach; Chile took a similar approach during the 1960s.

From a neostructuralist perspective, the recommendations resulting from such experience would involve regulation of interest rates at real positive levels and action by the public sector aimed at extending maturity terms and promoting credit allocation to productive activities, including lagged small entrepreneurs, rather than financing the transfer of existing assets and consumption.[25]

Foreign trade policy and macroeconomic effects. Finally, foreign trade policy has four effects that may be classified as macroeconomic, which we would like to highlight here.[26] Excessive protectionism restricts investment and its productivity by enclosing production within the limited domestic frontiers. This was the prevailing keynote in Latin America since the crisis of the 1930s.

The first point refers to the fact that protection of the domestic economy in past decades tended to be exclusively identified with import substitution policies. Thus, countries committed the costly error of protecting import substitution (1) without taking into account its negative effects on the relative prices faced by producers of exportables (anti-export bias); (2) without taking advantage of the support that the expansion of exports could involve for more efficient import substitution (complementarity between them in cases of economies of scale and specialization); and (3) without the encouragement to technological innovation resulting from vigorous nontraditional exports and gradually scaled-down protection to importables (X efficiency à la Leibenstein 1966; Bhagwati 1978; Agosín 1991).

These limitations were increasingly felt in Latin American economies in the 1970s. The technological lag, the underutilization of economies of scale, and the widening gap between domestic and external prices of certain manufactures became more visible. Thus, as countries of the region advanced toward a semi-industrialized economy, the promotion of exports acquired growing priority (Prebisch 1963, 1977; Bhagwati 1978). When the consequences began to be felt more strongly, with various lags, the countries resorted to tariff exemptions, various forms of drawbacks, and subsidies.

The cost of not acting in a timely fashion to activate export promotion cannot be defined independently from the degree of domestic progress in import substitution and the conditions prevailing in the international markets. The greater the advance of the substitution process, the greater the priority for complementarity with the promotion of exports. The timeliness with which this need is recognized has a determinant impact on the efficiency of the interrelation with international markets, an effect that accentuates rapidly when it involves smaller economies. On the other hand, the degree of openness of international markets affects the feasibility of import substitution and export policies. Throughout the 1960s and part of the 1970s, LACs found increasingly expanding and more accessible markets for their exports; therefore, policies that did not take advantage of such opportunity became much more costly.[27]

Second, indiscriminate liberalization of imports, within the framework traditionally prevalent in Latin America, changes relative market prices and the availability and diversity of goods in favor of consumption. Coupled with the credit facilities available in a liberalized financial market, a shift occurs from savings to consumption, either directly or through the financial system. In fact, owing to the financial reforms implemented during the 1970s in the Southern Cone, the latter tapped a markedly greater proportion of total savings, but then it reoriented a significant portion of these funds to consumption, which reduced effective domestic savings (Arellano 1985; Sarmiento 1985; Zahler 1988). It is illustrative that in their opening to the international economy, countries such as Brazil, Colombia, South Korea, and Taiwan did not indiscriminately liberalize consumer goods imports (Sachs 1987; Agosín 1991; Bradford 1992). What good is it for the consumer to have access to a wide variety of importables at international prices if this has a negative impact on domestic savings and investment, and if as a producer he is unemployed or bankrupt?

Because of this, it is advisable to use a gradual sequence of policies involving net positive pulls, for example, a stronger export-promoting inducement on the demand for resources—rather than the negative pulls of import desubstitution—supported with a financial system at the service of productive development. What is ultimately intended is to foster the efficient production of both exportables and import substitutes, amidst a dynamic investment process (Ffrench-Davis 1979: chapter VIII). The relative strength of positive and negative pulls determines whether adjustment is made below or along the production frontier, and how fast this frontier is shifted upward (Ffrench-Davis and Vial 1991; Sachs 1987).

Third, indiscriminate import liberalization in sectors where output differentiation is important contributes to segmenting domestic demand in different varieties and hampering the operation of local producers. This is important in sectors such as durable consumer goods and their parts and components, in which there are economies of scale and specialization. Therefore, trade policy should reconcile external competition with local utilization of these economies of scale and specialization.

Finally, in a world of "limited information" (Arrow 1981), an attribute of selective tariffs and export incentives is that they contribute to enhancing in the market the presence of sectors in which there are investment opportunities. Improved visibility mobilizes savings and capital formation. In other words, the efficient (that implies moderate) use of tariffs and export incentives not only enables the reallocation of resources, but also may contribute to expanding the production frontier.

Investment Opportunities and Development of Comparative Advantages

Latin America needs to be actively inserted into the world economy. It needs to systematically expand its exports, capturing external markets with profitable prices. This is an effective device to promote domestic productive development. The task of acquiring new comparative advantages plays a crucial role within this framework.

Given an appropriate macroeconomic framework, two groups of indirect policies can be distinguished that, through their effects on the optimizing decisions of both private and public enterprises, may help the market to identify and implement comparative advantages. One involves the various domestic policies that affect demand conditions and the availability and quality of productive resources. The other involves the various interventions affecting the relationship with external markets, such as trade policies. Lastly, a discussion is made on direct policies favoring the development of sectors intensive in acquirable comparative advantage.

Domestic Interventions

Here mention will be made of only some types of governmental actions that affect the development or acquisition of comparative advantages. A first group consists of public infrastructure such as the availability of water, energy, roads, ports, and harbors. Their location undoubtedly alters the profiles of market comparative advantages. Their nature as public goods and their indivisibility show how unfeasible a neutral public policy is in this respect. This is true regardless of whether the tariffs charged do or do not cover their production costs.

A second group involves public health, education, and technical training. The first affects labor productivity and learning capacity. An educational and training policy, depending on the skills and/or productive activities it focuses on, may have a decisive impact on the comparative advantage profile attained. Some coordination between supply and demand is critical for encouraging high rates of utilization and resource formation. Given the long maturity periods involved, waiting for observed market demand to determine supply, or for changes in supply to bring about a restructuring of the market demand for skills, could prove very frustrating for those affected, and could entail wasting national efforts. What is required is a harmonious and timely coordination between supply and demand.

A third group includes scientific and technological infrastructure and a research and technological development policy. It constitutes a decisive factor for a developing country. Experience indicates that the public sector plays a pivotal role in the results to be obtained in this area, and also that the selection criteria applied in its policies have a deep impact on the de- gree of endogeneity of national development (ECLAC 1992; Fajnzylber 1989a; Stewart 1982).

A fourth group deals with public policies that affect the demand structure. These include, for instance, state purchasing policies, as they discriminate according to the source and quality of supply; social policies distributing goods and services outside the market; and trade agreements negotiated with partner countries.

Many other elements, not dealt with here, may form part of a productive or industrial development policy (tax system, public enterprises management, environmental protection, regional development). Most of these topics, however, are dealt with directly or indirectly in the following chapters.

External Promotion Policies and Relative Prices[28]

In the experiences recorded in Latin America, the level and structure of trade has been controlled by many instruments. Indeed, most countries have at one time or another used various combinations of import tariffs, export tariff exemptions, multiple exchange rates, prior import deposits, foreign exchange controls, free zones, quantitative restrictions, domestic price stabilization mechanisms for tradable products, and antidumping regulations. Other instruments affecting trade have also been used, including various credit and tax mechanisms to protect import substitutes and exportables (Díaz-Alejandro 1976; Ffrench-Davis 1979). All policy tools mentioned affect relative prices faced by producers and consumers, as well as the level and composition of trade, and, therefore, modify market comparative advantage.[29]

Government intervention in foreign trade has resulted excessively from short term situations or crises, leading to protection under pressure by vested interests and the rescue of decaying or bankrupt industries. These situations obviously resulted in much irrationality, deterring productivity increases, with excessively high effective protection for some sectors and harsh detrimental rates for others. The lack of a rationally based tariff system means that the pressures just mentioned have greater probabilities of prevailing, hence the importance of designing a system that systematically embodies relatively objective criteria. This can be used in the processes of unilateral gradual liberalization or in trade agreements being negotiated by several LACs in the early 1990s.

The criteria applied most frequently to tariff design are seriously flawed. The fact of being limited to whether the goods are produced or not, or to origin (primary or manufactured) or use (consumption, interme- diate products, and capital), constitutes a hardly defensible position as a general rule.[30] The same applies to the criterion of protection according to degree of elaboration, without taking into account what the latter entails. All of these criteria have some basis, but not for use as general criteria. These must explicitly and consistently meet domestic development objec- tives and the obstacles this development faces.

The role of tariffs becomes increasingly more significant according to the magnitude of the imbalances and distortions of domestic markets, and to the difficulty of eliminating them by means of a first or second best al- ternative. The objective of trade policy within a suboptimal framework consists in the reallocation of productive resources in such a way as to re- duce the structural imbalances of the economy, and in generating invest- ment opportunities to encourage domestic capital formation. Conse- quently, tariff protection, as well as export incentives, should be contingent upon the nature and severity of these imbalances and the ca- pacity of various activities to contribute to their resolution.[31] This ap- proach, in an "nth best world," leads to the use of differentiated or selec- tive tariffs and subsidies, as opposed to the zero tariff in the orthodox approach.

Differentiating protection depending on the characteristics of eco- nomic activities has been little used in practice in LACs, despite the fact that it provides the most solid base for supporting a deviation from gener- alized free trade. Those aspects that are likely to be considered in their de- sign are illustrated by three groups of productive activity characteristics: labor and capital intensity, the infant activity argument and its capacity to improve productivity through learning by doing (Arrow 1962a), and the activity's externalities over the rest of the national economy. The various productive activities differ among themselves in these three respects; an example would be infancy, which requires temporary protection. In turn, the degree of development, the supply of factors, and the stage of indus- trialization of each country will affect the type of activity likely to be promoted in each case (Bhagwati 1978; Ffrench-Davis 1979, 1982, 1984; JUNAC 1981; Krugman 1986).

The preceding analysis proposes an integrated treatment of import substitution protection and export promotion. In this way, generally the same criteria for structuring promotion (or discouragement) would apply to both sides of trade. Thus the anti-export bias of traditional protection- ism is eliminated. In brief, then, the profile or structure of import tariffs should coincide with that of compensatory export incentives. That is, if a given economic activity is protected (unprotected) because of its beneficial (detrimental) effects on the domestic economy, it should generally also be encouraged (discouraged) to produce for external markets. This was one of the strategic features of the South Korean experience during the 1960s and 1970s, a period in which its economy underwent an amazing transformation (Bhagwati 1978; Bradford 1992; Fajnzylber 1989a; Sachs 1987).

The criteria mentioned here provide a basis for rendering the design of trade policy more objective, as far as possible, and subject to the capacity to implement the policy. Consequently, they constitute an attempt to provide a conceptual framework incorporating the salient features of developing countries.[32] This line of reasoning supports the deliberate differentiation between various groups of products, based on the divergence between social and market values in different activities. On the other hand, the same good should tend to receive similar treatment regardless of its target market (domestic or foreign). Competition with foreign products, abroad and domestically, takes place but with relative prices modified by the incentives profile.

Identification and Acquisition of Comparative Advantages

Distortions arising from standard differences between social and market prices may be corrected with policies such as those dealt with in the preceding paragraphs. Over and above the resulting price system, there is another characteristic of developing economies that strongly supports productive development policies in which the public sector plays a direct and active role. This feature refers to the infant nature of developing country economies, which gives rise to substantial dynamic externalities and "diffuse" comparative advantages that are difficult to pinpoint in a self-regulated market. The infant nature of productive development is associated, on the one hand, with the limited transfer of technologies already available in the world economy, and to obstacles to their absorption and diffusion in domestic markets. On the other hand, it involves market relations characterized by their changing nature and lack of transparency. As a result of this, development demands a major effort to acquire comparative advantages, as well as to identify those factors, areas, or sectors with greatest potential in order to focus such efforts on them.

In many cases the comparative advantages are difficult to identify, because they contain an acquirable component that is more important than the natural one. Thus, in economies undergoing a process of change, the visualization of comparative advantages does not constitute a variable that is generally defined and known, except in the case of goods whose advantages are based on favorable natural resources, climate, and geographic location or some quality already acquired (captive technology, outstanding personnel skills). These cases are far from covering the totality of eventually productive activities. On the contrary, there are many projects whose costs and benefits depend, to a large extent, on externalities or economies of scale or of specialization, which they are able to take advantage of, and on the availability of markets. It is therefore likely that the comparative advantages are diffuse in these cases, and that the market has difficulties in delivering a single and optimal response on its own. Therefore, the productive structure becomes distorted and the investment volume tends to be lower than the potential. In short, two negative conditions tend to arise: an inefficient allocation of resources and a suboptimal volume of these.

In these cases of diffuse comparative advantages, the economic authority may play an essential role as coordinator, selecting groups of products or strategic complexes or factors, in which efforts to generate dynamic externalities should be concentrated, advantage should be taken of economies of scale, and external markets should be pursued. Two alternatives exist besides that of an active state. These are the concentration and selectiveness of efforts to be determined either by transnational corporations or large national economic groups. The first option, as a sole alternative, runs counter to the objective of development with a national profile, and the second one goes against the objectives of equity and democratic development. In reality, the three should tend to concur simultaneously, but with a democratic and participatory state that possesses autonomy, vis-à-vis those groups, to design public policy.

In those areas where comparative advantages reside essentially on acquirable attributes, effectiveness demands selectiveness and concentration of efforts, no matter who is the acting agent. Consequently, this option differs from the orthodox approach in that it seeks to put into effect a deliberate process that fosters production, and differs from the traditional approach of indiscriminate import substitution, since it deals with a selective and coordinated effort and grants a leading role to exports.

Some selection criteria are:

1. Focusing attention on activities with acquirable comparative advantages. This implies excluding from the set of possible activities those sectors that presently exhibit removable problems, in aspects such as limited access to external markets, technology, or training. Sectors with comparative advantages easily identifiable by the market should also be excluded, since they obviously do not require any specific support for their market materialization, nor would it be justifiable to grant it.

2. Giving priority to sectors (and factors) with significant linkages and dynamic multiplier effects in productive or distributive spheres (García and Marfán 1987). A priority aspect in this sense should be the capacity of the activities to generate employment, along with rising productivity.

Based on these two points, a broad number of activities arise, undoubtedly larger than can be implemented. Therefore it is imperative to have a selective approach and choose a limited number of activities from this universe that are consistent with the financing and management capabilities of the government. Insofar as this is coordinated by the state in conjunction with the private sector, the area covered could be expanded. Market intervention is aimed both at contributing to a better outlining of comparative advantages, as well as to generating them in sectors where these depend primarily upon acquirable attributes in the productive specialization itself (learning by doing) or through the selection of areas of specialization.

The choice of areas should be done simultaneously with a series of concerted actions by the public and private sectors. In fact, the rate of return of a plant is subordinate to the eventual installation of other complementary activities, particularly in less developed areas. This complementation includes the production of common services, infrastructures, input supply and training, the creation of marketing channels and diffusion of knowledge, and negotiations to achieve access to external markets.

Selecting a group of associated products whose output is projected to be promoted in a coordinated way—and the concentration of state support—contributes in providing each investor with a more defined economic framework. In effect, the joint scheduling of the group of products—even when investment activities are undertaken by different public or private enterprises in their various forms of management and ownership—makes it possible to visualize more accurately the presence and extent of dynamic external economies than in an unregulated market. This approach is equivalent to the standard investment and strategic planning conducted by transnational corporations.

Naturally, an isolated public investor can experience the same difficulties as a private investor. The crux of the argument thus lies not in the relative efficiency of public and private entrepreneurs, which depends on other considerations, but that in the context described, the operation of the marketplace on its own is certainly not optimal. Consequently, there is room for intervening in it and, even with a certain margin of error, increasing its efficiency.

In short, in the presence of dynamic externalities and economies of scale and specialization, the act per se of selecting fields in which to concentrate investment, institutional development, labor training, research, infrastructure, negotiations for access to external markets, and technology becomes very important.[33] The greater the externalities and economies of specialization, the more diffuse the comparative advantages tend to be, and the greater the need to complement the market. Even random selection, providing that it is carried out among the fields of activities where acquirable dynamic components are significant, may contribute to effectively generate comparative advantages and afford greater investment opportunities. Evidence from semi-industrialized countries that have achieved sustained growth supports this hypothesis, as opposed to the shortcomings evinced by indiscriminate protectionism and unrestricted liberalization.

Likewise, the nature of selection could influence productive employment levels, the degree of sameness or differentiation of consumption patterns, regional structuring of production, and integration of the respective production process into the national or world economy. Thus, systematic research is required on the most appropriate criteria for identifying acquirable comparative advantages, and on the most suitable means for transforming them into acquired ones, in the presence of varied forms of structural heterogeneity.

Conclusion: The Challenge of the Future

The experience of the 1980s leaves in its wake various useful lessons on how to achieve more vigorous and sustained development.

1. *The Need for Macroeconomic Balances Functional to Productive Development.* Macroeconomic balances are a prerequisite in any approach seeking success. Major imbalances, both in terms of excessive and insufficient aggregate demand, are detrimental to vigorous investment and productivity increases. Therefore, an effective demand that is close to productive capacity (that capacity use consistent with expected relative prices) is required. Selective fiscal, credit, and trade policies could prove to be effective mechanisms for achieving this objective. A high exchange rate (depreciated), together with effective social coordination, would contribute in bringing activity levels closer to potential capacity. The subsequent high capacity utilization encourages a larger rate of capital formation.

2. *Reducing Net Transfers Abroad.* External debt servicing taps a significant proportion of the region's domestic savings. A reduction of net transfers, coupled with improved access to world markets, would make way for increased availability of productive investment financing.

3. *Expanding the Availability of Long Term Domestic Financing.* Achieving a high rate of capital formation requires the strengthening of a long term financial market, with pluralistic forms of entrepreneurial organizations having access to it, including small businesses, cooperatives, and labor communities.

4. *Increasing the Availability of Technology and Social Investment.* Promotion of the absorption and generation of technology is needed, as well as the improvement of education and training of increasingly skilled workers. On the other hand, in order to reduce poverty and invest in people, a relative enlargement of basic consumption is required at the expense of nonessential consumption. Tax reform becomes a crucial component.

5. *Placing the Financial System at the Service of Productive Development.* A rebalancing is needed between the power of agents with productivistic training and concerns and financierists (those specialized in financial activities and activities involving the transfer of existing assets). Both are needed, but in changed doses.

6. *Promoting New Dynamic Comparative Advantages in the Production of Exportables.* This implies boosting exports that have a pulling-up effect on investment and productivity through their linkages with the rest of the domestic economy.

Notes

1. The topic is further discussed by Ffrench-Davis (1988) in a comparison between neoliberal and neostructuralist paradigms.

2. It encouraged excessive indebtedness by advocating the liberalization of financial markets and by upholding indebtedness as "good business" that, once performed by private agents, would be self-regulatory.

3. More recently, the performance of savings has been analyzed by Arellano (1985), Marfán (1985), Massad and Zahler (1988), and Werneck (1988).

4. "Neutrality" is used here in the policy-objective sense, for example, free trade that treats all types of goods equally. However, neither the transition between the current situation and the policy objective, nor the effects on income distribution and capital formation, are neutral.

5. For example, the latter assumption implies that one generation will not become excessively indebted at the expense of upcoming generations.

6. For example, contributions by these specialists are very significant in connection with the implications of product differentiation, economies of scale, learning by doing, and dynamic externalities. See, for example, Krugman (1986, 1989). These contributions are of great relevance in a neostructuralist approach. Generally, these analytical developments tend to be ignored in neoliberal recipes.

7. For an in-depth study on the role of the state and the market in economic development, see Chapter 13.

8. In Hirschman's (1971) opinion the contrast between a comparatively high economic performance and the disenchantment expressed by many analysts was due to a "defeatist mentality."

9. See the various articles included in the works compiled by Ffrench-Davis (1983), Wionczek (1985), and Griffith-Jones (1988).

10. Ffrench-Davis and Marfán (1988) examine the similarities and differences in the adjustment experiences of various countries. The Chilean case is analyzed in Ffrench-Davis and Muñoz (1990).

11. Nineteen eighty-two was a year of transition in economic activity, as well as in external financing and investment, between the continuation of the boom in various countries in 1981 and the open, generalized recession of 1983.

12. Per capita domestic savings remained virtually constant, while its total level increased, rising from 23 percent to 24 percent of GDP for each period.

13. In many countries, external debt servicing has been predominantly a fiscal responsibility and has become a significant component of the public sector deficit. In various cases, the external debt was originally private, and it became a Treasury or Central Bank burden only after the 1982 crisis.

14. Gross fixed capital formation was close to 16 percent of GDP in 1983–1990, and the change in net transfers reached 5 percent. If capital depreciation is estimated at 6 percent, 10 percent of GDP would go to increase the capital stock, and the transfers shock would then amount to half of that figure. The coefficient of two-thirds corresponds to a 9 percent depreciation ratio.

15. The terms of trade steadily worsened between 1982 and 1989 (line 8), which coincided with the expansion of the exports' quantum. Improvement of the nonfinancial current account in a way that is compatible with economic development requires, among other things, greater access by Latin America to export markets. Access to these markets is threatened by protectionism and instability, including intraregional trade. Reciprocal trade dropped sharply, in response to the contraction recorded in the region's markets. Intraregional exports were, on average, 33 percent lower during the five-year period of 1983–1987 than in 1981. (Chapter 12 provides more information on trends in the terms of trade for the region.)

16. See Chapter 4 for a sharp analysis of stabilization policies.

17. "Practical orthodoxy is more dogmatic. It is embodied in business press editorials, in both private and public sector executives . . . and in some of the more politically or financially ambitious academicians" (Bacha and Díaz-Alejandro 1983: 16).

18. It is surprising that thirteen years after some of the most profound financial liberalization reforms were begun, those who conceived and guided them now state that "we are beginning to see that total liberalization of banks is undesirable vis-à-vis high and variable inflation" (McKinnon 1988: 38).

19. In conventional literature, a fundamental role is also assigned to wages. For example, the analysis of real exchange rate is linked to the real wage level, implying that any devaluation involves a drop in wages. In practice, however, there are other variables—such as activity level, increases in productivity, economic rents, the bargaining capacity of each party, and interest rates—that can open the way for a different relation between wages and the exchange rate.

20. In this respect, the orthodox recommendation of maintaining free access to the foreign exchange market, together with appreciated exchange rates, was "effective" in facilitating capital flight from Latin America in recent years.

21. See Ffrench-Davis (1979: chapters V and VI). A free exchange rate is advocated by closed economy monetarism. Open economy monetarism (the monetary approach to the balance of payments) advocates a fixed exchange rate, as that applied between 1979 and 1982 in the monetarism experiment imposed in Chile. Paradoxically, this proposal coincides with ultra antimonetarist approaches, which seek an exchange rate freeze for similar anti-inflationary purposes.

22. In practice, the relation is much more heterogeneous than the relative price between tradables and nontradables. Within tradables there is no single price determined by the exchange rate. There are transfers of category between importables and exportables, as well as changes in the borderline between importables and nontradables, which determines a more heterogeneous relative price profile.

23. It tends to have a greater inflationary impact, which must be compensated with policies that favor the concertation of prices and income. In the absense of this, economic policy is forced to overly depend on the restriction of aggregate demand. Adequately programmed, as part of a comprehensive set of economic policies, activating effects will probably prevail over the contractive impacts of a devaluation.

24. To avoid monetary instability, foreign exchange policy should be accompanied by stabilizing (ex-ante) or sterilizing (ex-post) mechanisms of fluctuating

capital movements and main export proceeds. See Ffrench-Davis (1979: chapters VI and IX).

25. This assumes that primary credit allocation affects the composition of its end use, which seems to reflect market reality.

26. We shall not examine the effect on the equilibrium exchange rate since it is well known. Its overall effect can be easily captured by a crawling-peg exchange rate policy and compensatory incentives to exports (Ffrench-Davis 1979: chapter VIII). Neither shall we consider the impact of foreign trade policy and the degree of openness on the transmission of external instability, which also has macroeconomic implications. See, for instance, Ffrench-Davis and Vial (1991).

27. A less promising situation came about in the 1980s, and something similar is forecast for the 1990s. In light of this, a constructive response is an active policy that seeks and opens up markets; in the foreseeable external market, regional integration processes and commercial and productive agreements between developing countries take on renewed importance as a means for promoting the trade of nontraditional exports.

28. The subject has been dealt with extensively in Aninat (1983), Ffrench-Davis (1979, 1982, 1984), and JUNAC (1981).

29. Differences have also been recorded between the effects produced by various instruments. The main ones refer to the degree of certainty regarding the protection they afford, the repercussions on the rest of trade, their impact on fiscal revenue and monetary liquidity, and the strengthening or weakening incidence on the transmission of economic instability.

30. Neither does the neoliberal option of a uniform tariff other than zero have an analytical base in a small country.

31. In macroeconomics, this position also applies to the case of a binding external gap that restricts the use of productive capacity, as occurred in the 1982 debt crisis. Trade policy should seek to affect the composition of aggregate demand, reducing the demand for tradables in such a way as to avoid generating significant decreases, either in domestic production requiring imported inputs or in productive investment (Ffrench-Davis and Marfán 1988). This involves concentrating restrictive measures on consumer goods imports. Despite the fact that in times of emergency efforts are made to save on foreign exchange, the policy does not intend to pursue the reallocation of resources to local production of all these goods. For this reason, an unequivocal signal must be given that these measures (or part of them, in some cases) are only temporary.

32. In addition, suggestions by Ramos in Chapter 4 regarding the need to create institutional counterbalances against the asymmetrical pressure for greater intervention, and of considering exports to be the true infant industry of the future, assume great importance in defining an optimal tariff policy.

33. As was mentioned in the preceding sections, the pricing system should play a crucial role as a planning and coordination instrument, even in the most strategic activities. After implementing a strategic decision, such as the selection of a productive area, countless decisions remain in connection with technology, scale of output, and supply of intermediate goods, in which relative prices should play a determinant role.

7

Environment and Natural Resources in Latin American Development

Nicolo Gligo

It is no easy task to address the issue of economic development in Latin America and its relation to the environment and natural resources. On the one hand, one of the principles underlying the paradigms that have prevailed throughout different periods has been "the abundant resources available in the region," a statement that, despite its relative and comparative correctness, is one of the main causes of environmental deterioration. On the other hand, the peculiar characteristics of peripheral and dependent development were translated into almost permanent instabilities, causing a great number of conflicts between societies and their physical environment. Another aspect to be considered is the impact of remarkable scientific and technological advances that are causing unprecedented advances in the use and value of resources.

To understand the links between environmental problems and economic development in Latin America, we must understand the role assigned to this region ever since the Spaniards arrived and how natural resources were used up until the last fifty years. Over this long period the changes that have taken place have been so momentous and the pace has been such that the continent's ecological reality has been modified. A historical perspective should enable us to understand the rural and urban processes, the greater intensity of which in the decades prior to the crisis has clearly influenced the transformation of the region's spaces.

The crisis clearly shows the inadequacy of economic thinking in relation to the environment. Environmental deficiencies in economic theories sharpen a series of conflicts in the conceptualization of goods, assets, and planning horizons vis-à-vis output growth. In the coming decade and those immediately following, the region will face increasing environmental challenges. It is possible to anticipate a setting marked by adjustment policies and the shadow projected by global ecosystemic changes. Therefore, establishing policies with higher environmental sustainability will become a

185

top-priority political objective that will demand efforts to identify the structural causes of the environmental situation.

In realistic terms, a change in the prevailing social formation should not be expected. Rather, we should accept that what will most probably happen in Latin America is a continuation of ideological and political structures inherent to a system of dependent capitalism. Accordingly, the possible changes proposed will probably be restricted solely to policies.

The dominant thesis in this chapter is that Latin America's relation of dependence has conditioned the region's environmental situation. Such conditioning stems from the imposition of a highly stratified social structure in which a large proportion of the population lives in poverty. This structure is the basic cause of the depressed environmental situations that affect urban and rural marginal populations. The system through which poor societies relate to their physical environment has created the descending environmental spirals generated by the survival efforts of populations trying to make the best possible use of available resources.

On the other hand, the concentration of economic power has fostered systems that use and abuse environmental resources by means of multiple legal and illegal tactics, causing serious overexploitation processes. The general structure described above has managed to efficiently integrate the specific structure for generating, implementing, and disseminating technology by fostering the use of technologies that are dependent on the continuation of power relations despite their environmentally negative traits.

The Environment and Development Prior to the Crisis

A Historical View

On territorial appropriation by colonizers. When the Spaniards came to Latin America, they found the region organized into agricultural empires. The most outstanding empires were the Inca empire in Andean territory and the Aztec and Maya empires in the territories of Mexico and Guatemala. The rest of the region was occupied by ethnic groups who survived by hunting and fishing and incipient agricultural processes. The Spaniards disorganized these territories by breaking up the existing social and economic structures.[1]

The reorganization and the way in which the environment was used were oriented primarily to mining since the Spanish Crown tried to seize the maximum amount of resources, especially gold and silver. The Indian population supplied the labor force to work the mines and related services. Agriculture developed as a means to provide supplies to population settlements and forts maintained in the area by the Spanish Crown. The need to produce energy, both for operations and transportation, also determined how land was used and organized.

The energy needed to treat minerals was obtained basically from forests located close to the mines and foundries. For that reason, and despite the fact that population density was low at the time—even lower than before the conquest when there was a large Indian population that later suffered from the effects of the conquest, wars, and illness—land was abused through severe deforestation practiced in order to produce the energy required by foundries. In addition, minerals were taken to the ports by animal traction: mules, donkeys, and horses provided the basis for this type of transportation. These animals grazed in vast stretches of land that were for the most part overgrazed.

The Spanish conquest marked aspects that were decisive in the environmental management of Latin America during colonial times. First, the old cultures—which had, to a large extent, managed to successfully integrate society and the physical environment—were taken apart, especially in the highland empires. Empires, aside from being plundered, were subjected to disorganization in social, demographic, and structural terms. Second, agricultural production was initially oriented to serve mining purposes. However, when new agricultural and livestock products were incorporated, the extraction approach applied in mining continued to prevail vis-à-vis the region's agricultural resources. Third, as new territories were discovered, the belief that Latin America's natural resources were virtually infinite became widespread. This idea lasted for centuries, and in the course of time, it had an extremely negative effect on extraction rates and concern for preservation.

Finally, the way in which the territory was organized to suit the crown's objectives also bears mentioning. In general, land was reorganized according to the Spanish interest in populating regions that had greater prospects for mining operations. Therefore, Mexico and the highlands of Peru and Bolivia attracted the main efforts and enterprises. Although crops were very important for self-consumption and exports, farming areas were small compared to those that exist today. Demand for self-consumption was limited to the needs of a very small population, and exports were subordinate to transportation and the limitations imposed by international trade.[2]

Aside from mining operations, the region was gradually organized into a property structure established through different types of land grants and endowments—*encomiendas, mercedes, sesiones, comunidades subsesiorales,* and the like—bestowed by the Spanish kings. The land tenure system was based mainly on traditional colonial haciendas, large landed estates, small landholdings, and agricultural enclaves. The way in which agriculture was run and the conviction that soil was unlimited were factors that influenced the existence of planting methods that were incompatible with soil conservation (Cunill 1974).

The emergence of a mercantile bourgeoisie was one of the fundamental causes of Latin American independence. Thus, one of the basic characteristics of this period was efforts of the new nations to become involved in international trade by exploiting their natural resources. Regional economies thus became increasingly linked to the frequent and violent variations of world markets. Therefore, the treatment of natural resources and the environment suffered the ups and downs of these instabilities.

In general, the appropriation of productive resources by national owners had no significant influence over the fact that natural resources continued to be treated as mining resources (Di Filippo 1977). Territorial space was organized according to an ownership structure based on large, landed estates and supported by three elements: seignorial monopoly over agricultural land, the paternalistic ideology inherent to the *encomienda*, and hegemonic control over power-sharing and representation mechanisms (García 1969). These elements had a much greater influence on social structures and land use than mining operations. The development of mining and exports was associated with the denationalization of these industries, which in most cases was accomplished through enclaves.

No significant pressure was exerted in favor of expansion into and penetration of inland territories. Except for some subtropical and borderline tropical areas, based on the boom experienced in some crops such as rubber, the most relevant intervention took place in the ecosystems of temperate areas. Intervention in the tropics was restricted to coastal areas and to the implantation of ecological enclaves such as cotton, coffee, cacao, and sugar. Thus, countries changed their temperate areas and highlands significantly without expanding toward arid zones and the humid tropics.

On the accelerated transformations of the past fifty years. The political impact, the readjustment of world economies, and the modifications derived from World War II prompted major adjustments in the region's economy in the postwar period that forced countries to redefine their development processes. Latin America attempted to define its re-insertion into a dynamically everchanging and developing world.[3] The region's option was to try to achieve industrial and urban development through a pattern known as industrialization via import substitution. Between 1950 and 1960 the region's gross domestic product (GDP) rose at an average annual rate of 5 percent. Evidently, a uniform analysis of the development of that form of industrialization in all Latin American countries is not possible, since different patterns were used and then adapted to the specific conditions of each country, and each pattern adopted its own pace. However, in general terms, this development model prevailed in Latin America, producing unprecedented economic growth. This form of development had significant influence over aspects of the environment and natural resources.

A first aspect is the structural change that was generated by the high priority granted to industrial development. Mining and agriculture were no longer the main concerns, and therefore these sectors of the economy were left unprotected. In the 1950–1960 period, the share of agriculture in the GDP dropped from 20 percent to 14 percent. The remaining sectors changed very little, while the industrial production of manufactures rose from 18 percent to 23 percent.

A second aspect that had a clear bearing on how the environment was treated was that industrialization was based, particularly at first, on exploiting the natural resources of individual countries. Despite incipient industrialization processes based on imports of foreign natural resources, Latin American countries generally tried to channel their industrial development processes to an intensive use of their own resources.

Modernization was the third outstanding aspect of the structural transformations that took place in the years after World War II. Latin American societies—which in the preceding decades were primarily rural—were violently and irreversibly transformed into predominantly urban societies. Moreover, the new development model was based mainly on socioeconomic polarization, a fact that had noticeable environmental consequences. On the one hand, a strong capitalist sector developed and consolidated, and, on the other hand, the greater part of the population was excluded from progress and had to struggle to survive by adopting different strategies. Informal sectors began to develop and became increasingly important in the region.

In the agricultural sector this two-tier configuration was even more evident. On the one hand, there was a modern capitalist sector based on highly productive technology with regard to labor and capital and low labor intensity; on the other hand, there was a peasant sector based on traditional technologies applied to diversified production, which formed the basis of peasant survival strategy. These characteristics had a strong impact on the physical space, with evident environmental consequences.

The productive processes applied involved a high cost in environmental terms, mainly because their environmental sustainability was not questioned. Moreover, demographic factors caused significant changes in the population's spatial distribution by creating urban concentrations and a growing demand for resources, especially energy and water. The two-tier configuration drove many poor peasants to the cities, which, in turn, intensified environmental problems; some peasants emigrated to agricultural frontiers where they started processes of agricultural development involving high ecological costs, while others stayed on their properties and were compelled to overuse resources in order to survive. We shall analyze this aspect later on in the context of the most significant processes that currently exist in Latin America.

From the 1950s onward, and together with the process of industrialization via import substitution, an important change took place in the region's population dynamics. In general, the population increased significantly, but the evolvement of demographic changes was uneven from the perspective of space. Large urban concentrations developed as well as vast areas of low or very low population density. The main effect of population growth was a simultaneous increase in the demand for food, energy, and industrial crops, with the concurrent effect on the region's areas and territories.

Environmentally Significant Processes in Rural and Urban Latin America

The structure of agricultural and land tenure systems has been definitive in determining the region's environmental characteristics. Notwithstanding the heterogeneous and differing features of Latin America's agricultural development, it is necessary to analyze certain environmentally significant processes: agricultural modernization, expansion of the agricultural frontier, peasant survival, and transformation of the urban space.[4]

Agricultural modernization. The process of agricultural modernization is understood as the momentum provided by capital and technology that tends to substantially modify productivity levels. This momentum is inclined toward homogeneity, since it tends to reproduce the technological systems and the combination of inputs used in the countries where these originated. Another characteristic of the process is that it produces expansion in certain areas, which prevents matching new technologies with knowledge of their ecological impacts. Technologies are applied without previous research studies; frequently, research only serves to verify the deterioration produced by inadequate technology. These characteristics, and the effects of the process, shall be described below. However, for the purposes of this chapter, modernization shall be understood as the overall process mentioned above, including all its characteristics and effects, which evidently go beyond the possibilities of a single theoretical approach. Thus, modernization should not be confused with technological and scientific progress; even certain undertakings that may be classified as inherent to modernization should be objected to from a technical or scientific perspective, such as, for example, pollution caused by intensive use of pesticides.

Given the peculiar features of the agricultural sector, the penetration of a new form of development has taken on special characteristics. In more permeable sectors, which lack the tradition or the weighty structural conformation of agriculture, this development pattern has managed to penetrate more quickly. Modernization processes in the manufacturing industry, for example, have speeded up when faced with the possibility of product obsolescence, a situation that does not occur in agriculture. In agriculture, the usual process is to shift from one product to another, but different responses to the development pattern are based on systems and forms that are suited to modernization, or others that offer more resistance to modernization.

Latin American agriculture has increased threefold in the past forty years. This growth stems from the extension of cultivated land and increased productivity. Natural conditions, on the one hand, and the characteristics of the progression of the development pattern, on the other, have helped to shift relative weight from one process to another—particularly in recent years—and will become especially important for future projection. In other words, the relative importance of land productivity in Latin America's agricultural output is increasing progressively and is directly related to the process of modernization. It should be noted that modernization and expansion are neither mutually excluding nor comparable processes. Modernization has penetrated all areas, to a lesser or greater extent; therefore, it is also present in some expansion systems. Furthermore, modernization is precisely one of the reasons why the agricultural frontier has expanded.

Several Latin American countries have tried to modernize their agriculture by applying different development strategies. The goal pursued by most countries has been to modernize agriculture by promoting greater reinvestment of agricultural surpluses, and by fostering capital investment, either from other sectors or from abroad. The dominant groups in the domestic agricultural sector have concentrated the greater part of investments in infrastructure, thus contributing to a global concentration that responds to the prevailing pattern.[5]

In areas favored by comparative advantages, the production of which is mainly oriented to exports, the phenomena and processes described above are extremely evident. In these areas agricultural modernization has received strong state support: irrigation works have been undertaken in places where investment is most profitable; agricultural activity has required, and been supplied with, energy; the demand for inputs has given rise to distribution centers. Increased output has made it necessary to build storage and packing centers or processing agroindustries. Agricultural machinery needs maintenance and repair shops. All these activities require skilled labor, and therefore training centers, schools, and health and trade services have been established. In other words, concentration encourages concentration.

Profitability is one of the chronic problems of Latin American undertakings. The prevailing pattern has also helped to increase dissimilarity in this aspect. On the one hand, there are export-oriented farms with comparative advantages that are able to generate a surplus; on the other hand, there are farms that produce for domestic consumption, have profitability problems, and produce almost no surplus, together with scores of subsistence small landholdings. There are also medium-sized farms. Some, influenced by the development pattern, attract surpluses, raise capital, and usually form associations or national or transnational trusts; others, however, lose capital, break up, are overexploited, and fall into subsistence economy.

By managing public investment, power groups—usually linked to the owners of highly profitable lands—have benefited from investment trends and received high subsidies. Several research studies point out that investments in infrastructure are paid only partially by the farmer, and the corresponding discrimination mentioned above has given rise to serious economic and social problems. Usually, resources assigned to public works are allocated by economic sector; in this allocation the weight of the hegemonic sectors has been decisive.

Preferential treatment has also been given to hegemonic sectors through other state policies such as prices, loans, and inputs. Furthermore, the model for generating technology has adjusted almost automatically to the products from these areas due to demand, their significance as generators of foreign currency, and the influence of transnational enterprises that handle technologies and offer technological inputs.

Therefore, the model fostering technological generation, adoption, and dissemination has tended to reproduce modernization in agriculture, make it more dependent on the use of technological inputs, and promote its specialization in terms of the international market and the new consumption patterns that prevail in domestic markets. Modernization surfaced so powerfully after World War II that it caused an important qualitative change in Latin American agriculture, both in modes of production and in social relations. Agriculture today is undoubtedly radically different than the agriculture of thirty years ago. Although traditional systems and forms are still maintained, the way the process is conducted has changed, with a clear dominance of modernizing forms that have forcefully influenced technological change in agriculture.

The technological model has promoted the use of technological packages (inseparably linked sets of procedures), thus fostering a process whereby ecosystems are built up and made as artificial as possible and made to depend heavily on energy subsidies (fertilizers and agricultural mechanization). The introduction of agricultural machinery is related to the possibility of displacing agricultural workers. On the one hand, population growth has meant a constant increase in the labor supply. On the other hand, the rigidity of labor demand in Latin American agriculture, together with special seasonal characteristics, has led to an extremely high rate of equivalent unemployment.[6]

The breakup of the large landed estate and small landholding complemental structure—which previously predominated in Latin America—worsened the problem of employment and, therefore, led to migration and the use and abuse of resources. It should be noted that the population in many areas consisting of small landholdings or held by small farmers has decreased; however, this smaller population has increasingly less access to agricultural work outside farms. Traditional, large landed estates, by adopting capital intensive technologies and mechanizing the work, have reduced job opportunities for peasants. The situation has become even worse due to successive land divisions that have caused small landholdings to proliferate.

Under these circumstances peasants have been forced to take certain measures to survive. First, they have tried to raise production rates by overexploiting the soil, thereby creating one of the main causes of erosion (see Table 7.1). Second, a considerable percentage of peasants has emigrated to urban centers, giving rise to a number of well-known problems. Third, these supernumerary sectors have moved to virgin areas. They have thus increased colonization processes (either spontaneous or directed) with the corresponding destructive effect on natural resources, which is added to the destructive effect of large penetration companies. Peasants usually complement the work carried out by these companies in exchange for using a piece of land by assuming a commitment to return it "clean." Given growing migration, deterioration has become noticeably worse: new lands are used for agricultural purposes when they are really more suitable for forest farming, livestock farming, or mixed activities. Ignorance about the new areas should be added to these deterioration factors. This lack of information is not limited to companies and colonizers; frequently, it also extends to technical and scientific staff. Thus, a phenomenon of unprecedented magnitude has taken place: the occupation of forest areas and tropical and subtropical savannahs, with the corresponding progressive and alarming deterioration.

Table 7.1. Erosion in Selected Countries, 1970–1986

Country	Area and Localization	Affected Area as % of the Total Country	Amount of Erosion (ton/year)	Erosion Rate (ton/ha/year)	Estimation Year
Argentina Brazil Paraguay	Cuenca del Plata	—	95×10^6	18.8	—
Peru	Entire country	100	1.9×10^9	15.0	—
Jamaica	Total land under cultivation (205,595 ha)	19	7.4×10^9	36.0	1980s
El Salvador	Cuenca de Acelhuate	2	—	19–190	1970s
Dominican Rep.	Región Boa	0.2	—	346	1970s

Source: World Resources Institute (1988) *World Resources 1988–1989*, New York: Basic Books Inc.

Despite demographic pressure—which promotes the spontaneous occupation of the land—major deterioration in tropical and subtropical forest
areas is apparently caused by the activities of large livestock companies,
which try to "clean" the ecosystem through precarious tenure or the use of
agricultural machinery with unparalleled power.

Expansion of the agricultural frontier. The expansion of the agricultural
frontier in Latin America has been basically induced by four factors.[7]
First, it has been induced by the survival needs of poor people driven from
farming areas and marginal urban zones. Peasant migrations are due to the
limited or nonexistent increase in labor demand, which is less than the
supply generated by population growth. Second, agricultural expansion
took place in response to demand for certain livestock and agricultural
products, either for export or consumption by the country's more developed and urbanized areas (Katzman 1975). Third, active state involvement
to encourage the occupation of new lands should be noted. This phenomenon dates back to the beginning of the Latin American countries and
was brought about by the concern of rulers to populate national territories
and "develop sovereignty." Together with the depletion of the easily
accessible lands, this process lost dynamism. State action was renewed as
of the second half of the twentieth century, particularly in Brazil, where
numerous colonization projects were carried out. Fourth, and more recently, speculation has stimulated the expansion of the agricultural frontier
in pursuit of profits (Mueller 1983).

Despite these four factors, and notwithstanding the fact that the expansion process continues, its relative importance in increasing agricultural output is inferior to that of increasing land productivity. However,
most Latin American countries grant great importance to the process of
expanding the frontier, due both to the growth of domestic agricultural
output and to social and geopolitical reasons. Strategies applied by countries that foster this process are based on the fact that Latin America has
vast stretches of yet uncolonized and virgin territory or territory used only
for fruit gathering, hunting and fishing, and selective harvesting of some
woodland species that fetch high prices. However, these potential resources have two limitations:

1. Great fragility and vulnerability of ecosystems. Expansion takes
place primarily in the humid tropics, mainly around the Amazon or in the
Atlantic areas of Central America and Mexico, where the fragility and tendency to deteriorate are obvious. Other ecosystems liable to be occupied
are tropical and subtropical savannahs and subtropical forests such as the
Orinoco and Chaco plains, which, despite being less vulnerable, are also
fragile and degradable. Semi-arid areas that present frontier phenomena

are even more difficult to manage due to the conditioning factors posed by water scarcity. Consequently, ecosystem degradation poses an additional problem: the loss of productive potential. This loss is not easily measured because expansion processes tend to make the agricultural output grow, which is what is actually computed. Nothing is said about the ecological cost involved in achieving a given growth in output.

2. Access difficulties. Almost all expansion areas are located in the continent's inland areas. This requires major investments in infrastructure for communication and transportation. This aspect is so relevant that in many countries the government can easily induce occupancy by building highways or establishing regular inland waterway routes.

Despite these limitations, one statement is irrefutable: countries need to expand their agricultural frontier. Hence, the question for the future is not how to clarify the antinomy of whether to "freeze" the frontier or expand it, but rather centers on clarifying how to expand the agricultural frontier while minimizing ecological costs in order to establish sustainable and feasible long term development areas.[8]

From the 1940s onward the processes of industrialization and urbanization and the demand for export products and livestock production were still the main causes of expansion, but the crisis of the farming sector also contributed strongly to the process. In traditional areas the new pattern led to the modernization of large landed estates and middle-sized undertakings, the introduction of capital intensive technologies, and, hence, to a progressive drop in labor demand, which, as already mentioned, drives farmers to the agricultural frontier or the cities.

Large, capitalist companies with important capital endowments can be found in the areas of penetration, and they can either stay in agriculture or take their business elsewhere if circumstances so warrant. These companies (particularly transnational corporations) rationalize their activity so as to maximize their invested capital without taking into account factors such as resource conservation or how long their ownership will last. Soil and forests are "harvested" with the concurrent environmental deterioration. Once these are depleted, the company expands the frontier either by leaving or selling the depleted land. The penetration rate has been very swift because all kinds of high-powered machinery have been used for land development. To the above we must add the availability of cheap fuel, which lasted until oil prices began to rise.

To these land development methods we must add traditional systems: large landed estates devoted to livestock production or forestry and livestock farming. In this combination, plots are assigned to peasants driven from traditional areas who clear the plots and later cultivate the land for some time. This land is then incorporated into a larger farm and new, undeveloped plots are assigned to peasants. Companies use all available methods to achieve their objectives: rentals, sharecropping, concessions, and the like.

The occupation of space has either been unplanned or executed through controlled colonization programs. Due to the specific conditions of newly incorporated areas, unplanned colonization has resulted from the implementation of specific policies such as the building of penetration highways. Unlike planned occupancy, this form of penetration is characterized by its low cost per colonizer and the fact that it contributes a high percentage of the total number of migrants.

As Pinto (1975) says: "Colonization processes are far from being a success; in socioeconomic terms, most of them are failures." In addition to factors such as insufficient financial support and training, poor organization, and lack of rational planning, these failures are attributed to the fact that ecological characteristics were not seriously considered and to the lack of adequate physical infrastructure.[9]

The expansion of agriculture's productive area has caused evident changes in ecosystems. Worthy of note among these are severe erosion and deforestation processes, both closely correlated, especially in sloping areas and/or in areas with water deficits. The magnitudes and rates of deforestation may be suitable indicators of the expansion of the agricultural frontier in the humid tropics. Unfortunately, these evaluations are complex and heterogeneous. Only some countries keep adequate records (see Table 7.2).

The expansion process has had other environmental effects, such as erosion, sedimentation of waterways, loss of genetic diversity, and climate changes. This raises the question of whether the contribution to domestic economies is sufficiently significant to warrant the irreversible deterioration of occupied areas. Several studies on the matter show indisputably that the contribution to the GDP generated in frontier expansion areas is quite limited. Apparently, the basic objective of colonization policies fostered in various countries in the region and the expansions induced is not the economy, but rather geopolitical goals—to populate certain areas—and survival strategy functions targeted at poor people in areas with growing social problems.

Peasant survival. The Latin American peasant world is heterogeneous, complex, and diversified. Nevertheless, there is a common pattern: the struggle to survive. The conditioning factors of the prevailing development pattern have turned this struggle into highly significant processes with regard to the environment. Many of these processes can be described, ranging from the problems faced by peasants in the highlands of Mexico or Central America, to those of the *Polígono das Secas* in Brazil and those of the Chaco plains. This study has selected the Andean highland peasants, due to their limited availability of resources, the size of the population involved, and the specific forms of social organization.

Table 7.2. South America: Forest Resources and Deforestation, 1980s

Country	Jungle and Forest Area		Deforestation 1980s	
	Open	Closed	Annual Amount	Annual
	(thousands of hectares)		(thousands of ha/year)	Rate (%)
Argentina	—	44,500	15.50	3.5
Bolivia	22,750	44,010	1.17	0.2
Brazil	157,000	357,480	23.23	0.5
Chile	—	7,550	0.50	0.7
Colombia	5,300	46,400	8.90	1.7
Ecuador	480	14,250	3.40	2.3
Guyana	220	18,475	0.30	0.0
Paraguay	15,640	4,070	2.12	1.1
Peru	960	69,860	2.70	0.4
Surinam	170	14,830	0.30	0.0
Uruguay	—	490	—	—
Venezuela	2,000	31,870	2.45	0.7

Source: World Resources Institute (1988) *World Resources 1988–1989*, New York: Basic Books Inc.

Most Andean highland ecosystems have been so affected by the action of humans that many are undergoing an obvious process of deterioration. Physical and climatic conditioning factors such as rainfall, rainfall distribution, temperatures, thermal ranges, frosts, and winds, in addition to soil elements such as the basic material of soils and geomorphology, have helped to establish low biomass ecosystems, vulnerable to disturbances—especially those caused by humans—with poor support and an exclusive type of fauna that is difficult to preserve.

Elsewhere in the world, high basins are scarcely populated or not populated at all; therefore, the analysis shall focus only on human actions on the physical environment rather than on the social and productive situation of resident populations. In the Andean area the problem centers on the need to survive and the development possibilities for local communities. These communities have to manage in a fragile and very vulnerable environment, in which the social, economic, and cultural transformations suffered since colonial times have led to complex readjustments in the ways of using and managing natural resources, with the resulting disturbances (Figueroa 1981; Universidad Nacional Agraria La Molina and Centro de Estudios Rurales Andino Bartolomé de las Casas 1986).

By analyzing the size of population settlements in these highland ecosystems, we may infer that these are the most important highland-populated areas in the world. Ecuador, Peru, and Bolivia have approximately twelve million inhabitants on lands located 2,500 meters above sea level or higher. In Ecuador the obvious ecological difference between the mountains and the coastal area marks a clear distinction between their ecosystems and populations. In Bolivia the move east is relatively recent, and population settlements in the lowlands, whether in Yungas, Llanos de Mamoré, or Chaco, constitute an obvious minority.

In Peru the problem is more complex, and therefore it is necessary to describe it. Analysis of data on the concentration of rural populations at different altitudes in Peru shows that 60 percent of the country's rural population is concentrated at the 2,000 to 4,000 meter level, 17 percent live on the coast, and 10 percent live in the jungle area. Obviously, when analyzing the entire population, these figures change due to the importance of coastal population centers, especially in Lima. However, concentration in coastal areas is under 50 percent. Ecological regions located at altitudes over 2,000 meters (Quechua, Suni, and Puna) account for 30 percent of the total population.[10]

In rural populations the most important components are joint-ownership communities of peasant families. In Peru, according to data from the ministry of agriculture, in 1980 there were 3,030 peasant communities representing 39 percent of the country's total rural population and 58 percent of peasant economies (Peru, Ministerio de Agricultura 1980). Of the total land held by the communities (19,023,394 hectares), 84 percent was located in the mountains (Gonzáles de Olarte 1984). Consequently, this relatively high population density exerts pressure to use fragile and scant resources. A type of vicious circle is created: resources deteriorate according to the extent to which they are overused, and therefore the availability of products decreases, whether they are used for self-consumption or for commercial purposes, which in turn leads to greater overexploitation.

A series of ecological characteristics make these spaces very fragile and vulnerable to human action. Since the major limitations are climate related, human activity has built up the environment by using it for livestock farming, handling wildlife, and adjusting and improving plant breeding. Most of these territories are drylands because irrigation is greatly limited due to its cost—lowlands with climates suitable for agriculture are always preferred—and also because of the natural limitation inherent to the soil and slopes. Since climates cannot be altered, there is a low probability of producing effects by modifying the great limitations—water, temperature, and energy. Thus, the artificial building up of the environment is very limited—except in the rare irrigated areas—and in general, if it is carried out with a conservationist approach, the basic characteristics of the ecosystem should not change radically.

The dramatic situation of the Andean highland peasants has been of constant concern to governments, social scientists, and planning experts. Aside from certain policies that have served to partially improve their status, the overall situation is very precarious. Peasant economies have not become incorporated into the capitalist development of agriculture as such. Peasant forms of agricultural production may be classified as mercantile and noncapitalist. Their articulation with the capitalist economy is through mercantile circulation.

This situation, described in general terms, offers several variations for insertion, according to the space occupied, organization of markets, and facilities for communication, storage, and distribution. But, despite these different levels of interaction, peasant economies constitute specific forms of peasant family subsistence in highland ecosystems. Therefore, it is important to inquire into how the prevailing development pattern in Latin America has influenced the highland peasants during the past years.

The development of agroindustries might be viewed as an important process in modernizing agriculture in Andean countries, especially in relation to exportable products and those that constitute their basic input; however, this development has helped to produce few new products. Many basic foodstuffs have remained stagnant or even decreased. After World War II the dependency of Andean countries regarding foodstuffs increased, and imported food has become increasingly more essential. Changes in consumption patterns have made per capita consumption increase with regard to several products—wheat, oil-seeds, rice, and dairy products, for example—while consumption of other products has dropped. Consequently, an element that apparently could have fostered agricultural development—agroindustrialization—fulfills this function only in relation to very few products.

The second important aspect to be considered in analyzing the situation of highland peasants is their physical location and their organization into communes, microregions, and regions, in the context of their relation with the central economies. Social organization among highland peasants is based on the community, which centers on family, community, and wage relations. The first arises in the midst of family land use; the second is based on reciprocal and collective obligations and work *(mingajos, faenas);* and the third, wages paid in money and in kind to complement income without necessarily entailing proletarization, is due to its relative importance.

The income of the various families that make up the community is not homogeneous, given the differences in resources available to each. Indeed—and this is a central aspect in this analysis—communal land does not cover a single, ecological floor, but rather it covers different altitudes. Family plots are located at different levels and each family can breed its own animals. Therefore, there are usually three major forms of land use: family-run plots; sharecropping between families from the same or different communities; and communal operations, usually livestock farming on grazing lands located in the uppermost areas. The differences in resource stocks that each family possesses give rise to different forms of production relationships. However, the basic fact is that different peasant families are organized into communities in a given territory and that their relationships arise from the need for labor integration and the exchange of products.

The development pattern that has prevailed over the past decades has had very evident effects on regional and microregional economies, particularly everything related to the commodities markets. On the one hand, the different valuations of agricultural products, the lack of incentives, and the relative deterioration of prices have resulted in lower monetary incomes for the peasant sector. In addition, the building of public roads and the arrival of agroindustries have made trade networks more complex, in which surpluses are appropriated in different stages. On the other hand, the undervaluation of local production has prevented certain products from reaching the market—some of which were an important part of everyday meals—because prices for these products have been either too low or practically nonexistent.

Consequently, changes in mercantile relations have led to marked differences between microregions. However, the greatest problems have arisen in the terms of trade between community members. Undoubtedly, in terms of the relative levels of productive specialization, economic modifications produce notorious differentiation processes among peasants. And at this point the environment appears as a basic determinant. In the past community integration and trade between different altitude floors was dependent on maintaining a self-supply equilibrium in the communities. Newly acquired purchasing power that provoked the overvaluation of some products (compared to previous situations) and the impact of the undervaluation of other products have broken up this self-consumption equilibrium, with consequent inconveniences. Some peasants have increased their income, others have reduced it and been forced to sell their labor to other communities in the microregion or even in other microregions.

However, the problem is not restricted to the above. Changes in consumption habits and the pressure for certain production inputs have led peasants to try to obtain higher monetary incomes, seek greater skills, and distinguish their capacity in their own community. And this is how the community's process of disintegration begins, together with clear processes of differentiation and proletarization.

The physical environment has had to bear the effects of several social adjustment processes. First, there have been attempts to increase cultivated areas; these have involved extending agriculture to higher altitudes, thus creating the risk of frosts, and, above all, of affecting sectors that are more fragile. Second, there has been a tendency to overuse the land—a frequent situation in peasant communities—which has produced severe erosion (Felipe-Morales 1987). Third, peasants have tried, within their own means, to intensify crops, and to adopt some technological innovations (fertilizers and use of pesticides).

Although peasant communities have felt the weight of the progression of this pattern, environmental conditioning factors and age-old social organization have evidently restrained its influence. Hence, the disintegration process takes on different forms, depending on various factors: the environment in which it takes place, the solidity and functionality of social organization, and the influence of urban centers, specialization, and culture.

Special mention should be made regarding the role of the state. With slight variations, the different states supported the expansion of capitalist development during the 1970s. There were contradictory policies, but agricultural sectors felt the weight of the influence exerted by a worldwide boom of modernization of the green revolution type. This greatly favored the model's penetration at the central level and produced serious alterations in regional economies based on peasant economies. The presence of the state has made itself felt at regional and microregional levels through the infrastructures and goods and services that have acted as regional income redistribution factors. However, due to the characteristics imposed by the development pattern, many of these infrastructures have intensified regional and intraregional differences.

Transformation of the urban space: expansion and metropolization. As mentioned above, one of the most important processes that has characterized the region during the past decade is the high rate of urbanization and metropolization. This has implied a major transformation of productive structures based on significant changes in economic, political, and cultural performances that have centered increasingly on urban areas (Sabatini and Jordán 1986).[11]

Growth rates and population settlement systems have differed greatly. Human settlements are the outcome of a series of distinct factors and processes that arise in different forms in the region's countries. However, some overall patterns may be identified in these settlements, such as original settlements on sea and river coastal areas. As mentioned previously, a remarkable fact in Latin America, rooted in pre-Columbian cultures, is that a significant part of the population lives in areas located between 2,000 and 2,500 meter above sea level.

Urbanization rates in Latin America are considerably higher than worldwide averages and even higher than other Third World regions. By the end of this century, these tendencies will make the region one of the most urbanized areas on earth. The dynamics of urbanization processes are based on the crisis caused by the development pattern prevailing in the rural sector. The acute process of eviction of rural inhabitants was the outcome of the agricultural development pattern based on reducing the labor force and increasing land productivity. This was the essential factor underlying the increase in urban population in the 1950s and 1960s. In the 1970s migration was not limited to rural-urban migration but included migratory movements from small urban centers to medium and large centers. At present, rural populations do not move directly from the country to large urban centers or metropolitan areas; instead, they tend to pass through these intermediate centers that, in demographic terms, are still quite dynamic.

The urbanization process in Latin America in the past decades developed further homogeneous characteristics. First, a strong concentration of population and economic activity, particularly industrial activity, developed in large metropolitan areas. Almost 40 percent of Argentina's population is concentrated in Buenos Aires, and 40 percent of Chile's population is gathered in the area of Greater Santiago. Mexico City and São Paulo are examples of megapolises that are almost impossible to manage. Second, another important characteristic has been the evident growth of precarious settlements in so-called marginal areas. This growth has occurred in both absolute and relative terms. In Lima marginal settlements represent 50 percent of the population; in Guayaquil the figure is even higher; in Caracas it is 35 percent; and in Santiago, Chile, 25 percent. Third, the concentration of political power and, in general, cultural modification processes in cities have changed lifestyles, especially consumption patterns. This phenomenon has determined how resources are used. The outcome in intermediate and large cities has been greater deterioration of the human environment and increased poverty.

According to *pobladores* (shantytown dwellers), environmental problems are closely linked to survival and minimum living standards. This perception normally differs from technical views. Areas developed for settlement by poor populations are poorly equipped, and the inhabitants are therefore subjected to serious risks derived from a precarious situation. People living on steep slopes are subject to landslides during rainy seasons; those that live near river beds run the risk of floods. Latin America registers an increasing number of these disasters due to this situation.

Precarious settlements in Latin America are affected by problems of living standards regarding basic needs. Lack of sewers causes serious health problems. Insufficient or totally lacking drinking water not only involves health risks but also a waste of time in fetching water, due to the limited number of water fountains or pipes available to the whole settlement. Soil pollution due to excrements or to closeness to sectors that discharge industrial waste is another factor that seriously affects the region's urban populations. Incomplete urbanization and the lack of pavement obstructs traffic and hampers individual circulation, in addition to the risks involved in walking through mud and its consequences for human health.

The serious problems of Latin America's urbanization process not only affect the poorer sectors; at present, they are spreading to the rest of the community. Air pollution is a process currently affecting all urban sectors; however, it is usually much more acute in areas near large industrial centers. Problems such as air pollution have reached critical dimensions in Mexico City, São Paulo, and Santiago, which are considered among the most air-polluted cities in the world.

Time wasted in transport is another aspect to be considered since it poses severe problems. Megapolization of Latin American cities and precarious public transport slow down traffic. Average speeds of 6 to 8 kilometers per hour for public buses are common in some sectors of Latin American cities. This has a negative effect on air pollution and is a considerable waste of time for people traveling to and from work.

The inference is evident that pollution problems stem from deficient management of both urban and industrial city waste. Perhaps this is one of the most postponed problems in Latin America—which must unavoidably be dealt with—where a major, relative backwardness may be found in relation to environmental management in other regions. The problem of urban waste has not been addressed comprehensively, and it is still a bottleneck that is hard to solve in Latin America. Major Latin American cities, particularly the poorer sectors, are being invaded by waste discarded haphazardly.

An extremely serious and growing problem in the region is the loss of agricultural land through urban expansion. We must remember that Latin American population settlements were established in areas with the best temperate and subtropical soils in highly fertile valleys that were selected by the Spaniards to resemble their native habitat. Many cities were established in highly productive irrigated lands. One of the characteristics of the urbanization process is a very low-density, horizontal expansion that has resulted in the use of vast areas of land for nonagricultural purposes. For example, Santiago, Chile, with four and a half million inhabitants, occupies an area that is two and a half to three times the area covered by Paris with eight million inhabitants.

Given the projections of the process of metropolization and urbanization in Latin America, it is certain that if, by the end of this century and the beginning of the next, land use systems are not regulated efficiently, the area in use will be extremely extended and have a very negative effect on agricultural production. A projection for the year 2000 calculated in Chile shows that only 2 percent of the continental area will be used for urban purposes. This 2 percent of the national territory is equal to approximately 1,500,000 hectares. It should be noted that irrigated land in Chile covers 1,600,000 hectares and that large cities, particularly those in the central zone, are located there. Therefore, we may infer that the country's most productive area (where 80 percent of production is generated) will be seriously endangered in the next few years. This is also the case in Mexico, Peru, Colombia, and most of the other countries in the region.

Environmental Deficits in Economic Thinking

Economic Theories and the Environment

In the past few years several studies have tried to analyze and interpret the relation between development and the environment. Many researchers believe that concern for ecological issues is quite recent, due to the environmental crisis that is affecting the region (García Hurtado and García D'Acuña 1980; Mansilla 1981: 9). However, this concern has existed for a long time. At present, it has probably been taken on by dominant sectors and decisionmaking centers because they have also felt threatened.

Undoubtedly, the debate on population growth and the availability of natural resources has attracted more attention than the progressive degradation of nature, or even pollution problems. The political crisis caused by the demographic problem and the pressure it exerts on resources gave rise to several studies on the subject throughout the world, particularly in Latin America.[12] Perhaps many of these studies, generated through evidence from other regions, may have helped to identify the region's environmental problems.

The lack of response and the limited or nonexistent treatment of environmental problems in classical and neoclassical economic theories motivated some individuals, particularly in the 1970s, to question these theories and motivated others to propose some supplements and modifications. Studies were centered on trying to challenge, from an environmental viewpoint, principles regarding the virtues of the market as the organizer of an efficient economy, and as a tool to detect environmental problems.[13]

These criticisms led to certain basic conclusions regarding the inclusion of environmental issues in development planning and management. The conclusion drawn was that the Pareto optimum proposed by advocates of neoclassical theory does not necessarily conform to the environmental optimum. This is essential to understand the rationale applied by decisionmakers to the use of resources.[14] On the other hand, many physical changes in the environment that exceed the limits of reversibility do not necessarily provide the corresponding economic evidence, which obviously complicates any analysis of the environment.[15] Furthermore, solving environmental problems through bilateral negotiation (the Coase Theorem) does not appear possible (Coase 1960).[16] These problems led classical and neoclassical theoreticians to proposes innovative approaches to correct the deficiencies described. Thus, there are some authors who hold that ownership systems determine the use of resources and are therefore the basic cause of environmental problems.

Although Marxist approaches do not explicitly acknowledge the importance of environmental problems—analysis is centered on social and political considerations regarding economies—they do delve deeper into the diversity of modes of production. These approaches therefore focus on analyzing the rationale underlying different systems for resource use derived from different technical and social relations. Furthermore, complex planning systems offer easier options for incorporating the environmental issue. However, different patterns in socialist systems give rise to a series of questions on the different solutions used to deal with environmental problems and management (Sunkel 1981).

Integrationist, or holistic, approaches have emerged, together with criticism of economic theories and the views of economists regarding the new challenges. Integral approaches to interpret development prospects are proposed, giving priority to treating the planet as an ecosystem while pointing out the physical limitations inherent to the development process. This led to the Club of Rome report—prepared at the Massachusetts Institute of Technology—which helped to open up the debate on world development prospects with zero population growth and a reduction of economic growth (Meadows et al. 1972).[17] Latin America replied to this proposal by endorsing the World Model suggested by the Fundación Bariloche. Instead of focusing on physical limitations, this model points to the need for redistributive strategies preferably oriented toward satisfying basic needs (Herrera et al. 1971).[18] In addition, a series of papers prepared according to neo-Malthusian viewpoints has been published.[19]

Global approaches centered on the polemic limits of growth were dealt with from the perspective of energy, by defining flows and transformations in terms of energy and proposing unidimensional analyses of their balances.[20] Other analyses explored the causes of environmental problems by associating them with technology, social organization, and economic structures.[21] These analyses gave rise to differing interpretations by developed and underdeveloped countries (Commoner 1976). The Founex report, prepared for the United Nations Conference on Human Environment, introduced the concept of human environment. Studies that have delved deeper into this concept clearly associate it with development strategies. In Latin America the effort to incorporate environmental issues in development approaches was complemented by introducing the concept of development patterns. The latter's behavior determines different environmental situations.[22]

From all these proposals, standpoints, interpretations, and studies, some conclusions may be drawn that should help to include environmental concepts to a greater extent in development theories and practice. On such a basis the different agents can avoid the lengthy learning process that they would face if these studies had not been carried out. The main conclusions are:

1. The market is not a suitable mechanism to detect the environmental aspects of development, and if any knowledge exists, it is limited or has a clear time lag. In the original neoclassical model the environment is a typical example of an externality and is consequently considered as such.

2. Physical, ecological, political, social, or economic laws cannot be classified on the same hierarchic level. The fact that social and political sciences cannot alter fundamental physical laws is easily understandable. However, this is not so evident when dealing with complex ecological laws. It is important to understand how these behave in order to understand their hierarchy with respect to social and political laws.

3. New requirements regarding resources and space do not automatically require a technological answer. At times, society is incapable of providing technological solutions to many of its problems. Thus, no optimistic predictions should be made on the basis of the myth of humanity's ability to react, since this poses the risk of irreversible catastrophes.

4. Ecosystems have a limited sustainability capacity, which, if exceeded, makes the ecosystem deteriorate. Economic development tends toward the limits of sustainability. This concept provides an interesting variable to interpret economic and social development, particularly regarding the time that it takes to reach the limits or to exceed them. From an environmental viewpoint this fact points to the importance of long term planning.

5. Sustainability is not a rigid concept linked exclusively to the limits of resource supply or, in other words, to the physical environment. Social and cultural capacity makes it possible to modify sustainability. That is why environmental management, conceived as the intelligent mobilization of society's social and cultural capacity to transform its physical environment, would make it possible to transform nature in positive terms and, consequently, modify sustainability.

6. There is a noticeable lag between the economic horizons of producers and the ecological horizons regarding the environment, which become particularly significant when the different rationales applied by different types of producers are analyzed.

*Controversy on the Concept of Goods, Planning Horizons,
and Growth-Equity*

Economic and environmental goods. The development pattern of the past decades promoted a dual form that helps the pattern of dependent capitalism to develop and increase its penetration. Analysis of the environmental issue has corroborated that capitalist companies in Latin America are, in general, trying to internalize benefits and externalize costs.

The internalization of benefits first involves an appropriation of certain environmental goods, which also are social goods, and the externalization of costs due to the lack of *ex-profeso* valuation of certain environmental goods. Serious theoretical efforts have been made to internalize costs, but in the light of prevailing theories and existing economic instruments, these efforts are a dead end: some instruments are refined so as to price invaluable goods, or those not easily valuable. This problem becomes more relevant in Latin America due to the structural instability that makes it very difficult to determine many basic economic parameters required to internalize costs. Therefore, the basic problem lies in the fact that many environmental goods do not pass through the economic circuit and therefore have no market price. Efforts to assign market prices are mere instrumental sophistications that do not contribute much to specific solutions.

Now, if the Latin American situation is analyzed in detail in relation to the penetration of the development pattern of the past decades, we will find that private appropriation of environmental goods not accomplished through the economic market has increased. Moreover, there have been some efforts to avoid internalizing some costs derived from the use of the environment that could be evaluated. Land is the most typical case. Land is a social good, but because it is appropriated privately in Latin America, it has a market value. However, the fact that someone privately owns a social good such as land does not necessarily mean that he/she owns the environmental goods surrounding that land. The landowner does not own the complicated interactions derived from the fact that the land is located in a given basin. It also does not mean that an individual owns part of the water cycle that obviously passes through the land nor that he/she owns part of the carbon cycle. Nor does it mean that the person owns the flora and roving fauna. All these goods do not pass through the market, or if they do, they do so very tangentially, as in the case of fauna. It is normal for landowners to feel that these environmental resources are an integral part of their property.

The use of natural resources and their depletion has worried theoretical economists who, rather than creating new theoretical proposals, have tried to observe and analyze the possibilities of making economic theories compatible with the specific realities of the different countries. In the United States in-depth studies on the depletion of natural resources appeared only after World War II. Almost all these studies hold that technological progress amply compensates for the depletion of the most productive sources of natural resources (Barnett and Morsen 1963). In other words, theoretical analyses state that the extraction rates of renewable and nonrenewable natural resources pose no problems because the market and the pricing system should regulate them efficiently. Evidently this entire proposal, as well as that suggested by Fisher and Peterson (1976), is incompatible with what is going on in Latin America and the world. And this analysis has been applied to the resources that actually enter the market. The position of theoreticians is much more uncomfortable with regard to efforts to bring into the market resources that are currently not in the economic circuit.

The contradiction between economic and environmental goods also appears with regard to the externalization of costs. In general, depending on the characteristics of the development pattern, environmental goods that do not pass through the economic circuit are obviously not considered internal costs but tend to become externalized. This requires no major efforts. However, efforts have centered on demonstrating that other goods, which may be quantified in economic terms, should be considered as externalities in Latin America. An example of this is the entire infrastructure or the artificial building-up of the environment to provide irrigation. For several decades Latin America has developed irrigation infrastructures that may be viewed as naturalized capital assets. It is frequently assumed that these goods and their maintenance correspond to operation externalities and that, from the private viewpoint, their maintenance has zero cost.

Environmental conflict in the economic planning horizon. The rationale applied by the main productive actors operating in the different economic sectors tends to overvaluate the short term to the detriment of the long term. This is logical if one considers that capitalist producers try to obtain the maximum profitability from their capital investment. In addition, producers mainly concerned with survival devote little thought to the long term. Short term overvaluation has created intergenerational problems because short term economic horizons enter into conflict with ecological processes. Despite all efforts, economic theory has not been able to provide an answer to this conflict. Baumol and Oates (1982) recognized this by saying that "when dealing with the allocation of resources over time, the issue of intergenerational equity inevitably comes up . . . which has not been solved despite the careful work of highly distinguished specialists in the matter."

Consequently, what are the signs, what are the signals available to economic theory that will enable it to update the value of future demand? Prices evidently play an essential role here, but these prices will be assigned in terms of the evolution of technology and future demand. In our continent we tend to underestimate future demand because we would first have to estimate an increase in terms of current trends and then a higher consumption level resulting from the needs of the future population. But according to Martínez Allier (1987), "the crux of the matter is to consider whether the inter-generational allocation of resources, particularly that of exhaustible resources, provides arguments against the methodological individualism of economic theory." According to Martínez, the basic methodological principle of economic science is still present in these studies. The only objective data for economists shall be the inscrutable appraisals made by individuals.

When dealing with exhaustible resources, we find an ontological difficulty regarding the methodological principle that the allocation of resources should respond to preferences manifested by economic agents: many significant economic agents are, as yet, unborn and therefore cannot express their preferences. But, if the trend observed in the past decades in Latin America could be projected twenty, thirty, or fifty years into the future, the situation will inevitably be overwhelming in terms of survival (Martínez Allier 1987). Therefore, we should assume that economic agents express their preference for an intergenerational allocation of exhaustible resources that has been decompensated with regard to the future. This clashes with the region's immediate and overwhelming problems, and it seems senseless—in political and realistic terms—to raise it. This fact is closely linked to the discount rate. Undoubtedly, the discount rate of the present value of future demand necessarily involves the area of ethics, an issue that must unavoidably be raised regarding future needs.

Ramsey (1928) said "let us not discount future enjoyment as compared to immediate enjoyment, a practice that is ethically unsustainable and which is simply the consequence of our lack of imagination." Statements such as this will necessarily be limited since the principle of diminishing marginal returns supposes some future increase in per capita consumption. According to Martínez Allier (1987),

> most economic growth models do not take into account Ramsey's moral principle: "Current sacrifices in consumption, that make an increase in investment possible, are compared to the present value discounted from increased future consumption, attributed to the supplementary investment of the present period. In addition, a radiant future is assumed and its present value is discounted; however, if we go beyond the closed discourse of an economy based on growth and go into an exhaustible resource economy, then it is impossible to determine whether the future shall be more or less prosperous that the present."

Indeed, instead of supposing a more prosperous future we find that the opposite is the case: a greater discount rate will produce a higher depletion rate and therefore a less prosperous future. "What really exists is an intragenerational conflict on the current value of benefits and future damages" (Martínez Allier 1987).

Economic lucubrations are more complex when considered in the context of Latin American resources and the region's economic structure based on the exploitation of its exhaustible resources. The present value of future demand in Latin America will possibly be poorer than its present value. In this context future demand should really be overestimated rather than underestimated. Economic agents cannot elude this moral dilemma. In this respect economics is seriously limited in overcoming this type of moral and ethical problems.

Economic growth of output vis-à-vis decreasing natural assets. Development may be defined as the transformation of society's natural, physical
environment (natural resources) into built-up means (fixed capital, infrastructure) by means of social effort (work and technology). In this process
productivity and living standards rise by increasing the amount of capital
available per inhabitant. At the same time, however, this process also tends
to deteriorate and deplete natural resources and even reduce fixed capital
and infrastructure, thus endangering increases in productivity and living
standards (Sunkel and Leal 1984). This is particularly relevant in Latin
America, where development has been based on exploiting natural resources and therefore has been related to evident processes of natural resource depletion. Yearly changes in macroeconomic parameters such as investment, savings, and interest rates correspond exclusively to the
management of economic flows. However, these flows result from using
natural resource stocks and the environment, in other words, natural assets. In this process natural equity is altered in both negative and positive
terms. Experience shows that equity creation processes exist vis-à-vis
serious equity deterioration problems. Except for some catastrophic cases,
annual changes are almost unnoticeable; consequently, equity appears as
a constant in short term planning. However, in the long term the influence
of flow variables can be very significant, so the relation between assets
and flows should be considered carefully in all planning exercises and the
management of development.[23]

Cumulative assets cannot be evaluated by working solely with flows,
which in turn prevents awareness of the possibilities of using the idle capacity of the man-made environment and the potential of society's physical environment. On the other hand, working with stocks entails quantifying assets and being aware of asset enrichment or deterioration.
Conceiving development in terms of transforming assets permits an in-
depth evaluation of the greater sustainability of certain long term policies,
on the one hand, and negative changes in productive capacity and living
standards, on the other. In Latin America both aspects are crucial with regard to political issues and decisions that the region's countries shall have
to deal with.

Environmental Challenges to Be Faced by
Latin America in the Coming Decade

Prospective Scenario for the Coming Decade

Probable effects of adjustment policies.[24] Different hypotheses have been
put forth regarding the environmental impact of the Latin American crisis
and its adjustment policies (ECLAC and Joint ECLAC/UNEP Development and Environment Unit 1989). No immediate negative effects have

been verified. However, serious negative effects are anticipated in the medium and long term if the adjustment's projections are not modified.

Adjustment policies intend, on the one hand, to reduce aggregate demand and, on the other, to modify the relative price of goods by reallocating expenses. The reduction of aggregate demand has involved a reduction or elimination of supervisory activities; the postponement, reduction, or elimination of investment and replacement works; and the minimization of studies on environmental impact and suggestions to eliminate or reduce special programs for marginal sectors.

Policies to modify the relative price of goods by the reallocation of expenditures have been implemented through currency devaluations, rising import tariffs, and other incentives. All these actions should influence the intensification of certain products, particularly export products, with the corresponding overexploitation of resources. This situation should be seriously considered in analyzing ways to include environmental management in different sectoral and regional domestic global policies. These considerations will be analyzed below.

The shadow of concern over global ecosystemic changes. In recent years developed countries have included in their agendas growing concern for the progressive instability of the planet due to global changes. Concern focuses particularly on climate changes caused by the higher levels of CO_2 in the atmosphere (greenhouse effect), the thinning of the ozone layer, the evident changes in the regulating functions of the seas due to pollution, and the loss of live resources in the humid tropics due to deforestation. Forecasts on these changes are quite worrisome because all studies, to some extent, conclude that if present tendencies continue, the world will face such cataclysmic changes in the coming decades that they could seriously threaten the fate of humanity. Obviously, Latin America and the Caribbean will affected by these changes, and due to the conditions of the region's ecosystems, some of the effects shall be particularly powerful.

This new factor will complicate the region's situation even further, not only due to the physical, economic, and social effects of the changes but also due to international pressure—headed by developed countries—to focus efforts on adopting measures against possible future catastrophes. Even now there is evident concern over the lung of the region, the humid tropics, and pressure for the conservation of these territories. The shadow of these problems may be projected on the region, leaving in the dark or semidark the structural causes: the prevailing development pattern that conditions the region's serious environmental situation and tendencies.

Furthermore, the search for urgent solutions to halt the negative trend of global changes will probably make it necessary to divert financial resources in order to solve these problems. And evidently in this case, resources will be reoriented to developed countries, which are primarily responsible for causing these global changes. The danger lies not only in how financial resources are used but also in the reorientation of priorities in environmental policy, science, and research in the region's countries. Latin America's cultural, scientific, and technological dependence is a well-known fact. The possible reorientation of priorities in the center will inevitably be reflected in the periphery. Links with research centers and individual researchers will be maintained only if the dependent part adjusts to the new circumstances, which is foreseeable in light of the historical experience of these social groups. In brief, the universalization of the environmental issue will tend to make the environmental situation even more acute by diverting attention toward the planetary issue.

Intensification of the economy-environment conflict. In view of the changes described in the preceding sections, it is logical to anticipate that in the coming decade permanent conflicts in the concepts of goods, planning horizons, and equity versus growth will become more intense. Most adjustment policies currently being implemented—and which will most probably be continued—are inseparably linked to privatization processes. In these privatization processes environmental goods are appropriated by the private sector, which results in the reduction or elimination of supervisory activities, and pressures to increase the profitability of investments and attract capital, which gives rise to efforts to externalize costs.

The possible scenario for the coming decade will be marked by a sharpening of the problems of poverty due to insufficient growth rates and regressive income distribution. In this context priorities will center on efforts to modify or reverse this situation. Unless environmental problems are clearly associated with these priorities, the trend will be to respond to short term social demands, and, if so, environmental sustainability will still be endangered. On the other hand, it is also possible that programs and environmental policies will appear in response to possible catastrophes derived from the heightening of deterioration processes. However, we may anticipate that these new actions will only occur as a reaction to catastrophes or in view of evidence that they pose an immediate threat.

With regard to the conflict between equity and growth, forecasts indicate that in order to grow the region will consume increasing amounts of its natural assets each year. This conclusion is derived from the most likely repercussions of adjustment policies.

Toward Policies of Greater Environmental Sustainability

The political role of the environment. It is difficult to insert environmental issues in development management without changing the basic structural causes that condition the relation of Latin American societies to their physical environment. It is even more difficult for the different productive actors to understand that Latin America's situation has changed drastically in the past forty years. Today, it is the environmental reality that turns against developmental processes, making progress difficult because its feet are increasingly made of clay. Does this then lead to the conclusion that nothing can be done? Do we have to witness or be part of the catastrophes that will make affected communities react and take drastic measures?

Important steps can be taken before catastrophes actually take place if there is awareness on the need to turn the environment into a significant political actor. For the environmental issue to be considered as such, political society, in its different expressions, must assume this problem and its corresponding potential. It is not possible for the miscellaneous aspects of this issue to be granted greater significance if the different sectors of society do not express this as a need for change. However, the different groups and classes that make up national societies have different views on the environment because this issue inevitably reflects the conflicts, structures, and social relations existing in different societies. Furthermore, since the physical environment is subject to private appropriation and since some of its resources are becoming increasingly limited, internal conflicts in national societies will undoubtedly have a conspicuous effect on the environmental issue (Gligo 1968b: 9–14).

To isolate the environmental issue by denying its political role is to deny the fundamental basis for it to really be included in development policy. Turning the environmental issue into a politically aseptic issue, however, will lead its proponents to promote sterile, technocratic, and inefficient efforts while decisions with deep, environmental implications will be made in society's political pressure spheres. On the other hand, since environmental problems are increasingly becoming a political issue, the discursive and rhetorical proposals that usually accompany plans and speeches will have to be confronted with the implementation of strategies, policies, and programs that contemplate using the environment more efficiently. The distance between what is said and what is done is still big, but it can undoubtedly be bridged if national societies and, particularly, the most affected classes demand better and more efficient environmental management.

Therefore, political decisions in benefit of society need to have maximum clarity in this respect. Ever since the environment became a political issue, it has moved within two easily manipulated extremes: on the one hand, the globalization of the environmental issue and, on the other, its technocratization and reduction to mere studies on environmental impacts. Globalization tends to generalize environmental problems by holding that the planet is in danger and proposing some debatable solutions (for example, zero growth). The earth's future is unquestionably in danger, but the causes, which originate mainly in industrialized countries, are precisely the causes that many apparently solidaristic planetary proposals try to conceal.

The environmental situation must be explained in light of the imposed development systems and the difficult and complex relations of dependence between countries. Latin America and the Caribbean cannot disregard their dramatic history of spoliation and poverty in order to advocate a better planetary environment to help the consolidation of the prevailing international economic order. The globalization of the environmental issue turns it into internal stand-taking in each country, thus distracting attention and concealing the basic causes of the environmental situation, such as inequalities in living standards and the poverty that afflicts considerable population segments.

At the other extreme, reductionism also tends to turn into an instrument for manipulation, generally used by minorities, always in collusion with technocratic sectors. This reductionism generally consists in dealing with the environmental issue through simplistic studies on environmental impact and including only this aspect in planning and development strategies. These studies are generally carried out in order to analyze possible negative impacts. The region's experience is not exempt from several instances in which studies—the results of which were known beforehand—were carried out with the sole, practical purpose of generating income for foreign consultants.

Conceiving the environmental problem as such and reducing it to the simple application of mere impact techniques and the economic evaluation of the physical impact is also an attempt to conceal the causes of the current environmental situation, this time by disguising it behind a scientific and technical image. If it is assumed that the environmental situation of Latin American countries will not follow the course of the abovementioned extremes, it can be easily seen that it should turn into an important instrument to adjust the region's future strategies.

If at present the environment has not, as yet, been granted due priority and importance, it is because it has not been acknowledged as one of the region's immediate, urgent, and top-priority problems. Indeed, the environment is disregarded in the context of the challenges posed by the pressure exerted by an important population segment that needs to improve food intake, income, and employment. Governments in general believe that the environment is a factor that affects living standards and that, if its importance is acknowledged, it could be improved once the pressing problems of survival, food intake, and employment have been solved. For most people the environmental issue will only become a political issue and form part of public opinion trends—as in European countries—once these other problems have been solved, at least to a significant extent.

We may agree on the reason why the environment has not, as yet, been granted priority. However, we may also foresee that in the coming years the environmental issue—inextricably linked to the structural, political, and economic crises of the region's countries—will assume a decisive role in development strategies. This is due to the fact that, unlike what happened in developed countries, the environment is a factor and a part of the crisis itself. In the region the environmental issue is not linked solely to living standards but also to the survival of an important part of the population. Therefore, if there is awareness of this fact, sufficient political pressure will be brought to bear to have this issue explicitly taken into account.

Any alternative strategy or substantial modification to any strategy currently being applied will necessarily have to include the environment. On the other hand, if the modifications we have described are not made, the crisis in the physical sustainability of current strategies will be accelerated, and the need to grant greater priority to the environmental issue will become even more evident. At present, however, governments, planning experts, and policy executors are not aware of the environment's crucial role. Many explanations deal with political views, but others deal with the management of methodologies, instruments, and, particularly, languages to communicate changes in the environment and their effects and perspectives.

Global policy adjustments. There are three global policies that in the future should have important consequences on the inclusion of the environmental issue in development management, in view of the need to wisely minimize or alter the effects of the adjustment policy. These policies are: science and technology, organization of public institutions, and education.[25]

With regard to science and technology, it should necessarily be reoriented in terms of the demand for the scientific knowledge needed to transform ecosystems and create a model to generate, adopt, and disseminate technology. By internalizing the environment, this model should reduce the ecological cost involved in the alterations caused by development processes. The amount of products that are produced, included into the area of pharmacopoeia, and used in transport increases every day. Very little is known about their effects on human health and on the health of ecosystems. The challenges created by the new biotechnology raise questions that need to be answered through significant scientific investments.

There is a vast field of action to be explored in relation to public, institutional policies and juridical issues since the region's institutional structure for dealing with the environment is, to a lesser or greater extent, weak.[26] The environmental issue in Latin America has been effectively incorporated in traditional sectors such as agriculture, mining, health, and housing. However, in dealing with environmental problems, there is a tendency to create a new sector dedicated to the environment. A solution of this kind inevitably tends, in the medium and long term, to leave the environmental issue out of development planning. Thus, the following is recommended in institutional terms:

1. To foster the establishment of organizations to coordinate environmental actions, in both sectoral and spatial terms, in the economy's different sectors, and in the territorial divisions of each country. This is one way to avoid establishing a sector dedicated to the environment.
2. To grant priority—in legal and budgetary terms—to the environmental issue by providing the financial resources needed to mobilize initiatives and projects and the laws and regulations needed to protect resources.
3. To establish agencies capable of encouraging forms of environmentally sustainable development that, at the same time, should be profitable, thereby generating permanent economic activities (recycling, waste treatment, energy-producing forests).
4. To grant priority to the environmental departments of sectoral and regional organizations responsible for the main social and economic decisions.

The institutional problem should not be confused with the real incorporation of the environmental issue. It has been confirmed that Latin American countries with ad hoc organizations and/or clear institutional allocation of explicit policies on the environment actually overuse and degrade resources. The institutional issue—in each case—should be a tool to execute strategies and policies that include environmental issues or specifically address the environment. There is no general conclusion on this matter. We can only point out that the arguments against environmental sectoralization could be similar to those against the establishment of an environmental ministry. However, each country should find its own solutions.

Nevertheless, not encouraging an environmental sector is not the same as rejecting environmental planning, policies, and lines of action; some studies tend to present a dichotomy between positions that advocate global incorporation of the environmental issue in planning and management and other environmental viewpoints. But an analysis of the region's environmental status clearly indicates the need for concerted action. On the one hand, it seems that the incorporation of environmental issues mentioned above is far from being a reality. This leads to omissions and gaps that are usually filled by planning environmental policies and lines of action through traditional domestic, sectoral, and regional action and organizations. On the other hand, Latin America's environmental situation is such that, aside from what could be achieved through adequate environmental management, implementing a series of environmental measures is essential in view of the imperative need to solve increasingly serious problems. Evidently, many of these measures emerge from ad hoc environmental policies.

As for educational policy, we must emphasize that it is vital to have an environmental education policy aimed at public opinion, either in the context of school or university education or implemented through nonformal structures.

Sectoral policy adjustments. The conclusion to be drawn from examining the Latin American situation is that the environmental issue is incorporated mainly at sectoral levels, either regional or national. However, this does not mean that establishing autonomous environmental agencies for policy implementation involves abandoning sectoral approaches because institutions can clearly correspond to the functions of a given sector.

The development of the agricultural—and farm forestry and livestock—sector should be carried out depending on the behavior and attributes of the live ecosystem and the degree to which it has been artificially built up. Any policy or line of action applied in this sector will probably affect the treatment given to resources and, therefore, will influence the ecological cost of the transformation. In Latin America, however, when environmental actions for the agricultural sector are proposed, these usually refer to erosion prevention and water and soil pollution caused by pesticides. The problem is much more complex, which is why the following aspects should be mentioned:

1. The complexity of modes of production prevailing in agriculture as a result of the resource tenure structure and cultural, social, and economic patterns;
2. The introduction of technological models that tend to make ecosystems extremely artificial, not taking advantage of the environmental supply, and subordinating agricultural development to the energy subsidies required by the degree to which the environment is man-made;
3. Ecosystemic specialization that is frequently inconsistent with natural aptitudes, but which is vital for manipulation by international and national purchasing powers;
4. Social problems related to the poverty of peasants that frequently lead to overusing the environment;
5. Competition for the use of soil between different lines of business, such as foodstuffs, energy, industries, and urban expansion;
6. Noticeable separation between economic, short term behavior and resource conservation.

Among secondary activity sectors, the industrial sector is undoubtedly very important in the relation between development and the environment. On the one hand, it is closely linked to the demand for primary sector resources, and, on the other, waste generation produced by the industrial process creates pollution problems, which in turn give rise to a series of environmental policies needed to prevent or solve these problems.

In marine ecosystems the situation is similar to agriculture. The exploitation of renewable natural resources involves a high ecological cost, further aggravated by limited knowledge of the behavior of ecosystems, above all, because it is very difficult to plan efficient control measures. In addition to all these problems, there are two aspects that pose serious difficulties in planning: controlling the changes produced by waste thrown into the ocean and dealing with pollution caused by oil spills and the exploitation of other nonrenewable natural resources found in the seabed. This leads to the conclusion that planning the processes that affect the sea is so complex that it requires extraordinary efforts.[27]

The environmental issue is also evident in social sectors: health, habitat, and basic facilities. It would be redundant to repeat the well-known deficits that affect all types of social aspects in Latin America, and which tend to get worse.

Urban policy adjustments. Extensive studies on urban development processes have not always granted due rank to the environment. Nevertheless, if there is a global understanding of the problem based on a systemic approach and further study into the issue of migration, social status, organization of space, sale of land, and transport, an adequate framework is established that makes it possible to include environmental issues in urban development policies.[28]

It is in the field of city planning where sectoral policies—particularly social policies—dealing with the environment are most frequently implemented. The greater relative importance of urban populations with regard to rural populations has helped to grant priority to the implementation of many social urban plans and programs to the detriment of rural populations. The collection of environmental problems provoked by accelerated urbanization and, particularly, the seriousness of some environmental problems in the city have driven urban planners to include, to a lesser or greater extent, the environmental issue.

However, some concepts should be clarified. Cities can be viewed as highly artificial urban systems that require a permanent supply of material, energy, and information and from which the waste resulting from their activities must be removed. However, despite the fact that cities are highly artificial systems, we should bear in mind that cities stem from an ecosystem that, despite the transformations to which it is subjected, preserves certain basic attributes and provides a given and permanent environmental offering. Consequently, a highly built-up environment must not become a factor to conceal the possibility of using the environmental potential remaining in the ecosystem. Notwithstanding these proposals and those suggested by city planners, the environmental issue in Latin America has been included in city planning and management in view of major environmental problems, which have become true bottlenecks in some cities, although in medium-sized and large cities the environmental issue is frequently incorporated implicitly in their design and management.

The growing power of local and municipal administrations and metropolitan intendancies in Latin America stemming from the acuteness of urban development problems, especially from environmental problems, requires processes that are more elaborate and more closely linked to regional and global sectoral planning. Therefore, it is increasingly important to analyze methods through which to include the environmental issue. In this regard the following considerations should be taken into account:[29]

1. The need to focus on the process of urbanization through an integral, historical, and long term approach must be acknowledged. Furthermore, human settlements should be viewed as centers that concentrate people, activities, and a built-up environment, and which give rise to and are the outcome of a constant flow of transformations in the use of material and energy;

2. Beyond familiar pollution problems, the sale of lands and the organization of transport systems become particularly important for planning the structure of space;

3. Transport policies have multiple effects on urban environments and the general demand for natural resources, particularly energy resources;

4. The representation of community interests is a form that has not been widely used. There have been remarkable experiences outside formal channels that have produced local solutions to environmental problems.

Appendix: Synopsis of Possible Effects of Adjustment Policies on Environmental Deterioration Processes

Adjustment policies	General purposes	Policy instruments	Immediate actions	Deterioration processes	Impacts and/or new processes	
					Short/medium term	Medium/long term
Policies aimed at reducing aggregate demand.	Reduce the fiscal deficit. Improve the trade balance.	Contraction of current expenditures and capital budget.	Reduction or elimination of supervision activities.	Invasion of protected areas for illegal extraction of valuable species.	Depredation and risk of losses of ecologically valuable species.	Conversion of protected areas to crops and grazing.
				Inadequate disposal of industrial wastes.	Urban pollution.	Pollution of farm, aquaculture, and recreational areas.
			Postponement, reduction, or elimination of investments in new projects, and in the repair and maintenance of existing facilities.	Deterioration of municipal and sanitation services and infrastructure.		
				Absence or deterioration of projects to protect and/or correct sedimentation processes, destruction of water courses.	Increased incidence of natural catastrophes.	Deterioration of physical infrastructure by silting-up of dams, equipment damage, etc.
			Reduction or elimination of activities on environmental impact evaluation and mitigation studies.	Project implementation disregarding prevention or minimization of negative environmental impacts.	Destruction of valuable ecosystems, unique formations and sceneries, etc., during project works.	Multiple deterioration processes.
			Reduction and/or elimination of special social programs.	More restricted access of poor sectors to health and education.	Higher incidence of diseases, undernutrition, and infant mortality.	Cultural deprivation.
		Reduction of internal credit.	Reduction of private sector investments and operations: depression of urban-industrial activities.	Idem. Interurban migrations and slum expansion.		
		Limitation of money supply expansion.		Fall in wages, unemployment and subemployment increase, food supply decrease with higher prices—causing greater urban poverty and limiting rural migration prospects.	Increased pressure on slope and agricultural frontier areas for fuelwood and cultivation.	Settlements in inappropriate areas.

Appendix: Synopsis of Possible Effects of Adjustment Policies on Environmental Deterioration Processes (cont.)

Adjustment policies	General purposes	Policy instruments	Immediate actions	Deterioration processes	Impacts and/or new processes	
					Short/medium term	Medium/long term
Policies aimed at modifying relative prices of goods, reallocating spending.	Improve balance of payments to better the position of tradable goods.	Exchange and trade policy instruments.	National currency devaluation.	Increase in the general price index, particularly food prices.	(Inflation is associated with the other social processes indicated in the first part of this synopsis, contributing to the same impacts.)	
		Incentives to mobilize production factors.	Increased import duties.	Intensification of nontraditional export crops.	Displacement of basic items of the low-income sector's diet.	Excessive artificialization and overuse of soils, producing erosion and pesticide pollution.
	Expand supply of tradable goods.		Various sectoral incentives.	Expansion of the agricultural frontier for crops and livestock farming.		Economical and cultural pressure on native groups.
				Pressure on forest for lumber, disregarding ecological capabilities.	Deterioration of fragile ecosystems and risk of losing valuable species.	Impoverishment of settlers.
						Destruction risk of fragile ecosystems.
				Idem.	Deforestation of river basins.	Idem.
						Acceleration of erosion and sedimentation in river basins.
				Aquaculture expansion in areas with other uses (biological reserves, mangroves, farming, etc.).	Deterioration and risk of coastal ecosystems destruction.	Interruption of hydrobiological cycles and loss of resources.
				Intensification in catches of diverse marine resources, even ignoring closed seasons.	Reduction of resource availability through overexploitation.	Depletion of marine resources.
				Expansion of mining exploitation areas or installation of new works ignoring environmental impacts.	Destruction of valuable ecosystems and formations.	Depletion of mineral deposits.
					Pollution.	Incentives for spontaneous settling in areas of expanding activities.

Notes

1. For more details, see Gligo and Morello (1980).
2. See Mellafe (1973) and Gligo and Morello (1980).
3. See Sunkel and Paz (1970).
4. The subject of agricultural development in Latin America is dealt with extensively in Chapter 10. See also Gligo (1986a).
5. See Gligo (1986a).
6. PREALC-ILO (1975) estimates that "equivalent unemployment" ranges from 20 to 40 percent of the rural labor force.
7. For more details, see ECLA/UNEP (1983) and ECLAC (1989c).
8. See Vidart (1980).
9. For more details on colonization programs, see Nelson (1973: 333).
10. For more details, see Dollfus (1981).
11. See ECLA (1982).
12. For more details, see ECLAC (1975), Fucaraccio et al. (1973), Meadows et al. (1972), and Chaplin (1972).
13. Milton Friedman is the most conspicuous representative of proponents in favor of acknowledging the market's virtues. See Friedman (1976); see also Ruff (1970).
14. See Georgescu-Roegen (1975).
15. See Daly (1971); see also Melnick (1981).
16. For the corresponding critique, see Mishan, Krutilla, and Galbraith, quoted by Melnick (1981).
17. See also Mesarovic and Pestel (1975).
18. The Bariloche (Herrera, et al. 1971) model concluded that (up to the 1970s) the obstacles to harmonious development for society were neither physical nor economic, but rather essentially sociopolitical. It held that desirable growth rates (4 to 6 percent) could be reached by reducing nonessential consumption, increasing investment, eliminating socioeconomic and political barriers preventing the potential use of land, implementing an egalitarian distribution of basic goods and services, and, in underdeveloped countries, implementing active policies to eliminate negative balances in international trade.
19. See Brown (1972) and Ward and Dubos (1972).
20. See Odum (1971) and Kneese et al. (1970).
21. See Sunkel (1981).
22. See Sunkel and Leal (1984), Sunkel and Gligo (1981), Sunkel (1981), and Gligo (1981).
23. See Chapter 2.
24. See Appendix for a preview of the possible effects of adjustment policies on processes of environmental deterioration.
25. Chapters 8 and 13 constitute significant progress in this direction.
26. See Koolen (1986).
27. Important measures are already being adopted in the region. See, for example, Vergara and Pizarro (1981).
28. See Unikel and Necochea (1975); see also Kowarick (1981) and Geisse and Sabatini (1981).
29. Some of these conclusions are drawn from the generalization of items included in ECLA (1982).

8

The Endogenization of
Technological Change:
A Development Challenge

Ennio Rodríguez

The paradox of technological change is that although most economic growth scholars point to it as being the main long term variable explaining growth (Solow 1957), the truth is that it is the most unknown of all variables. After dutifully recognizing its importance, most economists prudently ignore technological change in their considerations.[1] Nevertheless, because of its significance, the topic has become an important subject of independent research.

This chapter endeavors to revise and integrate the independent contributions as a way to overcome this vacuum in knowledge on technological matters. It is hoped that this effort will provide guidelines regarding the possibilities of creating a distinctive technological capacity that can instill dynamism and continuity into Latin American development. With these objectives in mind, section one reviews the theoretical and historical backgrounds of technological change. Section two covers recent transformations that fuel the current debate on the subject. Lastly, section three outlines the new view of technological change deriving from the strategic framework of development from within proposed in this book.

Theoretical and Historical Background of the Concept of Technological Change

The Emergence of Technological Change as a Subject of Study

Only recently has technological change and innovation become a subject of study in its own right. Concern for economic growth gained momentum after World War II, and increasing emphasis was placed on technological variables. Nevertheless, technological change was studied only because of its effects on economic variables considered to be significant, such as growth, trade, employment, and production. But study of it per se—analysis of the conditions underlying technological development and the dissemination of innovations, for subsequent discussion of its effects—did not take place until the late 1950s.

Technological change as a subject of study occurred in industrialized countries. The problem of the possible specific effects of technological change in countries lagging in development was not posed until even more recently. Despite early concern by the Economic Commission for Latin America and the Caribbean (ECLAC) with respect to the distribution of the benefits of technological progress, analysis was not aimed at determining the logic of technical progress; rather, it was equated with industrialization, and hence only the study of its distributive consequences in international trade and in the shaping of national structures was attempted. Subsequently, in light of the restrictions on development stemming from import substitution in Latin America, methodological concerns revolved around criticism of dependence and the consequences of peripheral development. Technology was seen as only one aspect contributing to the description. Later, with the return of the neoclassical agenda, the role of technological change was once again excluded from the analytical concerns of development.

The subject has gained importance in Latin America, but more as a reflection of concerns external to the region: the growing interest in technology within industrialized countries and the success of Asian countries, particularly Japan, in bridging the technological gap.[2] Industrial restructuring in central countries and Southeast Asian development form the backdrop for a Latin America that is debating between orthodoxy and heterodoxy. Discussions of short term economic policies reach greater depth, but the contributions in terms of structural change suffer political and conceptual lags.

The argument in favor of technological change becoming a new object of study with its corresponding discourse can be made from various angles:

1. One of the features underlying the emergence of a new object of study has been the appearance of textbooks. Among those in Spanish are the annotated bibliography of Nadal Egea and Salas Páez (1988) and the work of Sábato and Mackenzie (1988). Among those in English are Freeman's (1982) classic, already in its second printing, and the recent book by Coombs, Saviotti, and Walsh (1987).

2. Also prominent from the point of view of the sociology of knowledge is the emergence of research traditions with their conceptual preferences, such as the Science Policy Research Unit of the University of Sussex and, in another British university, the University of Manchester with its Departments of Management Sciences and Science and Technology Policy; so too the subject of technological management with its *Technology Management Publication*.[3]

3. The hypothesis of the emergence of a discourse on technological change is reinforced by the fact that numerous contributions have come from different disciplines. Economics has provided the main contributions from its many areas of specialization: industrial economics, production theory, labor economics, and macroeconomics. But political science has also contributed, particularly with its study of public policy, industrial sociology, the sociology of science, and economic history and management, particularly in technological management.

Despite these contributions, none of the disciplines have been able to subsume the topic as one of their own specializations. The subject of study ends up imposing itself with its own logic. As Coombs, Saviotti, and Walsh (1987) point out, "despite the fact that the subject can be dealt with from a variety of fields, some common features emerge that suggest an underlying unity of the technological change process." This logic that interweaves specific concepts is what renders it an independent object of study. This is not to say that it is not interrelated with other economic, social, and political processes. It is fragmented for analytical purposes, but only for a single aspect of analysis, in order to later be able to study the reciprocal determinations with other processes.

The emergence of the discussion on technological change is associated with the seminal works of Schumpeter (1928, 1934, 1939, 1943) and Kuznets (1930, 1940). The propositions that opened up a new agenda for research and policy revolved around the fact that competition between enterprises providing greater stimulus to growth was based on new products rather than on price or cost. Therefore, in order to study long term growth it was imperative to thoroughly understand the process of technological change. Thus, the notion of innovation[4] gained great importance, as did the typologies that classify innovations according to their impact into basic or radical and incremental or minor, or according to their reference to products and processes. The dissemination of innovations also became significant, as well as other concepts that have been emerging more recently, such as *technological trajectories, clustering of innovations, innovative swarms, technological paradigms, and technological systems.* This expanding conceptual swarm and the logic of its reciprocal determinations make up the dynamic discourse on technological change.

The importance of these concepts is that some suggest an agenda for research, while others attempt to find an answer to problems raised: understanding the origin of innovations of one or another type and the logic of their dissemination. Subsequently, discussion helps reveal their impact on variables such as business cycles, employment, labor organization, and international trade.

One of the characteristics of postwar technological change was the generation of great expectations regarding the possible impact of organized

innovation on economic growth.[5] It was the period of the professionaliza-
tion of research and development (R&D). At the time it was believed that
the lead of the United States rested on the magnitude of R&D expenditures
on military, space-related, and nuclear areas and the governmental policies that affected these technologies (Servan-Schreiber 1965). Nonetheless, the evaluations carried out showed that there was a lack of correlation
between R&D expenditures and growth, although there was awareness that
the interrelations were more complex (Coombs, Saviotti, and Walsh 1987).

The development of the theoretical discourse in terms of its relevance
and the problems raised fed on the historical process of technological
change itself. During the 1960s, the growth of R&D expenditures declined,
and there was greater concern for its effectiveness. There was an explicit
emergence of scientific policies concerned with channeling R&D expenditures according to economic and social objectives. In this context, studies
on the nature and conditions of innovation and technological change gain
importance, as do the ways in which these could be used by the economic
system, as well as the greater concern for specific problems of project assessment and R&D expenditure programming. In this way the possibilities for response by a new field of study coincide with some concerns
emerging from industrialized countries.

During the first two postwar decades, attempts were made in Latin
America to develop public awareness of the need to create a scientific and
technical infrastructure. Public programs included support for scientific research faculties and institutes in universities and the creation of national
science and technology councils. Nevertheless, the links between science
and technology and between technology and the productive sectors were
not raised: "Technology was not very important in this effort, because it
was assumed that once the capacity to produce science was started up,
it would flow continuously and would be incorporated without major difficulties into the productive structure that was anxiously awaiting it" (Sábato and Mackenzie 1988: 229).

The following decade allowed for some advances, mainly in the control of imported technology. However, Latin American countries remained
technology importers, with the exception of Brazil, which developed some
offensive innovation strategies. In the 1970s these views on scientific and
technological policies based on supply went on to include demand elements, which meant the incorporation of more actors into the scientific and
technological system. However, little progress was made in the absence of
clear policy decisions to advance the development of the system.[6]

In the 1990s, with the return to neoclassical thinking, consideration of
technology has experienced a setback in terms of its policy priority.[7] An
indicator of this reversal is the decrease in public expenditures on R&D,
which, in contrast with developed countries, has taken place in Brazil,
Mexico, Chile, Peru, and Venezuela (Fajnzylber 1989a: 34).

Structuralist Proposals for Technological Change

One of the factors motivating Latin American structuralist analysis was the disenchantment with the consequences of integration into the international economy on the basis of the individual decisions of economic agents as international price takers. Criticism of the theory of the comparative advantage of international trade was based on the unequal distribution of the benefits of technical progress.

ECLAC's view emphasized the dynamic aspects of economic development and, in particular, technical progress, in a context of noncompetitive markets that determined an unequal distribution of the possibilities of accumulation and consumption.[8] The policies proposed were intended to bring about structural change that would modify this unequal distribution of the benefits of technical progress. Economic development became synonymous with structural change. However, although mention was made of the possibility of changing Latin American insertion into world markets through industrial exports (Prebisch 1959), the emphasis was on import substitution and common markets, within the framework of other policies such as agrarian reform and the expansion of domestic markets.

It could even be argued that analytical emphasis was placed on the distribution of benefits from technological change and not on the issue of the conditions underlying the emergence of technological change. It is true that issues such as the accumulation of capital were raised, but only in order to discuss the distribution of the benefits of technical change in the international system. This distributive emphasis meant that technical progress as such was not dealt with and, consequently, did not lead to the proposal of technological strategies. Perhaps there was an implicit assumption that these would be a byproduct of industrialization strategies.

On the other hand, the pessimism surrounding the possibilities of exporting manufactures to developed countries could have derived from a belief that technological modernization would be somewhat subordinated to peripheral protected market conditions, which could be characterized by less than optimal techniques or adapted to the various supply of factors and entrepreneurial and labor traditions. In this interpretation ECLAC was the precursor of proposals for an appropriate technology. Particularly valuable are their analyses on the possible impact of technical change on employment under conditions of structural heterogeneity, in which technical change simultaneously creates and eliminates jobs, but the latter effect may be greater.[9]

ECLAC did not deal with the issue regarding the scientific and technological requirements to change the international insertion of a country or region from a primary goods producer to a producer of more technologically complex industrial goods. Greater weight was placed on an inward-looking strategy that favored domestic and regional markets, where technical change was more an outcome of industrial development than a prerequisite. The analysis made little headway in specifying the role played in technical change by the various institutions: enterprises, market, and state. The novelty consisted in incorporating dynamic aspects into the analysis to explain the evident historical fact of a capitalist system with a developed center and an underdeveloped periphery, in order to formulate alternative policies to the orthodox ones whose recommendations tended to reproduce the unequal benefit distribution pattern of the system.

Subsequently, the disenchantment with the results of import substitution gave rise to a criticism of dependence.[10] The inequality between center and periphery was expressed in the subordinate relations at the economic, political, and cultural levels, tending to produce national disintegration and transnational integration. Technological dependence was seen as one way in which transnational capitals dominated. This line of criticism underscored the need for isolation from the global system in order to reorganize peripheral society in all its dimensions. The characteristics of this reorganization depended on the degree of radicalism of the ideological positions, but they generally shared a strong anti-imperialist slant. The technological aspect of the reorganization was not fully worked out.[11] An important line of analysis arising from this position of stronger criticism of the role of transnational corporations was the discussion on the impact of patents (Vaitsos 1979) and the area of bargaining with major transnational corporations (Vaitsos 1979; Lall 1980).

The Orthodox Concept of Development and Technological Change

One of the most prominent facts in Latin American economic development has been the return of orthodox thinking, with an enormous focus on academic discussion but, above all, on policy formulation. The development conception of the new orthodoxy rests on two tenets: (1) the free operation of price signals as coordinating mechanisms and (2) the view that private economic agents are more efficient than public ones. Based on these premises, policy proposals seek to eliminate state intervention in price signals and to transfer public enterprises to the private sector. The discussion of institutional suitability for development begins and ends with the market.

Contrary to the new orthodox assumption, the theory of competitive markets states that the free operation of market forces is not sufficient for the invisible hand to operate; if technological knowledge can be appropriated and become a source of monopolistic revenue, the market does not yield optimal results.[12] Therefore, there is no such assumption that the proposed institutional scheme of the orthodox view is the most suitable.

Despite such formidable objections to the orthodox view of development in dealing with scientific and technological problems, there are those who insist on orthodox prescriptions. Their implicit sociological assumption is that a poorly operating market, or even one that should not exist, operates better than any institution. This is a metaphysical proposition. From a theoretical point of view, the limitations of the market as an institution for technological change have been amply pointed out.

First, it is a well-known fact that, if we take prices as given, private economic agents in competitive markets will tend to allocate suboptimal amounts of resources to scientific and technological development (Arrow 1962b).[13] Second, this shortcoming is not related to a poor operation, but, rather, it is the existence of the market per se that introduces the failure into the system (Cooper 1973). Optimal results in competitive markets presuppose the free availability of knowledge and production techniques. Violation of this assumption gives rise to the market of technological knowledge. By definition, these market transactions emerge due to the ignorance of one of the participating agents. Prices are determined under monopolistic conditions and, therefore, represent a rent. Third, according to welfare theory, monopolistic rents in this case involve transfers from economic agents willing to buy something of which they are unaware to agents who manage to appropriate technological knowledge. This transfer of welfare causes a reduction in overall welfare. If technological monopolies are found primarily in the developed world, the effect of international technological transactions is a transfer of welfare from the Third World toward developed countries (Cooper 1973).

Consequently, there are sufficient arguments for doubting that the institutional format of private agents and price signals is the most suitable one to solve the problems of allocating resources to scientific and technological development, and that transactions constitute a medium for technological change in competitive markets. It then becomes essential to study the conditions involved in the emergence of technological knowledge markets and the logic of firms for resource allocation under these conditions of uncertainty and noncompetitive markets.

Alternative formulations, based precisely on the analysis of the virtues and weaknesses of competitive markets, have required new analytical developments, policies, and strategy formulations to deal with the challenge of economic growth spurred by technological development. The analytical effort should be aimed at past experiences in an attempt to evaluate the possible contributions of alternative institutional formats. Consequently, it is not surprising that great weight has been given to the analysis of case studies and the history of economic development in this field of linkages between science, technology, and development.

Furthermore, it is a known fact that major discourses in economics sidestep the technological problem: (1) the neoclassical theory with its assumptions of free availability of knowledge and outputs known from the beginning to the end of the history of the economy and (2) the Keynesian analysis with its emphasis on short term macroeconomic variables. Thus, contributions from other disciplines become necessary, and often one must resort to a less abstract debate in order to deal with most problems.[14] From a conceptual point of view, it is important to scrutinize the linkages between scientific and technological development and economic development, but starting from an analysis of the determinants of technological change.

The Current Debate

Patterns of Innovation

In order to deal with the problem of the origin and dissemination of innovations, it is necessary to understand the logic behind innovations. The theoretical roots of the debate revolve around supply and demand factors, associated with Schumpeter and Schmookler, respectively. Schumpeter proposed two alternative hypotheses on the origin of innovations. In his first hypothesis it is the entrepreneur who is capable of taking generally known ideas that are unproven in the marketplace and implementing them. To do this it is necessary to overcome habits and institutions. It is the innovation of products rather than the innovation of processes that will give rise to new industries and have a greater impact. This innovative process is the basis for the destructive creation that characterizes capitalism (Schumpeter 1943). In his second hypothesis inventing becomes practically endogenous to firms; the growing institutionalization of R&D in large companies is recognized.

A second question that Schumpeter raises refers to the market structure that tends to generate more innovations. In his first hypothesis of technical change, the motivation for innovation emerges from the desire of competitively involved entrepreneurs to enjoy a potential monopoly as a result of the introduction of a new idea. In his second hypothesis, the monopolists or oligopolists are in a better position to raise the funds required for R&D. A related question, attributed to Galbraith, refers to the size of the firms that most encourage innovations (Coombs, Saviotti, and Walsh 1987).

Based on studies on investment, employment, and inventions in a number of sectors in the United States during the first half of the nineteenth century, Schmookler (1966) proposed a line of causality, opposite to the technological determination of Schumpeter ("technology push"), where the emphasis is on demand factors. The rise in demand tends to increase activities leading to invention, and the fluctuations in investment, in turn, depend on external factors rather than on the pressure from inventions. Despite the fact that Schmookler did not propose a determinism of demand, the literature has made him the representative of the theory of "demand-pull" (Coombs, Saviotti, and Walsh 1987: 96).

This set of hypotheses has given rise to countless empirical research and also, necessarily, to conceptual discussions. In terms of the relative weight of supply and demand variables on innovation, the current state of debate indicates that, based on research in the development of the chemical, synthetics, and electronics industries (Walsh et al. 1979; Walsh 1984; Dosi 1981), neither demand nor supply were found to predominate exclusively. The analysis based on investment patterns, scientific works, patents, innovations, and production allows the generalization that demand or supply factors tend to predominate in the various stages of the development of an industry (Freeman, Clark, and Soete 1982). The technological push tends to weigh more in the initial stages of the development of an industry, while demand factors tend to become more important in the more advanced phases of a product's life cycle.

On the other hand, results tend to invalidate the line of causality that states that market structure and firm size are explanatory variables of innovation (Kamien and Schwartz 1982; Scherer 1980; Soete 1979). Empirical studies show that there is as much variation in technological variables used as innovation indicators (R&D expenditures and number of patents) among different industries as among different firms within the same industry. This has led Coombs, Saviotti, and Walsh (1987: 114) to propose an alternative explicative variable: *technological opportunity* as the main determinant of various innovation patterns. In new sectors with high technological opportunity, first comers have an initial edge, which, as these technological opportunities materialize, could give rise to oligopolies.

The concept of technological opportunity stems from the recognition that in supply terms technical change is structured, which affects the incentives for the various growth strategies of firms. Technological opportunity refers to the existence of incremental, potential innovations of a technology in terms of the relation between its specification and performance variables (intensive opportunities), or when a technology with the same specifications has the possibility of being transferred to other technical systems where it can more efficiently fulfill the same functions that existing technologies fulfill. Microcircuits are an obvious example. An outcome of technological opportunity is that it allows the clustering of firms facing similar opportunities and thus permits the identification of behavior patterns that enable aggregation, not necessarily according to the market, but rather by technological type. Consequently, industries with a greater degree of technological opportunity will tend to show more research and greater technical progress.

A concept linked to technological opportunity is *technological trajectory*. By including technical change as endogenous, this conceptualization establishes the evolution pattern of a firm's behavior. In this sense Nelson and Winter (1974) define technological trajectory as a set of decisionmaking rules adopted by firms regarding the detailed features of their products and processes. It is hoped that these technological decision rules will give rise to stability in the short term and that they will be similar for firms operating with the same technology. This implies that most of the time there are restrictions that limit the range of technological options available to firms.

These concepts have provided the basis for the development of a research tradition on innovation dissemination models that attempt to incorporate the microeconomic elements that lead to innovation: the effects of firm size, the existence of decision rules that govern the behavior of firms, and the interaction of technological push and demand. These conceptual developments have opened up an important agenda for empirical research that has yet to be carried out (Coombs, Saviotti, and Walsh 1987: 120–133).

However, technological trajectory and technological opportunity refer to evolutionary processes and apply to the period in which the technology is maturing. This is when patterns and limitations emerge. Dissemination takes place within the limits determined by the subsequent evolution of a mature technology. Therefore, it is also necessary to give thought to the major breaks that mark the emergence of new technological opportunities.

Technological Break

Freeman, Clark, and Soete (1982) have argued that technological change does not only take place through evolution, and that the perceived discontinuities explain long term cycles observed in capitalism.[15] In their explanation they introduce the concept of *new technological systems* (NTSs): powerful sets of new technological trajectories derived from the advances achieved by core technologies. These technologies must be characterized by their wide applications to a large number of products and processes in many industries, thus generating related innovations. Furthermore, they must not only be powerful, but also their dissemination processes must be in clusters. No reference is made to the clustering of innovations, only to their dissemination, which is what can have a significant economic impact. Another characteristic of NTSs is that they are expected to have greater impact on infrastructure industries such as transportation, energy, or communications, where they can have a greater multiplier effect on other activities. The most recent example is that of electronic components and circuits and their use in consumer durables.

In explaining long term economic cycles, the interrelation between NTSs and employment and wage performance plays a pivotal role. The initial steps of NTSs take place in small enterprises or the departments of larger companies. Their initial impact is found in the development of new technological and management skills that will be commanded by the most dynamic sectors of the following long term cycle. Once the transit to the new cycle has occurred (the mechanics of this transit are not explained by the authors [Coombs, Saviotti, and Walsh 1987]), the NTS creates new jobs in new industries and also in older ones that benefit by their linkages with avant-garde industries. This expansion of employment and the scarcity of new skills required in the new industries push wages upward.

The turning point in the economic cycle is defined by technological, employment, and wage variables. First, decline in the output growth rates combined with institutional pressures for higher wages could result in inflationary phenomena. The drop in the economy's growth rate occurs as a result of the diminishing returns of technological trajectories, depletion of economies of scale, and market saturation of the new products. Second, as the new technologies mature, they tend to become more capital intensive—as is also the case in the other sectors—which causes the job destruction trait of the technology to prevail in relation to its potential to create new jobs.

As recession worsens, investment is increasingly directed at streamlining output and not at increasing production within a more competitive context. The recession increases unemployment trends that also arise from technological changes. This depicts the recessive phase of the long term cycle caused by the interrelation of the NTS with its outputs and employment markets.

However, as was mentioned, this explanation does not shed light on why, at a given point in time, an NTS becomes dominant. It is necessary to understand the factors underlying the clustering of the dissemination of a new set of technological trajectories. In other words, what are the technological, economic, and institutional reasons causing investment flows to abandon their previously normal channels and be directed at NTSs? The answer to this question is crucial from the perspective of economic development because it could identify the variables that are essential for a society to succeed in deliberately incorporating an NTS.

Pérez (1985) makes some headway in answering the question of how an NTS becomes dominant and determines a new long term expansive cycle. In her explanation the social and institutional context plays a pivotal role that makes it possible to formulate the concept of a technological and economic paradigm. Each cycle corresponds to a paradigm, and they become dominant when the following conditions are met:

1. A relative cost that is perceived as being low and declining
2. Apparently unlimited supply
3. A potential influence that permeates the entire productive sphere
4. A generally recognized capacity, based on a set of technological innovations, to reduce costs and improve the quality of capital, work, and products

Long term recessions occur when there is a lack of concordance between the technical and economic spheres and the social and institutional ones. This concordance arises from the existing institutional structure and social behavior patterns developed in concordance with the preceding paradigm (Pérez 1985).

This thesis clearly opens up a new research agenda. First, it becomes even more necessary to specify the social and institutional context. According to Pérez (1985), this includes the organizational and administrative patterns of firms, workers' organizations, and interest groups, together with the legal frameworks in which they operate. This specification, however, must necessarily resort to historical analysis and, therefore, refers to specific periods.

In this respect Piore and Sabel (1984) underscore social relations in an attempt to explain the current economic crisis. First, they highlight the *weltanschauung* of the production organization of standardized merchandise, so that competition is based on reducing costs and not on introducing new products. Technological trajectories are oriented toward the standardization of products and gaining an edge from economies of scale to reduce costs. The second aspect mentioned by these authors arises from the fact that mass production needs to find a stable environment that will allow the depreciation of high investment costs in inflexible fixed capital. This gives rise to various corporate strategies and the emergence of new roles for the state. However, the external world is much too uncertain to permit the realization of the benefits of mass production, which results in a trend toward crisis. There are two available options. The first is to try to generate the necessary stability so that mass production does not lead to a crisis by adopting a global Keynesian strategy to handle demand. The alternative is a change toward flexible specialization.

Flexible specialization is a different technological concept than the core technologies of Freeman, Clark, and Soete (1982). The line of causality is reversed. The option between mass production and flexible specialization will not be resolved by the implicit power of their embodied technologies. Resolution will occur in the area of social relations and will reflect the relative power of the different sets of social actors.[16]

Hoffman and Kaplinsky (1988) attempt to combine technological determinism and resolution of the conflict in the area of social relations to explain the major transitions in industrial history. The nature of technology is such that, under certain circumstances, it transforms social relations once it is applied, while in others, the maximum benefits of innovation can only be obtained if social relations are transformed beforehand. Moreover, these authors place great importance on specifying the labor process, since the social relations established there are particularly relevant to analyze technological change.[17] Analysis of the labor process also includes a cultural and ideological dimension (habituation); in other words, the dissemination of given innovations within the labor process or in machinery can be culturally determined and perhaps be subject to change through the manipulation of mass communications media or education.

Technological changes can be grouped into three kinds: (1) marginal changes that occur within a technological trajectory, (2) radical changes that give rise to new technological trajectories, and (3) revolutionary changes that modify both the production techniques and social organization of that production. According to this view of technological revolutions, Hoffman and Kaplinsky (1988) have proposed a division of industrial history into three periods.

In the First Industrial Revolution, the predominant role did not apply to the introduction of new techniques, but rather to new forms of organization of production that revolutionized productivity levels. It involved the organization of workshops with known techniques, but with wage labor and new forms of control of the production process. The Second Industrial Revolution was characterized by the introduction of machinery in production, so that the labor process began to depend on the assembly line and not on workers' skills. The possibilities for control and division of labor were increased, and large scale production was made possible. This revolution involved the introduction of new technology. Nevertheless, social and trade union conditions and market size determined its more successful dissemination in the United States than in Europe. In the Third Industrial Revolution, new techniques only constitute one aspect. Moreover, countries that have moved ahead in introducing them do not necessarily achieve the hoped-for advances in productivity. Social conditions and entrepreneurial and labor union reorganization are prerequisites for new technology to have an impact.

Technological potential emerges from innovations in storage, processing, and the rapid and low-cost transmission of information. Numbers, alphabets, and simple decision systems can be reduced to binary systems (infinite combinations of 1 and 0). Thus, countless information and decision systems can be interconnected because they operate on the basis of a common logic. The benefits of this new technology require that the different parts of the industrial organization of a plant or enterprise operate with a common logic. Design, production, and management are carried out with the aid of computers. The new revolution involves the introduction of interconnected systems. The organizational aspect is fundamental. Flexibility of major industrial complexes is sought to produce quality goods in the least time possible that can open up markets (flexible specialization). A very close relation is required between marketing, design, and production.

The large enterprises designed to benefit from the advantages of the Second Industrial Revolution must undergo major changes in order to participate in the third. Mass production has given place to flexibility. The axis went from supply considerations (maximum production of undifferentiated products) to demand. To achieve flexibility, the labor process needs to be modified so that workers have greater control over the process. This means reversing the trend toward a reduction of required skills and control exercised by the workers themselves. The assembly line logic under "Taylorist" managerial concepts that characterized the Second Revolution were based on conflicting relations between capital and labor. In contrast, new technologies give back to the workers the decisionmaking capacity in order to increase flexibility and improve quality control. Within this new framework, worker-management relations cannot be based on conflict. The labor process undergoes a change from conflict to consensus building.

Biotechnological Break

A series of changes have taken place in the biotechnological field. This is the result of innovations in a series of areas that threaten to bring about another technological break, owing to the consequences on the organization of production, R&D and its links with production, and the impact on a large number of productive sectors: agriculture, food products, mining, and pharmaceuticals. Therefore, a brief reference to the most important features is useful, particularly regarding applications to agriculture.

Prior to the present technological break, technical change in agriculture was based on research conducted or financed by public agencies with an extensive international network of research and dissemination. Various research centers were established in Latin America, duly connected to public networks in developed countries. As a result, technological development experiences and the dissemination of new techniques and natural material were accumulated on the continent. However, developments in biotechnologies modified the institutional format for R&D in agriculture and defined the priorities for development agendas of new technological trajectories in different directions than those under formats dominated by public interests.

Biotechnology is the utilization of living organisms for commercial purposes.[18] In fact, it refers to various fields of specialization that may be classified into: (1) cultivation of tissues, (2) transfer of embryos, (3) cellular fusion, (4) fermentation, and (5) genetic engineering.

Some of the consequences of the innovations occurring in these fields include (Rodríguez and Weisleder 1989):

• A change in the institutional organization of R&D, primarily in agriculture, with greater weight of private activity at the expense of public activity. This trend had the following three consequences: (1) The trajectories selected are those that promise to generate profitable innovations.

Subjects such as parasitosis in tropical agriculture or the problems of semi-arid agriculture may be omitted from research agendas; (2) Knowledge will not be freely available because most of the resources in research are geared to the objective of establishing technological monopolies. The free flow of science to build greater knowledge by the scientific community tends to be encumbered, and access to more knowledge becomes more difficult for newcomers; (3) Private research agendas may be tightly linked to the dependent consumption of successful products, for example, seeds that require the presence of certain pesticides.

• Associated with the greater weight of transnational private interests in R&D in agriculture, legal conditions were modified to allow greater private appropriation of biotechnological knowledge.

• One of the features of biotechnology emerged from the rapprochement between basic research and its applications, which increased the externalities in the communications between researchers and producers.

• Certain innovations have opened up large areas of possible applications. A single technique, such as the cultivation of tissues, may be used to greatly increase the efficiency of a large number of processes, such as fermentation or the reproduction of countless genetically identical plants.

• Technological trajectories emerged from major markets, from the needs of temperate agriculture, and from concerns such as chemical pollution. The results could reduce the need to use chemical pollutants in agriculture within temperate zones, which could probably lead to stricter regulations on the allowed level of chemical products, and in turn could eventually exclude tropical products.

• The comparative advantages of tropical agriculture are being eroded as a result of other factors besides those already mentioned: (1) It is possible, by cellular reproduction in the laboratory, to avoid the agricultural phase in the production of a given substance. Opiates are an example; (2) Fermentation processes have made it possible to obtain products by using raw materials that were unlikely only a few years ago. The best example is artificial sweeteners.

Thus, a technological lag in these circumstances could mean that: (1) technological trajectories do not respond to the conditions of lagging countries; (2) an erosion of comparative advantages could occur with loss of access to key markets; (3) the increasing private appropriation of technical knowledge by blocking the flow of scientific knowledge tends to consolidate the technological gap between developed and peripheral countries; and, (4) dependence on genetic material and on chemical inputs is heightened due to the characteristics implanted through genetic engineering.

However, the new technologies also offer important advantages: (1) the relatively low cost of installing avant-garde laboratories in some fields such as tissue cultivation or the diagnosis of illnesses and the preparation of vaccines permits a large number of countries to attempt to place themselves at the technological forefront; (2) the existence of qualified personnel in many peripheral countries; (3) the incipient nature of the industry, for which reason the entry costs are still not exceedingly high; (4) the existence of public research infrastructure, both in developed countries and in Latin America, that can deal with areas that are not necessarily profitable, such as the problems of small producers working in tropical conditions; and (5) the characteristics of technology that, by being so close to basic research, allows the rapid development of new applications.

A View of Technological Change from Within

To deduce the possible implementation of the preceding views, once they are seen from the perspective of development, a fundamental question—largely institutional in nature—must be answered: What institutions can contribute to science and technology so that they, in turn, can make a greater contribution to development?

Technological Change Institutions

In societies that are not centrally planned, the primary institutions that carry out or have an influence on technological change are firms, the market, and the state, although numerous other institutions also participate but in a much more subsidiary manner. Consequently, a large proportion of the studies on technological change are theories on the participation of the main institutional agents in the process.

The particular blend of institutional responsibilities in the technological change process depends on the society in question. However, it is possible to make some generalizations that even point to a characterization of center and periphery. Developed countries are characterized by the following:

1. The market tends to lose importance as the institution responsible for technological change. Market failures in technological transactions and the nature of competition—when technology is not only not shared but is at the same time the basis of competition—have led to a greater institutional importance of the other two institutions (firms and the state).

2. The relation between science and technology is increasingly narrower. Modern technology is characterized by being based on or related to science. The pursuit of two somewhat independent subsystems increasingly loses validity. The division of labor between public responsibilities in the case of basic science and private ones with their regulation and intervention system, for example, patents, becomes increasingly meaningless.

3. R&D takes place within the enterprises and is geared to relate science and technology in a regulated, systematic manner and at an increasingly greater scale. Its objectives can involve the innovations of new and improved products or processes.

4. Nevertheless, public intervention in the innovation process through explicit policies is justified precisely because of those market flaws: "The socialization of some of the risks and the uncertainty of technical innovation is difficult to avoid owing to the pressure of world competition, the externalities and the factors of scale in R&D, and the adverse consequences of *'laissez innover.'* Such socialization, however, implies the responsibility of developing an explicit rather than implicit national scientific and technical innovation policy" (Freeman 1982: 26).

The balance is different in peripheral countries:

1. Firms carry out little R&D. It focuses primarily on adapting and modifying imported technology, referred to as informal or implicit R&D, being small-scale in nature due to the lack of a systematic activity, differentiated from other firm activity (Sábato and Mackenzie 1988: 224).

2. National scientific and technological policies, in most cases, have not transcended the promoting of scientific activities, without ensuring that these eventually be transformed into innovations.

3. Consequently, despite its flaws, the main technical change institution tends to be the market. In view of the well-known fact that an overwhelming majority of R&D occurs in central countries and, consequently, innovations arise there, the international market is the principal supplier of the means to modify the techniques of peripheral enterprises. It should be mentioned, however, that the specification and control over technology imports is one of the areas in which interesting developments have occurred in Latin America (Sábato and Mackenzie 1988: chapter 7).

The possibility is set forth, then, that one of the reasons for the technological lag that characterizes the periphery may lie in the different institutional blend of technological change agents. The market is depended upon for the most important technological changes in productive sectors because the most significant endogenous efforts of firms do not transcend adaptive changes, and explicit policies have not succeeded in linking scientific development to innovations. Thus, the capacity of peripheral productive sectors to compete on the basis of new products or processes (the most dynamic element of capitalism, according to Schumpeter) is technologically limited by its innovative incapacity. That is to say, peripheral export products must compete in price; competition in domestic markets also tends to be based on price or oligopolistic arrangements. Therefore, the logic of entrepreneurial survival depends relatively less upon the innovation of processes and products, which makes it unnecessary to develop systematic, organized, and differentiated R&D. The vicious circle of underdevelopment leaves no room for innovation.

This view is consistent with Vernon's (1966) product cycle theory. According to this theory, new products tend to originate in high-income countries, due to the existence of demand and the skills for producing them. The innovator country exports them to other high-income countries, which will eventually produce them, and if they prove to be more efficient, they could even reverse the direction of the trade flow. As the product matures, its production becomes more standardized, and it is possible to transfer the technology to lower-income countries. At this stage international trade can go from low-income to high-income countries.[19]

The preceding analysis of technological change would explain why the skills to produce new products exist in high-income countries, which are, in turn, the conditions for generating new products. These skills depend on firms' systematic and organized R&D activity and public policies that socialize some of the risks of the process. The preceding discussion on technological change and product cycle is also consistent with the original ECLAC hypothesis regarding the unequal distribution of the benefits of technical progress in international trade between the center and periphery.

The firm. The neoclassical discourse refers to markets, and its fundamental question is: What are the necessary conditions for competitive equilibria to exist? The analysis of the firm's characteristics becomes subordinate to the aspects that are compatible with competitive balances. It is primarily a market theory (Machlup 1967) and not one of the firm per se. Its scant "realism" is tied to the fact that it does not attempt to explain a firm's behavior in the face of complex decisions arising from domestic factors and its milieu. The theory limits itself to forecasting behavioral responses to changes in prices according to the endogenous tendency toward equilibrium. It is thus that other aspects are assumed to be exogenous and constant in order to isolate the effect of changes in price. When the milieu variables are modified, the analysis of their impact is reduced to reactions in the face of price changes. Technological change cannot be reduced to price changes.[20]

Nevertheless, an important direction of the development of economic discourse refers to the way in which firms or industrial branches have adapted to selection techniques in the price formation process. This discussion puts neoclassical authors face to face with neo-Ricardian and Marxist writers. The debate has not been resolved, largely because it lacks a theory of price formation, except under competitive market conditions (Nadal Egea and Salas Páez 1988: chapter 2).

From a more general perspective, but with fewer possibilities for formal analysis, important contributions have been made to explain firm behavior in response to technological change.[21] The results obtained cannot be classified as a theory of the firm, and the analyses have necessarily required going beyond the institution of the firm. Other institutions such as research centers and scientific communities, as well as other elements of the milieu, also have an impact on technical change that takes place within firms.

From a developmentalist perspective, advances in understanding firm behavior in terms of R&D and the innovation that has occurred in developed countries have limited application because they presuppose the existence of behaviors whose origins need to be explained. The question posed from the perspective of development needs to be modified to include, as a starting point, how can innovative behavior emerge in firms, which is not the same as asking how these behaviors emerged in developed countries. Obviously, the contributions made in central countries are basic because they tend to explain the nature of behaviors that may be desirable to develop. Whence, from a developmentalist position, the scope of the research agenda broadens with the inclusion of the objective of explaining the technological lag and setting forth the requirements to close the gap.

The analysis of developed countries has followed two types of strategies. Coombs, Saviotti, and Walsh (1987), based on the theoretical developments within a number of disciplines, have attempted to explain decisionmaking aspects in R&D. A different methodology has been directed at building a typology of innovative behaviors in firms and of related variables based on abundant empirical studies, without attempting to constitute a theory of the firm. The most important is that developed by Freeman (1982).

Toward a theory of the firm. The initial method followed by Coombs, Saviotti, and Walsh (1987: chapter 2) was to apply administrative theories to technical change. Administrative strategies are formulated within contexts that include technological opportunities and limitations. These stem from the very characteristics of the firm, resulting from its past growth and the technical and economic factors surrounding it. It was found that decisionmaking in the face of incentives and constraints was complex and internally differentiated, often associated with conflicts within the firm and carried out within environments of uncertainty.

Subsequently, decisionmaking analysis was applied to aspects related to R&D (expenditure levels, degree of basic research, program structure and its objectives). Among the explanatory factors, mention is made of specific firm resources, technological opportunities, and industry and market structure. The authors are optimistic that models can be eventually developed to forecast some of the results of the behaviors generated by resource allocation decisions in R&D (Coombs, Saviotti, and Walsh 1987: chapter 3).

The analysis continues with a discussion of the organization and im-plementation of R&D and reveals a variety of management practices that seem to depend on tacit knowledge, ad hoc procedures, and accumulated experience in the field. These practices, occurring within a context of mar-ket uncertainty and organizational complexity, depend upon the actions of scientists and technological experts that are still tied to the control mech-anisms of the scientific establishment (Coombs, Saviotti, and Walsh 1987: chapter 4).

From an analytical point of view, it can be stated that even if there was a theory of the firm, it would be unable to explain technological change, since the latter is the result of the interrelation of various institu-tions and practices which, besides the firm, include the market and non-profit research institutions. This line of analysis is producing a growing body of literature around the concept of technological management as a "process that permanently establishes technological proposals, missions and objectives; that continuously evaluates their validity, perceiving and creating timely opportunities for achieving them; that detects and foresees problems and difficulties in achieving them, to shape and resolve them" (Machado 1988: 5). The concepts developed have allowed a series of prac-tical applications both in central countries and in Latin America. While in developed countries the emphasis is on improving management,[22] in Latin American countries (primarily Argentina, Brazil, Costa Rica, Mexico, and Venezuela) the stress is on promoting technological management devel-opment, in terms of both the adaptation and generation of new technolo-gies, through the deliberate promotion of management nuclei (Machado 1989; Machado and Doryan 1989).

However, the absence of an answer regarding public policy require-ments within contexts of technological lags has limited the impact of tech-nological management programs. "The absence of a global frame of ref-erence for technological management processes, both at national and regional level, have characterized these actions, among other flaws, by their inconsistencies, lack of communication and contradictory orienta-tions, which have prevented their results from contributing to the techno-logical development objectives of the region." (Machado 1988: 10).

Innovative strategy typology. Without attempting to explain the microe-conomic reasons why enterprises follow different innovation strategies, Freeman (1982) typifies these strategies and points to some of the prereq-uisites that must be present for enterprises to be successful in the strategies followed.[23] The possible types of strategies are the following:

• *Offensive strategy*: An offensive innovation strategy attempts to es-tablish a technical edge in the market by introducing new products before competitors do. To obtain this advantage, the firm will need to carry out very intensive research, capable of generating the unavailable scientific and technical information and guiding the innovation's course until the new product is launched into the market.

• *Defensive strategy*: A defensive innovator can put as much emphasis on R&D as an offensive one. The difference lies in the nature and timing of the innovations; voluntarily or otherwise, they do not occupy first place in the innovation but follow it closely.

• *Imitative and dependent strategies*: Imitative strategies follow offensive and defensive strategies from a distance and use well-established technologies. They must rely on certain advantages with respect to their predecessors, such as a captive market or lower costs. Their R&D is adaptive in nature and aimed at innovations in cost-reducing processes. A dependent strategy accepts a subordinate role with respect to a more powerful firm. It depends on its clients for specifications of new products and techniques. The dependent firm is linked to its clients by subcontracts or subsubcontracts.

• *Traditional and opportunist strategies*: The difference between a traditional strategy and a dependent one lies in the nature of the product. The traditional strategy is used in the case of products that are unlikely to undergo modifications, while dependent firms must change their products in response to requests external to the firm. Traditional firms are under no pressure from the market to change their products. The opportunist strategy refers to the possibilities that market niches may offer the imaginative entrepreneur under contexts of rapid change that may not require R&D or complex designs.

Center-periphery and innovative strategies. Peripheral firms tend to follow traditional or dependent innovation strategies. This prevents them from entering their products into the market at the initial phases of their respective cycles. Their survival strategies depend on cost advantages and are not based on their R&D.

The relation between science and technology is far from being direct. It is a complex interrelation and full of externalities. Although it is true that scientific knowledge is relatively available worldwide, in fact, access to the results of basic research is partly tied to the degree of participation (Price and Bass 1969). There are countless barriers that prevent benefiting from existing scientific knowledge. Among these, Freeman (1982: 174) has mentioned cultural, educational, political, national, and geographic barriers and those relating to trademark rights.

Nevertheless, the efforts by Latin American countries mentioned above to shore up their scientific systems have come up against the inability to articulate them with firms. This gap arises from the innovative strategies of peripheral enterprises that do not depend on their upper hand in the market to introduce new products originating from their endogenous innovative capacity. There is no demand for scientific developments because there are no offensive or defensive innovative firms. Entrepreneurial objectives in technological management remain within narrow frameworks of technological adaptation.[24]

For a peripheral country to close the technological gap requires the development of highly advanced scientific and technological infrastructure providing access to original research. However, converting this potential into products requires firms with suitable innovative strategies, for which it is necessary to depend less upon the market as a mechanism for technological change. Nonetheless, it is unlikely that firms will make this transition per se, without an adequate milieu of stimuli. Technological management nuclei must be promoted, but in a macroeconomic environment that streamlines innovative strategies.

Public policies. Government intervention in technology is an accepted fact in industrialized countries, both with respect to promoting technological change and in regulating it, particularly to avoid undesirable side effects or to introduce equity concerns. Nevertheless, although this is true for existing public interventions, every time a new intervention is proposed in countries like Britain, the entire ideological substratum of the discussion reemerges. In Asian countries, less concerned with ideologies, it has been easier to reach agreements on technological change objectives in order to deal pragmatically with decisions on the mechanisms to be employed. Their economic success is based on their technological strategy, as Freeman (1982: 190) points out: "Countries like Japan, which have followed a more consistent and patient technological public policy, have generally been more successful, although at a much lower scale of public expenditure in R&D, owing to the lack of significant military R&D."

Arguments in favor of intervention are analytically straightforward. In the technological area the social benefits or costs tend to differ from private ones. Therefore, in order to raise the general level of well-being, various forms of intervention are appropriate. Coombs, Saviotti, and Walsh (1987) put forward eight arguments to justify public policies for cases in which social benefits exceed private ones:

1. The scale of capital investment in R&D required by industries based on new technologies, particularly those in the lead, may exceed a firm's financial capacity or its level of risk tolerance. Possible instruments may include anything from subsidized credit to the creation of public enterprises.
2. The construction of comparative advantages in avant-garde sectors or the reconversion of lagging sectors in order to face international competition may require that public funds be made available to enterprises.

3. In strategically important social areas, it is possible that private companies will not benefit from investing in technological change, and yet it may be desirable from a social point of view (energy, transportation, telecommunications, and the like).
4. In most fields investment in basic research only produces dividends over the long term, which may underlie a private firm's preference for spending in applied research. Public funds for research thus become necessary.
5. There are areas of basic research that will hardly lead to innovation, but instead will provide the infrastructure needed by inventors, engineers, and industrial researchers. Enterprises do not tend to invest in this kind of research, thus making necessary the public presence.
6. In sectors where small units abound, such as agriculture, private enterprises may not have the financial capability or the skills to carry out R&D, and the market in general may not generate the incentives for them to undertake these activities.
7. In the area of public health, it is generally accepted that the market should not be the sole provider of services nor of R&D, although there are sectors such as pharmaceutical that in developed countries are dominated by private firms.
8. The defense sector requires public funds.

Another important field for public intervention refers to cases in which social costs exceed private ones (negative externalities). In principle, taxes and subsidies could be used to eliminate or reduce undesirable effects, as well as to generate sufficient information for consumers to become aware of the possible negative consequences. Nevertheless, it is less costly and more efficient to introduce regulations governing polluting activities, workers' security and safety, sanitary and safety product requirements, and the like.

A Strategy to Deal with Technological Lags

The structuralist theory of development emerged within the context of the Second Industrial Revolution. Insofar as technical change could be largely reduced to the introduction of new techniques, the technological problem could be incorporated into that of industrialization. However, if the market is relied upon as the mechanism for technological change, it will be most unlikely that endogenous innovation capabilities will be generated, perhaps with the exception of adaptive innovations. Consequently, the problem of technological lags must be set forth in a series of dimensions that involve many institutions besides the market.

First of all, it should be mentioned that the arguments put forward in developed countries favoring public intervention to promote technological change and prevent some of the possible excesses are equally valid when applied to peripheral countries. If breaching the technological gap is acknowledged as an objective, the innovative strategies of firms also need to be modified. This means modifying the milieu and the incentives to be faced, as well as explicitly promoting the development of technological management skills.

Public policies (macro level) should be geared to consolidating scientific and technological systems. They should also be primarily devoted to articulating scientific capacities with productive sectors, within a framework of long term decisions for product specialization and decisions in terms of the aggressiveness of innovative strategies that are sought in various lines of specialization. This involves deciding, on a strategic horizon, the innovative capacity required to selectively promote technological management programs and innovation dissemination by sector.

The most successful country in bridging the technological gap has been Japan, and thus deserves a brief mention. One of the interpretations regarding Japan's development states that its success can be explained by the transition of a significant proportion of traditional technological strategy enterprises toward imitative and later defensive and offensive strategies. Japanese national policy was designed to facilitate this transition (Freeman 1982). Government policies have backed managers' efforts at the firm level (Allen 1981; Peck and Wilson 1981).[25]

The most important group within the powerful Ministry of Trade and Industry (MITI) is responsible for following up world technological development and making recommendations to industry on future trends and their consequences (Freeman 1982: 222). According to these analyses and national development criteria, a recommendation was made as to the strategic sectors that were to gradually evolve in accordance with Japan's evolution and that of the world economy. These sectors have had ample support, which includes a wide variety of instruments ranging from direct recommendations to companies on products and areas for development, to subsidized credit.

National criteria for selecting strategic sectors and thus building comparative advantages without allowing these to be determined by international competition on the basis of existing comparative advantages are as follows (Sáez 1988):

- Income elasticity: the sectors with greatest income elasticity, so that in the face of an increase in world income, a deterioration of the terms of trade does not occur
- Relative technological progress: the sectors in which competitiveness could increase most rapidly if greater technological change were to occur
- Linkages: the sectors with the most linkages with the rest of the economy

- Employment: the sectors with greatest employment generation potential[26]

The weighting of the various criteria has been gradually modified over time. In the 1950s recommended sectors included basic industries such as steel and petrochemicals, characterized by their capital-intensiveness and by their avant-garde technologies at the time. Among the labor-intensive ones, the automotive, electronics, and machinery industries were selected. In addition to these selective policies, industrial policy also intervened in areas such as international trade, and in correcting imbalances in the relations between small and big business. In the 1970s the emphasis shifted to companies with an important R&D component and high aggregate value, such as machine tools and office equipment, among others. Lastly, in the 1980s priority was given to avant-garde technological industries to compete at the forefront of technological progress.

Technological policy was initially based on importing technology for the express purpose of developing an autonomous capacity to improve it and achieve the same level as the United States in the use of such technologies. One of the policies employed to promote technological adaptation was the direct action of the MITI to coordinate the formation of R&D joint ventures. These ventures were begun with government initiative and, in addition, received public funding. Their objective was to learn imported technology and disseminate it to companies (Yoshikawa 1988: 8).[27] Other instruments such as subsidized credit were used to ensure the dissemination of innovations.

Then, greater emphasis was placed on R&D, and it was possible to make headway in offensive and defensive innovative strategies. Nevertheless, the importance of permanently importing avant-garde technologies was underscored, since no country can reasonably hope to remain on top in all fields, for which reason adaptive skills continue to be paramount. It can also be inferred that it is crucial to identify the combination of products and processes used to modify the innovative strategy in the attempt to achieve the change from the most basic to the most sophisticated strategies. The relative weight given to developing offensive and defensive strategies, to mention only two, can be gradually modified over time.

Important efforts have been made in Latin America to analyze and streamline the technology importing process. As a starting point, it should not be indiscriminate but subject to objectives and conditions. Sábato and Mackenzie (1988: 221–222) indicate the following elements that must be taken into account in importing technology, in order to know its characteristics and be able to introduce the necessary changes for importing the most suitable technology:

- Nature: classification criteria refers to the sector in question, production, management and marketing; in production technologies a distinction must be made between incorporated and unincorporated technologies

- Sources: current but also potential suppliers
- Property rights: the rights that protect imported technology
- Costs: both direct and indirect and their effects on the balance of payments
- Quality: determine its relation with the local market and its own degree of obsolescence
- Social and ecological impact: assess its negative ecological impacts and its sociocultural consequences
- Diseconomies (negative externalities): in order to determine the importance of the diseconomies of the imported technology within the total technological flow
- Distribution by enterprise: to know which are the main importers

An important way of intervening, highlighted by Sábato and Mackenzie (1988: 243), refers to *qualitative technological protectionism.* This is based on the use of economic policy instruments to generate incentives for companies to use national technology. In particular, a very powerful instrument is the purchasing power of the public sector; this can give preference to local engineering and consulting firms and to local production, and it can even foster development of technological capacity to obtain a good or service.

The microeconomic dimension of dealing with technological lag includes technological management programs for the purpose of developing the capacity to effectively involve the technological variable in entrepreneurial decisionmaking. In the case of Costa Rica, the endogenization of the technological variable in entrepreneurial decisionmaking has been focused through two programs: (1) a technological management program aimed at creating management nuclei in strategic activities through major support to selected enterprises, with United Nations funding; and (2) a subsidized credit system for technological innovation projects in priority areas, with an Inter-American Development Bank credit (Doryan 1989; Machado and Doryan 1989).

Mesoeconomics, according to technological aggregation criteria, should set forth the corresponding strategies for the technological trajectories that are desired or not desired to be incorporated into the economy, according to the relevant innovation strategies. Significant conclusions concerning policies are emerging from this discussion that may guide decisions at an intermediate aggregation level between the company and macroeconomics. Technological aggregation enables making subsectoral or even cross-sector recommendations as, for example, those referring to the dissemination of innovations in microcircuits. The objective would be to create the conditions for benefiting from given technological opportunities, which in turn define innovative behavioral possibilities for companies.

Among these subsectoral actions, mention should be made by way of example of the Japanese efforts to develop R&D capacities and the dissemination strategies of innovations by subsector. Note should also be made of the need for organizational developments that transcend the company, but without necessarily including public policies. Examples of this include the commodity exchanges and the organizations that promote quality control, metrology, and standardization.

These three dimensions of the strategy to deal with technological lag (microeconomic, mesoeconomic, and public policies) require a diagnosis of current potential of productive, scientific, and technological systems and a prospectus of technological change at the world level to determine the possible impact on the potential productive structure according to different specialization scenarios. Strategy specification must include a discussion of the appropriate institutional format to achieve the proposed objectives. This is especially necessary in terms of the various innovative strategies to be promoted in selected technological trajectories, in many cases with increasing complexity.

With respect to the institutional organization for technological change and strategies and policies, the consequences become particularly relevant and meaningful once the characteristics of the microelectronic revolution and biotechnological innovations are introduced. The consequences of this Third Industrial Revolution demand much deeper social change than those indicated in the preceding paragraphs. It puts forth the social organization characteristics of production in accordance with the explicit objective of obtaining maximum advantage from the new technologies. The conditions for defining productivity in a society have transcended microentrepreneurial, mesoeconomic, and public policy considerations to include the organization of society itself. Flexibility, capacity of adaptation, and consensus-building processes will be requirements for a developed country. Concertation includes a series of dimensions: between companies of a same subsector, between public and private subsectors, and between workers and entrepreneurial organizations, both at a social level and at a level of the enterprise or plant itself.

According to the preceding argument, Latin American countries found themselves technologically lagging with respect to the Second Industrial Revolution. The gap today also extends to the Third Industrial Revolution. The unknowns this raises include consideration of what the necessary conditions would be for leapfrogging into the Third Revolution, or whether it will be inevitable to first go through the Second Revolution. Without attempting a satisfactory response, some considerations follow.

In view of such radical differences in the labor process between the Second and the Third Revolutions, it could prove advantageous to bypass the second and jump directly into the third. However, this means that leap-frogging stages now would require not only incorporating new technological trajectories, but also deep social and cultural changes, as a prerequisite for being able to introduce these new trajectories. Simultaneously with the introduction of technological trajectories, it would be necessary to develop innovative entrepreneurial behavior, in other words, new technological management capabilities. However, if the typical marketing process of the Second Revolution was not within reach of lagging countries, the difficulties of production based on flexibility and the adaptive capacity to market conditions would multiply the preceding problems. The impact of innovation possibilities would vary for different subsectors. For this reason, the possibilities of advancing to the technological forefront would differ. Studies on technological prospectives would be necessary in order for countries to define scenarios in innovative capacities, in accordance with potential technological trajectories.

A condition for being able to transform the corresponding technologies and labor processes is the cultural development of consensus-building. This change may require ideological transformations both in the relations between workers and factory management teams and even society. The role of trade unions and other workers' organizations should move toward establishing new bargaining schemes and making understanding possible. In general, due to the fact that competitiveness will tend to be socially defined according to the new technical and economic paradigm and increasingly less to the individual company level, the gap between countries that incorporate technological change and those that do not will be abysmal.

International reinsertion with products of greater technological content poses a series of challenges in public policy terms in addition to those dealt with in this chapter. However, there is a dimension that deserves comment. It involves the distribution of the benefits of technical change at the national level. The process of industrial reconversion can be synonymous with a concentration of property for the purpose of increasing the profitability of depreciated assets and of a greater division of labor within economic units of greater dimensions.[28] Alternatively, schemes will have to be proposed for organizing producers to allow for a greater division of labor, but without concentrating property. These organizations will, in turn, have to serve as the vehicles for technological innovation. This would allow for small and medium-sized businesses to partake in the modernization process. Mechanisms such as commodity exchanges and organizations that safeguard quality control, metrology, and standardization are also important ingredients to ensure that weaker companies are not excluded from the process.

Notes

1. Some economists have attempted to explain this paradox in terms of three factors: (1) the ignorance of economists in subjects such as natural sciences and technology, (2) their concern for the business cycle and employment problems, and (3) the lack of good statistics (Jewkes, Sawers, and Stillerman 1958).

2. Outstanding exceptions that maintained interest in the subject of technology in Latin America were, among others, F. Sagasti and J. Sábato.

3. According to Kuhn's (1970) sociology of knowledge, these are two important criteria in paradigm formation: text preparation—introducing basic conceptual developments as well as the research agenda—and the formation of research traditions.

4. An invention is an idea, design, or model for a new or improved product, process, system, or instrument, while an innovation is achieved only when a commercial transaction occurs that involves this new or improved product, process, system, or instrument. However, innovation normally refers to both invention and innovation as such.

5. The concept of technology refers to a body of knowledge on techniques, but it can also refer to the tangible expression of that knowledge in the physical equipment of production. Technical innovation describes the introduction and dissemination of new and improved products in the economy; while technological innovation describes the advances in knowledge (Freeman 1982). Technological change includes both technical and technological innovation.

6. As Lavados (1983: 41) points out: "The development of science and technology poses such a variety of problems and complexities, particularly in the current and expanded view of a scientific and technologic system, that little can be seriously done without a clear and sustained policy decision in this direction. On the other hand, if that policy decision does not exist, we shall continue to witness the weak, disjointed and inefficient efforts observed today in the majority of our countries."

7. An important exception is Costa Rica, which in 1986 established the Ministry of Science and Technology and has continued to reinforce the scientific and technological institutional system and its articulation with productive sectors (see Doryan 1989).

8. The incorporation of technological variables in explaining international trade is an important element in the current debate on international trade theories. The discussion focuses on whether the conventional theory of comparative advantages can accommodate technological variables or whether a greater methodological break is necessary. Nevertheless, the trend is clear. The technological variable tends to displace the supply of factors as determinant of trade flows. The explanation, however, focuses on trade flows and not on the institutional context in which the exchange of goods and technological know-how occurs (Coombs, Saviotti, and Walsh 1987).

9. ECLAC may be seen as the precursor of the work by Pasinetti (1981) and Stoneman (1983). It has generally been concluded that to compensate for the destruction of jobs with new job creation requires other changes that do not necessarily occur: "More recent theories and empirical evidence seem to imply that compensation, if possible, necessarily implies a changing composition of output and of the labor force amongst different industrial sectors" (Coombs, Saviotti, and Walsh 1987).

10. An excellent abstract of the criticisms to this process may be found in the first section of Chapter 2.

11. A major exception was Thomas (1974), who proposed the thesis that the technological problem was not particularly serious for small economies that attempted a self-centered development strategy. The minimums of scale had been gradually reduced and the technologies for basic industries were available in the market.

12. In the strict sense of socially efficient results: Pareto-optimal.

13. Arrow arrived at the conclusion that an optimal result in competitive markets was obtained only if the state assumed the responsibility for scientific and technological development (Arrow 1962b).

14. See, for example, Freeman (1982) and Coombs, Saviotti, and Walsh (1987).

15. Kondratieff (1944) and Schumpeter (1939) provide the theoretical background. The authors define themselves as "Neoschumpeterian."

16. This discussion on the interpretations of technological change can be summarized as attempts to get production forces or social relations to prevail as explanatory factors. Freeman, Clark, and Soete (1982) attempt an explanation based on production forces, in which social relations become malleable by embodied technologies. On the other hand, Piore and Sabel (1984), emphasizing social relations, presuppose a certain malleability of embodied technologies (Hoffman and Kaplinsky 1988).

17. For Hoffman and Kaplinsky (1988), the labor process is the system whereby human beings with different abilities meet up with various sets of machines. Emphasis is placed on the fact that the machines designed to carry out the same physical operations can be installed with different control systems, allowing workers greater or lesser control over the labor process.

18. An excellent introduction to the subject is found in *Development Dialogue* 1–2 (1988).

19. Vernon (1971) revised his theory based on the development of transnational corporations and the closing of the income gap between the United States and the rest of the world. This makes it possible for the introduction of a new product to be conceived and planned as a global operation from the start.

20. Nevertheless, the fundamental neoclassical premise of the analysis of the firm, the trend to pursue maximum profit, has been useful in analyzing partial aspects of the technological change process (Stoneman 1983).

21. The contributions have come from a number of fields, noteworthy among which are the works of Galbraith (1969), Mansfield (1968a, 1968b), Mansfield et al. (1977), Nelson (1971, 1977), Nelson and Winter (1976, 1982), and Gold (1971, 1979). An introduction to the current state of the debate can be found in Coombs, Saviotti, and Walsh (1987) following its progress in *Technology Management Publication*.

22. It has been stated that the difficulties in the United States in competing in the world economy may lie in deficiencies within technological management, despite remaining in a leading position in the generation of innovations. It is argued that managers have failed to fully understand the technologies they are trying to implement (Baker 1988: 809).

23. Coombs, Saviotti, and Walsh (1987) identify a distinctive cultural factor of firms that may be associated with their innovative strategies.

24. In his well-known analysis of the engineering industry in South America, Katz (1980) found that even the two most successful Brazilian companies in his sample operated in fields in which the technological frontier had not made significant leaps in recent years, which earlier had allowed them to approach international productivity levels.

25. Nevertheless, Japan's fast industrialization was accompanied by rampant environmental degradation and other negative consequences for Japanese life-style (Freeman 1982: 184).

26. In Latin America Rodríguez and Morales (1989) propose a series of criteria for defining the strategic and complementary activities for an industrial reconversion program. These criteria are then applied to the industrial sector.

27. One of the most mentioned successes of one of these ventures is that achieved in the Japanese semiconductor industry (Yoshikawa 1988: 8).

28. This could be the expected result from the external trade "shock" liberalization.

PART 3

PRODUCTIVE SECTORS

9

The Process of Industrialization: Theories, Experiences, and Policies

Oscar Muñoz Gomá

This chapter reviews the experience and interpretations of the industrialization process in Latin America after World War II.[1] This debate takes place at a time when industrialization has lost much of the appeal it had for governments immediately after the war. Since the 1970s, short term problems such as rising inflation, unemployment, foreign debt, and financial instability have been the major issues of concern to experts, international agencies, politicians, and governments. Strategies based on simple adjustment models for dealing with financial crises have plunged the region into stagnation and frustration.

Thus, the need to reformulate long term development approaches has gained momentum once more. New policies are required to allow Latin America to participate in worldwide modernization trends and productive transformation. At the same time, however, there is a general awareness of the failure of many strategies applied in the past. The world has changed, a new technological revolution is taking place, the balance of global economic power has shifted, and industrialized countries are undergoing strong structural adjustments, forcing them to pursue new policies and approaches. This situation undoubtedly affects the frame of reference and the development possibilities available to Latin American countries.

It is therefore essential to review the conceptual and practical foundations on which past industrialization strategies have been based. This will help us understand, and assess, the rationale underlying previous attempts at industrialization. New realities must be taken into account, particularly the experience of newly industrialized countries (NICs), such as South Korea and Taiwan, the impact of new technologies, and the new international economic order.

This chapter is divided into four sections. The first section deals with the topic of industrialization—why industrialization is relevant and what is meant by this concept. Some basic empirical data is included in this section to illustrate historical experiences. The second section reviews the main hypotheses that try to explain why industrialization takes place. This section will compare the structuralist and orthodox theories of the postwar decades. The third section deals with the experience of industrialization in Latin America. At the risk of oversimplifying matters, an attempt will be made to outline the main features of the process. The chapter ends by stating the main consequences to be derived from a neostructuralist approach.

Background Data on the History of Industrialization

Up to the early 1970s, the question of whether or not it was convenient and necessary for a country to become industrialized was not debated. This was taken for granted. It was part of the conventional wisdom at the time. In Latin America this assumption became widespread in the 1950s under the influence exerted by ECLAC and its pessimistic assessment regarding the benefits of the international economic system, which confined developing countries to the role of providers of raw materials for industrialized countries. The ideas set forth by ECLAC fell on fertile ground because the Great Depression of the 1930s and, subsequently, World War II caused such a disruption in social and economic structures that countries urgently required a new economic rationale to replace the old attachment of the nineteenth century's orthodoxy to free trade and the gold standard.

The doctrine of industrialization spread quickly; multiple advantages and benefits—mainly from the historical experience of industrialized countries, particularly European—were attributed to industrialization. It was seen as the quickest way to increase the availability of manufactured goods and the well-being of the population; to promote new and better-paying jobs in view of declining employment in agriculture and mining; to foster technical training and help master modern technologies; to create new sources of wealth; and to open up new opportunities for investment and capital formation other than the exploitation of natural resources. Industrialization could turn into a strategy for sustained economic development thanks to the technical features of industry: economies of scale, externalities, included physical infrastructure, transport and communications facilities, labor force training, and development of new institutions and entrepreneurial classes.

There were also sociopolitical arguments. If the excessive importance of primary exporting sectors was associated with dependency and the lack of sovereignty, industrialization would help to increase economic independence and sovereignty. Economic growth would be more dependent on internal efforts than on unstable external markets. Moreover, given the social movements that increasingly challenged and criticized the established sociopolitical system, industrialization would offer new opportunities for social mobility, modernization, and urbanization.

These assumptions were backed by the experience of advanced countries. In all of them, economic growth was associated with changes in productive structures, in other words, a sustained increase of the share of industry and manufacturing in the national product. Table 9.1 shows the calculations made by Kuznets (1966) on long term changes in the productive structures of industrialized countries. To name but a few examples, over a period of roughly one hundred years, industrial participation increased from 34 percent to 56 percent in Great Britain, from 24 percent to 52 percent in Germany, and from 17 percent to 55 percent in Sweden. The definition of industry includes mining, manufactured goods, building, transportation, and communications. These activities are supposed to use modern technology, are capital intensive, and require greater geographical concentration than agricultural activities. At present, this definition is open to debate, given that modern technology and capital intensity are rapidly invading agriculture and the service industry as well. In any event, even if we confine the definition to the manufacturing sector, economic growth is also associated with an increase in the share of this sector, as shown in Table 9.2. Australia is an extreme case of rapid industrialization in manufacturing, since the share of manufactures in the industrial aggregate rose from 14 percent in 1861–1865 to 51 percent in 1934–1938.

Table 9.1. **Industrial Countries: Composition of GDP by Major Production Sector (at current prices, in percentages)**

	Agriculture		Industry		Service Industry	
	Opening	Closing	Opening	Closing	Opening	Closing
United Kingdom						
1841–1901	22	6	34	40	44	54
1924–1955	4	5	52	56	44	39
France						
1872/82–1908/10	42	35	30	37	28	28
1954–1962	12	9	52	52	36	39
Germany						
1860/69–1905/14	32	18	24	39	44	43
FRG, 1936–1959	11	7	42	52	47	41
The Netherlands						
1913–1938	16	7	33	40	51	53
1950–1962	13	9	47	51	40	40
Sweden						
1861/65–1901/05	39	35	17	38	44	27
1901/05–1949/53	35	10	38	55	27	35
United States						
1869/79–1919/28	20	12	33	40	47	48
1929–1961/63	9	4	42	43	49	53

Source: Kuznets (1966: 90–91).

Table 9.2.   Industrial Countries: Composition of Gross Industrial Product
(in percentages)

	Mining	Manufactures	Building	Transport & Communications	Share in Overall GDP
United Kingdom					
1907	13	59	8	20	46
1924	10	61	6	23	52
1955	6	69	10	15	56
Italy					
1861–65	2	79	11	8	20
1806–1900	4	69	9	18	22
1951–55	2	74	11	13	48
United States					
1869–79	5	42	16	36	33
1919–28	6	57	11	26	39
1929	5	59	10	26	42
1961–63	3	66	12	19	43
Australia					
1861–65	46	14	29	11	31
1934	9	51	20	20	33

Source: Kuznets (1966: 131).

Studies by Kuznets in the 1950s and 1960s, and more recent ones by Chenery and associates, have repeatedly verified the relationship between per capita income and the share of industry in the national product. This relationship is present when country trends over the course of time are used or when a sample of countries with different income levels at a given point is used. Chenery (1960) described this situation in terms of the high elasticities observed in industry with respect to per capita income, which were greater than one and in some cases greater than two. These same studies have also shown that, as per capita income increases, some manufacturing activities are more dynamic than others. Chenery and Taylor (1968) identified three groups of industries according to their dynamism: (1) mature industries—foodstuffs, textiles, and leather—whose relative share in the national product increases when per capita income is fairly low and later becomes stabilized; (2) median industries—manufactures in rubber, chemicals, and oil—in which stabilization occurs at higher income levels; and (3) new industries—machine tools, equipment, transportation materials, paper and cellulose, and consumer durables—whose relative share increases more permanently. This statement must be qualified in view of the industrial evolution of the past twenty years, a subject referred to later on.

Another way to look at the appeal of industrial growth as a development strategy is to examine its effects on trade. An old argument of free-trade orthodoxy was that a country did not need to produce manufactured goods to benefit from their consumption. Through trade and specialization a country could exchange goods, which had been produced more efficiently, regardless of their nature (manufactured or not) for goods not produced domestically. This argument stemmed from the classical theory of comparative advantages. However, in recent decades manufactures proved to be the most dynamic component in world trade. Excluding fuels, because unsteady prices can cause distortions in comparisons, between 1960 and 1980 the share of manufactures in worldwide exports rose from 51 percent to 67 percent (ECLAC 1986). Conversely, the share of primary products fell from 48 percent to 31 percent over the same period. This happened at a time when world trade was going through one of its fastest growth periods. Therefore, even if a given country follows the theory of comparative advantages, it is more likely to stimulate economic growth and the availability of goods if manufactures are developed and traded than if it confines itself to specializing in its traditional primary products. It is no accident that developing countries with the most spectacular growth rates in the postwar years, such as South Korea and Taiwan, did so by following an explicit export-oriented strategy (Fajnzylber 1989b).

Therefore, there are plenty of conceptual and empirical reasons to maintain that industrialization is an efficient development strategy. This does not imply, however, that any type of industrialization policy will suffice to achieve this goal. These issues will be referred to later on.

Industrialization Theories

How does industrialization take place in a country that has a traditional and stable economic structure? First, reference will be made to theories that deal with this issue from the point of view of the role played by foreign trade in resource allocation. Second, some arguments will be considered regarding domestic demand and its composition, which influence the rate of industrial growth.

Industrialization and Trade

The most orthodox version of neoclassical theory on international trade did not view industrial development as a growth strategy. The important issue, for neoclassical theory, was to maximize real income, given the existing stock of productive resources. The implicit assumption was that, through international specialization and efficient allocation of resources via free trade, underdeveloped countries would increase their income, both in static terms and in the long term. This would make possible an accumulation of capital that would alter the existing boundary of production possibilities.

The most advanced version of this theory, proposed by Heckscher-Ohlin-Samuelson, held that this international specialization would, additionally, help reduce the income gap between factors of production. Countries with a large labor force and low wages would specialize in producing labor-intensive goods, and the demand for this factor of production would rise and wages would thereby increase. The opposite would happen to capital. Protectionism would prevent this effect by stimulating the local production of capital-intensive goods, a factor in low supply in countries with a large labor force and low wages; pressure to raise the price of capital would increase and wages would become stagnant due to persistent unemployment.

This theory has been under strong debate because of its basic assumptions and neglect of some dynamic factors. The latter—based on the theory of infant industries and learning effects—suggested that an alternative other than the free trade model, based on the protection of domestic industry, could be more efficient in dynamic terms. In other words, although this involved sacrificing real income in the short term due to static inefficiencies, faster technological change and learning effects originated by protecting industry could lead to a faster growth rate than the free trade system (Ffrench-Davis 1979).

This debate became animated in Latin America in the postwar years. After decades of depression and wars, there was pessimism in the region. Furthermore, in most countries accomplishments in export development achieved prior to World War I did not result in sustained industrial expansion, contrary to the frequent assumptions of neoclassical theory on comparative advantages. Thus, during the Great Depression of the 1930s, Latin American economies plunged into economic downturn. Sustained stagnation in international trade, intensified by World War II, strengthened confidence in the need to promote industrialization through an explicit state policy, whereby the state would play a more active role, even in business and financial activities, in an attempt to stimulate local manufactures. From ECLAC (1950, 1954), Prebisch (1950a, b, 1959) refuted the neoclassical theory of comparative advantages and the alleged benefits connected with specialization in the export of raw materials.

Reasoning for this approach was based on the theory of the deterioration of the terms of trade for primary producers, thereby allowing the benefits of technical change to concentrate in countries that produce manufactures.[2] The use of technical advances in primary exporting sectors would be detrimental to export prices because of a low income elasticity of demand. Under a free trade system, resources could not be reallocated to manufacturing because considerable differences in productivity with industrial countries would inhibit profitability. Besides, minimum scales were required to start production. Initially, state protection and support were required in order to develop investment efforts and industrial growth.

Nevertheless, industrialization strategies should be based on the industrial sectors' assimilation of technical change aimed at increasing productivity. This was the intention underlying the concept of development *from within*.[3]

Other authors followed Prebisch in proposing new industrialization strategies. Rosenstein-Rodan (1943, 1957) proposed the "big push" theory: if markets were too small to justify installing new industries with economies of scale, simultaneous investments in different sectors could be coordinated in order to multiply reciprocal demands, thereby allowing full use of economies of scale. Hirschman (1958) contributed his theory of intersectoral linkages that, despite a different temporal sequence to that proposed by Rosenstein-Rodan, concurred on the need to create self-reinforcing mechanisms for the demand of manufactured goods. Hirschman maintained the need to produce sequential imbalances in the supply side, thereby stimulating the production factor that he believed to be in shorter supply in developing countries: decisionmaking and business skills. Many other authors emphasized the importance of externalities in industrialization strategies.

Nonetheless, after a fairly successful period, it became increasingly evident that industrialization strategies based on protectionism and import substitution had serious flaws. These flaws were reflected in estimates of the so-called domestic resource costs needed to obtain a unit of foreign currency through import substitution, which turned out to be notoriously higher than their market price and cost through new exports. From a different angle, this result occurred because, as the industrial structure gradually shifted to goods with higher technological contents and greater capital needs, the gap between domestic and external costs increased. It was not possible to make full use of economies of scale; the skilled labor required for this type of production was unavailable, and the products involved were goods in which quality and design played a more prominent role than in prior stages. Only the largest countries in the region, such as Brazil and Mexico, were better placed to partially avoid these problems. In addition, these two countries followed highly dynamic industrial policies aimed particularly at improving the quantity and quality of domestic production factors.

Moreover, successful industrialization experienced by the NICs of East Asia, by promoting the export of manufactured goods, helped generalize a more critical attitude toward the Latin American experience. Thus, new literature appeared in the 1970s that extensively analyzed and compared, both theoretically and empirically, import substitution strategies versus export strategies. Although this literature shows widespread consensus regarding criticism of import substitution experiences, it also reveals discrepancies with regard to how exports were promoted in NICs.

The most orthodox approach (Krueger 1978a; Balassa 1981) favored the thesis of a close relation between the growth of industrial exports and a reduction in trade restrictions. In fact, a classification of trade systems was proposed—in increasing order of economic efficiency—which was divided into the following historical phases: phase 1, in which quantitative restrictions predominate; phase 2, in which some quantitative restrictions become price restrictions (for example, import quotas that turn into tariffs or advance import deposits); phase 3, in which restrictions operate predominantly through the price system; phase 4, which signals the start of trade liberalization; phase 5, noted for full trade liberalization and complete elimination of quantitative restrictions (for example, access to the foreign exchange market, which tends to subsist as far as phase 4) (Bhagwati 1978). Phase 5 would be the most conducive to export growth.

Structuralism itself anticipated criticisms to extreme forms of import substitution.[4] Prebisch (1977) had made this criticism as early as 1963. However, this approach differed from orthodoxy on the proper strategy to be followed. Orthodoxy held that rapid trade liberalization, such as the one carried out in Chile in the 1970s, was the best strategy. Development economists with structuralist leanings emphasized the fact that developing countries that had successfully promoted the export of manufactures had done so once they had mastered industrial skills and had acquired some experience through import substitution (Díaz-Alejandro 1974). Structuralist proponents also emphasized the need for the state and industrial policy to play an active role in creating new comparative advantages (Fajnzylber 1983). Under this perspective, the opening up of trade and export promotion are not viewed as equivalent to free trade, which is based on a policy of laissez-faire. The opening up of trade requires the support of an explicit trade policy. This is the accurate way to interpret the experience in East Asia—and also that of Brazil and Mexico, the two Latin American countries that had achieved earlier success in this respect.

Structuralism also emphasizes other aspects that help to account for successful endeavors in exports. These include: a vigorous international framework, such as the one that extended from the 1960s up to 1973; the exploitation of economies of scale to induce higher productivity; the adoption of best-practice technology; and a decided commitment by the state to sustain the strategy in the long term. This was reflected in stable foreign exchange policies—in real terms—and in policies aimed at compensating exporters for higher tax costs potentially incurred due to policies for the protection of local industry.

Recently, the so-called new international trade theory has gained prominence; it tries to account for trade patterns in manufactures based on the theory of industrial organization and, particularly, the existence of market imperfections, economies of scale, and learning effects (Krugman 1988). This theory is inspired by the fact that trade between developed countries—specialized in different branches of manufacturing—is the most dynamic component of worldwide trade of manufactured goods. The new theory holds that, while trade between countries with a different degree of development can be basically accounted for by the traditional theory of comparative advantages, trade between countries with a similar degree of development—specialized according to products and designs in a given line of industry—is random and more dependent on the trade strategies followed by companies and nations. Such strategies are determined by general industrial policies, by the determination to make full use of externalities and economies of scale, and also by scientific and technological policies, among other factors. The general conclusion for developing countries is that, while less vital than for industrial countries in accounting for trade patterns, it leads to stressing the importance of creating dynamic comparative advantages through policies that can raise international competitiveness.

A second conclusion to be drawn from this approach is that it opens up new possibilities to reassess the road to regional integration as a concerted integration strategy. In general, past attempts at integration failed due to many reasons, which will not be analyzed here (see, for instance, Lahera 1986). However, one of the major causes of failure was that production agents in each country feared losing the protected markets in which they held a sound position. The experience of advanced countries—that industrial development is not harmed by international competition when competition is directed at intraindustrial specialization on the basis of differentiated designs, products, and qualities—should lead to a new attitude regarding potential integration between countries with similar technological levels. Indeed, integration cannot replace national industrial policies intending to raise the level of international competitiveness, technological capacity, and industrial rationalization. But it may provide a highly favorable framework to advance toward modernization in a period strongly limited precisely by the circumstances of the international economy.

Industrialization and the Structure of Demand

The above discussion focuses on the effects of trade and industrial protection on resource allocation. A slightly different approach—which became very popular in Latin America in the 1960s—refers to the effects of demand and its structure on the prospects of industrialization. In economies marked by strong structural heterogeneity, the markets and demand are affected by segmentation. This tends to hinder vigorous industrial growth because the formation of vast conglomerates of actual consumers for manufactures takes place slowly.

Although this subject was raised by structuralism in Latin America—which viewed inequalities in income distribution as a serious obstacle to more advanced stages of industrialization[5]—it is interesting to find an analytical link with the staple theory of export growth. In the later years of the nineteenth century and up to World War I, several countries of the capitalist periphery had initiated a sustained process of industrialization, despite an increasingly liberal context. This of course took place earlier in the United States and Canada, but then also in Australia, New Zealand, in countries of the European periphery, and in Latin American countries such as Argentina, Brazil, Chile, and Uruguay. Although these late-developing countries had begun to participate in the international division of labor as providers of raw materials, they developed industrial capacities even within their primary structures.

Traditionally, the main theoretical interest had been placed on explaining why less developed countries did not become industrial nations. Therefore, those experiences raised the question why some peripheral countries were able to begin a process of industrialization. Traditional answers were in terms of exogenous factors such as inflows of foreign capital. The development of primary export trade was supposed to encourage foreign investment, thereby helping to disseminate capitalist modernization. However, this argument was not fully adequate; empirical evidence showed that foreign investment tended to converge particularly toward export sectors, thereby giving rise to substantial and isolated enclaves that were segregated from the economy as a whole. The crucial issue was why an internal transformation was being encouraged in the productive structure of some countries.

A neo-Ricardian revival helped analyze this issue. The main point was to acknowledge the heterogeneity of peripheral economies or, at least, their dualistic nature, which is determined by high differentials of productivity between production sectors, reinforced by segregated social relations among them. This problem is described and analyzed quite clearly by Lewis (1954), and also by the staple theory of export growth (see Watkins 1963). Lewis examines a traditional agrarian subsistence economy marked by a low land/labor ratio, whereas Watkins analyzes a staple exporting economy with a high land/labor ratio. Lewis's model requires an exogenous incentive to persuade redundant members of the peasant population to emigrate to a modern and more productive sector. If subsistence agriculture is capable of sustaining the process by generating farm surpluses for urban consumption, the process may go ahead and achieve sustained industrialization.

Watkins's model, however, starts with the existence of a dynamic export sector. The question is how export growth stimulates the domestic economy. The relevant parameters are the propensity to consume imported goods versus domestic goods by export earners. Additionally, the export sector generates backward and forward linkages à la Hirschman. Backward linkages stem from intermediate demand, producer goods, and the infrastructure required by the export sector: housing, communication routes, transport networks, railroads, and the like. Many of these are nontradable goods that must be supplied locally.

An essential parameter mentioned by Watkins is the social and property structure prevailing in the export sector. There are two typical cases: plantation agriculture, noted for its highly concentrated property structure and profound inequality in income distribution, and, at the other extreme, small family farms, which are marked by greater equality. In the latter there is a high probability that the propensity to consume local goods is higher than that for imported goods. The reverse could be true under highly inequitable income structures. Incidentally, this would help explain why some European countries—for example, in Scandinavia—were industrialized earlier than southern European countries. In the former, rural property structures based on family farms were historically predominant, and these were more egalitarian than southern Europe's feudal structures, thus favoring the growth of a domestic market for manufactures.

Nevertheless, the initial average income level is also relevant. This is crucial to create demand for manufactures. Relatively high income allows the allocation of a more substantial portion of household income to the consumption of manufactured goods. Subsistence income only permits consumption of basic foodstuffs. There is a Ricardian assumption in this analysis, as workers who live at subsistence levels do not play any dynamic role whatsoever as consumers of manufactures. Only entrepreneurs and landowners do.

However, analysis developed along a neo-Ricardian approach takes it as possible for workers to play a more active role in industrialization, as consumers of manufactures. It all depends on the level and growth of real wages, which, in turn, are influenced by the relative price of agricultural goods. This depends on the productivity of agriculture in the production of basic consumer goods. The higher this productivity, the higher the wage surplus over basic food that can be spent on manufactures. This is why fertile areas in temperate climates with larger amounts of land per worker tend to encourage the rapid growth of real wages in comparison to tropical areas with high population density (Lewis 1977). This idea would provide further backing for the explanation on the earlier industrialization, among peripheral countries, of Argentina and Australia, for instance, instead of Central America or India.

The complementarity between the basic analytical framework of the Ricardian paradigm and that of neo-Ricardian economists breaks down in one aspect: the role of effective demand. The problem of insufficient aggregate demand is absent from Ricardian analysis (though not in Malthus, who argued with Ricardo on this issue). There supply originates its own demand. The dynamic problem is that of income allocation between consumption and investment.

In neo-Ricardian and developmental approaches, the problem of the lack of effective demand for industrial growth shows up in its full extent. Furtado (1969b) analyzed this problem for Latin America. Kaldor (1975) also provided a discussion in theoretical terms. The theory that supply can generate its own demand is based on the assumption of perfect flexibility of relative prices. But there is a limit to this flexibility in developing countries that is determined by the high share of basic subsistence goods in workers' consumption. A situation of perfect flexibility of relative prices between foodstuffs and manufactures is equivalent to stating that real wages can adapt to any level. But that is not the case. Subsistence needs based on agricultural goods impose a rigidity on the distribution of the family budget of low-income sectors. Therefore, a deficit in the effective demand for manufactures is likely to emerge if their relative price cannot be lowered beyond a certain level. The potential deficit in the demand for manufactured goods increases in proportion to the propensity of urban workers to consume basic agricultural goods.

Classical English economists were not aware of the problem just described because the exports of manufactures made the problem irrelevant (Kaldor 1976). However, in the twentieth century this problem has been highly significant in developing countries, particularly from the 1930s through the 1950s when international trade stagnated, thereby making the exports of manufactures from developing countries very difficult. Similarly, agrarian regimes that did not favor productivity growth gave rise to cost pressures on manufacturing activities.

The staple theory of exports is an attempt to explain the beginning of industrialization in primary exporting countries even without state intervention or protectionism. This theory has been applied to Latin American countries that experienced early industrialization, such as Argentina and Chile (see Geller 1970; Muñoz 1977, 1986). However, as Watkins argues and Prebisch had pointed out previously, for industrialization to be successful (in other words, sustainable in the long term) it is necessary to develop new conditions, particularly on the supply side, such as raising investment, upgrading the labor force, improving business efficiency, achieving technological transformation, increasing productivity, and expanding exports of manufactured goods. Growth induced by primary exports is usually short-lived. This expansion period is crucial in order to reallocate resources and create dynamic comparative advantages.

The Industrialization Experience in Latin America

The process of industrialization in Latin America has been marked by unequal progress. First, some countries such as Argentina, Brazil, and Chile started industrialization quite early, in the latter part of the nineteenth century. Subsequently, during the 1930s, these three countries stimulated the process of industrialization by applying antidepression policies, whereas most other Latin American countries adjusted to the external shock without compensatory policies. After World War II, particularly in the 1950s, other middle-sized countries, such as Colombia, Peru, and Venezuela, began a process of industrialization; even Central American countries managed to develop considerably their industrial structures on the basis of a Central American common market.

In general, the results achieved by industrial growth in the entire region throughout the period 1950–1980 are satisfactory (see Tables 9.3 and 9.4). The annual growth rate of the production of manufactures ranged from 6 to 7 percent during that period. This is higher than the international growth rate of 5.7 percent and shows an even higher differential if only the United States and Europe are taken into account. Production of some intermediate industrial goods shows spectacular increases in the twenty-five years following 1960.

Table 9.3.   Latin America: Production of Some Intermediate Industrial Goods (eleven countries)

	1960	1970	1980	1985
Tires (millions of units)	8.7	20.1	45.3	—
Paper pulp (millions of tons)	0.6	1.9	5.2	—
Newspaper (thousands of tons)	140.3	281.4	404.7	693.0
Cement (millions of tons)	16.9	33.1	73.3	68.2
Steel (millions of tons)	4.8	13.1	29.2	36.1
Electric power (billions KWH)	67.4	150.0	366.2	480.5

Source: ECLAC (1989d).

Table 9.4.   Manufacturing Sector Growth, 1950–1988 (annual percentages)

	1950–1960	1960–1970	1970–1980	1950–1980	1980–1988
Argentina	4.1	5.6	1.6	3.8	-1.2
Brazil	9.1	6.9	9.0	8.3	1.1
Chile	4.7	5.3	1.1	3.7	0.0
Colombia	6.5	6.0	6.0	6.2	2.0
Mexico	6.2	9.1	6.9	7.4	0.0
Peru	8.0	5.8	3.3	5.7	1.0
Venezuela	10.0	6.7	2.0	6.2	1.7
Central America (5 countries)	5.7	8.6	5.2	6.5	-0.3
Seven other small countries	3.6	4.2	5.8	4.5	-1.4
Total for Latin America (19 countries)	6.6	6.8	6.2	6.5	0.5

Source: ECLAC (1980–1987) and data from ECLAC's statistics division.

In Latin America industrial growth was concentrated mostly in Brazil and Mexico, where industrialization achieved the highest annual rates, 8.3 and 7.4 percent, respectively, for the period indicated above. Venezuela also accomplished a high industrial growth rate, but then this dropped strongly due to the boom experienced in oil revenues. Colombia maintained a stable rate of development, averaging 6.2 percent in the 1950–1970 period. Southern Cone countries, on the other hand, only grew at moderate rates of approximately 5 percent in the period 1950–1970, which was followed by stagnation in the ensuing phase. In the 1980s the region was afflicted with industrial stagnation, and in many cases a process of deindustrialization took place as a result of adjustment processes implemented to deal with the foreign debt crisis.

From a broader perspective, the Latin American process of industrialization has achieved some successes while failing in other respects. It was already mentioned that, until the early 1980s, the general rate of growth for manufactures was satisfactory, showing a significant domestic effort to absorb technical advances and encourage capital formation. Nevertheless, it is generally agreed that industrial development has not been efficient in the use of available resources, mainly due to excessive protectionism. Most countries have been unable to develop the so-called endogenous cores of industrial activity capable of extending dynamism to other economic areas through their ability to spread innovation and creativity (Fajnzylber 1983). After several decades of industrialization, local business classes are still reluctant to undertake long term innovative projects. Economic policies have been marked by lack of stability and an inadequate understanding of their medium term effects. Perhaps the most important factor is that the economic policies have not managed to solve satisfactorily the complex relation between industrial growth and the external sector.

Industrial Policies and External Imbalances: The Early Stage

It is a well-known fact that industrialization policies began to be generally applied in Latin America due to the Great Depression of the 1930s. Countries that already had productive capacity in certain elementary industries adopted strict restrictions in order to make imports consistent with the purchasing power afforded by exports. Domestic demand was stimulated by expansive fiscal and investment policies. Various instruments that were used to achieve this purpose were frequently inconsistent. Imports were cut back by applying ad valorem customs tariffs that successively increased, fixed duties, import licenses, import quotas, or outright bans. Access to the foreign exchange market was controlled, and multiple exchange rate areas were established, which implied actual devaluations simply by shifting merchandise from one exchange rate area to another.

The most commonly used domestic policies were the expansion of public investment, particularly in infrastructure such as the building of housing and public works in general, with the primary aim to expand employment; long term loans to the private sector at subsidized interest rates; direct public investment by newly created state enterprises in strategic economic sectors that fostered the development of other related industries; natural resource surveys to determine location, quality, and quantities available; and state support for the use and dissemination of modern technology. In general, the criteria followed in applying these policies were largely in reply to the urgent need to replace the external supply of goods due to balance of payments restrictions and to create new sources of employment to replace jobs lost in the traditional export sector. Less emphasis was placed on the efficiency and long term effects that could be produced by some of the abundantly used instruments.

Positive responses to policy incentives developed, as was made evident by the fact that recovery throughout the 1930s and subsequent growth in the 1940s and 1950s reached considerable dynamism, even greater than that of industrial countries. Between 1929 and 1939 industrial production in the three major countries in the region, in addition to Colombia, Chile, and Uruguay, rose between 3 and 8 percent per year, whereas in the United States and Canada it remained virtually stationary (Díaz-Alejandro 1984). Subsequently, between 1936–1940 and 1955–1960 the Latin American industrial sector raised its growth to an annual rate of 6.2 percent (ECLA 1963). Nevertheless, as industrialization gradually progressed and became more diversified, some symptoms began to appear showing the need for strong policy corrections.

During the 1950s the classical problem of external imbalance took on a new nature. It was no longer solely a question of the cyclic fluctuations in the external demand for raw materials that characterized the old style of development based on primary exports. In addition to this was the relative and growing rigidity of imports that lacked the flexibility needed to adjust in situations of external shocks. Since industrialization in most countries sprang from domestic production of consumer goods and light intermediate goods, it created a dependency on the supply of imported capital and more sophisticated intermediate goods whose domestic production was not profitable. Thus, a process of import-intensive industrialization took place, thereby inducing a high income elasticity of demand for imports.

There was a second factor that increased the rigidity of the import structure: the high proportion of foodstuffs and basic consumer goods in total imports, which made the real value of urban wages very sensitive to the exchange rate. This was partially due to the protectionist policy in itself, which discriminated against agriculture and induced the reallocation of investment resources away from that sector to the industrial sectors, thus helping to slow down agricultural growth.[6] This phenomenon was already becoming evident as a consequence of the agricultural land tenure systems, which did not favor the formation of dynamic entrepreneurial agricultural agents, and the crisis of the 1930s, which strongly affected agricultural prices. Insufficient dynamism in agriculture—the annual growth rate reached only 2.8 percent in the 1940s and 1950s (ECLA 1963)—compared to a rapidly expanding industrial sector and the abundant rural-urban migrations that usually form part of this process, became a real deterrent to industrial development when food supply deficits had to be supplemented by increasing imports or through exportable goods, as was the case in Argentina. The rate of industrial growth was particularly affected in Southern Cone countries. However, "developmental" policies applied by Brazil and the fact that other countries—such as Colombia, Peru, and Venezuela—began a process of industrialization enabled the region as a whole to increase its rate of industrial growth to 6.6 percent in the 1950s (see Table 9.5). Thus, an internal imbalance in the production structure was transmitted to the external sector by creating a foreign trade structure that was not flexible enough to adapt to fluctuations in the balance of payments.

Table 9.5.   Share of Manufactures in GDP
             (percentages)

	1950	1960	1970	1980	1986
Argentina	21.4	24.2	27.5	25.0	25.0
Brazil	22.8	28.2	30.4	31.4	28.5
Chile	20.6	22.1	24.5	21.4	20.6
Colombia	17.2	20.5	22.1	23.3	21.9
Mexico	17.3	17.5	21.2	22.1	21.0
Peru	15.7	19.9	21.4	20.2	20.1
Venezuela	10.2	12.7	13.6	16.2	18.8
Central America Common Market (5 countries)	11.4	12.8	16.4	17.7	17.7
Total for Latin America (19 countries)	18.6	21.2	23.5	24.8	23.7

Source: ECLAC (1980–1987) and data from ECLAC's statistics division.
Note: Percentages of the total GDP, at constant 1980 prices for the period 1970–1986, spliced in 1970 with data for 1950–1970 at 1970 prices.

A third way through which industrial policies helped make the balance of payments more rigid was the disincentives to exports that resulted from import substitution policies. By overvaluing the currencies, without compensating exporters, these activities had to bear the brunt of effective negative protection measures that discouraged investment and diversification in exports. Thus, it has been possible to state that this industrialization model led to a faster growth of imports but to a slower growth of exports, thereby introducing a structural tendency to run a deficit in the balance of payments (Schydlowsky 1973).

Growing difficulties in financing the balance of payments led to rising foreign indebtedness and a stronger search for foreign investment. Although this helped finance the external deficit, it also helped increase the burden of interest payments and profits remittance abroad. Foreign debt service, as a share of current foreign exchange revenue, rose from 5 percent to 10 percent throughout the 1950s.

The Transition to Export Diversification

In the 1960s the idea that substantial reforms to foreign trade policies had to be made gathered strength in several countries. Problems with the balance of payments, and an increasing awareness that industrialization was not helping to make Latin American economies more independent and less vulnerable, reinforced the notion that a greater flexibility in the trade structure was required, that protectionism should be rationalized, and that it was necessary to diversify exports.

Several circumstances contributed to this evolution. On the one hand, ECLAC was promoting the establishment of a regional market in Latin America in the belief that industrialization could not progress much further due to the existence of what were then called "water-tight compartments." National markets in most countries were too small to permit full use of economies of scale. A process of gradual integration was then proposed, and the first measure was to establish the Latin American Free Trade Association (LAFTA).

The changes in world trade were no less important. Once the economic and financial difficulties of the postwar years had been mastered, developed economies went through an unprecedented expansion. It was thus possible to overcome the pessimistic attitude toward exports prevailing in the immediate postwar period, an attitude that had prevented nontraditional exports and manufactures from being viewed as feasible dynamic alternatives.

Several countries that had followed protectionist policies started to adopt export-promoting policies. Throughout the 1960s many countries gradually shifted toward policies promoting nontraditional exports and price corrections in an attempt to eradicate the most acute distortions (Chile in 1965, Brazil in 1967, Argentina in 1967, and Colombia in 1968). In general, these policies involved the following measures: (1) modification of tariff systems by replacing quantitative restrictions to imports with ad valorem tariffs and shortened lists of goods subject to import restrictions; and (2) programming of realistic exchange rate policies to avoid the currency overvaluation and instability that occurred in periods of high inflation.

One of the major instruments of this policy was exchange rate planning. Based on the premise that the exchange rate is a key signal to allocate output and demand between foreign and domestic markets, exchange rate planning is designed to improve the stability of the exchange rate's real value by permanent adjustment of the nominal exchange rate in accordance with internal and external inflation and the expected variations in competitiveness (see Ffrench-Davis 1979). The purpose is to avoid an accumulation of large disequilibria. This improves decisions of investors and eliminates erratic fluctuations due to speculation that affects foreign exchange markets.

The second component of trade reform referred to import restrictions. Quantitative restrictions applied in the 1950s created allocative inefficiencies, regressive distributive effects, and cumbersome administration procedures. Therefore, protection measures began to be replaced with ad valorem tariffs. However, tariffs do not avoid the anti-export bias derived from the effective negative protection that affects many export activities. This encouraged the application of tariff reforms to correct these distortions or, alternatively, to compensate for their negative effects on export activities either by tax refunds or through direct subsidies.[7] A third set of policies implemented to promote exports consisted of public investment in the necessary infrastructure, expansion of the export-producing capacity, or simply loans to finance pre- and postshipping loans.

The results of these policies are significant. They lead to a significant growth acceleration of nontraditional exports in the region, especially of manufactures. The contrast becomes evident if the growth rates of exported manufactures are considered: from 2.7 percent per year in 1955–1962 to 20.2 percent in 1962–1973 (ECLA 1979). Although world trade was booming in 1962–1973, Latin American growth was higher than the corresponding worldwide rate: the region's share in the trade of manufactures went from 0.8 percent in 1955 to 1.3 percent in 1975. This export dynamism continued in the next decade. Between 1970–1971 and 1983–1984 manufactures exported by LAFTA member countries grew by 21.2 percent per year and by 17.9 percent per year if Brazil is excluded (ECLAC 1987b, 1987c). Part of this growth, however, is purely nominal since it occurred during a period of high worldwide inflation.

On the other hand, the composition of exports changed since, in relation to total exports, manufactures increased from 3.6 percent in 1960 to 12.3 percent in 1970, 17.1 percent in 1980, and 23.9 percent in 1985 (ECLAC 1985). Estimates of the concentration of exports per product in each Latin American country shows that, with the exception of Jamaica, this indicator fell constantly from 1960 on in all countries. Brazil was the country that diversified its exports the most. The Latin American balance of trade for manufactures tended to become more even: while manufactured exports in 1960 were equal to 5.2 percent of imported manufactured goods, in 1970–1971, they rose to 19 percent and finally to 70 percent in 1983–1984 (or 39 percent if Brazil is not taken into account) (ECLA 1979; ECLAC 1987b, 1987c).

From the perspective of the origin of exports according to type of country, the highest share belongs obviously to the larger countries: Argentina, Brazil, and Mexico. Their share in the total regional exports of manufactured goods rose from 58 percent in 1965 to 68 percent in 1975 and 89 percent in 1983–1984. This shows the growing disparity of industrial competitiveness within the region (ECLA 1979; ECLAC 1987b, 1987c).

A factor that certainly played a significant role, initially, in the development of trade with manufactures was the creation of regional integration agreements. But they lost significance, particularly after the crisis of the early 1980s. In 1970–1971, 35 percent of the exports of manufactured goods from Asociación Latino Americana de Integración (ALADI) member countries remained within the region, but this ratio had dropped to 17 percent in 1983–1984 as a result of the adjustment processes that restricted the demand for imported goods in each country (ECLAC 1987b, 1987c).

It is worthwhile noting that products exported to the region (or to other developing regions) tend to be more capital and import intensive than products destined for industrial countries. For example, in 1970–1971, 51 percent of machine tools exported by ALADI countries as a whole was intended for the region, whereas only 20 percent of nondurable consumer goods was intended for the region. In the following decade these ratios dropped to 17 percent and 13 percent, respectively (ECLAC 1987b, 1987c). This shows the difficulties involved in competing in developed countries with products that require more modern technology and larger production scales.

Further analysis tried to identify factors that could explain the successful export diversification started in the 1960s. Díaz-Alejandro (1974) makes several points in this respect. In the first place the fact that it was the larger countries that were most successful is quite meaningful. On the one hand, these countries had adopted the more aggressive import substitution policies due to the possibility of exploiting economies of scale and, therefore, already had in place a stronger industrial base. This hypothesis assumes that it is very difficult to launch industrial activities that are oriented, from the start, toward exports. A learning process is first required, and this was achieved in the earlier industrialization stages. We should note, however, that this hypothesis is subject to opposing views. Balassa (1981), for example, emphasizes the opposite hypothesis, quoting some instances of Korea's experience in which technological mastery was achieved directly in exporting industries without going through an import substitution stage.

On the other hand, larger countries faced fewer difficulties in pursuing foreign exchange policies favorable to export growth because the tradable sector tends to be relatively smaller than in small countries. Furthermore, small countries have strong discontinuities in the hierarchy of their comparative advantages, and, consequently, global foreign exchange incentives do not produce the same effects as in large-sized economies with continuous comparative advantages and greater possibilities for making full use of economies of scale.

However, the same evidence provided by Díaz-Alejandro does not suggest that the larger countries followed very aggressive real exchange rate policies. Both in Brazil and Colombia the real exchange rate in 1969–1971 was not much higher than in 1960–1962. In Colombia it was only 4 percent higher, whereas in Brazil it was 2 percent lower. Rather than a high exchange rate, in absolute terms the essential aspect appears to have been the real exchange stability that was achieved through foreign exchange planning. The same evidence has been quoted for South Korea (Jones and Sakong 1980).

A third point worth mentioning concerning successful export policies relates government commitment with this objective. This means that the transition from the import substitution stage to the export stage was not achieved by dismantling the state apparatus or abandoning selective policies, but rather by changing the direction of many instruments used for direct promotion, such as subsidies, loans, and exemptions, plus correcting some gross distortions, such as those created by effective negative protection and overvaluation of the exchange rate.

Industrial development in Latin America came to a halt with the debt crisis of 1982–1983. It has been correctly said that the 1980s was a "lost decade" for Latin America. An annual industrial growth rate of a mere 0.5 percent reveals the widespread lack of growth in the region. Only a few countries (Chile, Colombia, and Venezuela) have managed to escape this virtual economic standstill. The paragon of Latin American industrialization, Brazil, only registered a scant 0.6 percent rate of industrial growth despite the fact that even in the most critical postwar years it managed to maintain significant rates of industrial expansion.

A combination of unprecedented phenomena has affected most of the regional economies: foreign indebtedness that exceeded all reasonable ability to pay; an unstable international financial situation, particularly in the United States; the rigid and unilaterally imposed adjustment programs designed to transfer a high share of domestic saving abroad; and social demands to recover real wage losses. All of these factors have unleashed the hyperinflationary processes that halted growth.

Beyond the specific events of the 1980s, widespread disappointment with past industrialization policies led to a more general belief that deeper changes had to be implemented and that renewed economic policies were becoming a necessity. Despite achievements, most Latin American economies continued to be especially vulnerable to the international economy and its fluctuations. State intervention did not always meet expectations, either because state capacity to act effectively was overestimated or because the state lacked the relative independence needed to impose policies consistent with the objectives of industrialization.

The Proposals

The circumstances of the 1980s proved beyond doubt that it was essential to renew the road to industrialization. Ten years of stagnation, the intensification of poverty, which at present threatens even the middle classes, and the unprecedented external indebtedness are all situations that must be dealt with through new development strategies. And as if this were not enough, the rest of the world is advancing toward a new technological and economic revolution that is changing the configuration of the international division of labor and most aspects of social, economic, and political life. In this worldwide reorganization, Latin America cannot afford to stay aside. New and creative approaches are required to allow Latin America a stronger participation in the current course being followed by the international economy and which should, at the same time, make it possible to successfully deal with the conditions that led to the recent stagnation.

In the past, particularly after the Great Depression and World War II, industrialization provided a path to overcome the no-longer-operative economic structures that had prevailed for half a century. This is still the way to free the region from its current structural crisis. However, the strategies and policies to be implemented do not have to be the same ones that were applied in the past. Domestic and international conditions have changed. There are lessons to be learned from past mistakes and the accomplishments of others.

Evidently, strategic measures of rectification cannot be identical for all countries in the region. The size of the economy is a vital variable in the range of possibilities and options available. Market possibilities in countries such as Brazil and Mexico, and to a lesser extent Argentina, differ greatly from those available to small-sized economies such as Uruguay, Bolivia, or Ecuador. While the former can make full use of economies of scale in a broad range of activities, the same is not true for the other countries, even for middle-sized countries such as Colombia, Chile, Peru, or Venezuela.

Industrial Policy Approaches

It was already mentioned that the new development strategies must take into consideration three fundamental factors faced by Latin America in the late 1980s: stagnation, increasing poverty, and the external debt burden.

These three critical problems indicate that the new strategies should address three major issues: stagnation must be countered by revitalizing available resources and the stocks accumulated in the course of several decades, primarily by making them more productive and internationally competitive; increased poverty should be countered with equity so as to redistribute a substantial part of growth in benefit of the poor; and the debt burden, which will continue to be serviced, despite being depreciated and rescheduled, should be dealt with through austerity, especially among higher-income groups.

These three approaches should be expressed in concrete policies. Equity will require new and more efficient social policies. Foreign debt service demands creative financial policies. Increased productivity and competitiveness must be a central focus in new industrial policies. The consistency of medium and long term policies with short term macroeconomic and stabilization policies is a requisite. But this consistency has to be achieved through the reciprocal adjustment of each of the policies rather than by imposing a purely short term rationale, which has been the dominant trend up to now. That is the purpose of the "adjustment with growth" policy currently being proposed in some neostructuralist circles (Meller 1989; Ramos, Chapter 4).

A renovated approach to industrial policy must be developed. Indeed, inspired by the conservative ideas promoted by the Reagan administration in the United States, Thatcher in the United Kingdom, and Pinochet in Chile, the need for industrial policies—as those applied after World War II in Europe, Asia, and Latin America—was contested.

Traditionally, industrial policy had been understood as the state's commitment to intervene in a discretionary manner in resource allocation by supporting—through subsidies and protection or direct public investment—certain sectors that were believed to be of strategic importance. This approach was based on the theory of market failures, the development theory of the 1950s and 1960s, and, particularly, the structuralist approach formulated by Prebisch. Another contribution came from the sociology of development, particularly in the work put forth by Cardoso and Faletto (1979), who revealed the obstacles faced by Latin American development due to the weakness or even absence of a modernizing industrial bourgeoisie. Thus, it was concluded that the state should intervene as an entrepreneur, a role that in other regions was played by an active and innovative business class.

This approach was challenged by successive trends in neoclassical thought. The first wave of criticism arose in the 1960s, exposing the excesses committed under the industrial policies applied in developing countries, particularly in Latin America (Little, Scitovsky, and Scott 1970). These excesses were: protectionism, which was redundant or unnecessary in many cases; the distortions in relative prices; the inefficiency of state-owned companies; and the prevailing bureaucratism that paralyzed business and foreign trade. Proposals were aimed at eliminating these excesses and gradually correcting the main distortions without challenging the role played by the state in encouraging and promoting development.

The second wave of criticism—conservatism—was more radical because it not only proposed deep changes, in the sense of implementing a speedy liberalization and deregulation of markets, but also proposed a fundamental reduction in the role played by the state, confining it to a subsidiary role, with the private sector as the driving force for development and the privatization of state-owned firms.[8] Even the roles of the welfare state and social policies were challenged.

The more successful countries in Asia and Europe that thrived after rebuilding their economies following World War II applied industrial policies that required some form of state intervention to increase productivity and international competitiveness. In East Asia such policies were noted for involving direct state intervention and the formulation of very specific sectoral priorities with a view to achieving development through export activities. This was accomplished through a concertation between the state and the major private economic groups, by means of a straightforward relationship established between both types of agents. In Europe, particularly in the smaller countries, policies were not so forthright and left more room for the markets in the framework of very open economies that became increasingly integrated into the European Economic Community, but in which the state still provided explicit support for technological development, investment in infrastructure, and for social and regional equilibrium. Equally important was the commitment of the state to macroeconomic and financial stability viewed as essential to encourage long term private investment. In some of the larger countries, such as France and Italy, the state participated more actively in sectoral priorities and in establishing a major public enterprise sector.

European industrial policies were backed by an institutionality that was compatible with social concertation, expressed through a system of social-democratic corporatism that induced social actors—entrepreneurs and workers—to negotiate according to their own interests and establish politically acceptable distributive patterns. In East Asia, particularly in countries that were under occupation after World War II, reforms to property systems made it possible to initiate modern industrialization processes with distributive equity, thereby avoiding the typical conflicts experienced in Latin America.

From a Selective Keynesian Approach to a Modified Neo-Schumpeterian Approach

The traditional Latin American approach to industrial policy could be characterized as a selective closed-economy Keynesian approach: an industrial policy based on protectionism and fiscalism according to which the main problem was to increase domestic demand for manufactures through the protection provided by tariff barriers and to expand supply through fiscal incentives such as subsidies, tax exemptions, and public investment. The sequence of this productive strategy ranged from the "final touches" added to traditional consumer goods (as Hirschman called them), to the mass production of the same, to intermediate goods, some capital goods, and consumer durables. An industrial policy approach was thus developed that tended to respond to a demand structure determined by fiscal incentives.

By comparison, the East Asian approach may be considered a modified, outward-looking Schumpeterian approach. In the long term the central purpose of industrial policy was to establish the institutionality required to strengthen and develop an innovative business class that could be encouraged to increase productivity and develop new forms of production, new forms of designing goods, the use of new materials, new locations, and even new products. The coincidence between many specific policies—such as protectionism or selectivity in the allocation of investments, for example—with strategies applied in Latin America is a relatively secondary issue. The main aspect is that, while the leitmotiv in Latin America was local market development, in Asia it was the mastery of entrepreneurial and technological abilities with the intention of conquering foreign markets. In East Asia public and private institutionality was aimed fully at accomplishing this goal. Lively and efficient state intervention was applied in an attempt to strengthen the private sector, through concertation and persuasion, by encouraging it to undertake the goals of industrial policy jointly determined by the public and private leaders.

An interesting variation, for Latin America, of this modified Schumpeterian approach is the course followed by what has been called the "Third Italy" (as opposed to Italy's industrialized north and its backward south): industrial development based on modern and internationally competitive small-sized firms, established in the more refined niches of the international market of traditional consumer goods (for example, high-quality clothing) or specifically designed capital goods that are not suitable for large-scale manufacture (for example, machine tools). This is a Schumpeterian approach because it is based primarily on the development of a new business class, either initially small-scale or formed by highly qualified technicians who made proficient and full use of an institutional and economic environment that favored this type of activity. This environment may be characterized by a social system strongly organized on the basis of families, grass-roots organizations, and municipalities, which enabled a high degree of decentralization in the mobilization of financial resources, technical training, and recruitment of skilled workers. Northern Italy's high degree of industrial development, which made available an efficient infrastructure for transport, communications, and public services, was also highly favorable to this process.

While the Keynesian approach emphasized fiscal discretionary powers and a centralizing approach to economic policy, Schumpeterian theory emphasized the crucial role played by entrepreneurs in a given institutional framework. Keynes developed his theory on the basis of the conditions of a depressed economy. He assumed that the general conditions of full employment and stability could be reestablished through expansive fiscal policies so that market rules would become effective once more and private investment could act as the engine of development. Keynes perceived the social role of the state in reestablishing full employment.

The selective Keynesian approach implemented in Latin America was a synthesis between Keynesian strategy, which viewed the state as an agent capable of promoting economic growth despite stagnation, and structuralism, which considered that protectionism and the selectivity of public investment policies were the instruments needed to begin a process of industrial learning. But this synthesis, which prevailed in Latin America until the 1970s, tended to ignore the other component of Keynes's original thinking: that once an economy recovers and investment begins to grow, markets must play a major role in the allocation of investments and in motivating the business sector.

From a development point of view, Keynes was criticized on several grounds. The arguments brought forth were market imperfections, the dynamic problems of growth in an open economy, and the inflationary biases in fiscal policies. In developing countries criticism referred to structural deficiencies of supply, particularly in the initial stages of industrialization. For this reason the Latin American synthesis developed an industrial policy approach to deal with these supply deficiencies. This was the structuralist component. But the Keynesian tradition of perceiving investment and growing demand as the key variables of growth continued to play an important role. Since developing countries have been affected by persistent difficulties in raising their rates of investment and savings, industrial policies arrived at the dead end imposed by the ceiling of available funds. In passing, they helped to provide empirical confirmation of the inflationary biases of fiscal policies.

By ignoring Keynes's initial proposal on the importance of "animal spirits" and the need for an economic framework to motivate the private sector to adopt a dynamic investment attitude, policies for the institutional development of markets were also overlooked. This may perhaps be a contribution of neo-Schumpeterian theory, which went through a revival in the 1980s, under the stimulus of the neoconservative policies.

Industrial Policy Viewed from Neostructuralism[9]

Industrial policies implemented in Latin America after World War II were inspired, as mentioned above, by a synthesis between structuralism and Keynesian theory. Structuralism emphasized market imperfections, missing markets, and market rigidity as the basis for state intervention directed at encouraging industrial development. Keynesianism emphasized the need to create and expand internal demand. In the 1980s progress was made in formulating a neostructuralist approach. This approach can be interpreted as a new synthesis based on different theoretical trends in terms of current realities. Neostructuralism may provide the basis to define new industrial policy approaches.

How can neostructuralism be defined? In the first place, by acknowledging that many of the rigidities and missing markets that were relevant in the 1950s have ceased to be so. Perhaps the main one was the rigidity of the agricultural goods market and the missing land markets. In countries where agrarian reform has been carried out, land markets have opened, thus allowing new agricultural producers who are much more moved by an enterprising spirit than the former owners of the vast agricultural properties of thirty or forty years ago. The supply of agricultural products has become more flexible. The use of modern technology in agriculture is gaining headway.

Other markets that undoubtedly have developed and expanded are capital markets. Notwithstanding the effects caused by the foreign debt crisis, the credit rationing that characterized the postwar period has given way to greater diversification in the financial markets, which undoubtedly offer better alternatives than those traditionally available to agents who formerly only had access to informal credit markets with exorbitant interest rates. This does not means that all the rigidities that have traditionally affected these markets have been eliminated, particularly with regard to long term financing.

At present, a vast infrastructure and a more highly developed market for productive services and human resources have been made available to business. It has thus been possible to improve the technical efficiency of business and reduce the traditional lack of business capacity that affected the region.

With the development of previously absent or highly imperfect markets, many policy recommendations based on orthodox neoclassical theory may be recovered by development policies and included in a more global approach. The latter, however, must continue to acknowledge the validity of important aspects of the synthesis between structuralism and Keynesian theory regarding the persistence of rigidities and discontinuities that cannot be solved spontaneously by the markets. Three issues fall into this category: the persistence and even the growth of social inequalities; the huge technology gap that separates the Latin American productive apparatus from the industrial world (and, at present, also from the "Asian Tigers"); the lack of mechanisms to ensure that environmental protection with relevant ecological effects is duly included in decisionmaking processes, particularly those related to savings and investment but also, and increasingly, in resource allocation.

Thus, neostructuralism emerges as a new synthesis of: (1) elements included in orthodox theory, but which lacked validity since many crucial assumptions were not fulfilled (the role of the markets, prices, and competitiveness), a situation that has changed over the course of time; (2) elements of the old structuralist theory that continue to be valid (social inequalities and structural heterogeneity—which are currently linked more to social, educational, and employment policies—and the technology gap, an issue that now becomes the chief purpose of industrial policy); (3) elements of Keynesian theory, including some traditional ones such as the role of the state in ensuring that the future is adequately considered in decisionmaking processes, and other less well-acknowledged ones, such as the need for international financial cooperation in facing the debt problem; and (4) elements of Schumpeterian theory, such as the role of the business class in absorbing and incorporating technological advances.

Evidently, this approach calls for greater analytical complexity and ideological pluralism. It is not by chance that this type of strategic combination is providing the inspiration for policy approaches in countries that have highly dissimilar political systems. However, we cannot disregard the many obstacles that may interfere with the implementation of this approach. The frequent identification of market liberalization policies with the authoritarian regime that ruled in Chile may frequently lead to confusion, such as a simplistic association between market policies and price adjustments with regressive income distribution effects.[10] Social demands, repressed for long periods, may lead to popular outbreaks that are highly destabilizing and harmful to the framework required by long term investment growth, as was the case in Peru in the late 1980s. The continued existence of extremely conservative ideologies or speculative behaviors by the business class acts against vigorous and creative involvement by these classes. Failure to reform the state apparatus can lead to destabilizing pressures from the fiscal sector.

From the outlook of industrial policy, neostructuralism conceived in this manner suggests several directions toward which efforts should be oriented. Fajnzylber (1989b; see also ECLAC/UNIDO 1989) summarizes this proposal very well when he says that Latin America needs to fill the "empty box" in the matrix of countries that are characterized as pursuing a development course that has made equity compatible with high rates of industrial growth and competitiveness. These are countries that, based on different combinations between state and market and from different ideological leanings, have raised productivity, developed an active export trade in manufactures, and increased real wages.

In contrast to traditional industrial policies, marked by a strong sectoral orientation and the state's entrepreneurial involvement, the new industrial policy proposals are based on making full use of the market, business initiatives, and international competition. The main role of the state is, consequently, to establish the necessary institutional framework to stimulate the creativity and vitality of productive agents, and to help them develop an ability for long term cooperation with the state and the workers. Specific sectoral options should be the flexible outcome of these initiatives and coordination, rather than a technocratic interference imposed by the state from above. The options should allow making use of the information afforded by domestic and foreign markets, instead of overlooking market trends.

An institutional framework of this type requires policies to overcome inequity, ensure macroeconomic stability, and provide the public goods essential to productive activities (the necessary infrastructure in material, financial, and service terms and also technological learning and development).

Conclusions

The main problem in this approach does not lie in the conflict between state and market but rather in how to establish a system of cooperation between economic and social agents in order to achieve sustained growth in the system as a whole. A clear conclusion is that without a minimum equity in income distribution, it is very difficult to establish this kind of long term cooperation.[11]

A second conclusion to be drawn is that it is not possible to modernize industrial policy in closed or highly protected economies, particularly in small-sized economies. While the first conclusion points to the need for the state to play a more active role with regard to distribution and social issues, the second conclusion emphasizes the role of the market and prices in the process of resource allocation.

Some positive results from the debate on development can be detected here. While structuralism highlighted the relevance of structures that prevented a more equitable distribution of the benefits of development, neoclassicism vindicated the importance of comparative advantages and foreign trade, which had been neglected during the decades of depression and after, and highlighted the fact that the state can also fail. Both contributions, together with the preceding reflections on the Keynesian and Schumpeterian heritage, converge toward a new strategic synthesis for a modern industrial policy that, nevertheless, must be formulated and completed with elements that have considerable relevance at present. These relate to: (1) the development of dynamic comparative advantages, technological mastery, and the restructuring of the production apparatus; (2) the institutionality needed for business to develop and be able to constantly adapt to changing market situations; and (3) the issue of the coordination of the business class with the rest of society to ensure a democratic consensus, which appears as one of the major demands for the 1990s. In each of these matters, the state must fulfill a crucial responsibility, not to impose solutions but rather to stimulate creativity in the search for solutions.

Notes

1. This chapter was written during 1989.

2. Chapter 12 contains an extensive analysis of the deterioration of the terms of trade for the region. In his innovative work on center-periphery relations, Ocampo has included theoretical data and empirical evidence in support of Prebisch's hypotheses.

3. See Chapter 2.

4. The substantial criticism by ECLAC of the import substitution process is quoted in the first section of Chapter 2.

5. The structuralist outlook on the debate over income distribution and growth has been skillfully dealt with in Chapter 3.

6. As pointed out in Chapter 10, this has meant resolving the conflict of distribution in favor of the cities. In Figueroa's opinion, this policy option, together with a series of structural problems that hinder development possibilities for the rural sector, has plunged this sector into a major crisis.

7. In Chile, for example, between 1961 and 1967 the mean level of nominal tariffs dropped from 83 percent to 48 percent, while the mean level of real protection decreased from 254 percent to 168 percent. At the same time, dispersion, measured according to the standard deviation of real protection, dropped by one half (Corbo and Meller 1979).

8. Cook (1988) provides a summary of conservative proposals.

9. Policy trends suggested here have been addressed extensively elsewhere in the book. See Chapters 6, 7, 8, 10, and 13.

10. Sheahan (1980) analyzes this subject.

11. Lustig and Salazar-Xirinachs, in Chapters 3 and 13, respectively, make some suggestions that apply to the issue of social pacts.

10

Agricultural Development in Latin America

Adolfo Figueroa

The severe crisis currently being experienced in Latin America should provide an opportunity for thinking about long term problems. An analysis should be made that would afford a much better understanding of the structural problems that beset the Latin American economy so as to prevent the economic and social setbacks that occurred in the region during the 1980s from occurring once again within a new economic development process.

The purpose of this chapter is to undertake this analysis, but only in connection with one economic sector: agriculture. (Hereinafter this term shall refer to both agriculture and livestock farming.) The chapter begins with a review of structuralist thinking in the 1950s on the obstacles faced by agricultural development in Latin America. Then the transformations that have taken place in the region as of the 1960s will be examined. In light of these changes in the region's agriculture, a reinterpretation of the structural problems of agricultural development will be made. Finally, the most important consequences of this analysis for economic policy design will be discussed. The chapter concludes with some thoughts on the role of the market and the state in achieving agricultural development in the region.

Structuralist Thinking in the 1950s

For structuralists in the 1950s, Latin American agriculture faced two essential problems in its development: (1) agricultural supply was relatively rigid, and (2) there was an oversupply of labor in the sector. Consequently, poverty was concentrated in the countryside. According to structuralism, the main cause behind this situation was the land tenure system. As Rodríguez (1980: 91) put it: "The land tenure system is characterized by the coexistence of large landed estates and small land holdings; both conspire against the expansion of agricultural supply and against the absorption of labor."

In the case of large landed estates, the economic rationale behind them was essentially a rent-seeking one, devoid of any entrepreneurial spirit. The only change that the large landholder undertook was to mechanize agricultural chores, which caused a shift in labor but had very little effect on the productivity of the land. For this reason, supply was inelastic. In small landholdings, on the other hand, the capacity to undertake technological innovations was lacking because everything was lacking, particularly land and capital. Thus, rudimentary techniques were conserved, which also led to rigid supply.

Evidently, the structuralist notion of *rigid supply* referred to the long term. Agricultural output could not increase continuously because the technological development that would constantly raise land productivity was lacking.[1] The structuralist argument is valid if in fact technological or land-saving institutional innovations exist. Only in that way is it possible to argue that the system of large estates and small landholdings poses an obstacle to agricultural development. The economic rationale of the large landed estate and the lack of resources of the small landholding would impede the adoption of these innovations.

On the other hand, structuralists proposed policies for developing land-saving technologies, since they considered land to be the scarcest factor in the region (with some notable exceptions such as Argentina and Uruguay). Their idea was that the greater the supply of new technology, the more the large estate and small landholding system would clearly become an obstacle to agricultural development. For them, neither large landed estates nor small landholdings corresponded to the optimum size for technological development. Both ownership structures were uneconomical and inefficient in dynamic terms. This explanation held a clear consequence for economic policy: the land tenure system had to be changed; technological modernization demanded it. Thus, proposals emerged for implementing agrarian reform programs in the region. Clearly, there was an economic argument underlying this proposal.

The problem of rural poverty would gradually be resolved as agricultural productivity increased; but this would not be enough. As Prebisch (1950b as quoted in Rodríguez 1980: 326) pointed out:

> If one recalls the considerable proportion of working population employed in [agriculture in Latin America] one would understand that the solution to the land tenure problem is only part of the general economic development problem. Whatever the solution to this, little headway will be made in increasing the standard of living of the masses that work the land . . . if the redundant population is not eliminated through technical progress and if that part that is not needed to work the new lands developed for cultivation is not reabsorbed into productively satisfactory activities.

Naturally, for structuralists the sector that should absorb the workers displaced from agriculture would have to be industry. Rapid industrial development would do the job. Industry would be the engine behind economic growth. The role of agriculture would be to produce the wage goods and free the workers required for industrialization. Thus, the development of agriculture would be subordinate to the needs of industrial development.

One must also point out that the structuralists recognized the different conditions in our countries and therefore did not propose a uniform treatment of the region's agricultural problem. Although they developed a set of generic propositions at the regional level, such as those indicated above, structuralists were very well aware of the differences between countries and regions.

Prebisch, for example, underscored the differences between countries in natural resource endowment and the availability of immediately usable lands. For this reason, he recognized two investment options: raising yields in lands currently in use and expanding farmed areas. The land tenure regime posed an obstacle to the first. And he concluded that "in regions where it is not land tenure per se that is holding back the agricultural process, but rather the lack of investment and technical action by the state, the solution cannot be the same as for others where land tenure is the major obstacle" (quoted in Rodríguez 1980: 327).

Main Transformations in Agriculture, 1960–1980

The ideas held by structuralists can be contrasted with the agricultural performance of the 1960s and 1970s. The next section will deal with the 1980s.

Agricultural Supply

In connection with agricultural supply, the region showed an average growth rate of 3.2 percent per year between 1960–1980 (FAO 1988). Indeed, it cannot be said that agricultural supply was rigid during those two decades. Moreover, this rate was higher than that of demographic growth, which was 2.6 percent per year for the same period. Thus, agricultural supply was not rigid either in absolute terms or in relation to demographic growth. And this result could even lead one to consider that agricultural performance was satisfactory.

However, an economic criterion needs to be established to evaluate the performance of agricultural supply. This could consist of comparing its growth rate to that of domestic demand. At what rate should agricultural output grow in order not to alter domestic prices or the proportions traded abroad?

The rate of expansion of domestic demand can be approximated in a very simple demand model as the sum of two rates: population growth and per capita growth of demand, where the latter is obtained by applying an income elasticity coefficient to per capita income growth.[2] The first component measures the population effect and the second the income effect. With the criterion indicated, the demand growth rate for the region in the period 1960–1980 would be around 4.4 percent per year.[3] Agricultural performance in the 1960s and 1970s now appears as lagging in the face of the buoyant global economy. In this respect, one can talk of the relative rigidness of agricultural supply.

Latin America has traditionally been a net exporter of agricultural products, but in the 1960s and 1970s the magnitudes decreased. The proportion of exports over imports decreased during this period (see Table 10.1). This fact is clearly consistent with the previous result showing that agriculture did not accompany overall development.

Table 10.1   Latin America: Transformation in Agriculture, 1962–1986

	1962–66	1967–71	1972–76	1977–81	1982–86
Share of Agriculture (percentage)					
GDP	17	15	12	11	11
Employment	48	40	36	32	29
Exports	51	48	44	38	33
Imports	19	18	15	14	15
Exports/Imports:					
Ratio for agricultural	2.9	2.7	2.6	2.4	2.7
Technological Modernization					
Consumption of fertilizers (kg/ha)	10	18	29	39	24
Mechanization: tractors/work force (thousands)	14	16	na	27	na

Source: FAO (1988, tables 4, 5, 6, 9, and 12).

Land Tenure

In any case, how can one explain the growth of agricultural output? For structuralists, the large estate and small landholding land tenure system was an obstacle to agricultural development. Was this system then modified? What changes occurred in the agrarian structure of the region during the 1960s and 1970s?

The studies that have examined the changes that occurred in the agrarian structures of the region over the past decades agree on some regularities in the events observed.[4] The "stylized facts" for the entire region could be summarized as follows:

1. Expansion of the capitalist form of production and the decline of feudal forms, all of this measured both in terms of output and farmed area. In various countries large landed estates have disappeared, owing to the agrarian reform programs (Bolivia, Peru, Nicaragua). In others, the transformation has been linked primarily to the development of technology and markets (Chile).

2. Expansion of peasant units. The number of peasant units has increased in most countries in the region. It is estimated that the augmented labor force—which increased in agriculture between 1950 and 1970—was distributed as follows: 24 percent as wage earners and 76 percent as peasant units. The pressure of the greater peasant population on scarce lands meant a decrease in the average size of holdings in peasant farming. Thus there is a trend towards smaller landholdings in peasant farming.

3. Capitalist production has increased in a greater proportion than peasant farming in output volume. In other words, peasant farming is increasingly less significant as a producer of goods in the economic system.

Technology

What has happened in terms of technology? Latin American agricultural output has increased—in part due to the extension of the agricultural frontier and in part due to the increase in productivity. Food and Agriculture Organization (FAO) (1988: appendix 4, table 5.5) study estimates indicate that the former component was the most important in the 1960s and 1970s, accounting for close to 60 percent of the increase in agricultural output (excluding livestock farming).

Yields have increased due primarily to the technological possibilities provided by the green revolution since the mid-1960s. The combination of improved seeds, greater use of fertilizers, and irrigation contributed to a significant increase in yields, particularly of irrigated lands. Table 10.1 shows that use of fertilizers increased almost fourfold in the region between 1962 and 1981. Mechanization also soared; the number of tractors per farm worker doubled.

The current technological context is very dynamic. The green revolution of the 1960s has been followed by that of cybernetics and robotics, genetic engineering, and biotechnology. All of these innovations are basically generated in central countries. The technological context of the 1950s was much more stable.[5]

Employment and Poverty

A fact that should be emphasized is the profound transformation in the rural labor market. As a result of technological changes that have exacerbated the greater seasonality of labor requirements in farming calendars, there has been an increase in the demand for temporary labor over permanent labor, while in terms of the temporary work supply, peasants compete with other workers, particularly those from the urban proletariat (for example, the *boias frias* in Brazil and the *golondrinas* in Peru). Thus, supply in the labor markets to which peasants have access is oversaturated.

As a result of the growing trend toward small landholdings, peasant farmers increasingly require an income in addition to that obtained from their holdings in order to scrape together a subsistence income. Thus, a growing proletarization or quasi-proletarization of peasants arises, in the sense that the wages earned for temporary work in the labor market, particularly the rural one, is becoming an increasingly important part of their total income. But, owing to the oversaturated supply in labor markets, wages cannot totally offset the impoverishment involved in the trend toward smaller landholdings. The result is evident: there is a trend toward greater peasant destitution.

With regard to overpopulation, the data show that the population involved in agriculture has not decreased. On the contrary, between 1960 and 1980 this population increased by almost 13 percent. However, since the total population of the region increased by close to 20 percent during the same period, as Table 10.1 shows, the proportion of the agricultural population decreased.

Although the farming population increased in absolute terms, in relative terms there has been a population shift away from farming. But during this period neither rural poverty decreased nor was industry the great employer of the displaced population. Of the 137 million persons who were classified as living in extreme poverty in Latin America in 1980, 82 million lived in rural areas and 55 million lived in urban areas (FAO 1988: appendix 2). Thus, the cities have filled up with poor masses employed primarily in tertiary activities. This fact contrasts with the original proposition developed by the structuralists.

International Trade

There were also transformations in international trade. Agriculture has lost relative importance in the region as a foreign exchange generating sector (see Table 10.1). Latin American agriculture, as that of other peripheral countries, has witnessed a decline in its share of international markets. In fact, this relative loss is part of a broader process: a change has occurred in the international trading patterns of agricultural goods.

Since the early 1970s, for example, world trade of foodstuffs has grown significantly, but imports have been more accelerated in peripheral countries and exports have been more rapid for central countries (World Bank 1986). As a result of this, central countries show ever more favorable trade balances of foodstuffs, while the opposite is true for peripheral countries. This is the case in Latin America.

Another characteristic of both domestic and international agricultural goods markets is that a small number of large corporations—usually transnational ones—act as brokers in these markets. Thus, these markets are run for the most part by oligopolies and oligopsonies, and the economic policy of our countries does not always take the strategies of these companies into account. There is ample literature in the region on these issues. Thus, there are works that show that transnational corporate strategies run counter to long term agricultural development and that what state policies have actually done is to support these strategies (Rama 1985).

Likewise, the United States operates as a leading price-setting exporter in international grains markets. This makes these markets very unstable because prices fluctuate in accordance with the domestic policy of that country (Mitchell and Ronald 1987). In general, international agricultural product markets are highly influenced by the agricultural policies of central countries (see Chapter 12).

In short, one can mention three basic characteristics of Latin American agriculture that exist today as a result of the transformations that have occurred since the 1960s. These are:

1. Social transformations in Latin American rural areas will primarily come from the changes in relations between capitalist agriculture and peasant farming. These relations are essential to understanding the social dynamic of Latin American agriculture.
2. Agriculture as a productive activity today has less relative importance in the overall economy of the region's countries compared to the 1950s and 1960s, both as a generator of foreign exchange and economic surplus and in the use of labor. Indeed, these trends are typical to economic development. However, the transformation of the productive structure has been incomplete in Latin America, since the relative loss of importance of agriculture has not been compensated by a greater dynamism of the industrial sector. This is particularly true with respect to the absorption of labor.
3. The international context is determinant for agricultural development in the region. Agricultural policies implemented by the central countries have a decisive impact on Latin American agricultural development.

Crisis and Agriculture: The 1980s

The economic crisis that Latin America went through in the 1980s was quite severe. Between 1981 and 1988 the region's GDP barely grew by 12 percent. Moreover, the 1988 per capita GDP was 7 percent below that of 1980 (ECLAC 1988b). As mentioned elsewhere, the 1980s constituted a "lost decade" for Latin America in terms of economic development.

The crisis was global. Although to different degrees, all countries in the region have been affected by the crisis. Also, virtually all economic sectors have seen a decline in their dynamism in these years. But agriculture was among the sectors that lost less dynamism. Thus, while GDP and manufacturing output grew between 1980–1987 at an annual rate of 1.8 percent and 0.9 percent, respectively, agricultural output grew by 2.4 percent (see Table 10.2). The most recent estimates by FAO, however, show that for 1981–1987 this rate was only 1.7 percent (FAO 1988: appendix 1, table 24).

Table 10.2. Latin America: Agricultural and Industrial Share of Total GDP (annual rates variance in percentages)

Year	Value of Total GDP			Value of Per Capita GDP			Percentage Share of Total GDP	
	Total	Agriculture	Manufacture	Total	Agriculture	Manufacture	GDP Agriculture	GDP Manufacture
1971	8.4	0.3	7.6	5.5	-2.3	4.8	13.3	23.2
1972	6.7	0.8	9.0	4.0	-1.8	6.2	12.6	23.2
1973	8.8	9.1	9.9	6.1	6.3	7.1	12.6	24.0
1974	7.0	5.2	6.5	4.3	2.5	3.8	12.4	23.9
1975	0.9	3.7	2.1	-1.6	1.2	-0.4	12.8	24.1
1976	5.7	2.2	7.0	3.1	-0.3	4.3	12.4	24.4
1977	5.1	6.1	3.8	2.5	3.5	1.2	12.5	24.1
1978	4.3	2.9	4.5	2.1	0.7	2.3	12.3	24.2
1979	6.4	2.4	7.5	3.9	0.0	5.0	11.8	24.4
1980	5.7	2.7	5.7	3.2	0.2	3.1	10.3	24.8
1981	0.7	4.8	-5.3	-1.6	2.4	-7.5	10.7	23.3
1982	-1.2	-0.5	-2.4	-3.4	-2.7	-4.6	10.8	23.1
1983	-2.5	0.6	-4.1	-1.7	-1.6	-6.2	11.1	22.7
1984	3.8	3.4	5.2	1.5	1.0	2.9	11.1	23.0
1985	3.7	4.7	4.3	1.4	2.4	2.0	11.2	23.1
1986	3.9	-2.8	6.4	1.6	-4.9	4.1	10.5	23.2
1987	2.5	6.9	2.0	0.4	4.6	-0.2	10.9	23.5
1970–1980	5.9	3.5	6.3	3.3	1.0	3.7	—	—
1980–1987	1.8	2.4	0.9	-0.9	-0.6	-1.7	—	—

Source: Prepared by Joint Agricultural Division based on national accounts data from ECLAC Statistics Bureau.

Explanations for the better relative performance of the agricultural sector have been given in various analyses (IDB 1986; Ffrench-Davis 1989). In terms of internationally nontradable agricultural goods, it is said that the drop in domestic demand for foodstuffs as a result of the recession has partly gone to prices and partly to quantities (while in industry virtually all would have gone to quantities). Also, the low income elasticity would make demand for foodstuffs fall proportionately less compared to industrial goods.

In terms of internationally tradable goods, it is said that adjustment policies have meant favorable measures for exports in general. And since in agriculture the proportion of tradable goods over nontradable goods is greater than for the rest of the economy, these adjustment and export-promoting policies have involved a relatively greater benefit for agriculture.

The statistical evidence is, in fact, consistent with the preceding argument. The volume of agricultural exports grew at 3.4 percent per year between 1982–1986, while agricultural imports only grew at 1 percent (see Table 10.3). This means that the production of nontradable goods grew at a lower rate than the sector average. Data for the 1980–1984 period indicate that, in fact, export crops grew at 3.1 percent and subsistence crops at 0.8 percent (IDB 1986). Thus, there has been a change in the productive structure of the agricultural sector.

Table 10.3.   Latin America: Foreign Trade Trends in Agricultural Outputs[a]

	Imports			Exports		
	Volume	Unit Value	Value	Volume	Unit Value	Value
1970	45	42	16	78	35	26
1971	47	46	18	74	36	25
1972	50	51	21	76	42	29
1973	55	63	32	80	59	42
1974	63	91	51	77	76	53
1975	55	85	47	72	79	57
1976	56	86	48	82	79	65
1977	63	83	52	100	81	81
1978	78	81	63	95	89	85
1979	82	96	75	98	95	94
1980	110	100	110	92	113	104
1981	107	104	111	110	92	102
1982	93	93	87	104	87	91
1983	101	77	78	121	80	97
1984	98	87	85	116	90	105
1985	100	75	75	127	79	101
1986	88	80	70	108	92	100
Yearly Average Growth Rates						
1970–1981			8%			3.3%
1982–1986			1%			3.4%

Source: ECLAC/FAO Joint Agricultural Division.
Note: a. Includes crops and livestock output.
1979–1981 = 100.

Clearly, the preceding analysis cannot be taken to mean that the recession and adjustment policies have been favorable to the development of agriculture. To reiterate, the preceding refers to agricultural performance *relative to the rest of the economy*; to be more precise, it is concluded that agriculture suffered less from the effects of adjustment. In this respect, if one observes agricultural performance during the crisis in relation to its own dynamism of previous decades, the result is completely different. The main characteristics of this performance are:

- Agriculture has lost overall dynamism. Its growth rate has declined with the crisis and adjustment policies (3.2 percent versus 2.4 percent, or 3.2 percent versus 1.7 percent, depending on the source used).
- Agricultural exports performance has been similar to that of the 1970s. Of course here one must consider the plummeting international prices during that decade (see Table 10.2). Proexport adjustment policies, particularly the increase in real exchange rates that took place in most of the countries, would have served to offset this drop (Ffrench-Davis 1989).
- The most important impact of the crisis and adjustment policies on international agricultural trade has occurred on the side of imports. From an 8 percent annual growth in the 1970s, it dropped to only 1 percent in the 1980s (see Table 10.3).

An important effect of the crisis has thus been the change in the agricultural production structure. Today, Latin American agriculture is aimed, more than before, at international markets. But the distributive effect of this change in the productive structure must be unfavorable, since the proportion of tradables to nontradables is lower in peasant farming than in capitalist agriculture.

The preceding data also lead us to conclude that, with the crisis, the per capita availability of food products declined in the region. This is evident if one combines the fact that per capita agricultural output decreased while the foreign trade balance increased, owing to the sharp drop in imports. ECLAC/FAO estimates show that the drop was around 10 percent between 1981 and 1986 (Ffrench-Davis 1989: table 7).

In short, the impact of adjustment policies on agriculture seems to have been unfavorable in terms of its overall dynamism—because its growth rate dropped—but favorable to agricultural exports and to import substitution, unfavorable to small-scale subsistence farming, which is where rural poverty is concentrated, and unfavorable to mass food intake because the per capita availability of foodstuffs decreased.

Reinterpretation of the Agrarian Problem

Old Topics with New Interpretations

Structuralist thinking in the 1950s focused its attention on two issues: agricultural supply and employment. Today, these concerns are still valid, although with new approaches or interpretations. Naturally, this is the result of the changes that occurred in the agrarian conditions of the region.

Two variables were proposed by structuralists to explain agricultural supply: the land tenure system and technological development. In current analyses other explanatory variables have been introduced, among which macroeconomic policy, international market conditions of agricultural products, and the role of transnational corporations in food agroindustries will be highlighted. Briefly, the analyses are as follows:

1. The effects of short term policies, particularly on the demand for agricultural goods and the terms of trade, have received growing attention by macroeconomists, who in their modeling clearly distinguish between agricultural and industrial sectors (Bacha 1981; Taylor 1983; Dancourt 1986).[6] The most important conclusion in this literature is that macroeconomic policies have a decisive impact on agriculture through exchange rates, effective demand, and public expenditures. These variables affect the demand and supply of agricultural goods.

2. The influence exerted by changes in international market conditions on agricultural development have also been analyzed in some detail, particularly the effects of changes in the agricultural policy of central countries. For example, the agricultural policy implemented by central countries leads to depressed prices for agricultural goods in international markets (Di Filippo 1987; FAO 1988). Agricultural development of Latin America thus becomes dependent upon the agricultural policy of central countries.

3. The growing participation of transnational corporations in food agroindustries affects the agricultural development of the region by modifying the productive structure and the consumption patterns of food products (Rama 1985).

New Emphases

New concerns have also emerged in economic thinking on Latin American agriculture. There are new issues to be reviewed and explained. The most important of these, in the author's opinion, are the following:

• The importance of technology in agricultural development has made it necessary to understand how technology is generated and disseminated.

Thus, a typically exogenous variable in the analysis of agricultural development of the 1950s has become an endogenous variable. A summary of the literature in this field can be found in de Janvry (1981) and Machado and Torres (1987). Innovations are partly generated by transnational corporations, where the prevailing rationale is monopolistic or oligopolistic. Another part is generated by international institutions (such as the Centro Internacional de Agricultura Tropical, CIAT; the Centro Internacional de la Papa, CIP; the Centro Internacional de Mejoramiento de Maíz y Trigo, CIMMYT; and the International Food Policy Reseach Institute, IFPRI), where the rationale is to centralize research at headquarters and disseminate it through official national centers in the countries. Thus, state resources are spent on disseminating and learning how to handle the imported technology and very little is spent on technological research to solve the specific problems of each country or region.

• Peasant economy is another topic that has been much discussed and studied. Its economic rationale, its role in the economy as a whole, and its dynamic are topics that have been studied in nearly all countries. A summary of some of these works is found in Ortega (1985). The peasant economic rationale is marked by it strong aversion to risk, and by its great, although subordinate, integration into capitalist economy. A more recent line of work explains the dissemination and learning processes of new technologies in peasant farming (Figueroa 1986b; Graziano da Silva 1981). There is a slow and unequal technological modernization of peasant farming, which is accounted for by market dynamism, state policies, and the quality of human resources, among the most important factors.

• Concern for natural resources, the environment, and the relations between the economy and ecology is another new line of study in the region. A special issue of *Pensamiento Iberoamericano: Revista de Economía Política* (1987) and FAO (1988) contain a discussion and an extensive bibliography on the topic.[7] Although, clearly, there is an environmental cost in the agricultural development process, there are successful experiences, such as the Mexican *chinampas* (small garden tracts in lakes) and the recovery of benched terraces in Peru, that show that it is possible to give new vigor to practices that have a positive impact on the environment.

• Problems related to food security constitute another, more recent, line of study in the region. An overall presentation of this issue can be found in Schejtman (1985) and FAO (1988). Few countries in Latin America have reached an adequate level of per capita food consumption, and virtually none have succeeded in eradicating malnutrition. Structural causes underlie this problem, such as unequal income distribution and limited food supply; but there are also short term instability factors, both in aggregate supply and in the real income of the masses.

Elements for a New Structuralist Analysis

Any theory that attempts to interpret how agriculture operates in Latin America has to start off by specifying the structural features of what could be referred to as the agricultural economy of Latin America. From the preceding sections on the transformations in Latin American agriculture and the new agrarian structure that has emerged, one can establish the essential elements that make up the context within which this agricultural economy operates. These elements could be the following:

1. The national economy in which it occurs is peripheral and is part of center-periphery relations.
2. The means of production are privately owned and are very concentrated.
3. There is overpopulation in relation to resources and technology in rural areas and also in the economy as a whole.
4. Two forms of production coexist: the capitalist and the peasant, which interconnect primarily through market relations.
5. Capitalist institutions in the countryside are not fully developed and rural markets are generally underdeveloped.
6. There is uncertainty in both the productive process and in trade, for natural and institutional reasons.
7. The supply of technological innovations is exogenous, but its adoption at a microeconomic level is endogenous.
8. Macroeconomic policy and the demand for agricultural goods is exogenous.

With these elements one could construct a theoretical body that would explain how agricultural economy operates in the region. In fact, several regional attempts have been made in this direction.[8] Here the main results from this literature will be used to discuss economic policy problems. As we know, economic policy cannot be formulated without a theory to back it up.

The economic rationale of economic units is, as economic theory maintains, a reply to the context in which they operate. The rationale, consistent with the overall economic environment indicated above for Latin America, could be summarized as follows: capitalist enterprises seek to maximize profits, but take into account the risks involved in each profit option they face; whereas peasant family units prioritize the minimization of risk, in other words, their behavior is one of aversion to risk, and subject to this they consider the available income options.

The endogenous variables relevant to the Latin American case are: prices and quantities of agricultural goods, employment, terms of trade, investment, and productivity. And in terms of the agrarian structure, one needs to explain both the distribution of income between wages, rents, profits, and peasant income, and the productive structure between tradables and nontradables.

On the other hand, the exogenous variables emerge primarily from the basic features of the Latin American agricultural economy indicated above. The concentration of property, the extent of market development, the degree of uncertainty, technological supply, macroeconomic policy, and the demand for agricultural goods are the main exogenous variables, and the agricultural policy design should be based on these variables. Each variable could be used as an economic policy instrument to modify the solution of endogenous variables in the direction desired.

The elements proposed here, although still incomplete for establishing a rigorous relation of causality, permit an analytical discussion of the main aspects of an economic policy aimed at agricultural development in the region. This will be done in the following section.

Economic Policy Proposals

Dilemmas and Objectives of Economic Policy

One of the main dilemmas faced by economic policy is how to obtain cheap foodstuffs and increase rural income at the same time. This conflict between countryside and city is the counterpart to the conflict between producers and consumers.

In central countries this conflict has been solved in favor of the countryside. Urban consumers pay higher prices than international market prices. The real income of consumers is already so high that this policy is socially feasible. In peripheral countries, and particularly in Latin America, the conflict has generally been settled in favor of the city. But here the conflict is dramatic: there is massive poverty in both the countryside and the city. Therefore, any solution to this conflict, favoring one or the other, keeps social tensions latent. And with the phenomenon of rapid urbanization the solution in favor of the city is more politically feasible because it is at least consistent with the electoral rationale of democratic regimes.

The apparent paradox whereby central countries have policies to protect their agriculture while in peripheral countries it is unprotected is thus simple to explain. Neither should we be surprised by the fact that, as a result of this protection, agriculture in central countries has developed swiftly, with a significant rise in technology and productivity that renders the central countries the major food exporters in the world. Agriculture has thus become one of the technologically advanced sectors in central countries. And since the international division of labor is increasingly based on differences in technological development, and therefore increasingly less on natural resource endowments, it should not surprise us that in these countries agriculture belongs to the export sectors.

It will be difficult to follow central country models in Latin America. It will not be possible to resolve the conflict in favor of the countryside, nor would this be appropriate. Economic policy should not attempt to change from one point to another in the social conflict curve (a negatively sloping curve between real urban and rural income). This would mean obtaining gains for one social group at the expense of another, and poverty is now distributed between countryside and city. The challenge for economic policy rests, rather, on how to shift the conflict curve outward and keep it so.

The parameters that determine the position of the conflict curve are the same as those that determine supply and demand conditions in agricultural markets. One would have to choose from among the exogenous variables that underlie the conflict curve those that can be used as policy instruments. The argument developed here is that policy choice cannot be confined solely to market liberalization. There are structural problems that must be overcome through state action.[9]

The Role of Macroeconomic Policy

One of the parameters of the conflict curve is the level of domestic demand. Higher real wage levels, for example, would increase this demand and shift the conflict curve outward, since the prices of nontradable goods would rise. Thus, real urban and rural income would increase in turn. Undoubtedly, the demand for tradable goods would also expand, which in turn would increase the net imports of the economy. This would require the use of another instrument to maintain the external balance. If not, the expansion of the conflict frontier would occur at a cost to the external balance. This result suggests that demand policy must be accompanied by supply-side policies for exportables. If agriculture itself is the way to bridge the external gap, then agricultural productivity has to increase. How can macroeconomic policy affect agricultural productivity?

Before answering this, take the opposite case of a drop in demand. One could say that a recession—a drop in the real income of the population—would reduce the price of nontradable agricultural goods, and with this it would modify the productive structure, shifting it toward tradables. Thus, the conflict curve would shift downward, but there would be a gain in foreign exchange. A devaluation would have similar effects. Its recessive effect would be similar to that described in the preceding case; but by changing relative prices directly, by making tradables more expensive, the productive restructuring would be reinforced toward tradables.

Thus, one could explain the evidence contained in section three as to the effect of the crisis on agriculture. There it was shown that the main effect of the recessive adjustment was to change the productive structure. This result means that tradables and nontradables are produced as if they were part of the same production frontier. They are interrelated.

The drop observed in the overall growth rate would, therefore, be related to the effects of the crisis on the supply side. The credit squeeze, the increase in costs due to devaluation, the reduction in public investment, and the greater uncertainty owing to higher inflation rates must have created a very unfavorable macroeconomic context for the growth of agricultural supply.[10] Short term macroeconomic policy seems to have a significant effect on agriculture, not only on the demand side but also on the supply side.

The main challenge to be faced by any agricultural policy is how to make productivity rise continuously. There can only be continuous agricultural growth if one can constantly raise productivity. Productivity, on the other hand, can only be raised if innovations—whether technological or institutional—are introduced. In both cases public and private innovations are required. In short, the basic issue is one of influencing the determinants of investment, particularly private investment. What incentives should be used to encourage farmers to invest more? Profitability is indeed one of these factors; but given the uncertainty under which farmers operate, two components of profitability must be considered: the mean and variance. What sort of influence could macroeconomic policies have on these two components?

A policy for favoring the average relative profitability of agriculture, relative to that of the other sectors, could be protection by tariff and foreign exchange policies. As mentioned before, this means leaving other sectors unprotected, without a net and substantial profit for society. If the industrialization policy in the region meant the subordination of agriculture to industry, here the opposite is not proposed. Other mechanisms must be used to arrive at that net profit. For example, policies aimed at raising agricultural productivity could achieve this objective.

One of the characteristics of agriculture is that in this activity the productive process is subject to great uncertainty, where the productive results have a significant random effect. This generates marked instability in prices and agricultural income even if everything else in the economic process is stable; in other words, there is a great risk to private investment. But this instability is usually exacerbated by macroeconomic policies. A central role of this policy should be, then, to reduce macroeconomic instability. Thus, incentives would be created for private investment even in high-risk sectors, as is the case with agriculture. For example, a devaluation of the exchange rate could give rise to macroeconomic instability by contributing to a higher rate of inflation. Thus, any positive effect it could have on agriculture, on the side of average profitability, would be lost on the side of greater variance. Stability and consistency are also necessary in macroeconomic policy per se. Erratic changes in these policies add to uncertainty in decisionmaking at microeconomic level, particularly for the long term.[11]

In light of this discussion, it seems evident that the current crisis and adjustment policies that have led to a macroeconomic context of recession and inflation could not have created a favorable environment for agricultural development. The drop in the growth rates of overall agricultural output in the 1980s is consistent with this hypothesis.

As was argued in the preceding section, the agricultural policies followed by central countries have a significant impact on Latin American agricultural development. What can be done to render this international framework less unfavorable to agricultural development in the region? In view of the export subsidies provided by central countries, Latin American countries could apply policies to restrict imports of these subsidized products. For example, the application of import tariffs would spread the benefits of low international prices among producers and consumers and not only consumers. Furthermore, the funds raised could be channeled into agricultural development programs in the country.[12]

In the institutional aspect, the General Agreement on Trade and Tariffs (GATT) "Uruguay Rounds" are underway, which constitute the main forum for negotiating and seeking solutions to the protectionist policies followed by central countries in their agricultural sectors. However, it should be remembered that a policy aimed at achieving greater diversification in production and agricultural exports is another efficient way of dealing with this challenge.

Sectoral Policies

Reducing uncertainty and risks. At the agricultural sector level, policies will be primarily supply sided. Demand for and prices of tradables are exogenous to the sector. How can the risk in agriculture be reduced at a macroeconomic level? Clearly there is no easy way to solve the uncertainty associated with agricultural production and trade. In fact, the problem of risk is already built into the rationale of producers. Economic behavior such as diversification, for example, reveals an aversion to risk. The producers themselves thus seek stability in their income and overall supply. But their behavior in terms of investment will be to demand a higher average profitability to offset the greater risk implicit in investing in agriculture.

A policy that could be followed, then, would be to establish mechanisms to spread these risks over the remainder of society so that they will not be assumed solely by the farmer. Price policies are one way of doing this. Guaranteed price programs and price ranges are the typical instruments used to achieve this objective. The experience with these programs has been quite varied in countries of the region. In various cases these programs have created greater instability than that which they sought to reduce; in others, such as in Chile, the price range policy seems to have been one of the main factors behind the notable burgeoning of agriculture in recent years, especially of basic crops. Clearly, the success of these programs will depend on the efficiency of the state in designing and implementing them.

Other ways of dealing with the problem are through technological and institutional innovations. The main idea in the former is to channel resources into risk-reducing technologies. It is interesting to continue with programs to develop new high-yield strains, but without disregarding their resistance to pests, frost, and the like. In designing genetic research, innovation-generating centers act as if the only thing of interest to producers is average yield but not variance. Technological innovations to reduce the average yield variance, whether in crops or livestock, would do much to reduce the economic risk implicit in adopting these new technologies.

A usual way for producers to deal with price variance is through stocks management, as is typically the case in industry. However, in the case of agriculture many products are perishable, which is why storage costs are so high. This is another example of the need to generate risk-reducing technologies, in this case through the development of postharvest innovations and services. Along this same line, it would be even better to introduce activities in the rural area aimed at industrializing agricultural products. The development of rural industrialization is clearly one way to reduce risk and, at the same time, raise and stabilize income and employment in the countryside. Very little has been done in this respect in Latin America.

The state, which is the largest investor in technological research, should include these criteria in its agenda when designing research. It is not that these efforts are not currently being made, but rather that they usually lack the necessary priority.

In terms of institutional innovation, the idea is to develop those markets that offer the producer the possibility of shifting or spreading risk to other private agents. Futures markets and crop insurance markets are nonexistent in the region. They do not exist because they do not generate an adequate private profitability. Development of these markets is thus a task for the state, at least in its initial phase. The latent demand is there.

The financing of investment. Financing could become another stumbling block for investment in Latin American agriculture over the next couple of years. The main sources of financing for the agrarian sector have up to now been external financial institutions and the public sector. Contributions by private domestic institutions have generally been very limited and selective, usually consisting of short term loans to major agricultural enterprises from the trading or export sector.

Over the next few years, external and public sector sources will tend to decrease their contribution to financing agricultural investment, a contribution that was already reduced during the crisis. The problem of the external debt and the attendant macroeconomic adjustments place limits on the expansion of all these sources of financing. And compensatory dynamism from private institutions is not to be hoped for. However, in the face of the little leeway that exists for raising investment levels, it is very important to pay special attention to increasing their effectiveness and yield, reallocating resources toward efficient sectors in the countryside and the economy in general. Undoubtedly, reallocation still provides considerable room for maneuvering.

In addition to what can be done to obtain greater funds from conventional channels and to raise investment efficiency, one can look to one of the options available domestically, particularly financing private investment. This option consists in increasing the efficiency of the financial market in rural areas. There is some consensus in the region on the potential that exists in rural areas for increasing the supply of funds to be loaned through rural savings (FAO 1988). To increase efficiency means in this case developing rural financial markets.[13]

It is evident that financial brokerage in rural areas is not an economically profitable activity. This is revealed by the fact that there are very few private capitalist-type institutions present. Cooperatives and rural credit unions have a greater relative presence, possibly because they need much lower rates of return to operate than do capitalist institutions. But even in this case their presence is not significant except in some countries and within given regions.

The factors that limit the development of financial markets in rural areas are connected, on the one hand, with the relatively high operating costs and, on the other, with state control policies on interest rates. In terms of the latter, interest rate policy must be handled from a longer term perspective—that of raising the supply of funds before subsidizing a favored group among those requesting credit (Graham, Adams, and Pischke 1984).

Operating costs are high because clients are highly scattered, transactions are small and numerous, operations are high risk, and capital turnover is slow. State policy could help to reduce these costs by improving rural infrastructure, particularly communications, and promoting the generation of external economies. What is needed is for the financial industry to establish itself and grow in order to thus reduce costs for those subsequently entering the industry. Public institutions, cooperatives, or rural credit unions can play a leading role because they are institutions that can operate where capitalist enterprises are not feasible.

In short, what is involved is to support the development of financial institutions and not spread subsidized credit, which is what private agricultural credit projects, international development financial institutions, and states usually do. Agricultural development projects funded by nongovernmental organizations (NGOs), for example, neglect the need for having in place financial intermediaries at local level who are capable of mobilizing part of the monetary surplus generated by the project. Consequently, after the project concludes the system begun cannot be reproduced.

In many cases external financial resources have the effect of displacing domestic resources (the effect referred to as "crowding out"), when their role should be one of complementing and reinforcing the policy of attracting resources within the rural area. External contributions should not be limited to injecting funds for loans, but rather should include technical assistance and personnel education on financial matters and on all that is needed for the technological and institutional modernization of the countryside. Development of financial markets in rural areas is another example of modernization and institutional innovation required to promote agricultural development. Technological innovations in the productive aspect must be somehow related to institutional innovations. One cannot advance without the other.

Public investment has an important effect on agricultural development because it improves the quality of production factors, contributing to increased private productivity and microeconomic efficiency. The greater infrastructure installed in rural areas also can help to develop markets and thus contribute to microeconomic efficiency. If this is true, public investment need not displace private investment, but rather it should serve to complement it.

Development of Peasant Farming

Structural Characteristics

Small-scale farming, organized under the form of peasant production, is defined by two characteristics: farming is done essentially by the family itself, and the size of the holding does not afford the peasant family an income above subsistence level.

In social terms peasant farming involves a significant proportion of the rural population in all Latin American countries. The notable exceptions are Argentina, Uruguay, and Cuba. The size that defines peasant farming is not easy to establish, but in most cases it seems to correspond to holdings under 5–10 hectares, depending on the country. Using this criterion, the average size for the region as a whole seems to be close to 2 hectares. It has been estimated that 25 percent of the total population of the region is composed of peasant families (Ortega 1985).

Peasant farmers not only operate on small holdings but also on lands of marginal quality. In fact, peasant farming takes place where capitalist agriculture is unfeasible: on the slopes of the Andes, in the highlands of Peru, Bolivia, and Guatemala, in the arid areas of Brazil and Mexico, and generally in nonirrigated farmlands.

Peasant farming is not only small-scale but is above all difficult. This means, among other things, that the degree of risk for the producer is greater. For this reason, and due to the instability of market prices and the fact that they are poor, the economic behavior of peasant families is characterized by a great aversion to risk. This behavior has two major consequences for economic policy: peasant economy is diversified as a way of minimizing risk, and its response to economic incentives is much more viscous.

Technological Potential

Despite the difficulties indicated, peasant farming now has great potential for development. Technological development in recent decades has generated innovations, such as hybrid seeds and fertilizers, that do not require large-sized holdings. Above all, technology has been generated to develop more innovations that are indifferent to the scale of production. This fact opens up great possibilities for small-scale agricultural development.

In actual fact, these innovations are already being adopted by peasants, although the rate is still low. Various studies have pointed out the great technological heterogeneity existing in peasant farming (Figueroa 1986b; Machado and Torres 1987). There is a marked difference in the rate of adoption of biochemical technologies among microregions, which, while ecologically similar, differ in the degree of technological modernization. A consequence of these technological gaps is the prominent differences in land productivity (see Table 10.4).

The microregions referred to as traditional in Table 10.4 are clearly the typical regions in rural areas of the four sample countries. The situation in the other Latin American countries is probably not very different. Evidently, there is great potential for increasing the productivity of peasant farming in the region. If it were possible to achieve a faster and more massive dissemination of the innovations used by peasant technological leaders to other peasant producers, the impact on aggregate output would be clearly significant.[14]

What are the main obstacles to the development of peasant agriculture? A factor that clearly limits the adoption of technological innovations is the scarcity of land. For most peasant families the size of their agricultural holding is suboptimal, both for the full employment of family members and for incurring the cost of adopting technological innovations. Indeed, despite the fact that some innovations are indifferent to the scale of

Table 10.4.   **Differences in Productivity and Adoption of Technological**
              Innovations in Peasant Farming in Peru, Brazil, Mexico, and Paraguay

Countries/Output	Microregions		
	Modern	Average	Traditional
Peru: potatoes			
Average yield (ton/ha)	8.3	4.0	3.7
Adoption of innovations: % of producers			
Pesticides	97	99	53
Fertilizers	98	99	35
Hybrid seeds	92	36	3
Brazil: beans			
Average yield (ton/ha)	1.1	0.4	0.1
Adoption of innovations: % of producers			
Fertilizers	100	90	0
Other chemical inputs	92	46	0
Mexico: maize			
Average yield (ton/ha)	3.1	2.0	0.9
Adoption of innovations: % of producers			
Chemical inputs	53	55	47
Improved seeds	78	65	0
Paraguay: cotton			
Average yield (ton/ha)	1.1	1.1	0.7
Adoption of innovations: spending on fertilizers, improved seeds, and pesticides, average (thousands of guaranies)	22	23	6

Source: Figueroa (1986b).

production, a minimum holding size is required. In many cases peasant families barely have a few furrows of land. Clearly, development of the agricultural unit is unfeasible here. Given the unequal land distribution that exists in the countries of the region, the development of peasant farming becomes an integral part of an agrarian reform program. This will be discussed further on.

Another limiting factor is connected to the innovation adoption process itself. Everything points to the fact that the technological learning process of peasants is very slow. The logistical learning curve of peasants seems to show a very long segment in its initial phase. This is primarily due to the fact that innovations are exogenous to the peasant economy, and to the cautious attitude of the peasant, stemming from the risk-minimizing rationale, in accepting an extraneous innovation. Some have confused this slowness in learning and in adopting innovations with a resistance to change.

There is another basic reason that explains this particular learning curve: the costs of learning are very high for peasants. Indeed, their information costs are high, but so are the costs of experimenting, to which even less attention has been paid. Recent studies show that all these costs are reduced when peasants have greater formal education (Figueroa 1986b). A very specific agricultural extension policy would be an instrument for speeding up adoptions. Its objective would be to substantially shift the logistic learning curve leftward. It should seek to reduce learning costs and thus partly substitute the role of formal education. In the long term this policy would have to be oriented to a specific form of generating technological innovations.

New technology is, on the other hand, more credit intensive. But small-scale agriculture is not only discriminated against in its access to credit by the state—which excludes it from its subsidized credit programs[15]—but it is also implicitly discriminated against by the market system. The unit cost of credit is greater for small-scale farming. Lenders face greater unit administrative costs when they lend to small-scale farmers, and they incur greater risk owing to the small amount of collateral. Therefore, the interest rate in a free market tends to be greater for small-scale producers.

This would be one of the reasons that explains what is seen in Latin America: the interest rate for informal credit is higher than that for formal credit. Because small-scale farmers operate primarily in the informal market, a state credit policy would have to compensate for this market discrimination. Thus, there are economic arguments for justifying a subsidized credit policy for peasant farming. A peasant credit program is needed to answer to the needs of peasant farming. The contents of such a program would have elements typical to each country, but one can suggest the main criteria:

1. Guaranty based on production and not on collateral security
2. Flexible use of loans for any of the activities undertaken by peasant economy, including financing the costs of entering labor markets and nonagricultural activities
3. Subsidized interest rates
4. Sufficiently extended terms to allow producers to experiment with new technologies and overcome annual income variations arising from changes in climate or the market without major difficulty

Undoubtedly, implementation of this program would require a very efficient institutional organization. It could be done through existing organizations or by creating new ones. For example, peasant banks could be created to this effect. What is important is for these institutions to operate by using another rationale and another system of incentives in their institutional operation. The success criteria of a peasant bank will be very different from those of a commercial bank and also from those of a state bank. Current state agrarian banks often exhibit schizophrenic behavior when they have to deal with medium- and large-scale farming and, at the same time, peasant farming. Institutional specialization by type of agricultural production (capitalist or peasant) seems to be most fitting in the dual agrarian structure that characterizes most Latin American countries.

Agrarian Reform

Although there are major differences between countries, the concentration of land ownership in Latin America is still very pronounced. The data, although imperfect for making valid comparisons between countries, coincide in showing that major concentrations occur in Brazil, Colombia, Guatemala, and Venezuela (FAO 1988: appendix 2).

Individual agrarian reform programs have already been implemented in various countries in the region. The greatest in scope were those in Bolivia, Chile, Cuba, El Salvador, Mexico, Nicaragua, and Peru. Regional program scopes are reviewed in Ortega (1985) and FAO (1988: appendix 2). Generally, agrarian reform programs have had the following characteristics: (1) they have benefited very few, leaving out significant portions of landless peasants, or those who own very little land; (2) cooperative organization for beneficiaries has not always been successful; (3) the effects on production have tended to be positive; and (4) beneficiaries have received little support in services (credit, technology).

Despite these advances and limitations, it is clear that agrarian reform still remains on the agrarian policy agenda of some regional countries.[16] What is new is the features that these programs should have, given the transformations that have occurred. As pointed out before, the land tenure structure in Latin America has changed in recent decades. The large estate and small landholding system has changed into the capitalist and peasant system. Large landed estates have given way in most cases to capitalist enterprises, whereas small-scale holdings have given way to the peasant family unit, which is linked to capitalist farming enterprises and the rest of the economy essentially through market relations.

Under these new conditions, the 1950s arguments of structuralists advocating agrarian reform have to be reinterpreted. Clearly, in cases where profit-oriented large landed estates lacking in entrepreneurial spirit still exist, the structuralist recommendation is still applicable. Agrarian reform would be in order there for reasons of efficiency and equity. In the capitalist-peasant structure, agrarian reform would be based on an argument of equity. Due to the fact that large enterprises are capitalist and have been significantly modernized, land redistribution would give rise to a conflict between efficiency and equity.

A very little known fact, despite its importance for agrarian restructuring, is the optimal size of holdings, not only for current technology but for the present technological revolution. On the one hand, the green revolution has in many aspects been neutral with respect to scale; but other aspects of ultramodern technology, such as automation and biotechnology, suggest the emergence of significant economies of scale. The scant empirical evidence available suggests that intermediate landholding sizes are optimal (FAO 1988). The case of Chile, for example, where the land market was allowed to operate after the agrarian reform, indicates this. The trend there has been toward medium-sized holdings (Muñoz and Ortega 1988).

In any case, the lessons to be learned from agrarian reform programs undertaken in the region are clear:

1. These programs require great political will in implementing them.
2. Peasant beneficiaries must actively participate in order to organize new forms of production more efficiently.
3. Programs for land redistribution must be complemented with other programs introducing technological innovations because the former should not be a substitute for the latter.

In actual fact, a reform program constitutes an instrument and a framework for rural development. Peasant farming development policies discussed above should be applied within an agrarian reform framework. Thus, one could ensure that agrarian reform also means an increase in productivity. The implicit conflict between efficiency and equity in agrarian reform could thus be mitigated. One could have more of both objectives. This would also afford greater political viability to agrarian reform, particularly in democratic contexts where future programs will be implemented.

Finally, one must not neglect the linkages between peasant farming and macroeconomics. All attempts to develop peasant farming without simultaneously increasing the demand for the goods it produces would be suicidal. Peasants primarily produce basic foodstuffs, and their productive structure is more intensive in nontradable goods. They are thus very dependent upon domestic demand. In this respect, greater real wages is a sufficient condition for expanding this demand. On the other hand, greater productivity (and income) in peasant farming would contribute to increasing real wages, since it would lead to a reduction of the labor supply in labor markets. The interests of workers and peasants become, in this case, complementary and could give rise to class alliances.

Some Conclusions Regarding Market and State[17]

Latin American agriculture generally operates in very specific contexts: high concentrations of property, overpopulation in relation to its resources and technology, an unstable macroeconomic environment, scant development of capitalist institutions in rural areas (particularly underdeveloped markets), an overall framework of center-periphery relations, and technology that is generated to a great extent in central countries. Under these conditions, economic policy aimed at boosting agricultural development cannot be reduced to a market liberalization policy, as advocated by current neoliberal approaches.

This reductionism, expressed in the liberal paradigm of "getting the prices right," has been taken to an extreme by making the entire argument revolve around a single correct price: the real exchange rate. For neoliberal thinking, a high real exchange rate is a necessary and sufficient condition to achieve agricultural development. However, as shown here, the experience of the region during these years of crisis suggests that a higher real exchange rate has the effect of modifying the agricultural production structure (between tradables and nontradables), but it does not lead to raising its output, at least in terms of overall growth rates.

The policy of respecting market prices could be a necessary condition, under certain circumstances, but it cannot be sufficient for agricultural development in Latin America. As shown, state involvement is justified in economic terms given the context under which the agricultural economy operates in the region. It is not only a matter of resolving market imperfections in terms of distortions between private and social costs, as is the case in natural resource management and the environment. It is also a question of reducing the strong inequality of income that results from structural elements, such as the excessive concentration of agricultural property, economic duality, and overpopulation.

It also involves state action that allows for the transformation of those elements that form the context and that prevent agriculture from being more dynamic, even if market prices are left untouched. For example, in this chapter it has been shown that agricultural development requires, in turn, more developed markets in rural areas. Thus, credit, securities, and futures and technology markets are underdeveloped (totally missing or incomplete), and they limit the expansion of agricultural productivity. In fact, in many rural areas in Latin America a liberalization policy would not make much sense since there are no markets to deregulate. The challenge consists, rather, in how to develop these markets, which the rationale of private agents has not succeeded in doing under current conditions.

The technological development of the agricultural sector is another clear example of how the market—on its own—does not guarantee efficiency in generating and disseminating technology. Institutional innovation is needed to organize the generation and dissemination of technological innovations. A technology to generate technology, which could be referred to as a *goal-technology,* requires state involvement.[18]

Finally, the development of peasant farming cannot be accomplished only via the market mechanism. The experience reviewed here shows that the market discriminates against small-scale farming: it increases the latter's transaction and information costs for its technological development in comparison to that of capitalist agriculture.

In short, agricultural development in the region requires policies that modify the current context toward another that is more appropriate for development. The distortions induced by economic policy are not the sole cause underlying the problem of agricultural development. Its causes are also structural, and these are perhaps most important over the long term because, among other things, they limit the efficient operation of the market. This requires economic policies that promote technological and institutional innovations. Market prices, although necessary, are not sufficient for this task.[19]

The "get the prices right" paradigm is insufficient. "Get the policy mix right" could better express the challenges involved in designing agricultural policy in Latin America. A correct combination of market policies and state participation must be sought. In other words, there is important room in agricultural development for joint action by the market and the state. This conclusion—reclaimed by the structuralist thinking of the region—presupposes that state involvement must be efficient. The state has to help solve the problems of agricultural development and not create them. The question is how to achieve greater efficiency of the state apparatus when it is also undergoing a crisis. This is a veritable challenge to the political talent of governments of the region. In any event, it does not involve a reduction or expansion of the size of the state, which is how the current discussion is phrased. Rather it involves modifying the state in qualitative terms toward a state that promotes the structural transformations such as those proposed in this chapter.

Notes

1. This notion contrasts with the current one, where *rigid agricultural supply* means that with a given technology and resources, production levels can barely increase. This is clearly a short term concept.

2. Demand may be considered as $D = AI'^{\alpha} p\beta N$, where D is the quantity of agricultural goods demanded, I is per capita income, P is the price vector, and N is population size. From this we obtain the following ratio in terms of growth rates: $D^* = \alpha I^* + N^*$, assuming that prices (P vector), income distribution, and other demographic and social factors remain constant.

3. This figure is obtained by applying an income elasticity of 0.6 to the per capita GDP growth rate, which was 3 percent per year, plus the 2.6 percent of demographic growth. The coefficient 0.6 is a very rough approximation based on studies on the demand for foodstuffs in urban areas. See, for example, Musgrove (1978).

4. The main studies consulted include de Janvry (1981), FAO/ECLAC works in López Cordovez (1985), FAO (1988), and the PREALC works in ILO (1987).

5. Chapter 8 provides a complete review of the role of science and technology in the development possibilities of Latin America.

6. The sources cited in this section are merely illustrative of the existing literature on the subject. An exhaustive bibliographic presentation is beyond the scope of this work.

7. Chapter 7 contains a broad presentation and discussion of the environmental issue and the role of natural resources in Latin American development.

8. A summary of agricultural development theories in the region can be found in Machado and Torres (1987). A perspective closer to the structuralist one is found in Figueroa (1986a).

9. Although there are significant differences between countries in the region, as indicated in the preceding sections, here economic policy issues that are generic to the region will be discussed. Indeed, a treatment by country or group of countries is beyond the scope of this chapter.

10. Public investment as a proportion of public expenditures declined significantly in the region during the crisis. In particular, the proportion of public expenditures directed at agriculture decreased from 8.1 percent in 1975 to 6.2 percent in 1980 and to 4.7 percent in 1985 for the region (FAO 1988: annex 1, table 16).

11. In Chapter 6 some basic guidelines are provided for macroeconomic policy aimed at creating a favorable framework for productive investment.

12. In Peru, for example, for some years wheat imported under the United States PL 480 program was subject to a tariff, and the funds collected were channeled into a program to develop the sierra. A more systematic and efficient effort along these policy lines would prove interesting.

13. Indeed, this proposal is intended for those areas where capitalist agriculture prevails. Areas with a peasant economy will have a lower potential owing to their very depressed state.

14. Estimates by the author for the Peruvian case show that raising peasant productivity to equal levels would mean a 15–20 percent increase in national food production; and between 50 and 100 percent for basic foodstuffs, depending on the product (Figueroa 1988).

15. The ECLAC/FAO Joint Agricultural Division estimates that subsidized state credit in eleven countries in the region does not cover more than 25 percent of agricultural units, almost exclusively supporting medium-sized and large units (ECLAC 1989, *Notas sobre la Economía y el Desarrollo,* No. 479 [July]).

16. The need for an agrarian reform program is evident in the cases of Brazil, Colombia, Guatemala, and Venezuela.

17. The topic has been extensively dealt with in Chapter 13.

18. For a complete review of these subjects, see Chapter 8.

19. The case of Chile is usually mentioned as one of successful neoliberal policy. However, for some economists it is the more active role played by the state as of 1983 that accounts for a good deal of this success (Muñoz and Ortega 1988).

PART 4

THE INTERNATIONAL CONTEXT

11

The New International Setting: Challenges and Opportunities

Winston Fritsch

The basic purpose of this chapter is to update the analysis of the strategic conditioning factors imposed by the international context on Latin America's foreign economic policy options. The first section recovers essential aspects of postwar Latin American structuralist thinking, in order to emphasize the importance that this school of thought attached to the analysis of the historical characteristics of the international setting in defining development strategy in dependent countries. The second section includes a brief retrospective analysis of the evolution of the Latin American economy's insertion into the postwar world economy, followed by a discussion of the characteristics of the emerging international setting that should determine the challenges and opportunities posed to Latin American economies in the management of their insertion strategies. Finally, the third section theorizes specific ways in which the region's different economies will have to redefine their relation with the world economy in the course of the next decade.

The International Setting in a Structuralist Analysis of Latin American Development

The proposals deriving from the so-called structuralist vision of the Latin American economic development process began to take shape and gained great influence during the first decade of the postwar period. Perhaps the most important of these proposals has been that both the acceleration of the growth rate in primary exporting economies and their reduced structural vulnerability to exogenous shocks may be achieved by stimulating industrialization. Its basic premise, supported by the historical experience of central countries, is that transforming the supply structure of primary exporting economies toward industrial products would have a strong effect on the economies' average productivity levels. In addition, increased

317

participation in revenue generated outside traditional primary goods export sectors oriented to the markets of the center would reduce the tendency toward external imbalance resulting from exogenous instability factors, which characterize dependent economies.

It may, therefore, be concluded that the proposal of deliberately introverted industrial promotion policies, or policies that intentionally repressed international trade, did not follow logically from the essence of structuralist analysis. The policies that were actually followed during the industrial boom phase created by import substitution in the region until the early 1970s, which are commonly associated with structuralist thinking, in fact came about as eclectic responses to a sequence of external shocks—beginning with the dramatic payment problems caused by the dollar shortage in the immediate postwar period—which justified adjustment policies based on the contraction of industrial product imports.[1] The basic premise of original structuralist thinking was simply that industrialization would reduce external vulnerability and create endogenous incentives to increase these economies' average productivity, a requirement to guarantee growth and overcome underdevelopment. As Sunkel says in Chapter 2, what was idealized was not simply an inward-looking development model, but rather a development model *from within* as a way of changing the asymmetrical relationship of international trade.

Furthermore, the great legacy of the structuralist school was methodological: the explicit recognition of the historicism inherent to the object of development theory and of the need for an all-encompassing vision of the development process.[2] This gave rise to the idea—central to the structuralist vision—that an analysis of the historical conditioning factors imposed by the international setting is crucial to understand the Latin American economic development process. Indeed, since colonial times, Latin American development has been understood as the region's process of integration into the movement of global economic expansion, the dynamic pole of which is situated elsewhere. Hence, the arrival at the idea that the effectiveness of domestic policies in the region depends essentially on the congruity of these policies with the global trends that condition their possibilities of insertion into the international economy.

Therefore, normative propositions of classical structuralism, especially their tactic emphasis on inward-looking development, have a place in history. How could it be otherwise, if they were deeply conditioned by a perception of the restrictions and opportunities created by the international setting in the immediate postwar period? Indeed, it is impossible to understand the structuralist proposal for industrialization by import substitution without reference to two commonly accepted premises on the evolution of world economy after World War II. On the one hand, the loss of dynamism in the international division of labor between the center and the periphery that was created during the Pax Britannica and, therefore, in international trade—within traditional models—was an engine of growth for peripheral economies. On the other hand, the viability of transforming the productive structures of the region's economies became evident from the historical experience during the period between wars. In those years an irreversible process of industrialization, still in progress, was already evident in many of the principal Latin American economies.

The updating of Latin American thinking on development in the structuralist tradition therefore requires the revival of the idea that a recovery of growth and reduced vulnerability to exogenous events demands, just as in the original analysis, structural changes aimed at maximizing the productivity growth rate. The economic rationale underlying this proposition—that is, the causal relationship between productivity increases and sustained growth—remains as valid today as it was in the period of the original structuralist analysis, given the nature of the twofold external restriction on the growth of the countries in the region, imposed by their large foreign debt, vis-à-vis the financing difficulties that they have had to face since 1982. The first restriction originated in the limit imposed on the levels of domestic activity by the need to maintain external balance. The second is the restriction on growth of installed capacity and, therefore, on long term product growth, created by the depressive effect on the economy's investment capacity caused by the real transfer of resources abroad for payment of the foreign debt.[3] Thus, while capital account balances remain depressed, the recovery of growth depends on maintaining a high exporting performance and increasing domestic savings levels as a proportion of total output.

The challenge is even greater because, in addition to these two imperatives of economic order for the recovery of sustained growth, these countries also face the political imperative of improving their population's standard of living, which has become more dramatic after a decade of stagnation. Furthermore, this should take place in a context in which increases in real wages at a rate above increases in productivity are incompatible both with continuing competitiveness of exports and the increase in the internal propensity to save. Therefore, a rapid increase in productivity becomes a necessary condition to meet the current historic challenge of recovering sustained growth, while making the restrictions imposed by foreign debt compatible with unpostponable distributive demands.

However, the most important step toward creating a new normative paradigm in structuralist tradition is to update the analysis of the international setting. This would make it possible to redefine the insertion of Latin American countries into the international division of labor in accord with the strategic objective of increased productivity. Under the influence of the historical conditioning factors mentioned above, the original structuralist analysis proposed a defensive redefinition of the links with the international economy, by creating industrialization incentives. It was expected that industrialization would automatically give way to gains in productivity.

Similarly, the revision of the old paradigm is obviously necessary for at least two reasons. First, the original analysis is outmoded after more than four decades of intense industrialization and far-reaching transformation in the ways in which Latin American economies enter the world economy, as described below. Second, and definitely most importantly, profound changes are now underway in the determinants of comparative advantage patterns, which, if they become more intense during the last decade of the century, may provoke radical changes in the postwar international division of labor trends.

Today's reality is entirely different from that discussed by structuralists in the postwar period, who could refer to Latin America as a whole as primary exporting countries, and who lived in a world in which for the past thirty years trade grew less than the overall product. The challenge today is to redesign adjustment strategies in a Latin America that is semiindustrialized in global terms but is increasingly heterogeneous, in a period in which world trade in manufactures is expanding at rates much higher than the overall product growth and in which, as discussed below, the process of internationalization of production is undergoing profound transformations.

The International Setting in Historical Perspective

This section is divided into two parts. The first part briefly describes the evolution of the Latin American economy's form of insertion into the world economy in the postwar period. The breaking down of this evolution into periods is basically determined by changes in the international situation, the restrictions and opportunities of which, to a large extent, determined the policies adopted in the region. The second part analyzes the principal characteristics of the new international setting emerging out of the 1980s.

The most distinguishing feature between the two periods is, without doubt, the greater international economic instability that emerged as of the early 1970s as result of the breakdown of the Bretton-Woods institutions and the combination of the oil shocks, rapid technological change, global macroeconomic instability caused by the imbalance in the North American current account, and the debt crisis in the developing countries. These changes affected countries' basic comparative advantages determinants and the strategic planning of transnational companies. The reactions of these two groups of agents—countries and companies—to this highly volatile environment determined the main transformations that are taking place in the world economy, which, in turn, will determine Latin America's options for foreign economic policy in the coming years.

Latin America and the World Economy in the Postwar Period

The evolution of Latin America's form of insertion into the flow of trade, direct investment, and international financing in the postwar period up until the 1980s can be divided roughly into three main stages.

The first stage includes the period of industrialization by import substitution, based on policies that created incentives that were strongly biased toward domestic markets, which were applied by most countries until the mid-1960s. The adoption of these policies was a natural response to balance of payments problems created by the dollar shortage and supply restrictions in industrialized European countries in the immediate postwar period, reinforced throughout the 1950s by the deterioration of the terms of trade of the countries in the region and by the inadequacy of financing flows. Indeed, despite the fact that up to the early 1950s some countries, such as the coffee producers, still benefited from the high prices of their basic export products, as of the end of the Korean War, there was a generalized downward tendency in primary product prices: in 1960 the region's export prices were some 20 percent lower than their 1954 peak. With the exception of Venezuelan oil, export volumes continued to stagnate, and the Latin American share of international trade dropped from 12 percent to less than 7 percent between 1950 and 1965. On the other hand, due to restrictions on the movements of capital in Europe until the end of the 1950s, which hindered the reconstruction of the international capital market, and because the supply of official financing from North America and the Bretton-Woods institutions clearly proved to be inadequate, direct investment—especially North American until the end of the 1950s—played an important role in the region's external financing.[4] This explains the adoption of policies that were relatively liberal toward foreign capital in industry, which, in conjunction with restrictive policies toward the import of manufactures, led to a high penetration by multinational companies.

Meanwhile, the appalling export performance of Latin America in this period cannot be attributed solely to the unfortunate behavior of prices and demand for the principal primary products exported by the region at that time. It was definitely reinforced by the adoption of overvalued exchange rates and selective and restrictive trade policy instruments, by which inward-looking incentive policies were introduced that contributed to isolating the region from the benefits of a world trade in manufactures that was in a phase of rapid expansion.

The reaction to this policy and the gradual reform of the incentives to tradables as of the mid-1960s mark the start of the second stage in the evolution of Latin American forms of insertion into the world economy, which lasted until the first oil shock and the growth crisis of central economies in the mid-1970s. Meanwhile, it is important to point out that, just as the international setting of the 1950s encouraged the adoption of defensive trade and exchange policies, the implementation of these reforms was encouraged by the particularly favorable external environment that existed at that time. The acceleration of growth in the Organization for Economic Cooperation and Development (OECD) led to an abrupt increase in the value of primary imports from less than 4.5 percent between 1955 and 1968 to more than 19 percent between 1968 and 1973.[5]

This improvement in the trade of primary products was accompanied by a substantial increase in the capital inflow into the region in the form of direct investment and, increasingly, money loans. The temporary relaxation of chronic external restrictions under which Latin American economies traditionally functioned, which was made possible by this favorable international environment, allowed the reduction of protection levels and anti-export bias, incorporating a battery of incentives to exports of manufactures into the arsenal of trade policy instruments. The effect of this greater neutrality on the structure of trade incentives was impressive. On the one hand, the age-old contraction of the participation of imports in the aggregate product, which had fallen by a third since the start of the 1950s, was reversed. On the other hand, between 1965 and 1973 the region's exports grew by an average of 10.8 percent per year, compared to an annual growth rate of 3.6 percent in the previous fifteen years. Exports of manufactured products grew at an impressive rate of 26.5 percent per year in this period, while the world trade in manufactures grew 16.4 percent per year. Indeed, the most striking feature of this period is the beginning of the process of diversification in the region's exports in the direction of manufactured goods.

As pointed out, this stage came to an end with the first oil shock in 1973–1974 and the ensuing recession in the central economies and global economic instability. It is also interesting to note that Latin American adjustment in the 1970s was relatively mild, in spite of significant asymmetries. Some oil-exporting countries benefited from the abrupt rise in oil prices, while the majority only managed to adjust by means of growing levels of foreign indebtedness permitted by the extremely accommodating attitude of international private financial markets. Others, such as Southern Cone countries, embarked on radical liberalization experiments, with extremely perverse effects on economic performance. Generally, the substantial levels of borrowing that these economies managed to attract allowed the current account adjustment to be extended over a more prolonged period, avoiding the need to reestablish exchange and trade controls such as those that prevailed in the 1950s.

After 1973 the region's export performance came to depend less on the reforms of domestic policies that were typical of that time. The greater instability in world trade caused by the uncertainty as to the future course of the parities between the principal currencies and, particularly, the strong fluctuations in growth and the increasing protectionism in central countries came to play a much more important role in the performance of Latin

American exports. With the exception of oil, the prices of primary products—which still represented almost half the region's total export income—fluctuated violently.

Consequently, since the viability of the adjustment-by-borrowing strategy depended on continued high export performance in the long term, the trend toward incentives policies for exports of manufactures was reinforced; and these exports, recovering from 1975 onward, grew at an average of 23.2 percent per year until 1979, nearly 5 percent above the world average. The transformations in the structure of Latin American trade in the 1970s were not limited to the diversification in the composition of export products; the region also experienced significant changes in the direction of trade. In this regard, a striking aspect was the increase in the share of nonoil exports destined for developing countries—due particularly to intraregional trade—as result, to a large extent, of these economies' faster growth as compared to the OECD after 1973.

This third stage ended with the debt crisis in the early 1980s, which marked the beginning of the current phase of recessive adjustment and stagnation. Some characteristics of the past decade are notable, such as the probably lasting collapse of loans flows—which suggests the occurrence of a cycle, similar to that faced in the 1950s, in which direct investment will again be important as a source of foreign currency—or the renewed importance of the OECD markets vis-à-vis the Latin American market, depressed by the sweeping recession that has befallen the region. But the most striking feature of this still-unconcluded and clearly transitional stage is instability and relative stagnation. A new international setting is emerging that may produce profound changes in the relation between Latin America and the world economy.

The New International Setting: Macroeconomic Instability and Structural Change in the World Economy

A broad consensus exists to the effect that we are living in an age in which an interaction of structural factors—linked to the recent acceleration in the pace and nature of technological and organizational innovation in the center and with expectations on the evolution of the unstable macroeconomic world situation—is steadily and decisively altering the determinants of strategic decisions by governments and transnational companies. However, although no consensus has been reached on the *direction* in which the increased instability affects the strategic reactions of these relevant agents, the design of plausible scenarios for these reactions is of crucial importance in defining the possibilities of inserting Latin American economies into the nascent international division of labor, and, therefore, in efficiently redefining long term policies in the region, especially trade and industrial policies.

The environment of world macroeconomic instability. Since the first half of the 1970s, the behavior of the world economy has been characterized by an instability unprecedented since the end of the Korean War. Meanwhile, both the immediate causes and the very nature of the instability have varied throughout these years. The period from the first oil shock up until the debt crisis was marked by large fluctuations in activity and price levels. This was caused by the combined effect of the collapse of the Bretton-Woods system and the oil shocks, in which the international finance system played a stabilizing role, allowing adjustment of current account imbalances created by these fluctuations. On the other hand, as of the first half of the 1980s, the world economy has entered a slow but sustained growth path with greater price stability, despite the fact that growing difficulties were observed in the financing of deficit areas—Third World debtor countries and, particularly, the United States—which warned of potential instability in international asset markets.

The main focus of this potential instability was the uncertainty, especially strong by the middle of the 1980s, as to whether it would be possible to ensure financing for the gigantic deficit in the North American current account. Projections of the evolution of the United States external imbalance showed that even after the substantial foreign exchange adjustment carried out as of 1985, if current parities were maintained and if currently projected growth and inflation rates for the United States and its principal trading partners were achieved, the current account deficit should start to grow again and exceed the current levels of nearly 150 billion dollars per year in the first years of the 1990s.[6] However, following the substantial dollar devaluation and the 1989–1990 slowdown in the United States, some important progress was made to correct this imbalance.

The most likely scenario is still one that combines sustained growth in the central economies—although at rates that are historically low—the rigidity of international interest rates, and additional devaluations of the dollar. This scenario, despite not being recessive, is not unequivocally positive for Latin American economies. Indeed, this scenario shows no significant improvements in the fundamental exogenous determinants of the balance of payments current account in these economies (the interest and growth rates of markets in the center). In addition, the definite prospect of a continued depression in the flow of voluntary financing—even assuming the optimistic scenario that the recent North American initiative manages to implement effective debt-reduction schemes—one may conclude that the region's economies will continue to face the threat of foreign currency restriction should they return to historical growth levels.

The exhaustion of possibilities for adjustment by contraction of imports and the prospects for continued world growth in manufactures indicate that in the course of the next few years the performance of exports of manufactures should be decisive for Latin American growth. This view suggests that today, in contrast to the postwar experience, overcoming the tendency toward external imbalance in a path of growth requires more, rather than less, trade. Thus, the important point here is to identify the opportunities available to increase the region's relative competitiveness. This takes us to the analysis of the profound changes in patterns of direct investment and the trading of manufactures that are currently in progress in the world market.

The tendency toward the internationalization of production. The combination of a wave of technological and managerial innovation and the growing economic instability discussed above gave rise to significant changes in the determinants of strategic decisions of transnational companies during the past ten or fifteen years and, therefore, to changes in the characteristics of the process of internationalization of production. The important and recent changes in the spatial and sectoral distribution of direct foreign investment flows within the central countries—with the rapid growth of Japanese direct investment in the electronics and automobile industries in the principal North Atlantic economies—still basically conform to the "Hymerian" dynamics, traditional in the North American and European postwar internationalization process.[7] This basically concerns the response of the leading Japanese companies in these markets—which control intangible assets that are crucial to the determination of competitive advantages, in the form of brands or technologies—to the real or presumed threats of higher protectionist barriers in their principal markets.

Furthermore, fundamental changes have taken place in recent years in the determinants of direct investment in the semi-industrialized periphery. The importance of domestic markets has clearly diminished vis-à-vis the exploitation of the recipient country's local advantages in the perspective of production for export. These changes are the result of two different influences. On the one hand, they reflect the so-called globalization process in transnational companies: the change in the spatial configuration of their operations as a way of replacing the traditional structure of relatively autonomous national or subregional subsidiaries with a highly integrated pattern of productive operations carried out in different countries. This process of vertical integration on a global scale seems to be irreversible. It represents the response of these large companies to the competitive pressures for restructuring their far-reaching industrial networks, which were created out of the world economic instability of the 1970s and were made possible by the reduction in costs of spatial coordination due to innovations in the telecommunications field.[8]

On the other hand, these changes also reflect the possibilities that direct investment offers to exporting companies with limited participation at the international level, and which still operate from a single national base, as a precaution against the effect of strong exchange rate fluctuations

on their international competitiveness or the effect of structural adjustment
to rapid increases in real wages—as has been particularly important in the
Japanese case. This has important implications for the analysis of the long
term evolution of world trade in manufactures, the dynamics of the process
of spatial reassignment of industry on a world scale, and the analysis of
medium term North and South direct investment flows. Therefore, in view
of the tendency toward further dollar devaluations, favorable conditions
should arise in the next few years for the increase in direct investment
from the principal European economies and Japan toward the dollar countries, as can already be seen. In the Japanese case, past and expected appreciation of the yen should contribute to the decisive acceleration of the
trend of falling competitiveness and to the migration of labor-intensive industries and imported raw materials. The most striking aspect of these
changes, in addition to the recently acquired Japanese leadership in sectors
such as the electronics and automobile industries, should be the internationalization of the country's industry—the production of which, outside
the archipelago, currently amounts to scarcely 3 percent of the total, in
contrast to almost 20 percent in the United States and former West Germany—and the possible vertical disintegration of the country's industrial
system in its transnational operations.[9]

The impact of these changes on the flow of direct investment toward
Latin America—firmly located in the dollar countries with low labor costs
and in various countries with a reasonable industrial infrastructure—
should, in principle, be favorable. Meanwhile, in spite of differing motivations, both the direct investment associated with the globalization process and that associated with the reassignment of exporting plants located
outside dollar countries have a common feature: they are both extremely
sensitive to the trade policy system of the recipient country. This may be
illustrated by comparing the propensity to export in North American subsidiaries located in the Asian NICs—where subsidiaries were clearly outward looking—and in Latin America, both shown in Table 11.1. The immense differences observed in the propensity to export reflect, to a large
extent, differences in industrial policy that affect the trade orientation of
foreign capital,[10] in the same way as the reduction of this difference in recent years reflects the reduction of the disincentives to exports of manufactured products in Latin America.

The trends in the dynamics of the internationalization of industrial
production discussed above therefore seem to point to two main conclusions. The first is that the realization of available opportunities for improvement in Latin America's export performance is closely linked to foreign capital policy. Indeed, at the end of the twentieth century, as in the
past, national strategies to encourage growth and diversification of exports
of manufactures in technologically dependent countries, such as in Latin
America, should not rest solely on national companies. The second is that,

in contrast to what happened in the past, the attraction of foreign investment will increasingly depend on minimizing the negative impact of distortions created by the protective structure of the region's economy on the plants located there.

Table 11.1. **Propensity to Export of the Subsidiaries of North American Manufacturing Companies (percentages)**

Country	1966	1977	1982	1986
All countries	18.6	30.8	33.9	38.3
Developed countries	20.4	33.1	36.6	39.3
Developing countries	8.4	18.1	22.0	32.6
Latin America	6.2	9.7	11.9	20.1
Asian NICs[a]	—	81.2	76.2	76.0

Source: Adapted from Fritsch and Franco (1988b: table 1).
Note: a. Hong Kong, South Korea, Singapore, and Taiwan.

Protectionism and market regionalization. The feasibility of increasing the degree of openness of Latin American industry, with a view to exploiting the opportunities created by the growing volume of trade in manufactures, obviously depends on a scenario of improved competitiveness and conditions of access to markets. However, the experience of the most industrialized Latin American countries demonstrates that supercompetitiveness in tight labor-intensive product lines leads to penetration rates in the markets of central countries that are incompatible with the pace of structural adjustment that is politically feasible in those countries, giving rise to protectionist measures directed at specific countries or products.[11]

In a given scenario of the evolution of protectionism in the North, the restriction of access to those markets can be minimized in two ways. The first is by the very process of globalization of the economies, given the political influence that transnational companies can exercise in terms of minimizing the damage caused by difficulties in access to the exports of their subsidiaries, or their vertically integrated associates, in their countries of origin.

The second and most important would result from a change in the nature of the products exported by the region's principal countries. The progressive substitution in those countries of products that are fairly unsophisticated, relatively homogeneous, relatively intensive in labor or natural resources, with price as the principal competitive factor, and where the major protectionist pressures are found—generally light consumer and semimanufactured goods—by differentiated consumer goods or industrial parts and components will have two important effects. The first effect is greater problems of adjustment and commercial difficulties due to the fact that the second type of products presents increasing opportunities for intraindustrial exchange with the central countries, as was clearly demonstrated by the intra-OECD trade experience in the postwar period. Second, growing technological sophistication in the composition of exports from the principal Latin American countries would increase their chances of complementing production structures of countries with less relative development in the region. Thus, from the perspective of the dynamism of Latin American exports, the growth in the composition of exports of manufactures in countries with greater relative development is not only possible, but essential.

Finally, the conditions of access are determined by the trade policies of our main partners. In spite of the difficulties that may be foreseen in the evolution of protectionist pressures in the central countries, their growth as a widespread, nonsectoral phenomenon is clearly associated with conditions of low rates of growth in domestic demand and exchange revaluation in those countries. This explains the growth of neoprotectionism in the North Atlantic during the recession of the 1970s and the emphasis of these pressures in the United States during the period of the dollar revaluation.

Meanwhile, from the mid-1980s on, continued growth, the realignment of exchange parities, and the start of a new round of multilateral trade negotiations under the General Agreement on Trade and Tariffs (GATT) at the end of 1986 largely contributed to reducing the threat of increased protectionism. The recently concluded review under the Uruguay round of talks shows that it is possible to achieve some effective progress in terms of liberalization of trade in agricultural products—both tropical and temperate—to the benefit of Latin America, as well as greater discipline in and multilateral supervision of the application of the nontariff barriers typically used against the exports of manufactures from developing countries.

Despite these positive developments, the impression persists that the formation of a free trade zone between the United States and Canada, together with the projected abolition of the remaining internal barriers proposed in the Single European Act, and the growing flows of trade and direct investment between Japan and its partners in the Pacific Basin will have a negative effect on Latin American trade. According to the latest version of the region's traditional export pessimism, these developments indicate a possible weakening of the multilateral trade system, which would break down into three blocks centered in the United States, the European Community (EC), and Japan, with particularly negative effects on the access of Latin American exports to these markets.

It is important to highlight the degree of exaggeration inherent in this type of prognosis. It is difficult to conceive an extension of a free trade zone centered in the United States including a significant number of countries of economic weight, with the probable exception of Mexico, or the few countries, such as Chile, with a liberal import regime, simply because to trade at North American prices implies adjustment costs equivalent to a unilateral liberalization decision. This decision is an alternative that is not only economically better but also less risky in political terms if one takes into account the possible reprisals by third parties.[12] Furthermore, the fear that the reduction of nontariff barriers within the EC will have negative effects on exports of countries outside the EC contradicts existing estimates that the effects of the change of direction of trade in these countries, resulting from the full implementation of the liberalization plans, will be substantially outweighed by the creation of trade arising from the 4–7 percent growth in the EC's aggregate product created by internal liberalization.[13]

It is also difficult to believe that the process of integration in the Pacific Basin, a natural result of the industrialization of the region's peripheral countries and the wave of Japanese investments in response to the adjustment pressures discussed in section two—and which will generate high rates of economic growth—could have harmful effects on Latin American exports to that region. However, the real threat posed by a larger European market and the natural integration of the Pacific Basin stems from the dynamic gains in productivity that will become possible for the companies located in these regions, which is very different than the threat posed by protectionism, which can be neutralized by increases in productivity in Latin America.

The actual dangers of unfavorable developments with regard to access by Latin American exports to these markets relate to the speed of depreciation of the dollar in relation to the main European markets. Simulations conducted by the OECD Secretariat show that a very rapid depreciation of the effective rate of the dollar, greater than the 15 percent needed to encourage a return to global macroeconomic stability, would have a devastating effect on the trade balance of European countries, with the exception of Germany. In the event of high levels of unemployment and relatively slow growth in Europe, this would certainly stimulate protectionist pressure in the EC, with the possibility of negative effects on the European integration, and might make the process of trade liberalization in agricultural products more difficult.

Conclusion: The Tendency Toward Divergent Insertion

Compared to the relatively stable environment of the world economy in the period of the original structuralist analysis, the basic features of the new international setting are a rapid and relatively unforeseeable change in the factors that determine comparative advantages in the different countries. In addition, in the course of the last four decades certain structural differences between the region's economies were accentuated. This makes it difficult to discuss future trends in the international insertion of Latin

America without an implicit consideration of the large degree of heterogeneity of its economies at the end of the twentieth century, which is evident both at the level of productive structures in the region's economies and in its form of participation in the world trade flow. On the one hand, the region contains large, semi-industrialized countries, which contrast with small economies that basically produce primary products. On the other hand, among the former are countries that are major exporters of manufactures (Brazil), oil (Mexico), and temperate agricultural products (Argentina). In addition, regardless of their size, South American countries are much less dependent on the North American market than other countries.

Apart from that, in contrast to the 1950s, in most countries in the region there is a clear perception that a solution to problems of external adjustment requires rapid growth in the export of manufactures. Indeed, after the failure of the Baker plan and the obvious limitations to the effectiveness of the new approach based on debt reduction, external financing problems should persist for some time in most debtor countries. Furthermore, despite the fact that central economies have lower rates of growth, unless unforeseeable destabilizing events take place, growth prospects in the world economy offer developing economies opportunities for insertion with rapid growth in the trade of manufactures.

Nevertheless, it is interesting to note that in contrast to the type of policy pursued by the great majority of Latin American countries until the 1960s—an inward-looking strategy, followed by greater neutrality of incentives—the common objective of maximizing export performance should produce different styles of trade, industrial, and foreign capital policies in the different groups of countries in the region. This is because the definition of a policy from within—as set forth in this book—can only be performed in terms of the perception of static and dynamic comparative advantages of each country. Naturally, these are decisively influenced by the specific features of their structural characteristics and their particular form of current insertion into the world economy.

It is clear that the global trends indicated earlier with regard to the functionality of the greater liberalization in trade policy and foreign capital systems should affect the region's economies uniformly. However, given the heterogeneity of Latin American economies, in the coming years a growing difference should become apparent in the styles of policies that define the relation between these economies and the world economy.[14]

The changes witnessed in recent years seem to indicate three distinct trends in liberalization strategies that will have to coexist. These may be classified as *orthodox, integrated,* and *selective.* The first would be characterized by the uniform reduction of current trade barriers and restrictions on foreign capital. This would be the strategy to be followed by the small countries in the region with a diversified market structure in at attempt to repeat the successful experience of certain small city-nations in Southeast

Asia (Singapore and Hong Kong), overcoming the limitations of the domestic market by looking toward the world market.

The second, in addition to the characteristics of an orthodox strategy, would be characterized by a deep integration of trade and an increase in industrial complementation with the North American economy. This would probably be the path followed by Mexico and various Caribbean economies that are extremely dependent on the United States market. Undoubtedly, in a similar fashion to the European integration experience, this option would require considerable financing for the structural adjustment of the economies that decide to integrate the North American market.

The third would be characterized by a sectoral liberalization process, oriented toward reducing the inefficiencies introduced by the current protective structure, combined with a low level of restriction on domestic operation but with strict demands on export performance by foreign companies. This would probably be the tendency in the semi-industrialized countries of South America. The term *selective* seeks to underline the fact that this strategy mixes elements of general trade liberalization with strategic policies to protect infant industries, based on efficiency criteria.

It is obvious that the effective choice between liberalization strategies will depend on the complex integration of advantages perceived by governments in adopting a particular style of policy in the context of international negotiations on trade and debt and the perceptions of the relevant domestic agents. Thus, for example, as long as the situation of a marked macroeconomic imbalance prevails in the majority of the region's economies, it is improbable that they will take the chance of implementing strategies based on a rapid and extensive liberalization of trade, even those limited to the sphere of regional integration. Likewise, exogenous events may radically change comparative advantages and, therefore, the strategy of specialization and international insertion in some countries. Dramatic examples of this type of contingency would be the effect on countries such as Uruguay and Argentina of liberalization of agricultural products in the round of GATT talks, or new oil-price fluctuations on the region's major producers. However, to sum up, what appears to be certain is that the search for trade advantages opened up by the rapid transformation in the world economy should mean that the options for insertion of the Latin American countries in the nascent international division of labor will contemplate a greater variety of national styles than in the past.

Notes

1. On the subject of the dollar shortage, a complete analysis of the difficulties and options involved in restoring the balance of payments equilibrium between Europe and the United States may be found in Johnson (1954). This work is quoted

by Ocampo in Chapter 12 on the terms of trade and the relation between the center and the periphery. Ocampo performs an interesting adaptation of these arguments to the context of the problematic Latin American economy.

2. For development of this point, see Sunkel and Paz (1970: 20 ff.).

3. For elaboration of this point, see Fritsch and Modiano (1988).

4. For a review of the characteristics of Latin America's external financing in the period, see Griffith-Jones and Sunkel (1986: chapters 5 and 6).

5. See Fritsch (1986: 234).

6. For recent projections, see Cline (1989).

7. See Hymer (1976).

8. For an informed analysis of this process, see Porter (1986).

9. For a more detailed analysis of this trend, see Fritsch and Franco (1988a).

10. As regards Latin America, North American investment is diversified and was originally oriented toward the domestic market in the classic "Hymerian" pattern. In Asia it was concentrated on light electronic equipment and was export oriented as a result of the creation of export processing areas and the extensive use of export requisites. For more information on the subject, see Blomström (1988: 22).

11. On this subject, see Abreu and Fritsch (1988).

12. This argument is developed in Fritsch (1989).

13. See Balassa (1989b).

14. See also Chapters 2, 6, 8, 9, 12, and 13 for the corresponding requirements for productive transformation and internal technology policies that support such proposals for external reinsertion.

12

Terms of Trade and Center-Periphery Relations

José Antonio Ocampo

The relations between developed and developing countries has been one of the dominant subjects in the Latin American literature on economic development. In fact, the concept developed by Raúl Prebisch and his followers, according to which the world economy is an asymmetrical system made up of developed countries at the *center* and developing nations at the *periphery*, has become a distinctive element not only of the ECLAC school, but also of the region's economic thinking in general.

This chapter takes up one of the central ideas of the center-periphery model—the deterioration of the terms of trade of developing countries—and analyzes it in light of other theoretical contributions and recent empirical evidence. The chapter is divided in four sections. The first section summarizes Prebisch's initial ideas on the subject. The second section reviews other theoretical approaches, including the Keynesian and neoclassical contributions, the literature on *unequal exchange,* and the recent modeling of North-South interactions. The third section summarizes recent empirical evidence on trends in the real prices of primary commodities in international trade and presents complementary considerations on postwar trends in the terms of trade of Latin American countries. The chapter ends with a short section of conclusions and policy implications.

The Prebisch Hypothesis

The hypothesis regarding the terms of trade of developing countries was initially formulated by Prebisch as an element in the analysis of the effects of economic growth on the structure of production at a world level. In a seminal article Prebisch (1951) took, as a starting point of the analysis, the widely held view according to which the relative size of the primary sector tends to decline during the growth process. As it is widely accepted, such a trend is associated with the low income elasticity of demand for

333

unprocessed agricultural goods, the substitution of raw by synthetic materials, and the increasing efficiency in the production of primary goods.[1]

According to Prebisch, such change in the productive structure has very important implications at world level because, for historical reasons, industrialization concentrated initially in central countries, generating from early in modern economic history an international division of labor whereby the periphery supplies raw materials to the center. Under these conditions, changes in the productive structure generate a systematic bias against developing countries. In fact, it implies that the contraction in the relative size of primary activities affects less developed countries (LDCs) more than proportionally. This fact tends to generate, in turn, a labor surplus in the periphery, as the redeployment of displaced workers to dynamic economic sectors faces several obstacles. The latter derive from political restrictions to international migration and the difficulties faced by "late" industrializers, associated with the great disparities in technology and capital availability with respect to the leading industrial centers.

According to Prebisch, if workers displaced from primary sectors in the periphery are not adequately absorbed, labor incomes tend to fall. Simultaneously, workers in central countries are able to raise their incomes during business upswings and protect them during world recessions. Thus, the reduction in the relative size of the primary sector generated by a dynamic world economy tends to depress relative wages in the periphery.

The adverse movement in relative wages tends to deteriorate, in turn, the terms of trade of developing countries. Evidently, relative international prices depend also on labor productivity in export activities. In Prebisch's view, however, the joint effect of the trends in wages and productivity implies that, whereas central countries are able to retain productivity improvements through higher real wages, those of the periphery are forced to "export" technological change through a deterioration in the factorial terms of trade (relative prices adjusted by productivity).

As it is widely known, the novelty of this approach was its departure from one the major hypotheses of classical economic thinking. Classical economists argued, in this regard, that the increasing demand for raw materials brought about by economic growth was bound to face the law of diminishing returns in agriculture. According to this hypothesis, the increased supply of agricultural goods could only come from lower-quality lands at increasing costs. As a result, economic growth would tend to raise the relative prices of food and raw materials. According to the classical model, the increase in the relative prices of agricultural goods would also tend to depress the rate of profit. Since in a capitalist system profits are the main source of capital accumulation, this would finally be reflected in a slower rate of economic growth.

Prebisch's seminal hypotheses, as well as those in his subsequent papers (in particular, see Prebisch 1959) and the parallel work by Singer

(1950, 1975), were widely disseminated in international academic and political circles. In retrospect, however, his pioneering work contained two complementary but different ideas. The first referred to the effects of the low income elasticity of demand for raw materials on the terms of trade of developing countries. The second was associated with asymmetries in the functioning of labor markets at the center and the periphery.[2] Although, in Prebisch's view, these asymmetries were related with the forms of specialization of the various regions, they also played a distinctive role in determining international prices.

The history of the controversy on the terms of trade of developing countries can largely be written as an extension of these two ideas by different schools of thought. Thus, the Keynesian and the neoclassical literature of the 1950s and 1960s stresses the role of income elasticities. Since the late 1960s, the analysis of unequal exchange and the more recent literature on North-South modeling focused, rather, on asymmetries in labor markets.

Theoretical Approaches

Keynesian and Neoclassical Formulations

The simplest Keynesian formulation on the effects of economic growth on the terms of trade was developed by Johnson (1954) a few years after the pioneering work by Prebisch.[3] Johnson's work had little to do with the controversies over developing countries. It referred, rather, to the debate on the difficulties faced by Europe in eliminating its balance of payments deficit with the United States (the so-called dollar shortage).

Johnson's model basically derives the conditions for equilibrium in the balance of trade in a growing world economy. In order to apply his scheme to the analysis of the relations between the center and the periphery, let us assume that there are only two regions in the world: North, or center, and South, or periphery. The North exports manufactured goods and the South raw materials. The demand for manufactures in world trade thus depends on the national income of the South and the relative price of raw materials versus manufactures. Likewise, the demand for raw materials depends on the national income of the North and the same relative price.

What is the effect of economic growth upon trade balances if the demand for manufactures is income elastic, while the opposite is true for raw materials? To answer this question, let us consider the case in which both regions grow at a similar rate. Under this assumption, the demand for manufactures in the periphery grows more rapidly than the North's demand for raw materials. There will thus be a relative abundance of primary products and a deterioration of the periphery's terms of trade. This deterioration would only be avoided if the raw material exporting region (the South) grows at a slower rate than the manufacturing region (the North).

This being the case, the income inelasticity of demand for raw materials would be reflected in a deterioration of the terms of trade or, alternatively, in a slower rate of economic growth of peripheral countries. Note that in the derivation of this principle, only the *income* elasticities of demand matter. *Price* elasticities determine, however, the magnitude of the variation in the terms of trade required to reestablish trade balances. Given the disparities in the demand for various goods, the deterioration of the terms of trade of raw materials will be higher the lower the relevant price elasticities.[4]

The foregoing analysis is based on the characteristics of demand for imports in various countries or regions that engage in world trade. Imports are, however, a residual demand, in other words, the difference between demand and production of a given product. Strictly speaking, therefore, they do not only depend on the characteristics of the final demand, but also on the domestic supply of import-competing sectors. It could very well be that, despite a high income elasticity of demand for manufactures in the periphery, the increase in the domestic supply of these goods could result in a growth of imports slower than that of national income. In fact, this was precisely the basic defense given by Prebisch to an import substitution industrialization policy in LDCs, as a way to counteract the deterioration of the terms of trade of the periphery.

Similarly, even if the demand for raw materials is income inelastic, world imports can be elastic if the North's supply of these goods grows at a sufficiently slow rate. This indicates, therefore, that greater trade latitude by the center for products exported by the periphery has a favorable effect on the latter's terms of trade. On the contrary, protectionism in the North tends to depress the relative export prices of developing countries.

The neoclassical theory of trade offers a complete framework to analyze the combined effect of supply and demand factors that affect the terms of trade of developing countries. As it is widely known, the general model used by this theory assumes perfect competition, no imperfections in factor markets, and full employment of productive resources at a world level.

The effects of economic growth on the terms of trade in this model were developed by several authors in the 1950s.[5] However, most of these articles consider the case of an individual country that grows facing a stagnant external supply and demand for internationally traded goods. As is evident, these are not the most favorable conditions for economic growth, since to prevent this expansion from deteriorating the terms of trade of the growing country, its export supply must not increase or, alternatively, the country must be a small agent in the world economy. The latter is possibly true for most countries in the South, but certainly not for the periphery as a whole. In any case, the corresponding model can be used to analyze what happens when two trading regions grow simultaneously.

Under these conditions, there are three types of factors that affect the terms of trade. First, as in the Prebisch-Singer analysis or the Keynesian model, world relative prices depend on the income elasticities of demand for different traded goods. Thus, as in the preceding models, the terms of trade of countries specializing in the production of income-inelastic goods would tend to deteriorate.

Second, if the rate of technical change is similar for the same sectors in different countries but varies across sectors, the terms of trade of those countries specializing in sectors for which productivity increases at a faster rate would tend to deteriorate.[6] If the assumption regarding technical change in the same sector in different countries is not met, the effects of productivity increases on international prices are uncertain. Generally, however, the terms of trade of a region will tend to improve if the rate of technical change in its import substitution industries is faster than in the rest of the world, whereas they will tend to deteriorate if productivity in its export activities increases more rapidly than in other countries. This indicates that the countries are forced to "export" to the rest of the world productivity increases that take place in their export industries, and, on the contrary, that they benefit more than proportionally from technical changes in their import substitution sectors.

This peculiar corollary of neoclassical theory reflects the fact that in a supply-demand equilibrium model, increases in export availability tend to depress the terms of trade, whereas the opposite is true if the demand for imports is reduced. It is worthwhile to note, however, that this conclusion only holds when the region under analysis is large enough to affect international prices. If the region is small, the terms of trade are independent of the domestic supply and demand of the various goods. Therefore, a small country benefits equally from productivity increases in its export and import substituting industries.

The third set of variables that affects the terms of trade in this model is the relative supply of productive factors. In this respect, it should be recalled that, according to neoclassical trade theory, countries tend to specialize in the production of those goods that use intensively the factors in which they are relatively well endowed. For this reason, an increasing supply of those factors that are relatively abundant in a specific region tends to depress its terms of trade; on the other hand, the terms of trade would improve if economic growth increases the supply of factors that are relatively scarce in that region. The most salient feature of economic growth is, of course, the accumulation of capital, including human capital. This factor indicates, other things being equal, that economic growth has an adverse effect on capital-rich (developed) countries. On the contrary, the factor of production that becomes increasingly scarce as the

world economy grows is land (natural resources). Thus, as classical economists argued, factor accumulation would tend to improve the terms of
trade of primary-producing countries.

The net effect of these factors on the terms of trade of developing
countries is, of course, uncertain. Generally, however, it can be argued
that, whereas demand factors have adverse impacts on raw material producing regions, supply accumulation has the opposite effect. In this way,
neoclassical analysis combines some of the effects suggested by Prebisch,
Singer, and the Keynesian School, which are detrimental to raw material
producers, with those that led classical economists to argue that economic
development tends to increase the relative prices of primary goods. On the
other hand, contrary to hypotheses much in vogue, neoclassical analysis
indicates that the periphery as a whole benefits much more from technical
change in import substitution rather than in export activities.

Unequal Exchange

In Keynesian and neoclassical theories, the terms of trade are jointly determined by supply and demand. In other words, relative prices constitute
the basic adjustment mechanism of international trade. The theories of unequal exchange developed since the late 1960s constitute a break with this
type of reasoning, as they claim that in the long run international prices
are determined solely by supply conditions. They thus return to the concept, widely defended by classical and Marxist economics, according to
which equilibrium prices are determined exclusively by production costs.

In Emmanuel's (1972) initial formulation, the concept of unequal exchange was associated with the difference in Marxist theory between *values* (direct and indirect labor content) and *prices of production*. His model
assumed that in the world economy there is a strong tendency to equalize
the rates of profit across countries, but the same is not true of real wages.
This assumption reflects a relatively high capital mobility at an international level combined with the political obstacles to labor migration. Given
these conditions, goods that have the same (direct and indirect) labor content—the same value in Marxist terms—have a much higher price of production in central countries, due to higher real wages. The equalization of
profit rates together with major wage disparities thus imply that higher
labor-values from developing countries must be traded internationally for
lower labor-values from developed countries. In this way, a transfer of
value takes place from the periphery to the center.

This formulation obviously depends on the validity of Marxist value
theory and the solution to the so-called transformation problem (of labor-
values into prices of production). Nonetheless, irrespective of this framework, the concept of unequal exchange can be associated with the hypothesis whereby the terms of trade are essentially determined by wage

disparities between developed and developing countries (see, for example, Emmanuel 1972: appendix 4; Braun 1973). In this respect, the analysis of unequal exchange is similar to Lewis's theory of the terms of trade (see Lewis 1977). Both can be considered, moreover, as a return to Prebisch's original idea whereby the terms of trade of developing countries are determined by the asymmetries in the functioning of labor markets.

Formulated in this way, the central idea of the theory of unequal exchange is very simple: with high capital mobility, the international terms of trade are determined by relative wages and labor productivities in export activities. Thus, an increase in real wages tends to improve the terms of trade of the region where it takes place, whereas an increase in labor productivity in the export sector has the opposite effect. Obviously, this analysis is only applicable to a region and not to an individual country. A wage increase in a specific country that does not have as a counterpart a similar process in competing countries only reduces its international competitiveness.

When considering trends in the terms of trade, these theories thus refer the analysis to the determinants of wage disparities between central and peripheral countries. This implies, in turn, that such trends are totally independent of the type of goods each region produces and, thus, of income elasticities of demand. In this way, the deterioration of the terms of trade may take place even if the periphery exports manufactures. In other words, the terms of trade are not associated with the type of goods each region exports but, rather, with labor market conditions in the different regions of the world economy. As will be seen, however, the type of goods does affect other variables, particularly relative employment levels.

What determines the relative wages of central and peripheral countries? On this subject there is a wide range of alternative hypotheses in the literature. The simplest and most complete formulation is that of Lewis. According to Lewis, wage disparities reflect the opportunity cost of labor in each region in the production of foodstuffs. "The terms of trade are bad only for tropical products, whether agricultural or industrial, and are bad because the market pays tropical unskilled labor, whatever it may be producing, a wage that is based on an unlimited reservoir of low-productivity food producers" (Lewis 1977: 37). According to this analysis, higher labor productivity in food production increases real wages and, therefore, improves the terms of trade of the region where it takes place. On the contrary, technical change in export sectors is totally exported to the rest of the world through a deterioration of the terms of trade.[7]

In the Marxist literature on unequal trade, there is no consensus on the determinants of relative wages. In Emmanuel's theory, there is a virtuous circle of wages and development in central countries: high wages increase consumption, which in turn encourages productivity improvements and product innovation. In peripheral countries, on the contrary, low wage levels generate a vicious circle of low demand and dismal innovations. Thus, development follows the curve of consumption, giving rise to a series of virtuous and vicious circles that reproduce or widen inherited wage gaps.

In Bettelheim's (1972) formulation, virtuous and vicious circles are also present, but the essential role is played by the preservation of precapitalist forms of production that block the development of the productive forces in the periphery. This fact is associated with the obstacles to late industrialization, but also with the political and ideological domination by central countries. For Amin (1973, 1974), low wage levels in developing countries are determined by the pressure exerted by major labor surpluses. Following similar formulations by Latin American dependentists (for example, Sunkel 1973), and unlike Lewis's theory of the subsistence sector, this surplus is largely the result of the penetration of capitalism into traditional agricultural societies; in other words, it is an effect rather than a cause of underdevelopment. On the other hand, high wages in the North reflect the formation of a labor aristocracy, largely based on the exploitation of peripheral countries through unequal exchange.

The work by Braun (1973) constitutes one of the most interesting attempts to integrate the literature on unequal exchange with some hypotheses derived from the ECLAC school. In effect, Braun assumes, following ECLAC, that there is a basic complementarity between foreign exchange earnings and production in peripheral countries. Under these conditions, if the external demand for the periphery's exports is reduced, developing countries are forced to devalue their currencies to generate additional export earnings. However, for the periphery as a whole, devaluation increases export supplies and, thus, deteriorates its terms of trade. Such deterioration will be stronger the more inelastic the demand for the periphery's export products, due to the nature of the goods involved or to protectionism in the North.

As we have seen, the basic hypothesis of all brands of unequal exchange theories indicates that in the long run international prices are determined by production costs and, thus, independently of demand. This implies that, unlike Keynesian and neoclassical theories, relative prices do not adjust supply-demand imbalances in international trade. What variable plays that role? To answer this question, it is necessary to introduce balance of payments equilibrium conditions into the classical scheme of price determination set forth by unequal exchange theories.

In complete models of this kind, variations in employment and production adjust supply-demand imbalances (Bacha 1986: chapter 15; Ocampo 1986). Let us assume that the demand for peripheral products is reduced as a result of technical change in central countries (substitution of natural raw materials by synthetic products, for example). In the short run, the periphery's terms of trade will be depressed, to adjust existing supplies to reduced Northern demands. In the long run, however, the price of Southern exports will increase if production costs are unchanged. The result will thus be a reduction in employment in the periphery until export supplies adjust to the reduced Northern demand.

The introduction of additional equilibrium conditions has major implications for the analysis of unequal exchange. First of all, it indicates that, other things being equal, the income inelasticity of demand for raw materials should be reflected in the slower growth of developing countries rather than in a deterioration of their terms of trade. Moreover, it implies that wage increases have quantity as well as price effects. Let us assume, for example, that wages increase in the periphery. According to the preceding considerations, their terms of trade will improve. However, the higher relative prices of the periphery's exports will have an adverse effect on Northern demands. The improvement in the terms of trade will thus be at the expense of lower production and employment levels in the South. Moreover, export income will only increase if Northern import demand is price inelastic. On the contrary, a wage increase in the North will adversely affect the periphery's terms of trade, but will increase Southern employment. Despite the adverse terms of trade effect, Southern export incomes could increase, if Northern import demand is price elastic.

A similar analysis can be undertaken to consider the effects of technical change in export industries. According to the unequal exchange theory, the entire increase in productivity will be reflected in the long run in a deterioration of the terms of trade of the country where it takes place. However, cheaper exports will have a positive effect on external demands and, thus, on production and employment levels in the region where technical innovation occurs. The net effect on employment would thus be favorable if external demand is price elastic.

North-South Modeling

The most recent contributions to the topic of this chapter are associated with the dynamic modeling of interaction between developed and developing countries. This literature may be seen as the application of the growth models developed in the 1950s and 1960s to the analysis of international trade. It has important affinities with the unequal exchange literature. This similarity is reflected in three different ways. First, emphasis is placed on structural differences between central and peripheral countries. Second, attention is focused on the characteristics of the countries or regions rather than the goods they produce. Finally, as will be seen, demand does not play any role in the determination of the equilibrium terms of trade; thus, in the long run, it has quantity (production and employment) rather than price effects.

A common characteristic of the models that have received the most attention in the literature is the assumption that the South is a Lewis-type economy.[8] This implies that there is an unlimited reservoir of workers in the subsistence food-producing sector; real wages are thus determined by the opportunity cost of labor in such activities. Capitalists' profits are a surplus between export income and subsistence wages. They are also the only source of savings and capital accumulation. Economic growth in the South is thus determined by the relation between the terms of trade, profits, and investment. An improvement in the terms of trade increases capitalists' profits, investment, and growth. On the contrary, a deterioration in the terms of trade has an adverse effect on growth.

Assumptions regarding the characteristics of developed countries vary in the different models. Findlay (1980, 1981) assumes that the North is a neoclassical economy.[9] This implies that there is full employment and that productive factors (capital and labor) can be substituted in production processes. As is well known, in a model of this kind, economic expansion is determined by the "natural" rate of growth, in other words, by the rate of increase of the labor force.[10] Savings rates are assumed to be identical for capitalists and workers and do not affect the rate of growth. However, increasing capital availability due to higher savings is reflected in the use of more capital-intensive technologies and higher real wages in the North.

In Taylor's (1983: chapter 10) alternative model, the North is, rather, a Kaleckian economy.[11] Labor unemployment and excess productive capacity allow production levels to adjust to variations in aggregate demand. Workers consume all of their income. Savings come exclusively from profits, which are generated by a markup on variable production costs. Given the mechanism of price and profit formation, the rates of profit and savings rise when aggregate demand increases. Demand is essentially governed by investment dynamics, which depends on profit incentives and the "animal spirits" of capitalists. In this way, the growth rate of the North is determined by the relation between capitalists' savings and investment decisions. If the "animal spirits" are dynamic, the rate of growth will pick up, but the opposite will take place if the savings rate (profit margins) increase.

Despite the different ways of modeling the developed countries, Northern economic growth is determined in both cases by its own macroeconomic dynamics, irrespective of its terms of trade and Southern dynamics. The North is, therefore, the locomotive of the world economy, to which the peripheral economies adjust. On the other hand, given the relation between the terms of trade, profits, and growth in the South, the first of these variables is precisely the mechanism by which economic growth in the developing countries adjusts to that of central economies. Thus, if the locomotive speeds up, the terms of trade of the South improve to allow their capitalists to accumulate at a faster rate. On the other hand, if the Northern locomotive slows down, the terms of trade of developing countries deteriorate.

In the long term, the essential determinant of the terms of trade of developing countries is, thus, the rate of growth of the center: the "natural" rate of growth if the North is a neoclassical economy or the relation between the "animal spirits" and capitalists' savings (markups) in a Kaleckian economy. Thus, as in unequal exchange analysis, demand does not affect international prices in the long run. Nevertheless, it does affect relative production and employment levels in the various regions that make up the world economy. Assume, for example, that there is a reduction in the Northern demand for goods produced in the periphery. In the short run the Southern terms of trade will deteriorate, leading to lower profits, investment, and growth rates. In the longer term the terms of trade of developing countries will return to their initial level, but the period of slower growth in the South will be reflected in a permanent deterioration of its relative production and employment levels.

What is the effect in these models of higher wages or productivity? Since the Northern wage is an endogenous variable,[12] it is only worth considering the impact of an increase in real wages of the South. Given the assumptions of both models, such increase must be associated with productivity improvements in Southern subsistence activities. Higher wages will depress the rate of profit, investment, and growth in the periphery. In order to ensure that growth in developing countries adjusts to that of the Northern locomotive, the rate of profit must recover through an improvement in the terms of trade. Thus, in the long run, as in unequal exchange models, higher Southern wages will improve the terms of trade of developing countries. Nonetheless, such improvement reduces Northern demand for Southern exports and, thus, reduces relative Southern employment.

Productivity improvement in the export sectors of developing countries has, on the contrary, an adverse effect on their terms of trade. Indeed, higher export productivity increases profits and growth in peripheral countries. In order to ensure a long-run rate of expansion similar to that of the North, their terms of trade must deteriorate. It should be noted, however, that such a trend in relative prices will tend to increase Northern demand for the periphery's exports. Relative employment and export earnings of the latter region could thus improve if its products face an elastic demand in the North. On the contrary, since the rate of developed countries is independent of relative export prices and productivity levels, technical change in the North does not affect the international terms of trade. Productivity improvements are thus totally transmitted to Northern real wages.

North-South models thus confirm Prebisch's basic intuition: developed countries are able to translate productivity improvements into higher real wages, whereas developing countries are forced to "export" technical change in their export sectors through a deterioration in their terms of trade. This asymmetry is a reflection of structural differences in labor market conditions, particularly the regulatory effect that unlimited labor supplies exercise on Southern real wages. For this reason, the South only benefits to the full extent from technical change in nonexport activities.

The Terms of Trade in Practice

The evidence accumulated in recent years tends to confirm the long-run deterioration of raw material prices (Spraos 1983; Sapsford 1985; Sarkar 1986; Di Filippo 1987; Evans 1987; Scandizzo and Diakosawas 1987; Grilli and Yang 1988). In effect, although such a trend is not confirmed for some subperiods and commodities, existing evidence indicates that, on average, real prices of raw materials have tended to fall since the last two or three decades of the nineteenth century. This has also been the trend for raw materials other than oil and for most commodities in the period following World War II.

Such evidence is summarized in Table 12.1. For the early decades considered, the information refers to the terms of trade of Great Britain, which is considered a typical exporter of manufactures and importer of raw material. Following Prebisch, the inverse of the British terms of trade can, therefore, be used as an adequate indicator of the international price of raw materials relative to manufactures. The corresponding series overlap, since the 1870s, with those measuring directly the relative price of commodities in world trade.

The evidence summarized in Table 12.1 indicates that real raw material prices improved throughout most of the nineteenth century, thus supporting the basic intuition of classical economists. According to Sarkar (1986), this pattern was particularly evident until the 1850s, and was followed by a period of transition of two decades during which the real prices of raw materials did not show any clear trend.

Since the 1870s or 1880s, however, the evidence is consistent with a long-run deterioration of real raw material prices. According to the series and period selected, the rate of decline fluctuates between 0.5 percent and slightly under 1 percent per year. Indeed, the only series that indicates a different performance is that estimated by the United Nations. Curiously enough, this series shows a deterioration of raw material prices both in the forty years that preceded World War II and in the decades that followed it. For this reason, if it is extended up to 1980 and trends are adjusted by a structural shift in the real price of raw materials during World War II, this series also shows an annual deterioration of 0.7 percent throughout the twentieth century (Sapsford 1985).

The long-run deterioration of raw material prices is also confirmed in Figure 12.1. This figure shows the historical trend of real prices of raw materials throughout the twentieth century, according to World Bank estimates. As this figure indicates, relative short term fluctuations aside, the real prices of raw materials have experienced three marked cycles over

Table 12.1. **Estimates of Trends in the Real Prices of Raw Materials**

Author	Source of data	Characteristics	Period	Trend (% per year)
Sarkar (1986)	Imlah	Terms of trade of Great Britain	1801–1881	-0.87[b]
			1882–1913	0.42[b]
	Schlote		1801–1830	-0.64[b]
			1882–1929	0.89[b]
Spraos (1983)	Prebisch	Inverse of the terms of trade of Great Britain	1876–1938	-0.95[b]
	United Nations	Real price of raw materials at international level	1876–1938	-0.64[b]
	Lewis		1871–1938	-0.46[b]
	United Nations		1900–1970	0.13[a]
			1900–1938	-0.73[b]
			1950–1970	1.52[b]
Grilli and Yang (1988)	World Bank (variables weights)	Real price of raw materials including fuels	1900–1986	-0.52[b]
		Real price of raw materials excluding fuels	1900–1986	-0.63[b]
		Real price of tropical drinks	1900–1986	0.63[b]
		Real price of cereals	1900–1986	-0.68[b]
		Real price of other foodstuffs	1900–1986	-0.54[b]
		Real price of agricultural raw materials other than foodstuffs	1900–1986	-0.82[b]
		Real price of metals	1900–1986	-0.84[b]

Notes: a. Significantly different to zero with 95% confidence.
b. Significantly different to zero with 99% confidence.

the century: a rise during the first two decades, followed by a collapse in the 1920s and early 1930s; a recovery from the mid-1930s to the Korean War, followed by a drop in the 1950s and 1960s; finally, a rise in the early 1970s followed by a sharp drop, particularly marked in the 1980s.

Within this cyclical pattern, there is a clear long-run deterioration of nonoil commodity prices. If oil is included, this pattern also emerges and is even slightly more pronounced up to the early 1970s. The two oil price hikes in the early and late 1970s altered the evolution of the general price series over the past two decades. Nonetheless, since 1986, the plummeting of fuel prices has depressed the overall index to levels that are not incompatible with a long term deterioration of commodity prices as a whole.

Aside from oil, a few raw materials do not share the general long-run decline in real commodity prices. As Table 12.1 indicates, this trend has been common and relatively uniform throughout the twentieth century (declining rates of between 0.5 percent and 0.8 percent per year) for grains, other foodstuffs, nonfood agricultural raw materials, and metals. On the other hand, the real prices of tropical beverages have tended to rise

Figure 12.1. Real Prices of Raw Materials (1977-1979 = 100)

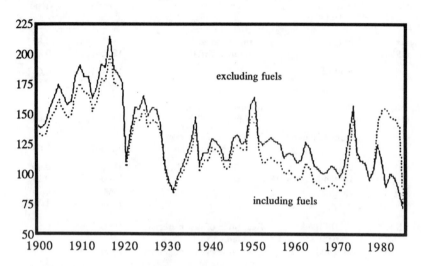

Source: Grilli and Yang (1988).
Note: Series with variable weights.

throughout the century at a annual rate of 0.6 percent. A more detailed analysis of the World Bank series, undertaken by Scandizzo and Diakosawas (1987), indicates that the declining trend is the general rule for most of the fourteen commodities that make up the price index of primary goods, excluding fuels. However, there are some commodities for which real prices have shown a long term improvement, particularly coffee and tin. For lead and zinc, there are no significant long run trends, whereas, for cocoa, the post–World War II upward trend has clouded the real price decline that took place during the first four decades of the century.

The performance of the various raw material prices in the years following World War II is shown in Table 12.2 and in Figures 12.1 and 12.2. The downward trend of the real price index for real commodity prices, excluding oil, is apparent. In fact, it has been interrupted only briefly by two booms, in the immediate postwar period and in the early 1970s. As Table 12.2 shows, the downward trend (1.3 percent per year) is much more pronounced than for the century as a whole and accelerated dramatically in recent decades (4.5 percent annually in 1974–1987). This trend also covers all product groups included in the table, with the sole exception of wood. In the case of oil, the trend in prices is strongly upward for the period 1948–1987 as a whole, but nil when the period following the first oil crisis is considered.

Figure 12.2. Real Prices of Raw Materials Other than Oil (1980 = 100)

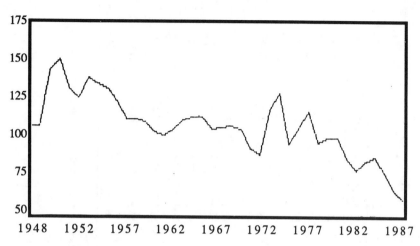

Source: World Bank (1988)

Although the trend noted tends to confirm Prebisch's main hypothesis, it is difficult to weight with existing evidence the role played by different theoretical explanations of such evolution. In any case, most analysts (e.g. Spraos 1983; Evans 1987; Grilli and Yang 1988) reject a simplistic hypothesis according to which such deterioration simply reflects an underestimation of quality improvements of manufactures. In fact, as emphasized by these authors, such improvements have also been significant for primary goods.

The evidence on income inelasticity of demand for raw materials is widely known. This factor may thus have played an important role in this process. It should be emphasized, however, that this feature is more characteristic of agricultural rather than mineral products (Lewis 1977; Adams and Behrman 1982: chapter 2). On the other hand, the evidence on widening income gaps between developed and developing countries is also well known (see, for example, Bairoch 1981) and must have played a role in the long term price deterioration of those commodities that are primarily produced in developing countries. As is obvious, this income gap cannot explain price trends for temperate agricultural goods. In the latter case, the high rate of technical change in relation to that of industrial production in developed countries is part of the explanation (Evans 1987).

Table 12.2. Real Prices of Raw Materials

	Real Price Index (1980=100)										Trends (% per year)	
	1948-49	1950-54	1955-59	1960-64	1965-69	1970-74	1975-79	1980-84	1985-87	1987	1948-87	1974-87
Oil	26.2	22.5	21.5	15.9	13.6	25.4	59.3	101.0	58.5	44.9	4.03c	0.56
Raw materials other than oil	107.4	137.2	122.2	106.4	109.0	106.9	103.2	87.4	67.2	59.2	-1.30c	-4.46c
Agriculture Total	117.3	147.7	124.6	107.0	101.2	104.8	107.9	88.1	67.3	55.9	-1.45c	-4.74c
Foodstuffs and drinks												
Total	114.8	138.4	119.7	102.3	99.5	106.2	111.6	88.3	68.7	58.5	-1.21c	-5.01c
Drinks	93.9	150.3	136.6	98.5	92.1	86.1	133.9	92.4	84.2	46.2	-0.99c	-2.68a
Cereals	157.5	162.3	123.8	119.4	129.1	135.0	108.6	91.2	57.8	60.1	-1.88c	-7.54c
Fats and oils	182.8	174.3	137.9	132.5	128.2	147.7	120.7	97.1	57.0	53.2	-2.01c	-5.90c
Other foodstuffs	82.8	88.4	84.8	83.9	76.3	94.7	77.0	75.1	56.5	61.8	-0.71c	-4.82c
Nonfoodstuffs	126.4	181.3	141.8	123.8	106.8	99.2	94.2	87.3	62.5	90.2	-2.20c	-3.69c
Wood	41.2	54.2	45.1	52.9	56.3	59.8	67.4	85.3	76.5	60.9	1.63c	2.26b
Metals and minerals	95.9	127.6	131.8	115.7	138.6	121.7	98.8	86.1	64.8	63.3	-1.30c	-4.82c

Source: World Bank (1988a).

Notes: Trends have been estimated using semilogarithmic regressions. The slopes obtained have been converted to equivalent annual rates.

a. Significantly different to zero with 90% confidence.
b. Significantly different to zero with 95% confidence.
c. Significantly different to zero with 99% confidence.

This evidence aside, it is unclear what effect technical change has had on raw material prices. Scandizzo and Diakosawas (1987) found very little evidence of an inverse relation between real prices and productivity by hectare for tropical beverages (coffee, tea, and cocoa) and sugar, although they did find such correlation for some grains (maize and wheat). The results of this study indicate, on the other hand, that real income by unit of land has remained approximately constant over the long term for grains and increased at a rate of 0.5 percent per year for sugar and 1 percent per year for tropical beverages. It should be pointed out, however, that the latter rates are below standard-of-living improvements in developed countries throughout the twentieth century (2 percent per year), and are barely equal to the average increase of per capita income in the periphery (for estimates of long term standard of living improvements, see Bairoch 1981).

The causes underlying the marked deterioration experienced by the real commodity prices in more recent decades are clearer, and involve both long and short term factors (see, for example, World Bank and IMF 1987; Maizels 1987; Helleiner 1988). According to existing studies, the most important underlying factor has undoubtedly been the severe recession experienced by the economies of developed countries in the early 1980s and the laggard subsequent recovery in Western Europe, which concentrates half of the world's raw material imports. Structural changes in the central economies (relative growth of the service sector, in particular) have also had a major impact on recent trends, as well as the effects of recent technological innovations in manufacturing, which have significantly reduced the raw material intensity of production processes.

On the other hand, at the onset of the 1980s, most commodity-producing sectors had accumulated substantial excess capacities, associated with investments made in the 1970s under expectations of world economic growth and improvements in real raw material prices, which did not materialize. The adjustment processes adopted by virtually all developing countries in the 1980s and the pressure by the multilateral credit agencies on LDCs to eliminate distortions leading to low domestic relative prices for traditional exports have encouraged the oversupply of raw materials in recent years and may reinforce it in the near future. On the other hand, international commodity agreements have weakened, as the proposals to design funds to regulate raw material prices have made no headway. Finally, agricultural and trade policies of developed countries have continued to distort world commodity rates for those goods in which they play a significant role as producers (grains, sugar, meat, and dairy products).

Given the importance attributed by unequal exchange and North-South literature to the characteristics of countries rather than the goods they produce, it is important to have an accurate idea of trends in the prices of manufactures exported by developing countries. Unfortunately, existing evidence on such trends is scanty. Table 12.3 summarizes available data, which cover only a relatively short period and may thus not reflect long term trends. The United Nations 1960–1980 series refers to the prices of manufactures exported by LDCs to developed countries, deflated by average export prices in the opposite direction. As can be appreciated, the price trend during this period was upward and more favorable than that for agricultural goods exported by the periphery.

Table 12.3. Estimates of the Terms of Trade of Developing Countries, by Type of Product

Source of Data	Product or Group of Products	Period	Trend (% per year)
United Nations	Foodstuffs	1960–1980	0.31
	Agricultural raw materials other than foodstuffs	1960–1980	-1.05[a]
	Fuels	1960–1980	7.47[a]
	Manufactures	1960–1980	0.77[a]
International Monetary Fund	Raw materials of developing countries	1957–1987 1968–1987	-0.78[a] -1.52[a]
	Manufactures	1968–1987	-0.88[a]

Sources: United Nations (1975, 1981) and IMF (1988).
Notes: United Nations series refer to the price of exports from developing countries to developed countries, deflated by the price of exports from developed countries. IMF series refer to raw materials exported by developing countries and to the unit value of exports from developing countries where the sale of manufactures in 1980 amounted to over 50% of the total exports, deflated in both cases by the unit value of exports from developed countries.
a. Significantly different to zero with 99% confidence.

The most recent data shown in Table 12.3 and Figure 12.3 indicate that from the late 1960s through the 1980s, there has been a deterioration in the real price of manufactures exported by developing countries. Such trend has, nonetheless, been more favorable than that for raw materials exported by LDCs. As Figure 12.3 shows, the collapse experienced by commodity prices since the mid-1980s has been shared by manufactures exported by the periphery. Thus, the hypothesis according to which international price trends follow common patterns associated with the characteristics of the exporting countries cannot be rejected. Nonetheless, given the short period covered by the series on LDCs' manufactures prices, it is impossible to know to what extent their evolution in 1968–1987 is merely a reflection of a short term trend and impossible to evaluate their performance in relation to productivity.

Finally, Table 12.4 and Figure 12.4 explore the evolution of the terms of trade of Latin American countries in the postwar period. Although the

Figure 12.3. Real Prices of Raw Materials and Manufactures Exported by Developing Countries (1980 = 100)

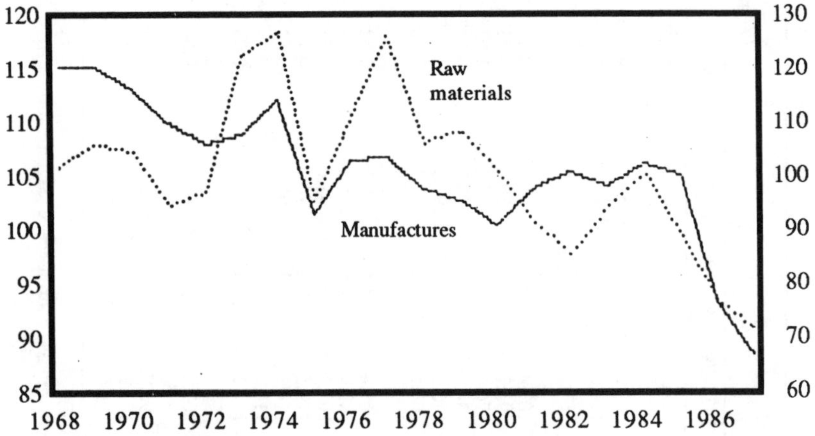

Source: IMF (1988)
Note: The characteristics of this series are shown in Table 12.3.

price trend for raw materials has been reflected in the evolution of the relative export prices of these countries, its impact has been less pronounced than often asserted. This fact seems to confirm the statistical results obtained by other authors (Grilli and Yang 1988; Dornbusch 1985), according to which the deterioration of the prices of raw materials is only partly reflected in the terms of trade of LDCs. This fact is associated with the favorable performance of the prices for some primary goods that play an important role in the exports of some countries (particularly oil, coffee, and tin), the growing importance of manufacturing exports, whose prices tend to evolve more favorably, and the importance of raw materials in the import structure of some countries in the region.

As Table 12.4 shows, the deterioration in the terms of trade in the postwar period is only statistically significant for half of the countries included; however, except for Ecuador[13] and Uruguay, it is less pronounced than the downward trend for raw material prices, excluding oil. Also, for five countries (Bolivia, Colombia, Costa Rica, Peru, and Venezuela), the terms of trade have improved in the long run. The major export of these countries has been a commodity that did not follow general trends in international prices.

For the more recent period, 1974–1987, the deterioration of the terms of trade is a common feature in Latin America. However, it is only significant

Table 12.4.   Terms of Trade of Latin American Countries

	Terms of Trade Index									Trends (% per year)	
	1945–49	1950–54	1955–59	1960–64	1965–69	1970–74	1975–79	1980–84	1985–87	1945–87	1974–87
Latin America	66.0	77.4	69.8	60.3	58.4	71.9	92.3	91.0	85.2	0.75c	-0.74b
Large countries											
Argentina	126.6	109.8	88.2	99.5	98.5	107.8	94.4	91.6	77.2	-0.68c	-2.18c
Brazil	109.9	180.6	150.4	124.5	116.7	128.1	130.8	85.5	89.0	-1.06c	-4.03c
Mexico	90.0	91.6	76.5	62.2	61.7	79.6	74.7	92.7	82.3	-0.1	0.74
Medium-sized countries											
Colombia	68.2	106.3	94.6	78.5	73.9	80.9	107.4	92.6	94.6	0.4a	0.03
Chile	98.8	108.7	107.9	107.7	146.4	149.4	91.7	84.2	80.3	-0.41a	-2.9c
Ecuador	113.3	160.1	136.3	114.2	107.0	81.4	76.6	94.1	80.1	-1.53c	1.07
Peru	81.0	89.9	79.4	74.3	86.1	106.4	84.8	90.8	87.9	0.31b	-0.72
Uruguay	181.7	219.5	162.6	184.8	174.1	184.4	115.8	94.8	97.9	-1.83c	-3.25c
Venezuela	35.6	43.8	43.0	32.2	24.8	32.0	66.6	102.0	82.1	2.18c	3.01b
Small countries											
Bolivia	25.2	25.3	27.7	31.3	43.6	43.4	68.8	96.4	88.5	3.82c	4.33c
Paraguay	—	—	111.1	127.9	123.1	135.9	143.9	104.6	115.1	—	—
Costa Rica	60.3	110.1	108.7	87.3	87.3	86.3	103.3	87.8	91.6	0.37a	-0.44
El Salvador	64.9	116.8	115.2	81.1	83.9	103.4	119.5	87.4	74.9	0.12	-3.66c
Guatemala	88.0	141.5	138.1	94.6	95.3	104.0	114.1	87.7	91.2	-0.5b	-1.79b
Honduras	98.2	111.9	108.1	99.2	106.2	106.7	111.2	93.0	82.3	-0.29b	-2.73c
Nicaragua	76.3	138.2	112.9	96.5	99.6	110.6	112.1	91.9	90.7	-0.03	-2.06c
Averages											
Large countries	104.6	133.7	110.9	95.6	91.8	105.5	102.6	89.4	84.4	-0.68c	-2.12a
Medium-sized countries, excluding Venezuela	96.6	121.6	107.7	100.6	111.2	114.6	93.2	90.2	86.7	-0.44c	-1.28b
Central America	77.9	124.0	119.0	91.5	93.8	100.8	111.7	89.1	86.8	-0.14	-1.99b
Latin America (weighted)	87.5	112.2	96.3	82.9	81.1	91.4	94.0	92.1	84.5	-0.21a	-1.05c

Sources: 1945–1970: ECLAC (1976); 1970–1984: ECLAC (1987a); 1984–1987: ECLAC (1988d).
Notes: a. Significantly different to zero with 90% confidence. b. Significantly different to zero with 95% confidence. c. Significantly different to zero with 99% confidence.

Figure 12. 4. Terms of Trade of Latin American Countries

Large Countries and Total

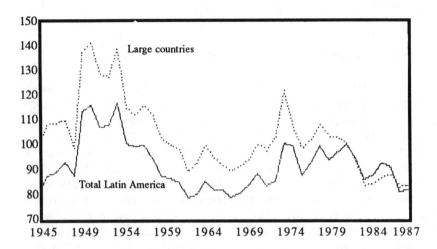

Medium-Sized and Central American Countries

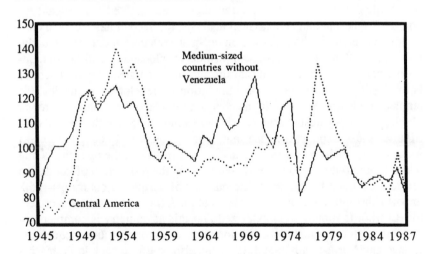

Sources: 1945-1970, ECLAC (1976); 1970-1984, ECLAC (1987a); 1984-1987, ECLAC (1988d).

Note: Subaggregates and the total refer to national terms of trade weighted by each country's share of Latin American exports in 1980-1984.

for approximately half the countries in the region, and for all of them, it is less marked than real price trends for raw materials, excluding oil. In any case, the terms of trade of most countries of the region in 1985–1987 were the lowest in the postwar period. This was particularly true of Argentina, Brazil, Chile, Ecuador, and Uruguay.

Conclusions and Policy Implications

As was pointed out in the first section of this chapter, the postwar controversy on the terms of trade of developing countries can be largely understood as an extension of the two basic hypotheses advanced by Prebisch in his seminal 1951 article. The first is associated with the income inelasticity of demand for raw materials under conditions in which, for historical reasons, peripheral countries have specialized in the production of those goods. The second is related to the differential impact of productivity improvements in central and peripheral countries due to basic asymmetries in the functioning of labor markets. Such asymmetries imply that, whereas developed countries are able to retain technical change in their export sectors through higher real wages, developing countries are forced to "export" productivity improvements through a deterioration in their terms of trade. Both hypotheses contradict the classical idea, also supported by neoclassical analysis, according to which raw material prices tend to increase in the growth process.

While the first of Prebisch's hypotheses has received theoretical support by Keynesian and neoclassical analysis, the second has received considerable backing in the literature on unequal exchange and, more recently, in North-South modeling. As a complementary element, North-South models indicate that, to the extent that the surplus generated in export sectors is the basic source of capital accumulation in developing countries, the terms of trade are the essential mechanism by which the economic growth of the periphery adjusts to the Northern locomotive. Some theoretical contributions also support the idea that, whereas technical change in export sectors tends to deteriorate the terms of trade of LDCs, the opposite is true when productivity improvements take place in the production of goods and services destined for the domestic markets of peripheral countries—both import substitution (as in the neoclassical model) or in the subsistence sector (Lewis). It should be emphasized that this asymmetry is complementary but different from that developed in the literature on unequal exchange and North-South modeling. It can also be traced back to Prebisch's seminal contributions.

On the other hand, empirical evidence indicates that real raw material prices have deteriorated in the long term, both if one takes as a reference the past 110–120 years or the post–World War II period. In both cases, there are, however, some commodities for which this trend has not materialized. In addition, although the experience of the periphery as an exporter of manufactures is more recent, the evidence since the late 1960s indicates that the real prices of Southern manufacturing exports have also experienced a downward trend, less marked than that for raw materials. In this way, one cannot reject the hypothesis according to which the trend of peripheral export prices has been associated with the characteristics of the exporting countries rather than the goods they sell to the North. Finally, empirical analysis also shows that in the postwar period real commodity price trends have not been totally reflected in the evolution of the terms of trade of Latin American countries.

What are the policy implications of these results? To the extent that the deterioration of the terms of trade is limited to primary products, there is major support for industrialization strategies in the periphery. Some support is also provided to commodity price supporting schemes. However, the postwar experience with different regulatory regimes has not proven satisfactory. Besides, it is unclear whether commodities agreements can alter long-run price trends.

It is important to emphasize that the defense of an industrialization strategy that stems from the preceding analysis does not presume anything in relation to the inward- or outward-looking orientation of such policy. This election depends on many factors, most of which are beyond the scope of this chapter. The most important are associated with the size of the national market, the soundness of integration processes underway, the labor intensiveness of export versus import substitution sectors, and the importance of the externalities and the dynamic economies of scale in tradable activities.

As the recent literature and other chapters in this book indicate, many of these factors lean toward greater emphasis on export sectors in the current stage of Latin American development. Moreover, in the absence of sound integration processes, the costs of deepening import substitution industrialization in small economies can overcome the disadvantages implicit in the deterioration of the terms of trade of raw materials, even justifying a commodity-exporting strategy. In any case, the models and empirical results presented in this chapter clearly indicate that the difficulties of an export approach increase if the center places obstacles to exports from the periphery, if the Northern locomotive slows down, and if the deterioration of the terms of trade is extensive to Southern manufactures.

Independently of the nature of the products exported and the development strategy adopted, there are additional implications that derive from the theoretical analysis presented in this chapter. The first relates to the greater benefits peripheral countries capture from technical change in nonexporting activities. This result has obvious implications for a development strategy. This conclusion is only valid, however, for the periphery as a whole or for large LDCs. This means that there is a contradiction between incentives to innovate in a single country and in the periphery as a whole. While for a small country such incentives are neutral across sectors, most productivity enhancement in export sectors is thwarted when other countries undertake similar efforts. On the contrary, benefits from technical change are enlarged when innovations concentrate in those sectors in which the periphery is a net importer of goods and services from the center.[14]

A second set of results with major policy implications is associated with the effect of macroeconomic adjustment on the terms of trade of the periphery. As Prebisch stated in his seminal work, and other models have explicitly shown (see, in particular, Braun's contributions), it can be stated that adjustments in external variables, particularly the exchange rates, are precisely the mechanisms through which the terms of trade adjust to their long term trend. As in the aforementioned case of technical change in export activities, efforts undertaken by individual peripheral countries to improve their competitive export capacity by devaluation may thus be frustrated through a deterioration in the terms of trade if it takes place simultaneously in several countries. The corresponding costs will be higher the lower the Northern price elasticity of demand for LDC exports. Higher adjustment costs are thus likely to be borne by countries that have great difficulties in articulating into the world market through manufacturing exports. This result has major implications for a strategy of joint response to a generalized balance of payments crisis in LDCs. It also may be very important for the design of the external aid policy of developed countries.

Notes

1. The best-known modern formulation of this hypothesis is that of Kuznets (1966). See also the recent work by Chenery, Robinson, and Syrquin (1986).
2. For an excellent synthesis on this subject, refer to Chapter 5.
3. For more recent formulations of this theorem, see Spraos (1983) and Thirlwall (1983).
4. However, dynamic stability requires that the sum of the price elasticities of the demand for imports in the two regions be greater than one. This requirement is known as the Marshall-Lerner condition.
5. In particular, see Rybczynski (1955), Bhagwati (1958), and Findlay and Grubert (1959). There are many textbook versions of this analysis. See, for example, Ffrench-Davis (1979: chapter 3).
6. Strictly speaking, the conclusions that follow are valid only when technical change is neutral, in other words, it does not affect relative factor use at constant factor prices. If technical change is not neutral, relative prices will be affected by both technical change and the increased availability of those factors that are used less intensively with new technologies. The effect of relative factor supplies is considered in the following paragraph.

7. Few attempts have been made to formulate alternative models along this line of analysis. See, however, the work by Bardhan (1982), in which he tests Lewis's hypothesis using alternative assumptions on wage determinants at the center and the periphery.

8. For alternative models, not considered in this chapter, see Burgstaller (1985) and Vines (1984).

9. See some extensions of this model in Findlay (1989), Saavedra-Rivano and Wooton (1983), and Kiguel and Wooton (1985).

10. In a neoclassical model, the "natural" rate of growth also depends on the rate of increase in productivity. This assumption can only be introduced in North-South models such as those considered here when this rate is similar and leads to proportional increases in real wages in both regions. Given the assumptions on the characteristics of the South, this would require that productivity increases at a similar rate in the subsistence sector of developing economies. As this assumption is not tenable, increases in productivity are considered in the following pages as isolated (once for all) processes, which may take place in either central or peripheral countries.

11. See also Dutt (1984).

12. In the neoclassical model, real wages depend on productivity and capital availability, determined, as was shown, by the rate of savings. In the Kaleckian model, they depend on productivity and profit margins. The effects of increases in productivity will be analyzed below. According to the preceding considerations, an increase in the savings rate in the neoclassical model, with its attendant effect on real wages, does not affect the terms of trade. On the other hand, as was also shown, an increase in the profit margin in the Kaleckian model reduces the rate of growth of the world economy and, thus, depresses the terms of trade of developing countries.

13. This case is paradoxical, since oil has been the major export of Ecuador since the 1970s. It could thus reflect problems in the terms of trade series for this country.

14. These results should spark an intense controversy on future industrial policy, in order to define an efficient pattern for the international insertion of Latin American countries. In this respect, Chapter 9 provides an interesting and valuable contribution to the debate.

PART 5

THE STATE

13

The Role of the State and the Market in Economic Development

José Manuel Salazar-Xirinachs

The economic history of the twentieth century has been characterized by a sustained increase in the scale and scope of economic intervention by the state in a wide range of countries. In developing countries (DCs) this expansion has come about in an even more compressed and rapid form, particularly in the second half of the century. The tendency to expand the state and take on more functions in the DCs is due to a variety of reasons, which include the need to build nation-states after becoming independent from the colonial empires; the acknowledgment of strategic aspects in development style; the need to guide and accelerate the processes of economic, political, and social transformation; and the need to safeguard income distribution and compensate for the negative effects of economic change.

In addition, the economic diagnosis that inspired development economics in the postwar period emphasized the countless imperfections of market systems in conditions of underdevelopment, both in the countries themselves as well as in the international economic system. The success of Keynesian policies in fighting unemployment and the stagnation of the 1930s and 1940s and the success of the Marshall Plan for the reconstruction of Europe after the war encouraged faith in cooperative and planned efforts, guided by the state, to bring about economic and social transformations. Finally, the successful takeover of power and state control, first in the Russian and Chinese revolutions and subsequently in other countries—inspired by Marxist conceptualizations of capitalism—kindled faith in the use of the state as an instrument of change for the benefit of the oppressed and excluded classes.

Factors such as the ones described above led to the formulation of different economic policies and strategies; however, all of them had in common the fact that they assigned a fundamental role to the state as the promoter of economic development. This approach was also encouraged by a high degree of confidence in the state's capacity to make rational economic interventions that were both economically and socially desirable.

During the 1980s and up to the present, a radical change in thinking on the role of the state has taken place. Criticisms and documentation of the negative effects of state intervention have proliferated. Faith—apparently boundless in some cases—in the state's capacity to intervene in the economy in a rational and socially beneficial way has changed into an intellectual atmosphere of profound skepticism as to the motives, abilities, and suitability of state intervention, and to a reaffirmation of the benefits of market forces and private enterprise.

However, as Lipsey (1991: 11) has observed:

> Although the old interventionist, import-substitution policies are discredited, "policy *laissez faire*" has not taken place everywhere. Japan and the successful NICs are widely perceived to have followed a policy that is a curious blend of free market and government assistance. Other countries are seeking to follow this lead with policy mixes suitable to their own circumstances. . . . While the U.S. and the U.K. espouse "policy *laissez faire*," much of the rest of the world is dedicated to what can be called "government-assisted, free market economies." Both approaches share in common the goals of privatization, deregulation, avoidance of major distorting interferences in relative prices and encouragement of competition, both domestically and through relatively liberalized trade.

One way to organize this broad assortment of arguments on the role of the state, on the one hand, and criticisms of development strategy, on the other, is to arrange the debate around an explicit evaluation of *standards of rationality* (the market and paradigms that interpret historical experience), which economists use as benchmarks to evaluate development policies. An explicit analysis of economic standards is a suitable way to define the topics that separate the different outlooks on the correct economic incentives for development. In particular, it may lead to a convergence of conceptions on the role of prices and the market, and therefore of what could constitute effective forms of state intervention and planning to promote economic growth.

This chapter examines the relative role played by the state and the market in Latin American development policies from this perspective. Section one contains a review of the main features of thinking—within the Economic Commission for Latin America and the Caribbean (ECLAC) school of thought and the structuralist movement—on the state and the market in the 1950s. Section two is devoted to examining some aspects of the expansion and the role of the state in the postwar period. Sections three and four analyze the the criticism to both development strategy and the role of the state from the neoliberal and neostructuralist perspectives, respectively. In doing so, some of the fundamental theses of development economics are retrieved, particularly those that emphasize the imperfections and asymmetries of market structures and their implications for market behavior and performance. Nevertheless, much of the criticism and some of the policy recommendations made by the neoliberal aproach are also recognized as valid, particularly the emphasis on incentive systems and the benefits of creating adequately regulated markets instead of substituting them.

Two main conclusions are reached. First, after a decade of fierce disagreements on the role of the state and development strategy, there now seems to exist some convergence on the role of the state between the traditional approach of development economics and the less extreme neoliberal positions, based on pragmatic reasoning and the correctly interpreted lessons of history. This consensus is well described by what Richard Lipsey calls "government-assisted, free market" policy mixes. Second, however, the recent drive toward the formation of free trade areas in Latin America, which propose to integrate as partners countries with wide disparities in their levels of development, suggests that at some point in the liberalization process, the paths dictated by the neoliberal and neostructuralist approaches will diverge on a number of important issues.

The State and the Market in Structuralist Thinking During the 1950s

In his presentation of the "Economic Survey of Latin America, 1949," Prebisch (1951: ix) indicated that "any analysis of the special problems that affect Latin American economies, as well as the analysis of changes that have occurred in the Region, have to overcome a major handicap: the lack of knowledge on the economic structures that exist in the various countries, on general trends in their economic development, and the nature of their problems in economic growth." Analyses carried out in ECLAC and by structuralists during the 1950s can be viewed precisely as an attempt to overcome this handicap, since they identify the principal development trends and the evolution of economic structures. The central pillar of this attempt consisted in characterizing the nature and behavior of markets—both at the center and on the periphery—and their interaction, and in developing policy actions based on this assessment.

The policies proposed, intended to improve real per capita income and living standards, emphasized four major areas: (1) increased productivity by promoting industry, technology, and the diffusion of technological progress, a subject extensively analyzed by ECLAC; (2) expanded capacity to save and to import; (3) the need to intervene in trade in order to build comparative advantages, given the asymmetries between the center and the periphery and the need to reduce external vulnerability; and (4) the importance of a strategic perspective in peripheral countries, allowing the state to play a leading role in defining and implementing this strategic outlook (Prebisch 1951).

As Sunkel points out in Chapter 2, these subjects were at the heart of the concerns of Prebisch, who originally proposed the theory of development *from within* (Prebisch 1951: 4) to emphasize domestic supply and structural factors, the importance of inducing an endogenous industrial and technological movement—based on the generation, accumulation, and diffusion of technological progress—and the role of increases in productivity.

While the outlook of the ECLAC school of thought is often correctly identified as an approach that fosters market intervention, it should be noted that several of the original ECLAC documents not only contain warnings against the dangers of excessive intervention, but also emphasize the importance of markets, private initiative, and an enterprising spirit. In addition, the documents pay explicit attention to suitable types of intervention. Thus, the first chapter of one of the most influential documents of the time is entitled "International Cooperation in a Development Policy Based on Private Enterprise" (ECLA 1954a). It is worth quoting at length how the

> balance between the participation of free enterprise and the state [in] economic development in Latin America depends, to a large extent, on private entrepreneurial activity. This idea is generally accepted in Latin America, even in countries noted for certain state interventions which hinder free enterprise. State interventions are not usually the consequence of an ideological position, but rather the result of a series of special circumstances: first, the Great Depression, then the Second World War and subsequently inflation. These interventions were almost always aimed at regulating, one way or another, the behavior of individual entrepreneurs; and, despite some positive results, the adverse developments which accompany these regulations are normally more important than their potential advantages, in addition to the opposition that they arouse due to the complications inherent to an excessive bureaucratic apparatus. . . . This in no way implies that economic development should be the result of a spontaneous interaction between economic forces. It is necessary to combine private enterprise with resolute state policies, and with a type of intervention aimed at promoting development by creating conditions that, one way or another, can guide and encourage entrepreneurial activity without restricting individual decisions. For this purpose, the state therefore resorts to monetary, foreign exchange, fiscal and customs policy and to its basic investments (ECLA 1954a: 7).

The paper even goes so far as to note that "basic state investments have led to an enlargement of the state's sphere of influence which, in some cases, could have improperly encroached upon the activities of private enterprise" (ECLA 1954a: 7). It criticizes the prevailing international finance and cooperation system for not guaranteeing easy access to international sources of capital and technology to national entrepreneurs, and for making these resources available almost exclusively to governments. Finally, it argues that "balance should not be achieved . . . by cutting back state investment, but by giving the greatest possible assistance to private enterprise investors, and, for this purpose, state investment in capital stock is essential" (ECLA 1954a: 8).

The major functions of the state according to structuralist thinking in the 1950s are the following:[1]

1. The design and implementation of an investment program combining public investment in infrastructure (social capital stock) and direct production with private sector investment, taking into account the incentives and motivation needed to stimulate private investment.
2. Measures to encourage the growth of national savings, with emphasis on fiscal policy.[2]
3. The design and continuous adjustment of a trade policy and a protection policy for the domestic market to stimulate industrialization through import substitution: "This substitution process normally requires protective and promotional measures to stimulate private enterprise and to place it in a position in which it can compete with more productive foreign activities" (ECLA 1954: 10).
4. Actions—both domestic and international—to diminish the economy's external vulnerability: This "makes structural changes advisable, not only with a view to import substitution, but also to generally strengthen and diversify the domestic economy" (ECLA 1954: 11).
5. Financial intermediation and orientation of credit to productive sectors and to real investment, with regard to resources from domestic sources and the attraction and channeling of international financial resources.
6. "An economic development policy . . . requires the state to carry out a profound and continuous activity in technology. . . . The state's technical activity with regard to industry has still not been systematically developed and organized—save for some rare although commendable instances. Therefore, the state—together with universities and technical institutions, on the one hand, and business concerns on the other—has to take on this responsibility which offers plentiful possibilities of international cooperation" (ECLA 1954a: 11–12).

Thus, although the structuralism of ECLAC affirmed that "there are fundamental reasons for the state to intervene in economic development," this vision supported "a combination of private enterprise and vigorous state action" in which a broad margin was left for private enterprise to develop (ECLA 1954a: 10). In addition, warnings were issued on the dangers of excessive intervention, and attention was given to the relevant forms and types of action.

The Development Crisis and the Role of the State

Despite the preceding reservations and shades of meaning concerning relevant forms and types of action, in practice, Latin American states experienced a sustained process of expansion in the scale and scope of intervention and a sharp increase in the size and importance of the state in the economy. This expansion process took on characteristics that were unforeseen by structuralism. They arose as a result of several factors, mainly the pressure exerted by different social groups demanding intervention on their behalf—and their success in defending rents and privileges resulting from such intervention—and the disposition of governing elites to have the state solve distributive conflicts and assume a broad range of development responsibilities.

The inability in many countries to manage conflicts through concertation and democratic mechanisms (political exclusion) and the features of the development model, particularly its inability to productively incorporate the growing labor force (economic exclusion), among other factors, made the power structures inflexible and led to a period of direct military intervention in the state, under what some authors have called a "bureaucratic-authoritarian" state model (Malloy 1976; O'Donnell 1978; Stepan 1974, 1978).

In the economy, interventions were directed at encouraging industrialization and modernization through the import substitution model. This was supplemented with a strong emphasis, and considerable fiscal spending, on basic infrastructure, health, education, communications, and activities in which the state played the role of investor and entrepreneur (ECLA 1972; Assael 1973). Although it is a historical fact that state-owned companies played an important role in the growth process and in reinforcing national and independent states in the region (ECLA 1971), it is also clear that "for various reasons the government-controlled sector has grown in areas which are neither strategic nor top priority, thus frequently creating inefficiencies which involve greater social costs than the ones that were trying to be avoided" (CLAD 1988: 2).

The severe macroeconomic imbalances that accompanied development strategy, the failure of the state's developmental approach to fulfill the redistributive duties that the structuralist agenda assigned to it, the inability to solve conflicts within the bounds of concertation and democracy, and the pressure exerted by the world economy—particularly in the 1970s—sharpened by still highly vulnerable economic structures, led to a major crisis in the development model. This resulted not only in a strong critical examination of the state's role but also of the overall development strategy pursued in the postwar period.

These criticisms have arisen from several conceptual perspectives, notable among which are *neoliberalism* and a vision that evolved in development economics and can be called *neostructuralism*. The main aspects of the diagnosis and policy recommendations made by each of these perspectives on development strategy and the relative roles of the state and the market are analyzed below.

Neoliberal Criticism of Development Strategy and the Role of the State: A Neostructuralist Evaluation

The reassertion of liberalism was based on new developments in economics, development experience, and political philosophy. As regards economics, the neoliberal vision is based on a reassertion of price and market theory as a benchmark or standard for policy evaluation and prescription. The use of the price paradigm and general equilibrium theory have led to fundamental questions such as: What is the correct incentive (price) system for growth and development? and, How are correct prices to be set? Prices thus became one of the basic topics of development economics, not only in redefining development strategies, but also in regard to the role of the state and the nature of market interventions.

This vision is also supported by interpretative paradigms of the development experiences of different countries. Paradigmatic cases have changed throughout the history of thinking on development. In the 1960s India was a paradigmatic and influential case. After that, the "Brazilian miracle" was discussed for a short time. Fascination with the "Japanese miracle" has been more lasting. The Southeast Asian experience became a source of inspiration for neoliberalism from the 1970s onward and, according to some authors, of empirical support for their theses. According to Lal (1983: 32), for instance, several decades of experience with import substitution policies and the abuse of these policies, combined with the exporting success of the Southeast Asian countries, have provided the empirical support for the "incontrovertible case" for "liberalizing financial and trade control systems and moving back to a nearly-free trade regime." Thus, in contrast with the theoretical discussions of the 1950s, the new argumentation in favor of free trade refers to a wide-ranging body of empirical literature and comparative studies of the trade regimes in various developing countries.[3]

New contributions in political philosophy have also strengthened the case for a small state with greatly reduced functions and a relative strengthening of private, individual, and/or communal spheres of action. Proponents of these new trends argue the case for the moral superiority of the market and hold that only a minimal or subsidiary state is necessary (Nozick 1974; Paul 1982).

The main components of the neoliberal development strategy are the following: (1) liberalization of foreign trade so as to pursue an outward-oriented development strategy (which is viewed as equivalent to free trade), replacement of quantitative restrictions (quotas) with tariffs, and adoption of low and uniform tariffs as a transitional policy; (2) avoidance of major distorting interferences in the price system, with the principal thesis that a nondistorted price structure maximizes growth and encourages economic development; (3) reduction in the size of the public sector, including privatization, elimination of fiscal deficits, and reduction of tax burdens; (4) privatization of the majority of the productive activities of the public sector; and (5) market liberalization and deregulation, particularly the financial and labor markets.

Liberalization and Trade Orientation of the Strategy

As regards the trade regime, this approach has strongly argued a series of interrelated points that can be summarized in the six following theses or propositions:

1. *Anti-export bias:* Import substitution or inward-oriented policies produce a bias in the incentive system against exports, in other words, a trade orientation biased in favor of the allocation of resources toward the domestic market and against foreign markets.[4]
2. *Neutrality of incentives:* The anti-export bias and other government-induced distortions in the incentive system—in contrast to what Balassa (1982a) denominated a "neutral state of affairs"—are the main obstacles to export expansion and economic growth in countries that have pursued import substitution policies.[5]
3. *Competition:* Competitive pressures exerted by the world market lead to a high rate of technological innovation, a dynamic learning process, and output increases to the efficient production possibility frontier.
4. *Outward orientation and export promotion:* Developing countries ought to adopt export promotion or outward-looking policies, in other words, deregulation and free trade policies. The external trade system should not be meddled with to solve what are basically domestic distortions.
5. *The "ideal," "correct," or "optimum" price-incentive system:* This system is the one least distorted by state intervention and closest to the perfect competition-evaluating standard used to measure distortions.

6. *Selectivity and protection of infant industries:* Like many other economists who sustain this approach, Balassa (1982a) justified his opposition to selective (tailor-made) policies and deliberate discrimination on the grounds of "ignorance as regards interindustry differences in social benefits," and would only allow for modest levels of protection for infant industries. Similarly, Lal (1983: 32) argues that "bureaucrats and planners have shown a lack of foresight that would have swiftly bankrupted a private agent." Baldwin (1969) provides a strong statement of the welfare theoretic case against the use of protection as an instrument for infant-industry promotion.

7. *Evidence:* The preceeding theses are backed by the experience of the newly industrialized countries (NICs), especially the Group of Four in Southeast Asia (Hong Kong, South Korea, Singapore, and Taiwan), which are examples of the indisputable advantages of pursuing a strategy of market liberalization and free trade.

The mainstream of neoclassical literature on development strategy and trade regimes insists particularly on theses 4, 5, and 6. Neostructuralism accepts that export promotion and reaching out to wider markets are important, a subject on which a consensus has been reached. However, neostructuralism rejects the strategy of eliminating the anti-export bias simply by introducing free trade (thesis 4); it views the competitive process differently (thesis 3); it emphasizes endogenous market distortions and therefore rejects the idea that the ideal incentive system is simply that which minimizes government-imposed distortions (thesis 5); and, finally, it has strongly challenged the interpretation of neoliberal economists regarding what happened in Southeast Asia.

These different approaches to trade policy and incentives imply important differences as regards the role of the state in export-promotion strategies. While neostructuralism clearly separates the issue of the sources of demand to stimulate growth—domestic versus foreign markets —on the one hand, and the justification of an active or supportive role for the state and of selective intervention, on the other, in the neoliberal approach the two issues tend to become confused.

Indeed, neoliberalism has tended to rigorously equate export-promotion policies with (1) free trade policies based on the principles of static comparative advantages, (2) no state intervention in the price system, and (3) in some cases a laissez-faire policy and the absence of an active and promotional role for the state. Balassa (1982a: 48), for example, explicitly denies that planning, technological, or marketing strategies, or an active promotional role, have played an important part whatsoever in the economic success of Southeast Asia.[6]

In conclusion, while neoliberal criticism of development strategy has to be commended for insisting on the importance of using foreign markets as dynamic sources of demand and the importance of freer trade regimes, this approach has shown a questionable tendency to equate outward orientation with laissez-faire and the absence of active supporting functions by the state or other institutions. The neostructuralist contribution to this topic is examined in section four.

State Intervention in the Price Mechanism

Intervention in the trade regime is merely a specific application of basic microeconomic theory used to evaluate economic and development policies. This method is based on the use of the Perfectly Competitive Economy (PCE) as an ideal reference model or benchmark against which reality is compared. This "efficient utopia" is the basis for appraising and measuring divergences, distortions, or biases between the optimal and the actual. The design of policy remedies to improve the economic system and establish adequate prices is based on this standard of efficiency of an idealized market.

In principle, there is nothing wrong with using an ideal norm or standard to assess economic situations or the actual performance of a given system. This standard can even be used as a model toward which society should advance. Furthermore, it can be held that this methodology is advisable in the social sciences insofar as it helps to clearly specify the model or blueprint toward which progress is proposed. From this hermeneutic outlook, clearly defined ideal models may contribute to economic and political debate and help elucidate the options available to society.[7]

If it is agreed that the method of using an ideal norm against which economic and social performance or situations are compared is, in principle, legitimate and fruitful, we are left with two fundamental objections. First, there is the question of feasibility, since it can be argued that the usefulness of such a procedure is undermined if there are good reasons to believe that the ideal standard is unfeasible or unattainable, that is, if this is a utopia the premises of which cannot be fulfilled under any imaginable scenario. Second, there is the problem of strategy for change, since this methodology tells us nothing about the problems of transition from the initial situation toward the efficient utopia or ideal model. It is at this point that many of the most important problems arise.

Regarding the feasibility of the PCE, it would be naive to suggest that it is proposed as a realistic ideal that we should strive to attain. No self-respecting economist would make such a claim. After all, utopia is, by definition, outside history. Yet, when economists proclaim the advantages of free trade, liberalizing or deregulating markets, and opening up the economy to international competition instead of captive markets or "artificially sheltered" activities, they do this on the grounds that with such policies reality would be brought closer to the Perfectly Competitive Norm, and that the world would benefit from the good properties of efficiency that characterize the economic model of perfect competition. This methodological paradox has led Stigler (1975: 103) to argue that "economists have long had a deeply schizophrenic view of the state" and of the design of economic policies.

Nevertheless, it is not possible to reject this method of economic evaluation because, as Hahn (1973) has said, if we did not have the PCE, we would have to invent it. Thus, there is no definitive solution to the paradox pointed out by Stigler. On the one hand, Elster (1984: 128) is right that "if the standards of rationality are set too high, the result may be irrationality." On the other hand, persuasion regarding economic arguments is clearly an interpretative process, which differs considerably from what McCloskey (1986) has called the "official rhetoric" about economic method. Therefore, the solution would seem to lie in not losing sight of the limitations of the PCE as a model for evaluating economic policies under specific conditions, so as not to abuse it, and not to accept conclusions that do not follow from the assumptions of the model. In other words, the problem consists in finding the proper way to relate the perfect competition assessment standard and the notion of Walrasian General Equilibrium (WGE) to the real world.

In more instrumental terms, three basic questions arise. Under what conditions is it legitimate to expect remedial policies based on the use of the PCE to work as the model predicts? Under what conditions will liberalization or deregulation policies produce a (liberalized) equilibrium with more desirable features than the (distorted) initial equilibrium? How, and to what extent is it possible, in practice, to structure markets in such a way as to permit their theoretical virtues to actually materialize? Faced with the task of evaluating and defining policies for state intervention in the price system, economists—whether of neoclassical or neostructuralist inclination—will inevitably have to provide satisfactory answers to these questions. The possibilities and limitations involved in using the PCE and WGE models as instruments for policy-setting and assessment can be analyzed from two complementary perspectives: (1) the General Theory of Distortions and Welfare (GTDW),[8] and (2) general equilibrium. The latter perspective will be discussed in section four.

The general theory of distortions and welfare. Changes in the terms of the debate on development and industrialization policies that took place between the 1950s and the 1980s have been closely linked with a revival of the propositions associated with the GTDW.[9] It is in terms of the GTDW, seen by some economists as providing "the grammar of arguments about policy" (Hahn 1973), that the modern case for free trade and the rationale for liberalization policies are generally formulated. The second-best theory of welfare economics is also the theory that tries to answer our earlier question on the problems of transition from the initial situation to an ideal or more efficient world.

Furthermore, the so-called *dirigistes* or "those seeking to argue the case for increased government intervention" have been scorned by Lal (1983) for not using this framework to "bolster their claims."[10] However, it is well known that in a world of imperfect competition the use of GTDW logic presents serious difficulties. The first difficulty is purely practical. The single, best-known optimal policy rule is that correction of the distortion at its source is always the first-best policy intervention. The practical difficulty of insisting on free trade and relying instead on domestic interventions via first-best production or employment subsidies, as this optimal policy rule would require, is that LDCs do not normally have control over their public finances (McKinnon 1979a: 439).

A more profound difficulty is the fact that this line of reasoning does not consider a series of key factors and causal mechanisms that link trade with growth, such as: the sources of nonprice competitiveness, asymmetries in the access to and dissemination of knowledge, the dynamics of technical change, and the influence of increasing returns. Insofar as the growth process depends on these factors, an approach that concentrates solely on price distortions will necessarily be partial and incomplete. This does not imply that second-best arguments are faulty on their own premises, nor that they lack analytic authority. What it does mean is that when these arguments are used to justify free trade as the engine of growth, one is tresspassing the limits within which the truth of their propositions is applicable. That is, one is abusing the norm by stepping beyond the field of validity of the underlying economic standard.

A third difficulty has long been familiar in development economics. In a classic article, Lipsey and Lancaster (1957) demonstrated that in an imperfect economy restoring some but not all the conditions that would exist under perfect competition would not necessarily bring about an improvement in welfare. The relevance of this conclusion was recently expressed by Krueger (1984a: 551) as follows: "Analysis of the welfare effects of alternative trade (and other) policies becomes exceedingly complex when it is assumed that not all distortions can be removed. When attention is focussed on the effects of varying one policy instrument, holding distortions elsewhere in the system in place, the general theory of the second best indicates that anything can happen."

On the same subject, Stiglitz concludes that:

> Unfortunately, the standard welfare analysis has little to say about modern industrial economies, where technological change and information problems (explicitly excluded from the traditional analysis) are of central importance. We do not have, nor is there likely to exist, a welfare theorem for such economies possessing the generality of the fundamental theorem of welfare economics. . . . What we do have is a number of

"insights" and "examples," which serve more to make us cautious in applying standard welfare economics than to provide us with a basis for policy prescriptions (Stiglitz and Mathewson 1986: xx).

In spite of the foregoing, neoliberal criticism of state intervention in the price system has tended to be unilaterally obsessed with government-imposed or exogenous distortions. There has been a tendency to avoid theorizing on the overall economic system and to avoid asking, as the appropriate use of the theory requires, how the system will behave when what is liberated is a set of markets plagued by endogenous or intrinsic market distortions.

Development theory in the 1950s began precisely this way, conceptualizing the endogenous and structural characteristics of the market, and drawing conclusions as to market behavior and performance under these structural conditions. In contrast, the neoliberal outlook has frequently gone so far as to forget the basic premises with which development economics started out in the 1950s, in other words, that there are multiple phenomena that constitute prima facie evidence of structural imbalances and a highly imperfect market system. To wit: the characteristic and chronic shortage of fixed capital to make productive use of the labor force; the lack of savings, finance capital, and foreign exchange; the segmentation, concentration, and monopolistic power of markets; and deficiencies in information, foresight, and expectations.

In conclusion, there are no grounds in economic theory for a policy seeking to eliminate all government-imposed distortions, whether in the trade system or the field of domestic interventions, while ignoring endogenous distortions and specific market structures.[11] Valid policy recommendations have to be based on an analysis of the interaction of both policy-imposed and endogenous distortions. The correct prices for a development strategy cannot simply be assumed to be equal to those present in a theoretical distortion-free economy, which operates in Walrasian equilibrium.

Empirical evidence of distortions and their effects. As Krueger (1984a: 555) has pointed out: "Despite the importance of distortions in theory, relatively little empirical work has been undertaken to estimate their magnitude or their effects. . . . An interesting question, on which there is to date no evidence, is how great distortions must be to be judged significant."

An influential study is the analysis of the impact caused by price distortions on growth in a sample of thirty-one developing countries in the 1970s, presented in the *1983 World Development Report*, by the World Bank. Different types of price distortions were combined in a "composite distortion index," which was regressed against GNP growth rates. The main conclusion was that price distortions hinder growth. It was found that while in the 1970s the average GNP growth for the thirty-one countries was close to 5 percent per year, the countries with low price distortions grew roughly an additional 2 percent per year. Whereas countries with high price distortions registered an annual growth that was 2 percent lower than average.

Agarwala (1983) discusses some methodological problems with this exercise. Other weaknesses have been underlined by Evans and Alizadeh (1984). Nevertheless, for our purposes, the point to stress is the fact that, according to this study, only 34 percent of the variation in growth of the thirty-one countries is accounted for by the composite distortion index. The other two-thirds can not be explained by prices, and there are large deviations between actual and predicted growth rates. The main reason why only one-third of the variation in the growth process is accounted for by price factors is that, as structuralism has maintained for many years, economic systems are dominated by different aspects related to structures, institutions, and imperfect competition, which determine performance. These systems bear only a slight resemblance to the perfect competition standard used as the benchmark to define and measure distortions.

The Impact Caused by the Size of the State: A Dead End?

Some versions of neoliberal criticism of the state view problems from the standpoint of the size of the state. However, as Kliksberg (1988: 7) argues: "Apparently, the problem is solely a question of size. There is a tendency to foster the myth that if size is reduced, ipso facto, efficiency will be attained."

The inadequacy of raising the problem in these terms originates, first, in the difficulties of developing a consistent theory that links growth with the different size variables of the state that can be defined (the tax burden, relative weight of spending as a proportion of GDP, number of state-owned companies, public sector employment, fiscal deficits, and the like). The structural forces that account for the increased size of the state are so diverse that they can only be covered by a series of ad hoc hypotheses on some of the basic causal relationships that may be operating, and it would be pointless to try to define a set of adequate indicators regarding the optimum size of the state. Second, it is evident that a large state can be weak in regulating markets and providing the necessary incentives for economic growth, while a small state can strongly develop these functions.

Third, although some comparative analyses based on size indicators may be of interest for specific purposes, and some partial hypotheses may be developed, there is no reliable evidence linking this type of indicator with overall economic efficiency or with rates of economic growth. Surprisingly, the evidence that does exist suggests that the size of the state has a positive effect on economic growth. Using internationally comparable figures for production, investment, and the size of the state, in a sample of 115 countries over two decades (from 1960 to 1980), Ram (1986) drew the following conclusions: (1) the size of the state has a positive effect on economic performance and growth; (2) the size of the state causes an effect of "positive externality" on the rest of the economy; (3) this positive externality effect was stronger in the 1970s; and (4) the positive effect of size on growth appears to be more important in countries with smaller incomes.

Regardless of the strength of such conclusions, one should be skeptical about the usefulness of addressing the subject from a reductionist approach to the size of the state. An approach that analyzes the state's management capacity in government-owned companies, its power to regulate markets, its ability to alter economic incentives, and the institutional mechanisms and processes needed for decisionmaking appears to be more useful than an attempt to determine the optimum size of the public sector based on a series of unhistorical indicators without the support provided by a clear theory of their impact on economic growth.

Privatization

Neoliberalism strongly favors privatization policies. The concept of privatization has been subjected to widely differing interpretations. It has been used to cover a broad range of actions, among which three basic categories can be identified: (1) sale of assets and state-owned companies (SOCs) to the private sector (denationalization or destatization); (2) contracts for the private sector to provide goods and services previously furnished by the state, financed either with public funds or authorized as concessions; and (3) deregulatory action, in other words, allowing competition in markets characterized by monopolistic advantages, legal restrictions, or other barriers to the entry of private companies.

Limiting the discussion to the first category, privatization is mainly justified based on criticism that emphasizes the poor performance of SOCs, the negative fiscal effects of companies that run deficits, and the shortcomings and inefficiency of state management. While cases of public enterprises that run deficits and are inefficiently organized undoubtedly abound, it should be emphasized, nevertheless, that drawing general conclusions on the performance of public enterprises is no easy task.[12] An adequate evaluation should take into account the wide array of reasons and objectives that gave rise to nationalization or the establishment of several types of state-owned companies. These include accelerating industrialization and mobilizing resources, regulating natural monopolies, extracting rents from international trade, and other strategic aims and objectives. Strictly speaking, the performance of these companies should be evaluated according to the explicit objectives associated with each company. If rigorous criteria of financial profitability are applied, it is hardly surprising that the evaluation is negative.

To illustrate some of the problems of evaluation, we can refer to one of the most frequently mentioned objectives in favor of privatization, which is at the heart of arguments on the relative role of state and market: greater efficiency. Conceptually, different types of efficiency should be clearly identified, particularly *productive efficiency* (production at a minimum cost) and *economic efficiency* (the efficiency of the entire economy, defined as the optimum allocation of resources combined with an undistorted price system). For example, an unregulated monopoly—whether government-owned or private—that maximizes its profits may be efficient in productive terms, but not necessarily economically efficient. Any corporation—either private or state owned—may be productively efficient but economically inefficient if it operates under a strongly distorted price system. This situation typically occurs under protectionist regimes or those with high production subsidies. In these cases economic inefficiency is not attributable to the company's status as a state-owned or private entity. However, as Marcel (1989: 11) has pointed out, "the most fervent supporters of privatization are used to equating efficiency with financial profitability, so that the poor performance of many state-owned companies in this respect will support their criticism of state management."

In general, the only conclusion that can be drawn, either from economic theory or from the available evidence, is that productive efficiency, economic efficiency, and profitability tend to coincide only in highly competitive markets. Under conditions that differ significantly from competitive markets, financial profitability loses its value as a criterion to evaluate productive efficiency, and productive efficiency may, in turn, depart considerably from economic efficiency. Nevertheless, financial profitability does demonstrate whether public enterprises depend on the national budget to continue operating.[13]

Due in part to these difficulties and others of a methodological nature, there are relatively few reliable comparative studies on the performance of state-owned companies and their relative efficiency compared to private companies. In a comparative study of state-owned industries in thirteen countries, Ayub and Hegstad (1987) conclude that: (1) financial results differ radically among public enterprises in the same country, and within the same industry in different countries; (2) rates of financial return are relatively low in industrial state-owned enterprises; and (3) they have tended to be less profitable than private companies in the countries sampled, even within certain industries. Nevertheless, the authors warn of the difficulties involved in this type of comparison.[14]

Yarrow (1986) reviews the evidence from twenty-eight studies and, based on a distinction between industries where competitive conditions exist and those where they do not, concludes that market structures are more important than ownership to explain the comparative performance of companies.

These considerations, which emphasize the structural and institutional aspects of the markets in which public enterprises operate, lead to three basic conclusions: (1) the argument that privatization will lead to increased economic and productive efficiency is more convincing for those that operate in competitive markets, or where competitive conditions could be created; (2) eliminating distortions and raising competitiveness, whenever possible, seems to be a complementary condition that contributes to the potential beneficial effects of privatization, in terms of economic efficiency; and (3) privatization under highly protected conditions, or where there are barriers to the entry of competition, will only have the effect of turning public monopolies into private monopolies. In this case it would not be possible to state with any certainty that economic efficiency would increase. This result is possible, of course, but it would be determined by the regulatory framework and the political and institutional circumstances in which these regulations are to be applied.

The evaluation of the results of privatization provides no conclusive answers, nor does it allow this type of policy to be considered as a panacea. This is partly due to the fact that the experience in this field is so varied that it does not allow for easy generalizations. It is also partly due to the fact that multiple—and often conflicting—objectives are expected from privatization. In each case the conclusions depend on the type of objectives believed to have priority. For example, in some specific cases of privatization, in which high priority is given to reorganizing the company in financial terms and obtaining the highest possible price for its assets, without restricting the number or type of new owners, it is frequently found that privatization helped to concentrate wealth, or has given rise to monopolies under private control. Even the fiscal impact may be negative when, as is often the case, profitable state-owned companies have been privatized. Nonetheless, the focus of attention in this area has led to many creative and innovative ways of organizing production and services in private hands.

Deregulation

The subject of deregulation appeared and developed powerfully in Latin America, especially in relation to financial markets. In the context of financial reform programs inspired by the views of McKinnon (1973) and Shaw (1973) and subsequent developments, the principal deregulation measures include: (1) liberalization of interest rates; (2) dismantling of quantitative and selective credit control mechanisms (portfolio ceilings), thus granting greater latitude to financial institutions to allocate credit on commercial criteria; (3) reducing and standardizing minimum reserve requirements; (4) lowering barriers to the entry of new financial institutions and national and foreign banks; and (5) relaxing the regulation, supervision, and control of the financial system.

The results of the experiences of financial liberalization in Latin America have been widely discussed.[15] The general conclusion is that results differ greatly from expectations, and that they had negative effects on several fields. Notable among these is the fact that although "financial deepening" grew strongly in most cases, the increase in intermediation tended to concentrate in short term assets. Thus, although financial savings rose, national savings not only did not rise but actually fell in several cases. In addition, interest rates often rose excessively. In Chile high interest rates, together with high levels of indebtedness, created a vicious circle that eroded the ability to pay, and led to delinquency, refinancing, and bankruptcy of many companies. A financial crisis of major proportions forced the government to abandon its rhetoric of commitment to market discipline and to intervene in the private financial sector through rescues and nationalizations, to such an extent that Díaz-Alejandro (1985: 1) observed sarcastically that Chile had "shown the world another route to the de facto nationalization of the financial system."

Various authors attribute the failure of financial liberalization efforts to inconsistent macroeconomic policies (lack of adequate coordination in policies regarding wages, credit, and foreign exchange) and to an incorrect sequence in liberalization measures applied to capital controls, trade controls, legal regulations, and fiscal policies (Edwards 1984b; Dagnino-Pastore 1984; Sjaastad 1983; Dornbusch 1984; Harberger 1985).

The record of financial reforms in Latin America provides important lessons, regarding not only the order and sequence of liberalization, but also the relative roles played by the state and the market in economic development and the importance of adequate regulation. One basic conclusion stands out: "Ten years after these reforms were first implemented, the evidence indicates that they were, to a large extent, a failure" (Edwards 1984b: 1). This fact has had the healthy effect of persuading neoliberal economists to propose second-best arguments more carefully, and to adopt a more cautious approach in making policy recommendations. For instance, one of the fathers of these reforms, and one of the most fervent advocates of liberalization and deregulation, honestly acknowledged that the Chilean experience "amounts to a quite humbling lesson for economists" (Harberger 1985: 460).

Principal Theses Proposed by New Structuralist Thinking on the State and the Market

The relevance of structuralism as a school of thought depends on whether it is able to propose an agenda of major problems and derive operational proposals from this agenda that can be integrated into feasible strategies to be carried out by existing social actors. Some of the principal components of the neostructuralist agenda are reviewed below, as well as their relation to the role of the state. This review clearly shows the richness and relevance of this school of thought for Latin America's reality. It should be noted that the assessment standard used by neostructuralism includes, but is much more complex than, the Perfectly Competitive Economy. This standard includes a considerable amount of nonprice factors and qualitative elements that determine performance, and which are characteristic of the neostructuralist view of reality.

Markets as Institutional Structures and Development from Within

As mentioned in section one, the essential part of Prebisch's thesis on development from within in the 1950s was his emphasis on internal supply factors, the importance of creating an endogenous industrial and technological momentum—based on the generation, accumulation, and dissemination of technological improvements—and raising productivity. This approach led naturally to emphasizing the need to develop a strategic outlook in peripheral countries, allowing the state to play a leading role in defining and implementing it.

Neostructuralism holds this same analytic approach and affirms that the chief economic problems in developing countries are endogenous and structural. Nevertheless, considerable progress, in analytical and empirical terms, has been made in the 1970s and 1980s in the analysis of markets, and in the identification of a broad range of structures and behaviors present under conditions of imperfect competition. Neostructuralism is strengthened by these developments, many of which stem from its own contributions.

One way to organize the main elements that occupy the attention of neostructuralism is from the perspective of general equilibrium theory. In terms of the properties and assumptions of Walrasian General Equilibrium, any real economy—but especially an underdeveloped economy—may be defined, as in Table 13.1, according to the following features: (1) an incomplete set of markets; (2) existing markets characterized by imperfections, segmentation, and market power; (3) imbalances, rigidities, and agents lacking full information, so that they make mistakes, learn (clumsily), or find themselves involved in strategic games with a much wider set of variables than mere prices; (4) a set of prices that is far from providing 100 percent of the information needed by the agents to make decisions; and (5) learning processes, processes of technological change, and externalities that mean that increasing returns in various sectors and industries may be large in relation to the size of the economy.

**Table 13.1.   Characterization of a Real (Underdeveloped) Economy
in Terms of the Perfectly Competitive Economy**

Perfectly Competitive Economy Walrasian General Equilibrium	Real Underdeveloped Economy
Complete set of markets	Relatively empty economy Incomplete set of markets due to: Public goods Lack of futures markets, uncertainty Abundant externalities
All markets are perfectly competitive	Existing markets are characterized by: Intrinsic or endogenous imperfections and segmentation Various degrees of market power, concentration, oligopoly, and imperfect competition between agents
Equilibrium exists and all the markets are cleared (after the Walrasian auctioneer has performed well)	Disequilibrium is endemic due to bottlenecks, rigidities, and agents who make mistakes, learn, and become involved in games in the absence of an auctioneer
Information: prices provide 100% of the information that the agents need to make decisions	Prices are not the only relevant indicators: this implies more externalities There are differences in information (of both price and nonprice varieties) between the agents
Constant returns to scale (or increasing returns that are small relative to the overall size of the economy) are needed for equilibrium to exist	Learning, technological change, and externalities mean that increasing returns may be large in relation to the size of the economy

These categories assemble the main types of deviations (distortions) from the perfect competition model, and correspond to the basic structural elements of markets that have traditionally occupied the attention of structuralism.[16] This characterization leads to a reassertion, in modern terms, of the strategic perspective regarding development, productive transformation, and trade that inspired development economics from the outset. Without denying the importance of prices, this perspective includes the real complexity of learning processes, the search for information, and decisionmaking under conditions of uncertainty, assigning a major role to technological change in the growth process.

Hence the neostructuralist thesis was developed that in order to grow proper prices or liberalization will not suffice. The market must be complemented by willful coordination by the state or public policy institutions, which includes—within the limits of their administrative competence—the following types of functions:

- *Classical and normative functions:* These include providing public goods—a legal framework, a police force, the security of its citizens

—maintaining macroeconomic balances, certainty as regards property rights, and equity in the distribution of income. They also include eliminating or compensating for undesirable structural distortions, whether these are price distortions or distortions related to the distribution of property or asset endowments, and access to economic opportunity.

* *Basic functions:* These include the basic infrastructure required for transport and communications, health, education, housing, and the like.
* *Auxiliary or support functions:* These include providing support for the economy's structural competitiveness and developing measures to improve market functions and behavior. They involve such things as the promotion of missing markets—for example, long term capital markets, crop insurance markets, and other risk management mechanisms; strengthening and improving incomplete markets—for example, enhancing the dissemination of and access to information; eliminating segmentation; eliminating or compensating for market imperfections derived from externalities, learning processes, or returns to scale; and developing scientific and technological infrastructure.

These categories include the main strategic action areas considered relevant by neostructuralism in the formulation of development strategy. In addition, neostructuralist thinking on intervention is typically framed within an approach to economics that takes into account the interaction between economic policy measures and the social actors that determine their viability. Thus, neostructuralism avoids the trap of a simplistic or willful view of intervention, based on a state-market dualism, with an idealized view of both institutions. For example, the argument that the likelihood of government failure is greater than that of market failure, and that governments are systematically more myopic than markets, has been widely used to justify a preference for market mechanisms over state intervention. Neostructuralism argues that it is useless to try to solve this dilemma by arguing in favor of one or the other position, since the list of failures or mistakes of markets and governments is potentially infinite, as is the list of successful decisions. Neostructuralists would agree with Kay (1987: 8) when he argues that:

> The idea that it is possible to trust unregulated market forces to lead to the best of all possible worlds is just as naive as the expectation that, if markets are eliminated, altruistic, omniscient and super-human regulators will achieve the same result. The reality is that both market and government imperfections are endemic in modern economies. It is foolish to stress one instead of the other, or even to debate which is the most important. The policy challenge is to develop institutions that can solve market imperfections and which, at the same time, avoid or diminish the possibility of failures in regulation.

Neostructuralism emphasizes the great variety of intermediate group-
ings or coalitions that exist between the individual and the state (cooperatives, associations of producers, tradespeople, labor unions), which form
a rich and varied network with substantial power over economic decisions
and the feasibility of economic policy.[17] This structural, institutional, and
organizational perspective has caused emphasis to be placed, with new analytical tools, on topics that have traditionally been essential in Latin
American economic thinking.

Restoring Basic Macroeconomic Balances[18]

One of the state's classical functions has been to maintain basic macroeconomic balances. Nevertheless, together with its distributional role, it is
one of the areas where the state has failed most. A widely commented
upon inadequacy of structuralism was its limited concern with the management of short term macroeconomic variables and its concentration on
long term aspects. In contrast, a recent review of neostructuralism argues
that it is now "perhaps guilty of the opposite: strong emphasis on short-
term analysis and comparatively little emphasis on the long-term" (Lustig
1988a: 48).[19]

Neostructuralism's contributions on inflation have centered on designing economic policy packages to restore stability while minimizing
social costs and negative effects on production and employment by means
of so-called heterodox shocks. These focus economic policy instruments
on neutralizing inertial processes or mechanisms that propagate inflation,
and on eliminating distributive struggles by freezing prices and salaries
(Alberro and Ibarra 1987).

Although by shifting its focus to short term problems neostructuralism
filled a vacuum in its line of thought, the results of the heterodox shocks
have not been praiseworthy. Hyperinflation in Argentina, for example,
shows that Frenkel (1987: 330) was hasty in concluding that "the 'Plan
Austral' has been an effective instrument to offset possible hyperinflation." Paradoxically, it could be argued that the operation of the Austral
Plan for eighteen months, and its subsequent failure, shows the relevance
of neostructuralist diagnosis and the importance of concertation mechanisms to control distributive struggles.

Disinflation produced by the Austral Plan exacerbated the distributive
struggle because: (1) by reducing the fiscal deficit and eliminating monetary emission, the state and all those who profited from fiscal chaos and
subsidies were forced to observe budgetary restrictions; (2) the inflation
tax and the associated subtle financial mechanisms for the transfer of revenues among transactors were eliminated; and (3) agents were able to understand price signals more clearly and better calculate the value of their
income, which made them more aggressive in their attempts to maintain or

increase their income shares. In other words, as Frenkel (1987: 329) holds, the elimination of the inertial component of inflation made the structural inconsistencies at the root of Argentina's economic problems transparent: the closed and overprotected character of the economy, the rigidities of supply, and the sectoral push for incomes.

Democratic consensus and concertation were finally too fragile to enforce cooperative rules of behavior on the different social actors. As Ibarra (1987: 30) has pointed out, "the real 'Achilles' heel of income policies in general, and those followed by heterodox strategies in Latin America in particular, was the lack of institutionalized mechanisms for social concertation."

It is obviously the responsibility of the state to coordinate and lead the institutional mechanisms for concertation that make possible certain stabilization policies. As a generalization, it may be said that restoring macroeconomic balances requires: (1) the reduction of transfers abroad; (2) anti-inflationary policies that deal with expectations, but with suitable handling of social concertation and consensus to make possible the commitments of different social sectors; and (3) domestic policies that reduce fiscal deficits and restrict demand, but which simultaneously stimulate production of tradable goods and services and exports. These three elements are necessary but not sufficient conditions for the adjustment with growth strategy proposed by neostructuralism. It also requires a reformulation of industrial strategy into a clearly defined productive transformation strategy.

Industrialization and the Promotion of Exports

The neostructuralist reformulation of the industrialization strategy.[20] According to the structuralist approach, Latin America followed what might be called a Keynesian growth strategy, which secured the market (the demand side) by protection measures but neglected productive efficiency (the supply side). The reformulation of the growth and industrialization strategy faced by the region requires a change of strategy in both aspects. On the demand side, once the "easy stage" of import substitution has been completed, the limitations of the domestic market (due to the size of the economy and the distribution of income), as well as the scarcity of foreign exchange and the debt burden, raise the urgent need to use exports as a dynamic source of demand and economies of scale. On the supply side, the relative neglect of productive efficiency when production was intended for a captive domestic economy, in addition to the new competitiveness that has become mandatory in the world market, makes it necessary to follow a Schumpeterian approach, the central objective of which is to mobilize entrepreneurial and management capacities, increase efficiency, modernize and reconvert the industrial plant, and develop sectors with high productivity and competitive advantages.

Hence, for neostructuralism the principal problem of trade policy is not simply opening up the trade regime, or bringing about outward orientation or neutrality in the system of incentives, but also determining how to accelerate the achievement of international competitiveness and facilitate adjustment without sacrificing the industrial base that was built through import substitution. Open economies compete on the basis of access to technology, thus the thesis that development policy requires profound and persistent work in the field of technology and human resources is reaffirmed. Neostructuralism holds that both the state and the private sector must play active promotional roles in this Schumpeterian approach.

Comparative advantages, competitiveness, and new theories of international trade.[21] Neostructuralism, both in its assessments and its proposals, has been strengthened by the development of new theories of international trade, which include uncertainty, imperfect competition, and technological change as basic premises of their models (Krugman 1986, 1987, 1988; Kierzkowski 1984; Greenaway and Tharakan 1986; Brander 1986; Stegemann 1989).

This new approach is based on the formalization of aspects of trade that structuralism emphasized in its analysis, but which it had not formally included in its trade models. As Krugman (1986) puts it, the new theories of international trade arose from the combination of an old idea and a new approach in the formulation of models. The old idea refers to increasing returns and the structural conditions of markets, and the new approach is the application of the theory of industrial organization in the area of international trade, particularly as regards the interdependent and oligopolistic nature of a large part of international trade.

At an empirical level, the new theories explain phenomena of trade patterns and international specialization, both at the macro level of aggregate trade flows and at the micro level of market structures and technology, which cannot be easily explained with conventional models. With regard to trade flows, conventional models are incapable of explaining the growing role of intraindustry and intracompany trade. Indeed, the majority of international trade does not take place between countries or sectors endowed with different resources—for example, between a center specializing in manufacturing and a periphery specializing in primary products—for which a theory based on different resource endowments may be adequate. Rather, the bulk of these flows increasingly corresponds to two-way trade in different goods that, nonetheless, can be classified in the same industrial sectors and are produced with similar factor endowments and production functions. At a micro level, most manufacturing industries are characterized by some degree of increasing returns, especially if dynamic economies of scale associated with R&D and the learning curve are taken into account. As Lustig (1988a: 38) points out: "Although these ideas were not developed with the same rigor when structuralist thought was born, they are the background to Prebisch's statements to the effect that the best way to achieve sustained growth was by encouraging industrialization."

Thus, in a steadily increasing part of international trade, a country's endowment of production factors and natural resources is not what determines what the country specializes in or is most successful at in international trade. In practice, in a framework of adequate incentives, certain factors have been more important, such as economies of scale, generalized accumulation of technological capacities, the ability to obtain information and identify market opportunities, an enterprising spirit, investment in human resources, and the organizational factors needed for decisionmaking and financial intermediation.

From this perspective, the international competitiveness of an economy is more than the mere outcome of the average competitiveness of each company. It is also the result of other structural factors that cover a series of economic and institutional phenomena that may be seen as externalities, and which give rise to the concept of *structural competitiveness* (OECD 1986). This concept holds that a company's competitiveness obviously reflects successful management by company executives, but also the strength and efficiency of the productive structure, the scientific and technological infrastructure, the nature of capital investments, the existence and quality of support services (financial, engineering, design, transport), and other externalities that favor both the company and the entire industry. All these factors give shape to dynamic competitive advantages and constitute strategic areas in which the state can play a fundamental role by supporting and integrating the efforts of the entrepreneurial and other sectors in a coherent strategy to accelerate productive transformation, improve flexibility, and promote the dynamic efficiency of the economy.

Promotion of exports, selectivity, and the new technoeconomic and organizational paradigm.[22] In general terms, three basic forms of producing an outward-oriented trade system can be identified: pure neutrality, compensated neutrality, and expanded compensated neutrality. The first consists in equating the profitability of sales on the domestic market with that of external markets (in other words, eliminating the anti-export bias) by establishing a free trade, zero tariffs, and nontariff barriers system, which eliminates, to the greatest possible extent, all measures to protect domestic industry. A trade system that maintains a certain degree of protection for the domestic market but which compensates the export sector with specific incentives is called compensated neutrality. Finally, a system of expanded compensated neutrality is one in which net incentives to export are granted so that in given sectors sales of the same product have a higher profitability on the external market than on the domestic market. Net export incentives (proexport bias) may be temporarily justified as a mechanism to promote infant export industries.

Neostructuralism supports a strategy based on eliminating anti-export biases and irrationally high tariffs. However, using the terminology introduced above, it is not in favor of pure neutrality, but of compensated or even expanded compensated neutrality, as a transitional strategy. That is, it supports deliberately discriminatory incentives for exports and selective or tailor-made policies for infant industries. In addition, it emphasizes the need to develop clear productive transformation and modernization strategies at the subsectoral level in order to strengthen structural competitiveness and facilitate the adjustment process.

It is precisely in the institutional and technological fields and in the study of institutional mechanisms for managing development where neostructuralism is making important contributions. The new technoeconomic paradigm is emphasized both at the level of the overall economy and at the level of individual companies and organizations. At the level of companies and the productive process, this new paradigm is based on two major components: (1) information technology based on microelectronics (computers, telecommunications, electronic control of equipment, and computerized manufacturing systems); and (2) a new model of management and organization based on concepts of maximum flexibility and agility of response, minimum inventories, and zero defects (Pérez 1988a). These two components come together in a new model of productive efficiency, and "their adoption, in one area after another, is establishing levels of productivity, quality and capacity of response significantly higher than the levels which, up to now, determined competitiveness in different markets" (Pérez 1988b).

In terms of the overall economy, this paradigm is based on recognizing the importance of information and adequate institutional ways to deal with an intrinsically uncertain world. The application of this institutional and organizational perspective to the Southeast Asian experience has resulted in a wide-ranging literature. The fact that the range of incentives has been less distorted in Southeast Asia than in countries that have pursued strongly protectionist policies is not forgotten in this literature, but it is devoted more to documenting institutional aspects, strategic planning and selection mechanisms, technological and marketing strategies, and the administrative arrangements that allowed the "correct" incentives to be applied and maintained.

In an excellent and detailed analysis of the Korean case, Yusuf and Peters (1985: 9) conclude that:

> Planning à la Eastern European economies or even China was never attempted by the Korean government. But planners utilized the entire register of policy instruments that economists of a dirigiste persuasion had

> labored to compile and there was no reluctance at all to intervene in pursuit of industrial, export and growth objectives. In many respects, Korea is a paradigmatic case of a managed economy in the non-socialist sense of the term. . . . Investment (in Korea) was not the outcome of market signalling but to a large extent deliberately contrived by the government.

Also referring to Korea, Sen (1983: 752) concludes that, "if this is a free market, then Walras's auctioneer can surely be seen as going around with a government white paper in one hand and a whip in the other."

For their part, Pack and Westphal (1986) point out the crucial function that the South Korean government has played in improving the dynamic efficiency of the Korean economy and in internalizing information externalities through coordinating decisionmaking, extensive consultation with private agents, and consensus building on resource allocation. "The Korean government can be seen as having achieved integrated decisionmaking, by acting as a central agent mediating among agents, forcing and facilitating information interchange and insuring the implementation of the decisions reached" (Pack and Westphal 1986: 12).

Furthermore, although there were instances of "government failure," the behavior of this central agent is best seen as following a "bounded rationality" (Herbert Simon's term). That is to say, not a classical optimizing rationality but a pragmatic rationality involving an important element of learning over time. Thus, on decisions concerning infant industries,

> there was necessarily a great deal of ex ante uncertainty about which were the "optimal" choices. The uncertainty was progressively resolved through accumulating additional information during the implementation of the choices made. Information gained during the process of establishing an infant industry was cast into its implications for expected export performance, with comparison of revised expectations being used to reformulate detailed strategies. The knowledge gained often implied that initial choices needed revision. What was entailed was an evolving strategy (Pack and Westphal 1986: 44).

This perspective opens up a wide forum for the debate of institutional forms, decisionmaking between and within organizations—including the state and its components—and the economic coordination mechanisms, which extend beyond the price system, and which determine the economy's dynamic efficiency and the possibility of creating comparative advantages.

Toward a Strategy to Reform the State

Latin American states are characterized as being overloaded with demands, facing a deterioration in management and service administration in connection with the objectives of that administration, and being in a weakened and vulnerable financial situation, which makes them subject to recurrent fiscal crises. As stated earlier, it is not easily justifiable to characterize the state as being too large, since the issue is not so much its size but its capacity for management and concertation. While in some countries financial aspects were strengthened and corrected in the 1980s, the overload of demands continues, in part, because the very development strategy that has been pursued assigns a large number of functions to the state. An inventory of relevant points for the transformation of the state and its role in Latin American development is outlined below.

The central function of the state. The central economic function of the state may be defined as devising a strategic vision of the development process, maintaining basic macroeconomic balances and an appropriate investment climate, reordering incentives and relative prices in the economy in a manner that is consistent with this vision, and achieving the constructive commitment of all social and political sectors to this strategy, by means of dialogue and concertation. A state that is efficiently organized around this central function could be called a *concerting state*, and it can be argued that this is what is suitable for this new stage of development in Latin America, characterized by the revival of democracy and increasing private sector responsibility in the development process.[23]

Strengthening of basic and classical functions and reduction of productive functions. Latin American states need to strengthen their *basic functions* (infrastructure, health, and education) and their *classical functions* (a legal framework, a police force, the security of their citizens, a foreign relations policy, macroeconomic balances, equity, the avoidance of key bottlenecks with regard to foreign exchange, savings, and investments) while at the same time substantially reducing the burden of their *entrepreneurial or productive functions* (administration of companies and direct production of goods and services). The need to mobilize resources for priority projects, in view of the incapacity of the private sector to do so, was one of the fundamental motivations for the states to become involved in productive and entrepreneurial activities, for the establishment and expansion of state-owned companies, and for the latter to be viewed as development agents. Nevertheless, the process of growth and modernization has advanced, and an entrepreneurial-managerial class has developed with sufficient resources and initiative to assume risks. Capital markets and financial intermediation have also improved substantially, a development that makes it more feasible than in the earlier stages of economic development for the private sector to mobilize resources. The new relative roles of the state and markets can be described as a government assisted, market-oriented approach, in which the private sector has to assume an increasingly leading role with adequate government support.

Support functions for competitiveness and exports. As explained, the competitiveness of an economy is more than merely the average competitiveness of each company. The policies of opening up to international competition and insertion into world markets, either unilaterally or in the context of the integration of free trade areas, strongly suggest that the Latin American states should strengthen what could be called *auxiliary functions*, or functions to support the structural competitiveness of the economy. These include: the improvement in the quality of the factors of production, particularly human resources and technological innovation; development, under an adequate regulatory environment, of markets directly associated with production (capital markets, consultancy markets, markets of perishable goods); development of efficient mechanisms for financial intermediation and access to credit; scientific and technological infrastructure; and other support services for productive modernization and exports.

Public finances. The task of restructuring state finances, with regard to both the restructuring of spending and the consolidation of its sources of income, should be one of the focal points in the neostructuralist agenda. One of the most daunting tasks will be to grapple with the fiscal implications of trade reform. With regard to spending, the following actions stand out: a restructuring that takes into account the accumulation of social debt, in other words, the need to avoid adjustment fatigue caused by the reduction in social spending and the deterioration in social conditions; reinforcing the managerial and administrative capacities, including the capacity for establishing priorities and developing selective actions; adequate definition and financing for a public investment program; and reducing financial subsidies except for those that have a genuine redistributive effect and are socially justified, or subsidies that may be justified temporarily as incentives for technological innovation, investment, learning, and exports.

The strengthening of these functions does not imply the growth of the state, but an improvement in its management. One of the conditions for this to occur is to make salary policies flexible so that the state can attract and retain managers and professionals of sufficient caliber, by means of salaries competitive with those paid by the private sector, but with clear performance requirements similar to those of the private sector. To achieve this without an overall increase in spending requires rationalization measures in other areas, including staff reductions. The subcontracting of goods and services previously provided by the state or the transfer of some activities to the private sector play a crucial role in this process.

Improving the management and efficiency of state-owned companies. Although privatization can make an important contribution, it is no panacea.

There is much that can be done, and has been done, to improve the efficiency of state-owned companies and services, including the banking system. The relevant areas of strategic action include (Pérez Salgado and Kliksberg 1985; Trivedi 1988; Bennett 1988; Martin 1988):

1. The elaboration of strategic plans, including a revision of objectives and instruments, should be undertaken. Frequently, the growth of SOCs, their incursion into new areas, and the creation of subsidiaries and new departments cannot be attributed to explicit policies on the part of the governments but, rather, is the outcome of initiatives implemented by the managers. The motivations have been diverse: processes of vertical integration or diversification that seem to be logical extensions of present activities, pressures from groups and regions for investment projects, and the like (Vernon 1987). In addition, managers have often used a variety of strategies to weaken the control of regulatory agencies (ministries, comptrollers) and widen their field of action in the running of the SOCs. The efforts of the managers to achieve autonomy illustrate the difficulties faced by governments in establishing effective control mechanisms. This tension has, in many cases, led to detailed systems of control and ex-ante authorization of spending, which not only have a negative effect on the management of the SOCs, but also degenerate into senseless routines (Vernon 1988).

2. Granting increased financial and management autonomy is necessary. This includes the ex-post revision of the management and control systems by focusing on the main variables and not on details. For example, a budget and control operation centered mainly on the authorization and supervision of current expenditure totals, total indebtedness, and investment would avoid any negative macroeconomic impact due to excesses in these areas, and at the same time, it would introduce flexibility to the field of action of management and the running of state-owned companies. The chief executives of state-owned companies should be capable of assigning resources internally, according to the priorities of the strategic plan, ensuring that they stay within the overall limits compatible with macroeconomic programming.

3. The complement to the type of reform suggested in 2 is that there should be more transparency in companies and in their actions with regard to the public. In other words, mechanisms should be developed for the control, supervision, and evaluation of state-owned companies, on the part of the users and the public in general, which would serve as a quality control mechanism in the running of the company and its services.

4. Mechanisms should be introduced to better optimize the prices and rates established for state-owned companies, similar to those of private sector companies, and social or subsidized prices should only be allowed in very well-defined and exceptional cases.

5. The sale of some assets to the private sector, the elimination of some functions, the subcontracting and tendering out to the private sector of goods and services, and the privatization of nonstrategic productive companies are all fundamental instruments in the reform of the state. Note that privatization is proposed as an instrument to improve state management in its relevant functions, to terminate functions that are nonessential or which the private sector can perform better, and to allow the reorientation of the state's actions to what was defined above as auxiliary functions in order to improve structural competitiveness. That is to say, privatization is not proposed as an end in itself. As with public investment, for which prioritized programs are routinely produced, the reform of the state requires an inventory of projects for public disinvestment, subcontracting, and the like.

6. Creating new attitudes, rationalizing spending and privatization, offering competitive salaries, and allowing user groups to explicitly participate in the control and supervision of management are all necessary but not sufficient actions to improve public sector management. These actions must be accompanied by legal changes to define and disentangle fields of action. Public management is often constrained by a maze of laws, rules, regulations, directives, and other practices that, on the whole, create a difficult environment for efficient management.

7. Finally, the improvement of management will, in the end, depend on the possibility of forming a solid national consensus on the main direction of change. In democratic societies, only the critical power created by the type of consensus developed by a concerting state will make possible the institutional reform that in some cases might meet fierce resistance.

Final Observations:
Elements of a Neostructuralist Intervention Policy

As discussed in the introduction, an appropriate way to formulate the topics that separate the different perspectives on the relative role of the state and the market, and of intervention in the price system, is to explicitly organize the debate around the standards of rationality used by economists to evaluate economic and development policies. The previous sections suggest that the assessment standard applied by neostructuralism includes, but is more complex than the Perfectly Competitive Economy used by neoliberalism, since it also includes other qualitative elements that are characteristic of the neostructuralist view of reality.

Three basic elements summarize the traditional emphases and characteristics of the neostructuralist evaluation standard: (1) a realistic and perceptive position on the nature of markets, organizational structures, and the determinants of technical progress and efficiency; (2) an emphasis on the distributive aspects of development, including access to entitlements of resources, distribution of property rights, and flows of income; and (3) attention to the mechanisms of participation of agents in economic decisions and policies and their relation to the state (inclusion-exclusion, democracy, concertation).

Given the need perceived by neostructuralism for an active supportive role by the state and the importance of its normative functions, it is mandatory for this approach to spell out in detail the social rationality criteria that guide its intervention strategy. Some of the elements that should be present in what could be called a neostructuralist optimum intervention strategy are described below.[24]

1. *The Price Paradigm:* With the reservations and limitations indicated earlier, this is an indispensable element to analyze the performance of markets and the consequences of state intervention in the price system. A fundamental question, consistent with the neostructuralist view on markets, is: How should markets be structured and regulated in practice so that their theoretical virtues can, in fact, materialize? The promotion of efficient markets thus should become one of the main points on the neostructuralist agenda. It should be noted, however, that in an institutionalist approach, which takes into account the concept of transaction costs (the costs of drawing up and implementing contracts), Pareto's criteria of efficiency lose their meaning, since it is no longer possible to specify the state structure of minimum cost for any given level of economic transactions or production (see North 1984).

2. *The New Technoeconomic and Organizational Paradigm:* This approach means that very high in the neostructuralist agenda should appear the modeling and understanding of institutions and organizations, and of the factors that determine the economy's structural efficiency and competitiveness. This breaks down into several priority areas: the role of flexible strategic planning mechanisms; decisionmaking processes and the implementation of plans of action in a changing and intrinsically uncertain world; and the importance of management, or complexity handling, including the ability of both public and private agents to reach agreement in a complex environment (Kliksberg 1989). The formulation and implementation of policies from this perspective is one of the principal instruments for the improvement of management and efficiency in development policies.

3. *Establishing Intervention Priorities:* Given the overload of demands and functions on the state in Latin American countries, and the limits to its administrative ability and management, the intervention strategy must establish priorities for action in the course of time and make use of concertation mechanisms to reach agreements with the private sector and the users and consumers of services, in order to ensure that the priorities decided upon have been met. Interventions to improve entitlements, access

to the stock of resources, and flows of income for the various national sectors occupy an important place in the neostructuralist normative schema.

4. *Clear and Transparent Rules of Intervention:* Interventions (exogenous or policy-imposed distortions) must not be so impenetrable as to prevent the social evaluation of their impact. The ideal would be the removal of distortions, while simultaneously this policy is complemented with measures to improve the markets and the conditions of competition. Compensation of distortions for one sector is at the same time a distortion for other sectors; therefore, if there are many compensations in the economy, it is difficult to determine whether one sector is a net beneficiary of economic policy or not. Thus, there is a loss of transparency regarding social costs and benefits, and a socially rational planning process is rendered impossible.

5. *The Agenda for Intervention in the State:* The principal elements of a strategy to reform the state were examined in the previous section. One criterion for this intervention must be the decentralization and depoliticization of conflicts as a way to: reduce the overload of demands and functions with which the central government is burdened; understand local peculiarities and promote local participation; and achieve more efficient state management. At the same time, however, decentralization imposes severe demands on management in terms of coordination and implementation.

6. *Automatic Mechanisms for Economic Counterbalancing:* Pressure to intervene in the market tends to be unidirectional—pressures for more rather than less intervention—for one fundamental reason: the benefits of intervention are usually concentrated in a few participants (coalitions, pressure groups), while the costs are spread out among many (consumers, taxpayers), all of whom offer less resistance. The opposite occurs with the benefits of reducing intervention, which are normally spread out over many participants who for this reason exert less pressure in favor of change, while the costs are concentrated on relatively few, frequently highly vociferous participants. Given this asymmetric pressure in favor of intervention, it is essential to create automatic counterbalancing mechanisms. These mechanisms might include: (1) establishing ceilings for fiscal spending on certain types of subsidies, so as to make it necessary to optimize the amount of fiscal resources that are applied (for example, export subsidies); (2) establishing ceilings to the average value of a differential tariff system in such a way that each time a tariff increases another must decrease in compensation, thus creating an institutional counterbalance to the natural rising trend; and (3) including legislated automaticity in the phasing out of subsidies or other measures intended as temporary.

7. *Concertation:* According to neostructuralism,

neither a neoliberal state nor a traditional interventionist state will be capable of fulfilling the difficult functions demanded of them in a situation of crisis and transformation; only a democratic and participatory state will be able to do so. . . . [Furthermore,] to insist solely on the lack of public efficiency is not the most appropriate response. The real problem is to increase overall efficiency, both public and private, of the economy. . . . What is needed above all is to gradually give shape to a new arrangement of state interests, both public and private, that will make it possible to establish a "virtuous circle." Therefore, it would be necessary to change planning and markets—albeit applying criteria of social rationality—instead of insisting on their antagonism (CLAD 1988: 2).

In conclusion, the balance of state and markets proposed by Latin American neostructuralism can appropriately be described as a "government-assisted, free market strategy," using as criteria for intervention the elements discussed above.

Notes

1. See ECLA (1954: 10) and Rodríguez (1980: 181).
2. For a detailed review of this topic from the perspective of ECLAC, see ECLA (1972) and Assael (1973).
3. See Little, Scitovsky, and Scott (1970), Krueger (1978b), Bhagwati (1978), Balassa (1982a), and World Bank (1983).
4. The anti-export bias and other price distortions are measured according to distortion indexes such as the nominal protection coefficient, the effective protection coefficient, the effective subsidy rate, and the triangles method to measure consumer and producer surpluses.
5. The concept of anti-export bias is the criterion used by Balassa to distinguish between development strategies: "The distinction between outward- and inward-oriented development strategies is based on the absence, or presence, of a bias against exports."
6. Krueger insists that a free trade policy based on principles of static comparative advantages is precisely what is needed in order to take advantage of dynamic considerations (Krueger 1982: 139). On the other hand, as Westphal (1984) has pointed out, in posing the problem in more cautious terms, Bhagwati and Srinivasan (1978: 17) seem to want to detach themselves from those who have argued the case with complete conviction and confidence.
7. One author who has defended the use of utopias in social and economic debate from a socialist viewpoint is Geoff Hodgson (*The Democratic Economy: A New Look at Planning, Markets and Power*, Middlesex: Pelican). Hodgson argues that the reluctance, in a considerable portion of socialist thought, to define a realistic model of a "feasible socialist society" has had harmful effects on radical politics and social science. This aversion comes from the very concepts of Marx and Engels, who throughout their lives opposed utopian socialism, and believed, incorrectly according to Hodgson, that schemes or detailed proposals (blueprints) were unnecessary. See Giddens (1982).
8. This topic has been more fully discussed by the author in Salazar-Xirinachs (1986).
9. The GTDW is the title of a classic article by Bhagwati (1971) in which the author, in a single theoretical framework, summarizes a long series of scattered results obtained by several economists, among which Harry Johnson and the "Delhi Trio"—Bhagwati, Ramaswani, and Srinivasan—stand out.

10. Lal states that "any economic justification for a *dirigiste* policy not based on the logic of second-best welfare economics must be incoherent, and akin to the miracle cures peddled by quacks which are adopted because of faith rather than reason" (Lal 1983: 16).

11. Hence the dubious validity of the following statement by Balassa, presented as the main conclusion of his review on the analyses of disequilibria in developing economies: "Removing distortions in product and in factor markets reinforce each other. In particular, the favorable impact of trade liberalization is enhanced if distortions in capital markets are *simultaneously* removed and vice versa" (Balassa 1982b: 1036).

12. For a review of criticisms regarding the performance of the SOCs, see Hemming and Mansoor (1988) and World Bank (1988b: chapter 8). Bennett (1988) provides an excellent review of the theoretical and practical problems faced by different criteria to evaluate the performance of the SOCs.

13. For an analytic evaluation of profitability indicators and a critique of the various comparative studies in existence, see International Monetary Fund, Public Finance Office, *Non-Financial State-Owned Companies: General Report and Case Studies*.

14. The authors hold that, for the reasons described below, comparisons of performance between state-owned and private companies are not conclusive and should be considered as merely indicative or illustrative: (1) SOCs are often assigned social or strategic purposes that affect their financial performance; (2) in many countries the public sector includes companies that run deficits and that the government acquired for noneconomic reasons; and (3) the sector of state-owned companies is often dominated by basic industries with slow growth rates, such as iron and steel, cars, fertilizers, and cement.

15. See Arellano (1984), Díaz-Alejandro (1985), and Corbo and de Melo (1987). Zahler (1988) provides an excellent review of the experience and results in the Southern Cone.

16. Even if these elements do not necessarily completely destroy the concept of equilibrium, they are sufficiently important to require caution in the use of this concept and in the use of the associated concept of distortion with regard to equilibrium. See Kaldor (1972, 1979).

17. Hirschman (1981), Ibarra (1987), Muñoz (1988), and Olson (1982) analyze, from different perspectives, the influence exerted by coalitions and pressure groups, and their interaction with the state in the performance of economic systems.

18. See Chapter 4.

19. The following sections differ from this analysis and suggest that there is also a very wide literature that, although diverse, has a structuralist slant, or should be seen as part of that school of thought, with important instrumental contributions on aspects of development strategy in the medium and long term.

20. See Chapter 9.

21. Chapter 12 is relevant to the discussion of these topics.

22. See Chapter 11.

23. The role of the state in creating consensus for the tasks entailed by development is analyzed in PREALC (1988) with regard to income and employment and by Muñoz (1988) and Salazar-Xirinachs and Doryan (1989) with regard to industrial policy. Kliksberg (1988) and various CLAD publications also discuss the topic extensively.

24. I wish to thank Joseph Ramos for his observations and enrichment of the following points on the optimum intervention strategy of neostructuralism.

References

ABREU, M. DE P. and W. FRITSCH (1988) "Market Access for Manufactured Exports from Developing Countries: Issues and Prospects" in J. Whalley (ed.) *Rules, Power and Credibility*, London: CESIER/University of Western Ontario.

ADAMS, F. and J. BEHRMAN (1982) *Commodity Exports and Economic Development*, Toronto, Ontario: Lexington Books.

AGARWALA, R. (1983) "Price Distortions and Growth in Developing Countries" in *World Bank Staff Working Papers*, No. 575, Washington, DC.

AGOSIN, M. (1991) "Reforma comercial y crecimiento: una reseña de la temática y evidencia preliminar," *Pensamiento Iberoamericano*, No. 20, July–December.

AHLUWALIA, M. S. (1976) "Inequality, Poverty and Development" in *Journal of Development Economics* 3 (December): 307–342.

ALBERRO, J. and D. IBARRA (eds.) (1987) "Programas heterodoxos de estabilización, Presentación" in *Estudios Económicos*, Special issue (October): 3–11, Mexico: El Colegio de México.

ALLEN, G. C. (1981) "Industrial Policy and Innovation in Japan" in C. Carter (ed.) *Industrial Policy and Innovation*, London: Heineman.

ALTIMIR, O. (1975) "Estimaciones de la distribución del ingreso en América Latina por medio de encuestas de hogares y censos de población: Una evaluación de confiabilidad." Proyecto conjunto CEPAL/Banco Internacional de Reconstrucción y Fomento sobre Medición y Análisis de la Distribución del Ingreso en Países de América Latina, mimeo, Santiago, Chile.

——— (1981) "Poverty in Latin America. A Review of Concepts and Data" in *CEPAL Review* 13 (April): 67–96.

——— (1982) "La distribución del ingreso en México: 1950–1977" in C. Bazdresch, J. Reyes Heroles, and G. Vera (eds.) *Distribución del ingreso en México. Ensayos*, Mexico: Banco de México.

——— (1984) "Poverty, Income Distribution and Child Welfare in Latin America: A Comparison of Pre- and Post-recession Data" in *World Development* 12 (March): 261–282.

——— (1986) "Estimaciones de la distribución del ingreso en la Argentina, 1953–1980" in *Desarrollo ecónomico* 25 (January–March): 521–566.

AMIN, S. (1973) *L'echange inegal et la loi de la valeur*, Paris: Editions Anthropos.

——— (1974) *Accumulation on a World Scale*, New York: Monthly Review Press.

ANINAT, A. (1983) "El arancel extero comun y la integración andina," mimeo, Santiago.

ARDITTO-BARLETTA, N., M. I. BLEJER, and L. LANDAU (1984) *Economic Liberalization and Stabilization Policies in Argentina, Chile and Uruguay*, A World Bank Symposium, Washington, DC: World Bank.

ARELLANO, J. P. (1984) "De la liberalización a la intervención: el mercado de capitales en Chile 1974–83" in *Colección Estudios CIEPLAN* 11 (December): 5–49.

—— (1985) "Políticas para promover el ahorro en América Latina" in *Colección Estudios CIEPLAN* 17 (September): 127–151.

—— (1986) "La Literatura Económica y los Costos de Equilibrar la Balanza de Pagos en América Latina" in Cortázar (1986).

ARIDA, P. (1986) "Macroeconomic Issues for Latin America," in *Journal of Development Economics* 22 (June): 171–208.

ARIDA, P. and A. LARA-RESENDE (1985) "Inertial Inflation and Monetary Reform in Brazil" in J. Williamson (ed.) *Inflation and Indexation: Argentina, Brazil and Israel*, Cambridge, MA: MIT Press.

ARROW, K. (1962a) "The Economic Implications of Learning by Doing" in *Review of Economic Studies* 29 (June): 155–173.

—— (1962b) "Economic Welfare and the Allocation of Resources for Invention" in National Bureau of Economic Research, *The Rate and Direction of Inventive Activity*, Princeton, NJ: Princeton University Press.

—— (1979) "The Limitations of the Profit Motive" in *Challenge: The Magazine of Economic Affairs* (September–October): 23–27.

—— (1981) "La limitación del conocimiento y el análisis económico" in Ffrench-Davis (1981), vol. 1.

ASCHER, W. (1984) *Scheming for the Poor: The Politics of Redistribution in Latin America*, Cambridge, MA: Harvard University Press.

ASSAEL, H. (ed.) (1973) *Ensayos de Política Fiscal*, Mexico: Fondo de Cultura Económica.

AYLEN, J. (1987) "Privatization in Developing Countries" in *Lloyds Bank Review* 163 (January): 15–30.

AYUB, M. A. and S. O. HEGSTAD (1987) "Management of Public Industrial Enterprises" in *The World Bank Research Observer* 2 (January): 79–101.

BACHA, E. (1979) "Más allá de la curva de Kuznets: Crecimiento y cambio en las desigualdades" in Muñoz (1979).

—— (1981) *Análise macroeconomica: uma perspectiva brasileira*, Rio de Janeiro: IPEA/INPES.

—— (1983) "Apertura financiera y sus efectos en el desarrollo nacional" in Ffrench-Davis (1983).

—— (1986) *El milagro y la crisis: economía brasileña y latinoamericana*, Lecture 57, Mexico: Fondo de Cultura Económica.

—— (1987) "La inercia y el conflicto: El Plan Cruzado y sus desafíos" in *Estudios Económicos*, Special issue (October): 167–215, Mexico: El Colegio de México.

BACHA, E. and L. TAYLOR (1973) "The Unequalizing Spiral: A First Growth Model for Belindia," Discussion Paper No. 15, mimeo, Brasilia: University of Brasilia.

BACHA, E. and C. DÍAZ-ALEJANDRO (1983) "Los mercados financieros: una visión desde la semi-periferia" in Ffrench-Davis (1983).

BAER, W. and I. KERSTENETZKY (eds.) (1964) *Inflation and Growth in Latin America*, Homewood, IL: Irwin.

BAIROCH, P. (1981) "The Main Trends in National Economic Disparities Since the Industrial Revolution" in P. Bairoch and M. Levy-Leboyer (eds.)

Disparities in Economic Development Since the Industrial Revolution, London: Macmillan.

BAKER, M. (1988) "Understanding the Technology Being Managed: A Short-term Solution" in *Technology Management Publication*, No. 1.

BALASSA, B. (1977) *Policy Reform in Developing Countries*, Oxford: Pergamon Press.

——— (1981) *The Newly Industrializing Countries in the World Economy*, New York: Pergamon Press.

——— (1982a) *Development Strategies in Semi-Industrial Economies*, Baltimore, MD: Johns Hopkins University Press.

——— (1982b) "Disequilibrium Analysis in Developing Economies: An Overview" in *World Development* 10 (December): 1027–1038.

——— (1989a) *New Directions in the World Economy*, London: Macmillan.

——— (1989b) "Implications of Europe 1992 for the World Economy," mimeo, Washington, DC.

BALDWIN, R. E. (1969) "The Case Against Infant-Industry Tariff Protection" in *Journal of Political Economy* 77 (May–June): 293–305.

BARAN, P. (1957) *The Political Economy of Growth*, New York: Monthly Review Press.

BARDHAN, P. (1982) "Unequal exchange in a Lewis-type World" in M. Gerzowitz et al. (eds.) *The Theory and Experience of Economic Development*, London: Allen and Unwin.

BARNETT, H. J. and C. MORSEN (1963) *Scarcity and Growth: The Economics of Resources Availability*, Baltimore, MD: Johns Hopkins Press.

BARRO R. and H. GROSSMAN (1971) "A General Equilibrium Model of Income and Employment" in *American Economic Review* 61 (March): 82–93.

BAUMOL, W. and W. OATES (1982) *La teoría de la política económica del medio ambiente*, Barcelona, Spain: Antoni Bosch.

BENNETT, A. H. M. (1988) "Theoretical and Practical Problems in Determining Criteria for Performance Evaluation of Public Enterprises" in *Public Enterprise* 8 (January–March): 18–27.

BERGSMAN, J. (1982) "La distribución del ingreso y la pobreza en México" in *Distribución del ingreso en México. Ensayos* 1, Cuaderno 2, Mexico: Banco de México.

BERRY, B. and M. URRUTIA (1976) *Income Distribution in Colombia*, New Haven, CT: Yale University Press.

BETTELHEIM, C. (1972) "Theoretical Comments" in Arghiri Emmanuel, *Unequal exchange*, New York: Monthly Review Press.

BHAGWATI, J. (1958) "International Trade and Economic Expansion" in *American Economic Review* 48: 941–953.

——— (1971) "The Generalized Theory of Distortions and Welfare" in J. N. Bhagwati, *International Trade: Selected Readings* (1982), Cambridge, MA: MIT Press.

——— (1978) *Foreign Trade Regimes and Economic Development: Anatomy and Consequences of Exchange Control Regimes*, Cambridge, MA: Ballinger Press.

BHAGWATI, J. and T. N. SRINIVASAN (1978) "Trade Policy and Development" in R. Dornbusch and J. A. Frenkel (eds.) *International Economic Policy: Theory and Evidence*, Baltimore, MD: Johns Hopkins University Press.

BIANCHI, A., R. DEVLIN, and J. RAMOS (1987) "El Proceso de Ajuste en América Latina, 1981–1986" in *El Trimestre Económico* 54 (October–December): 855–911.

BITAR, S. (1988) "Neo-liberalism Versus Neo-structuralism in Latin America" in *CEPAL Review* 34 (April): 45–62.

BLOMSTRÖM, M. (1988) *Transnational Corporations as Instruments for the Exports of Developing Countries*, New York: UNCTC.

BLOMSTRÖM, M. and B. HETTNE (1984) *Development Theory in Transition, The Dependency Debate and Beyond: Third World Responses*, London: Zed Books.

BONEO, H. (1985) "Privatización: Ideología y Praxis" in H. Boneo (ed.) *Privatización: Del Dicho al Hecho*, Buenos Aires: Ediciones El Cronista Comercial.

BOSCO PINTO, J. (1975) "Humanismo y colonización" in *Desarrollo rural en las Américas* 7 (January–April): 21–31.

BOURGUIGNON, F. (1989) *Optimal Poverty Reduction, Adjustment and Growth: An Applied Framework*, draft, Washington, DC: World Bank.

BOURGUIGNON, F., W. H. BRANSON, and J. DE MELO (1989) "Adjustment and Income Distribution: A Counterfactual Analysis" in *National Bureau of Economic Research*, Working Paper Series No. 2943, Cambridge, MA.

BRADFORD, C. (1992) "The East Asian Development Experience," in Grilli, E. and D. Salvatore (eds.) *Handbook of Economic Development*, North Holland Press.

BRANDER, J. (1986) "Rationales for Strategic Trade and Industrial Policy" in Krugman (1986).

BRAUN, O. (1973) *Comercio Internacional e Imperialismo*, Buenos Aires: Editorial Siglo Veintiuno.

BROMLEY, R. (1979) *The Urban Informal Sector: Critical Perspectives on Employment and Housing Policies*, Oxford: Pergamon Press.

BROWN, L. (1972) *World Without Borders*, New York: Vintage Books.

BRUNO, M., G. DI TELLA, R. DORNBUSCH, and S. FISCHER (1988) *Inflación y Estabilización: La experiencia de Israel, Argentina, Brasil, Bolivia y México*, Mexico: Fondo de Cultura Económica.

BRUNO, M. and S. PITERMAN (1988) "La Estabilización de Israel: Una reseña de dos años" in Bruno et al. (1988).

BRUTON, H. J. (1977) "Industrialization Policy and Income Distribution" in Frank and Webb (1977).

BRZOVIC, F. (1989) "Economic Crisis and Environment in Latin America and the Caribbean." Presented at Proyecto sobre Cooperación Técnica para la Integración de Consideraciones Ambientales en la Planificación del Desarrollo (November).

BURGSTALLER, A. (1985) "North-South Trade and Capital Flows in a Ricardian Model of Accumulation" in *Journal of International Economics* 18 (May): 241–260.

CANAVESE, A. and G. DI TELLA (1988) "¿Estabilizar la inflación o evitar la hiperinflación? El Caso del Plan Austral, 1985–1987" in Bruno et al. (1988).

CANITROT, A. (1981) "Teoría y práctica del liberalismo. Política antiinflacionaria y apertura económica en la Argentina, 1976–1981" in *Desarrollo Económico* 21 (July–September): 131–189.

——— (1983) *Orden social y monetarismo*, serie Estudios CEDES, No. 7, Buenos Aires: CEDES.

CARBONETTO, D. and E. KRITZ (1983) "Hacia un nuevo enfoque del sector informal urbano" in *Socialismo y Participación*, Lima: Ediciones Socialismo y Participación.

CARBONETTO, D. and E. CHAVEZ (1984) "Sector informal urbano: heterogeneidad del capital y excedente bruto del trabajo" in *Socialismo y Participación*, Lima: Ediciones Socialismo y Participación.

CARDOSO, F. H. (1977) "Originality of a Copy: CEPAL and the Idea of Development" in *CEPAL Review* 4 (Second half): 7–40, and in Ffrench-Davis (1981), vol. 2.

CARDOSO, F. H and E. FALETTO (1979) *Dependency and Development in Latin America*, Berkeley and Los Angeles: University of California Press. First published in Spanish (1969) *Dependencia y desarrollo en América Latina*, Mexico: Editorial Siglo Veintiuno.

CHAPLIN, D. (ed.) (1972) *Population and Growth in Latin America*, Lexington, MA: Heath.

CHENERY, H. (1960) "Patterns of Industrial Growth" in *American Economic Review* 50 (September): 624–654.

———— (1961) "Comparative Advantage and Development Policy" in *American Economic Review* 51 (March): 18–51.

CHENERY, H. and L. TAYLOR (1968) "Development Patterns Among Countries and Over Time" in *Review of Economics and Statistics* 50 (November): 391–416.

CHENERY, H., S. ROBINSON, and M. SYRQUIN (1986) *Industrialization and Growth: A Comparative Study*, Oxford: Oxford University Press.

CHU, K. and A. FELTENSTEIN (1978) "Relative Price Distortions and Inflation: The Case of Argentina, 1963–1976" in *IMF Staff Papers* 25 (September): 452–493.

CLAD (1988) "El rol de las empresas públicas en el contexto de la reestructuración económica en América Latina" in *Boletín Informativo*, No. 29 (April), Caracas: Centro Latinoamericano de Administración para el Desarrollo.

CLARK, C. (1951) *The Conditions of Economic Progress*, London: Macmillan.

CLINE, W. (1972) *Potential Effects of Income Redistribution on Economic Growth: Latin American Cases*, New York: Praeger.

———— (1975) "Distribution and Development: A Survey of Literature" in *Journal of Development Economics* 1 (February): 359–400.

———— (1989) *American Trade Adjustment: the Global Impact*, Washington, DC: Institute for International Economics.

COASE, R. (1960) "The Problem of Social Cost" in *Journal of Law and Economics* 3 (October): 1–44.

COBURN, J. F. and L. H. WORZEL (1985) "El problema de la empresa pública. ¿La privatización es la solución?" in Boneo (1985)

COLANDER, D. C. (ed.) (1984) *Neoclassical Political Economy: The Analysis of Rent Seeking and DUP Activities*, Cambridge, MA: Ballinger.

COLECCION DE ESTUDIOS CIEPLAN (1988) "Neoestructuralismo, neomonetarismo y procesos de ajuste en América Latina," No. 23 Special issue (March).

COMMONER, B. (1976) *The Poverty of Power*, Alfred A. Knopf.

COOK, P. (1988) "Liberalización y política de desarrollo industrial en los países menos desarrollados" in *El Trimestre Económico* 55 (January–March): 3–40.

COOMBS, R., P. SAVIOTTI, and V. WALSH (1987) *Economics and Technological Change*, London: Macmillan.

COOPER, C. M. (1973) *Science, Technology and Development*, London: Frank Cass.

CORBO, V. (1985) "Reforms and Macroeconomic Adjustment in Chile During 1974–1984" in *World Development* 13 (August): 893–916.

CORBO, V. and P. MELLER (1979) "Estrategias de comercio exterior y su impacto sobre el empleo: Chile en la década del 60" in *Estudios de Economía* 13 (First semester): 1–33.

CORBO, V. and J. DE MELO (1987) "Lessons from the Southern Cone Policy Reforms" in *The World Bank Research Observer* 2 (July): 111–142.

CORTÁZAR, R. (1984) "Restricción externa, desempleo y salarios reales: perspectivas y conflictos" in *Colección Estudios CIEPLAN* 14 (September): 43–59.

——— (ed.) (1986) *Políticas macroeconómicas. Una perspectiva latinoamericana*, Santiago: Ediciones CIEPLAN.

CORTAZAR, R., A. FOXLEY, and V. E. TOKMAN (1984) *Legados del monetarismo. Argentina y Chile*, Buenos Aires: Ediciones Solar.

COURIEL, A. (1984) "Poverty and Underemployment in Latin America" in *CEPAL Review* 24 (December): 37–62.

CUKIERMAN, A. (1988) "El Final de la Elevada Inflación Israelí: Un experimento de inflación heterodoxa" in Bruno et al. (1988).

CURRILL, P. (1974) "Variables geohistóricas en la destrucción de los parajes geográficos chilenos" in *Encuentro nacional sobre problemas del medio ambiente en Chile*, ECLA.

DAGNINO-PASTORE, J. M. (1984) "Assessment of an Anti-Inflationary Experiment: Argentina in 1979–81" in Arditto-Barletta, Blejer, and Landau (1984).

DALY, H. (1971) *Steady State Economics*, San Francisco: W. H. Freeman and Co.

DANCOURT, O. (1986) "Políticas agrarias y reactivación económica" in A. Figueroa and J. Portocarrero (ed.) *Priorización y desarrollo del sector agrario en el Perú*, Lima: Pontificia Universidad Católica del Perú and Fundación Friedrich Ebert.

DE JANVRY, A. (1981) *The Agrarian Question and Reformism in Latin America*, Baltimore, MD: Johns Hopkins University Press.

DEMERY, L. and T. ADDISON (1987) *The Alleviation of Poverty Under Structural Adjustment*, Washington, DC: World Bank.

DE SOTO, H. (1986) *El otro sendero*, Lima: Editorial El Barranco.

DEVELOPMENT DIALOGUE (1988) Special issue "The Laws of Life," C. Fowler, E. Lachkovics, P. Mooney, H. Shaud (eds.), Uppsala: Dag Hammersjöld Foundation.

DEVLIN, R. (1985) "La Deuda Externa vs. el Desarrollo Económico: América Latina en la Encrucijada" in *Colección Estudios CIEPLAN* 17 (September): 69–100.

DI FILIPPO, A. (1977) "Raíces históricas de las estructuras distributivas de la América Latina" in *Cuadernos de la CEPAL*, No. 18, Santiago.

——— (1981) *Desarrollo y desigualdad social en la América Latina. Ensayos*, Lecturas de El Trimestre Económico, No. 44, Mexico: Fondo de Cultura Económica.

——— (1987) "El deterioro de los términos de intercambio treinta y cinco años después" in *Pensamiento Iberoamericano: Revista de Economía Política* 11 (January–June): 357–383.

DÍAZ-ALEJANDRO, C. (1974) "Some Characteristics of Recent Export Expansion in Latin America," Yale Economic Growth Center Papers, No. 209.

——— (1975) "Trade Policies and Economic Development" in Ffrench-Davis (1981), vol. 1

——— (1976) *Foreign Trade Regimes and Economic Development: Colombia*, New York: NBER/Columbia University Press.

——— (1981) *Latin America in the 1980s*, New Haven, CT: Economic Growth Center, Yale University.

——— (1984) "Latin America in the 1930s" in R. Thorp (ed.) *Latin America in the 1930s: The Role of the Periphery in World Crisis*, New York: St. Martin's Press.

——— (1985) "Good-Bye Financial Repression, Hello Financial Crash" in *Journal of Development Economics* 19 (September–October): 1–24.

DOLLFUS, O. (1981) "El reto del espacio andino" in *Perú Problema 20*, Lima: Instituto de Estudios Peruanos.

DORINGER, P. B. and M. J. PIORE (1971) *Internal Labor Markets and Manpower Analysis*, Lexington, MA: Lexington Books.

DORNBUSCH, R. (1984) "Commentaries on Recent Experience in the Southern Cone" in Arditto-Barletta, Blejer, and Landau (1984).

—— (1985) "Policy and Performance Links between LDC Debtors and Industrial Nations" in *Brooking Papers on Economic Activity*, No. 2.

—— (1988) "Mexico: Stabilization, Debt and Growth," mimeo (April).

—— (1991) "Special Exchange Rates for Capital Account Transactions" in *Exchange Rates and Inflations*, Cambridge, MA: MIT Press.

DORNBUSCH, R. and S. EDWARDS (1989a) "Macroeconomic Populism in Latin America" in *National Bureau of Economic Research*, Working Paper Series No. 2986, Cambridge, MA.

—— (1989b) "Economic Crises and the Macroeconomics of Populism in Latin America: Lessons from Chile and Peru." Paper presented at the IASE meeting, March 30–April 1, 1989, Bogota, Colombia.

DORYAN, E. (1989) "¿Administrar el status-quo o desarrollar a Costa Rica?" in E. Rodríguez, *De cara al nuevo milenio*, San José: EUNED.

DOSI, G. (1981) *Structural Adjustment and Public Policy Under Conditions of Rapid Technical Change: The Semi-conductor Industry in Western Europe*, Brighton: University of Sussex Research Centre.

DUTT, A. (1984) "The Terms of Trade and Uneven Development: Implications of a Model of North-South Trade," mimeo, Florida International University (April).

ECLA (several years) *Serie distribución del ingreso*, Statistics and Quantitative Analysis Division.

—— (1950) *Economic Survey of Latin America, 1949*, New York: United Nations.

—— (1954a) *International Co-operation in Latin American Development Policy*, New York: United Nations.

—— (1954b) *El desarrollo Económico del Ecuador*, Mexico: United Nations.

—— (1956) "Some Aspects of the Inflationary Process in Chile" in *Economic Bulletin for Latin America* 1 (January): 45–53.

—— (1961) *Economic Development, Planning and International Cooperation* (June), United Nations.

—— (1962) "Inflation and Growth: A Summary of Experience in Latin America" in *Economic Bulletin for Latin America* 7 (February): 25–56.

—— (1963) *The Economic Development of Latin America in the Postwar Period*, Santiago.

—— (1966) "The Process of Industrial Development in Latin America." Presented at Simposio Latinoamericano de Industrialización, March 14–25, 1966, Santiago.

—— (1969) *América Latina: El Pensamiento de la CEPAL*, Santiago: Editorial Universitaria.

—— (1971) "Public Enterprises: Their Present Significance and Their Potential Development" in *Economic Bulletin for Latin America* 16 (First semester): 1–62.

—— (1972) "Las tareas de la política fiscal y tributaria a la luz de los problemas del desarrollo de América Latina" in Assael (1973).

—— (1975) "Population, Environment and Development: The Latin American Experience," *Economic Bulletin for Latin America* vol. XIX, Nos. 1 and 2, United Nations, New York.

—— (1976) *América Latina: Relación de precios de intercambio*, Santiago: ECLA.

—— (1979) "Analysis and Prospects: Latin American Industrial Development." Presented at Segunda conferencia latinoamericana de industrialización, September 1979, Cali.

—— (1980–1987) *Statistical Yearbook for Latin America and the Caribbean.*

—— (1982) *Report of the Regional Seminar on Metropolitanization and Environment*, Santiago.

ECLA/UNEP (1983) *Expansión de la frontera agropecuaria de América Latina*, Madrid: ECLA/CIFCA.

ECLAC (1984a) "Estabilización y Liberalización Económica en el Cono Sur" in *Estudios e Informes de CEPAL*, No. 38.

—— (1984b) "La superación de la pobreza: Una tarea urgente y posible." Documento del Proyecto Interinstitucional de Pobreza Crítica en América Latina patrocinado por Naciones Unidas/CEPAL, (May).

—— (1985) "Crisis and Development: The Present Situation and Future Prospect of Latin America and the Caribbean," vol. 3, Reunión de Expertos sobre Crisis y Desarrollo en América Latina y el Caribe Santiago, (April).

—— (1986) "Tres Ensayos sobre Inflación y Políticas de Estabilización" in *Estudios e Informes de CEPAL*, No. 64, Buenos Aires: ECLAC.

—— (1987a) *América Latina: Indices de comercio exterior, 1970–1984*, Santiago: ECLAC.

—— (1987b) *Integración e industrialización en América Latina: más allá del ajuste*, Santiago.

—— (1987c) "International Economic Relations and Regional Cooperation in Latin America and the Caribbean" in *Estudios e Informes de CEPAL*, No 63.

—— (1988a) *Economic Panorama of Latin America 1988* (September).

—— (1988b) "El desarrollo social en los años noventa: Principales opciones." Paper presented at Seminario sobre Opciones de Desarrollo Social para los Años 90, November 13–18, 1988, San José, Cesta Rica.

—— (1988c) "Preliminary Balance of the Latin American Economy 1988" in *Notas sobre la economía y el desarrollo*, No. 470/471 Santiago, (December).

—— (1988d) *Economic Survey of Latin America and the Caribbean: 1987*, Santiago: ECLAC.

—— (1989a) "La Deuda Social en América Latina y el Caribe" in *Notas sobre la economía y el desarrollo*, No. 472/473 (January–February).

—— (1989b) "The Dynamics of Social Deterioration in Latin America and the Caribbean in the 1980s." Paper presented to the Reunión Preparatoria Regional para el Octavo Congreso de las Naciones Unidas sobre la Prevención del Delito y Tratamiento del Delincuente, May 8–12, 1989, San José, Costa Rica.

—— (1989c) "Planificación y gestión del desarrollo en áreas de expansión de la frontera agropecuaria" in *Libros de la CEPAL*, No. 21.

—— (1989d) *Statistical Yearkbook of Latin America and the Caribbean, 1988*, United Nations.

—— (1990a) "Magnitud de la pobreza en América Latina en los años ochenta." Document presented to the Proyecto para la Superación de la Pobreza (sponsored by UNDP), Santiago.

—— (1990b) *Changing Production Patterns with Social Equity*, Santiago.

—— (1992), *Social Equity and Changing Production Patterns: An Integrated Approach*, Santiago, April.

ECLAC/UNIDO (1985) "Informe No. 1" in *Industrialización y desarrollo Tecnológico*, Santiago, (September).

ECLAC/UNIDO (1989) "Informe No. 6" in *Industrialización y desarrollo tecnológico* (June), Santiago.

ECLAC and JOINT ECLAC/UNEP DEVELOPMENT AND ENVIRONMENT UNIT (1989) "Crisis, deuda externa, políticas macroeconómicas y sus relaciones con el medio ambiente en América Latina y el Caribe." Reunión de Expertos de Alto Nivel Designados por los Gobiernos sobre Cooperación Regional en Asuntos Ambientales en América Latina y El Caribe, March 27–29, 1989, Brasilia, Brazil.

EDWARDS, S. (1984a) "The Order of Liberalization of the Current and Capital Accounts of the Balance of Payments" in *Essays in International Finance*, No. 156, Princeton, NJ: Princeton University.

——— (1984b) "The Order of Liberalization of the External Sector in Developing Countries," mimeo (June), Los Angeles, University of California and National Bureau of Economic Research.

ELSTER, J. (1984) *Ulysses and the Sirens: Studies in Rationality and Irrationality*, Cambridge-Paris: Cambridge University Press—Editions de la Maison des Sciences de L'Homme.

EMMANUEL, A. (1972) *Unequal Exchange*, New York: Monthly Review Press.

EVANS, D. (1987) "The Long-run Determinants of North-South Terms of Trade and some Recent Empirical Evidence" in *World Development* 15 (May): 657–671.

EVANS, D. and P. ALIZADEH (1984) "Trade, Industrialization and the Visible Hand" in *The Journal of Development Studies* 21 (October): 22–46.

FAJNZYLBER, F. (1983) *La Industrialización Trunca de América Latina*, Mexico: Editorial Nueva Imagen.

——— (1989a) "Industrialization in Latin America: From the 'Black Box' to the 'Empty Box'" in *Cuadernos de la CEPAL*, No. 60, Santiago: ECLAC.

——— (1989b) "Sobre la impostergable transformación productiva de América Latina," unpublished document.

FAO (1988) *Potencialidades del desarrollo agrícola y rural en América Latina* (Principal report and five annexes), Rome.

FEI, J. C. H. and G. RANIS (1961) "A Theory of Economic Development" in *American Economic Review* 51 (September): 533–565.

FEINBERG, R. and R. FFRENCH-DAVIS (eds.) (1988) *Development and External Debt in Latin America*, Notre Dame, IN: University of Notre Dame Press.

FELIPE-MORALES, C. (1987) "La erosión de los andenes en zonas pobladas de altura" in *Pensamiento Iberoamericano: Revista de Economía Política* 12 (July–December): 97–108.

FELIX, D. (1977) "Income Inequality in Mexico" in *Current History* (March): 111–114.

FFRENCH-DAVIS, R. (1974) "Mecanismos y objectivos de la redistribución del ingreso" in Foxley (1984).

——— (1979) *Economía internacional: teorías y políticas para el desarrollo*, Mexico: Fondo de Cultura Económica.

——— (ed.) (1981) *Intercambio y desarrollo*, Lecturas de El Trimestre Económico, No. 38, vols. 1 and 2, Mexico: Fondo de Cultura Económica.

——— (1982) "Foreign Trade, Industrialization and Development Policies" in R. Ffrench-Davis and E. Tironi (eds.) *Latin America and the New International Economic Order*, New York: MacMillan, Oxford, and St. Martin's Press.

——— (ed.) (1983) *Relaciones financieras externas. Su efecto en la economía latinoamericana*, Mexico: Fondo de Cultura Económica-CIEPLAN.

——— (1984) "Desarrollo y promoción de la producción: El rol del arancel selectivo" in *Estudios e Informes de la CEPAL*, No. 37, Santiago.

———— (1988) "An Outline of a Neo-structuralist Approach" in *CEPAL Review* 34 (April): 37–44.

———— (1989) "Ajuste y agricultura en la América Latina: Un examen de algunos temas" in *El Trimestre Económico* 51 (April–June): 377–406.

FFRENCH-DAVIS, R. and D. RACZYNSKI (1987) "The Impact of Global Recession and National Policies on Living Standards: Chile, 1973–1987" in *Notas técnicas CIEPLAN,* No. 97 (March).

FFRENCH-DAVIS, R. and M. MARFÁN (1988) "Selective Policies Under a Structural Foreign Exchange Shortage" in *Journal of Development Economics* 29 (November): 347–369, and *Notas Técnicas,* No. 126 (February 1989) Santiago: CIEPLAN.

FFRENCH-DAVIS, R. and O. MUÑOZ (1990) "Economic development and instability in Chile: 1950–89," Colección Estudios CIEPLAN 28 (June), and in S. Teitel (ed.) *A New Development Strategy for Latin America: Departures on Hirschman's Thought,* IDB/Johns Hopkins University Press, Baltimore, 1992.

FFRENCH-DAVIS, R. and O. MUÑOZ (1991) "The Latin American Economy from the 1950s to the 1980s," in P. Meller (ed.) *The Latin American Development Debate,* Westview Press, Boulder, and in Colección Estudios CIEPLAN 23, Santiago, March 1988.

FFRENCH-DAVIS, R. and J. VIAL (1991) "Trade Reforms in Chile" in *The World Bank Economic Review,* forthcoming.

FIELD, G. S. (1979) "Desigualdad y desarrollo ecónomico" in O. G. Muñoz (comp.) *Distribución del Ingreso en América Latina,* Buenos Aires: El CID Editor, S.A.

FIGUEROA, A. (1972) *Income Distribution, Employment and Development: The Case of Peru,* Nashville, TN: Vanderbilt University.

———— (1981) *La economía campesina de la sierra del Peru,* Lima: Pontificia Universidad Católica.

———— (1986a) "Producción y distribución en el Capitalismo subdesarrollado" in *Economía* 9 (June–December): 63–82, Lima. An approach centering more on agrarianism was presented at the international seminar, "La Agricultura Latinoamericana: Crisis, Transformaciones y Perspectivas," organized by GIA and CLACSO, September 1–4, 1988, Punta de Tralca, Chile.

———— (1986b) *Productividad y educación en la agricultura campesina de América Latina,* Rio de Janeiro: ECIEL Publication.

———— (1988) "Productividad agrícola y Crisis Económica" in *Economía* 11 (June–December): 9–34.

FINDLAY, R. (1980) "The Terms of Trade and Equilibrium Growth in the World Economy" in *American Economic Review* 70 (June): 291–299.

———— (1981) "The Fundamental Determinants of the Terms of Trade" in S. Grassman and E. Lündberg (eds.) *The World Economic Order: Past and Prospects,* London: Macmillan.

———— (1989) "North-South Models and the Evolution of Global Interdependence" in G. Calvo, R. Findlay, P. Kouri, and J. de Macedo (eds.) *Debt, Stabilization and Development: Essays in Memory of Carlos Díaz-Alejandro,* Oxford: Basil Blackwell.

FINDLAY, R. and H. GRUBERT (1959) "Factor Intensities, Technological Process and the Terms of Trade" in *Oxford Economic Papers* 11 (February): 111–121.

FISCHER, S. (1992) "Macroeconomic Stability and Growth," *Cuadernos de Economía* No. 87, August.

FISHER, A. C. and F. M. PETERSON (1976) "The Environment in Economics: A Survey" in *Journal of Economic Literature* 14 (March): 1–33.

FISHLOW, A. (1972) "Brazilian Size Distribution of Income (On the Emerging Problems of Development Policies)" in *The American Economic Review* 62 (May): 391–402.

———— (1985) "The State of Latin American Economics" in *Economic and Social Progress in Latin America* (1985 Report), Washington, DC: Inter-American Development Bank.

FOSTER, J. E. (1984) "On Economic Poverty: A Survey of Aggregate Measures" in *Advances in Econometrics* 3: 215–251.

FOXLEY, A. (1974) "Redistribución del consumo: efectos sobre la producción y el empleo" in *El Trimestre Económico* 41 (April–June): 327–355.

———— (1982) *Latin American Experiments in Neo-Conservative Economics*, Berkeley: California University Press.

———— (ed.) (1984) *Distribución del ingreso*, Lecturas del Trimestre Económico, No. 7, Mexico: Fondo de Cultura Ecónomica.

FOXLEY, A., E. ANINAT, and J. P. ARELLANO (1980) *Las desigualdades económicas y la acción del estado*, Mexico: Fondo de Cultura Económica.

FRANK, C. R., Jr., and R. C. WEBB (eds.) (1977) *Income Distribution and Growth in the Less-Developed Countries*, Washington, DC: The Brookings Institution.

FREEMAN, C. (1982) *The Economics of Industrial Innovation*, London: Frances Pinter.

FREEMAN, C., J. CLARK, and L. SOETE (1982) *Unemployment and Technical Innovation*, London: Frances Pinter.

FRENKEL, R. (1983) "La apertura financiera externa: el caso Argentino" in Ffrench-Davis (1983).

———— (1987) "Heterodox Theory and Policy: The Plan Austral in Argentina" in *Journal of Development Economics* 27 (September–October): 307–338.

FRENKEL, R. and J. M. FANELLI (1987) "El Plan Austral: Un año y medio después" in *El Trimestre Económico* 54, Special issue (September): 55–118.

FRIEDMAN, M. (1976) *Price Theory*, New York: McGraw Hill.

FRITSCH, W. (1986) "Latin America's Export Growth Imperative in the 1980s: Can the United States Help Achieve It?" in K. J. Middlebrook and C. Rico (eds.) *The United States and Latin America in the 1980s: Contending Perspectives on a Decade of Crisis*, Pittsburgh, PA: University of Pittsburgh Press.

———— (1989) "The New Minilateralism and the Developing Countries" in J. Schott (ed.) *Free Trade Areas and US Trade Policy*, Washington, DC: Institute for International Economics.

FRITSCH, W. and E. M. MODIANO (1988) "A restriçao externa ao crescimento económico brasileiro: uma perspectiva de longo prazo" in *Pesquisa e Planejamento Económico* 18 (August): 271–296.

FRITSCH, W. and G. H. B. FRANCO (1988a) "Investimento direto: tendencias globais e perspectivas para o Brasil," Texto para Discussao 195, Río de Janeiro: Departamento de Económía, PUC/RJ.

———— (1988b) "Foreign Direct Investment and Patterns of Industrialization and Trade in Developing Countries: Notes with Reference to the Brazilian Experience," Texto para Discussao 206, Río de Janeiro: Departamento de Economía, Pontificia Universidad Católica.

FUCARACCIO, A. et al. (1973) *Imperialismo y control de la población*, Buenos Aires: Ed. Periferia.

FURTADO, C. (1966) *Subdesarrollo y estancamiento en América Latina*, Buenos Aires: Edición Universitaria.

———— (1969a) *Um proyecto para o Brasil*, Rio de Janeiro: Editorial Saga.

––––––– (1969b) "Desarrollo y estancamiento en América Latina: un enfoque estructuralista" in A. Bianchi (ed.) *América Latina, ensayos de interpretación económica,* Santiago: Ed. Universitaria.

GALBRAITH, J. K. (1969) *The New Industrial State,* Harmondsworth, U.K.: Penguin.

GARCÍA, A. (1969) *Dinámica de las formas agrarias en la América Latina,* Santiago: ICIRA.

––––––– (1984) *Industrialización para el desarrollo equitativo,* serie monografías sobre empleo, No. 39, Santiago: PREALC/ISS.

GARCÍA, N. and M. MARFÁN (1981) *Incidencia indirecta de la industrialización latinoamericana sobre el empleo,* serie trabajos ocasionales, No. 38, Santiago: PREALC.

––––––– (1987) *Estructuras industriales y eslabonamientos de empleo,* Mexico: PREALC/Fondo de Cultura Económica.

GARCÍA HURTADO, A. and E. GARCÍA D'ACUÑA (1980) "Las variables ambientales en la planificación del desarrollo" in Sunkel and Gligo (1981).

GARCÍA-ROCHA (1986) *La desigualdad económica,* Mexico: El Colegio de México.

GEISSE, G. and F. SABATINI (1981) "Renta de la tierra, heterogeneidad urbana y medio ambiente" in Sunkel and Gligo (1981).

GELLER, L. (1970) "El crecimiento industrial argentino hasta 1914 y la teoría del bien primario exportable" in *El Trimestre Económico* 37 (October–December): 763–811.

GEORGESCU-ROEGEN, N. (1975) "Energy and Economic Myths" in *Southern Economic Journal* 11 (January): 347–381.

GERSCHENKRON, A. (1965) *Economic Backwardness in Historical Perspective,* New York: Praeger.

GIDDENS, A. (1982) *Profiles and Critiques in Social Theory,* London: Macmillan.

GLIGO, N. (1981) *Estilos de desarrollo, modernización y medio ambiente en la agricultura latinoamericana,* serie estudios e informes, No. 4, Santiago: CEPAL.

––––––– (1986a) *Agricultura y medio ambiente en América Latina,* San José: Ediciones SIAP/EDUCA.

––––––– (1986b) "Naturaleza y crecimiento, ambiente y desarrollo: El salto cualitativo" in *Ambiente y Desarrollo* 2 (May): 9–14, Santiago.

GLIGO N. and J. MORELLO (1980) "Notas sobre la historia ecológica de América Latina" in *Revista de Estudios Internacionales* 49 (January–March): 112–148.

GOLD, B. (1971) *Explorations in Managerial Economics,* New York: Basic Books.

––––––– (1979) *Productivity, Technology and Capital,* Lexington, MA: Lexington Books.

GONZÁLES DE OLARTE, E. (1984) *Economía de comunidad campesina,* Lima: Instituto de Estudios Peruanos.

GRACIANO DA SILVA, J. (1981) *Progresso técnico e relaçoes de trabalho na agricultura,* São Paulo: Editora Hucitec.

GRACIARENA, J. (1983) "La industrialización como desarrollo. Políticas industrializadoras, orden social y estilos neoliberales" in *El Trimestre Económico* 50 (July–September).

GRAHAM, D., D. ADAMS, and J. D. PISCHKE (1984) *Undermining Rural Development with Cheap Credit,* Boulder, CO: Westview Press.

GREENAWAY, D. and P. K. M. THARAKAN (eds.) (1986) *Imperfect Competition and International Trade: Policy Aspects of Intra-Industry Trade,* Sussex, England: Wheatsheaf Books.

GRIFFITH-JONES, S. (ed.) (1988) *Managing World Debt,* Sussex, England: Wheatsheaf Books; New York: St. Martin's Press.

GRIFFITH-JONES, S. and O. SUNKEL (1986) *Debt and Development Crises in Latin America: The End of an Illusion,* Oxford: Oxford University Press.

GRILLI, E. and H. YANG (1988) "Primary Commodity Prices, Manufactured Goods Prices, and the Terms of Trade of Developing Countries: What the Long-run Shows" in *The World Bank Economic Review* 2: 1–47.

GROSSMAN, G. M. and E. HELPMAN (1989) "Growth and Welfare in a Small Open Economy" in *National Bureau of Economic Research,* Working Paper Series No. 2970, Cambridge, MA.

GUNDER FRANK, A. (1969) *Capitalism and Underdevelopment in Latin America: Studies of Chile and Brazil,* New York: Monthly Review Press.

GURRIERI, A. (1980) *La Obra de Prebisch en la CEPAL,* Mexico: Fondo de Cultura Económica.

HAHN, F. (1973) "On Optimum Taxation," *Journal of Economic Theory* 6, No. 1.

HARBERGER, A. C. (1985) "Observations on the Chilean Economy, 1973–1983" in *Economic Development and Cultural Change* 33 (April): 451–462.

HELLEINER, G. (ed.) (1982) *Economic Theory and North-South Negotiations,* Toronto: University of Toronto Press.

———— (1988) "Primary Commodity Markets: Recent Trends and Research Requirements" in K. A. Elliot and J. Williamson (eds.) *World Economic Problems,* Washington, DC: Institute for International Economics.

HELLER, P. S. et al. (1988) "The Implication of Fund-Supported Adjustment Programs for Poverty. Experiences in Selected Countries" in *Occasional Paper No. 58,* Washington, DC: IMF.

HEMMING, R. and A. M. MANSOOR (1988) "Privatization and Public Enterprises" in *Occasional Paper No. 56,* Washington, DC: IMF

HERRERA, A. et al. (1971) *Catástrofe o nueva sociedad? Modelo mundial latinoamericano,* Fundación Bariloche, Bogotá: Centro Internacional de Investigaciones para el Desarrollo.

HERRERA, J. and C. VIGNOLO (1981) *El Desarrollo de la Industria del Cobre y las Empresas Transnacionales: la Experiencia de Chile* (April), mimeo, ECLA.

HEYMANN, D. (1986) "Inflation and Stabilization Policies" in *CEPAL Review* 28 (April): 67–97.

HIRSCHMAN, A. (1958) *The Strategy of Economic Development,* New Haven, CT: Yale University Press.

———— (ed.) (1961) *Latin American Issues,* New York: The Twentieth Century Fund.

———— (1968) "The Political Economy of Import-Substituting Industrialisation in Latin America" in *The Quarterly Journal of Economics* 82 (February): 1–32.

———— (1971) *A Bias for Hope: Essays on Development and Latin America,* New Haven, CT: Yale University Press.

———— (1981) "The Social and Political Matrix of Inflation: Elaborations on the Latin American Experience" in A. Hirschman *Essays in Trespassing: Economics to Politics and Beyond,* Cambridge, MA: Cambridge University Press.

HOFFMAN, K. and R. KAPLINSKY (1988) *Driving Force: The Global Restructuring of Technology, Labour and Investment in the Automobile Components Industries,* Boulder, CO and London: Westview Press.

HYMER, S. (1976) *The International Operations of National Firms: A Study of Direct Foreign Investment,* Cambridge, MA: MIT Press.

IBARRA, D. (1987) "Política y Economía en América Latina: el trasfondo de los programas heterodoxos de estabilización" in *Estudios Económicos*, Special issue (October): 13–38, Mexico: El Colegio de México.

IDB (1986) *Economic and Social Progress in Latin America, 1986 Report*, Washington, DC.

IGLESIAS, E. V. (1981) "Development and Equity: the Challenge of the 1980s" in *CEPAL Review* 15 (December): 9–46.

ILO (International Labour Office) (1970) *Hacia el pleno empleo*, Geneva: ILO.

——— (1972) *Employment, Incomes and Equality. A Strategy for Increasing Productive Employment in Kenya*, Geneva: ILO.

——— (1975) *Generación de empleo productivo y crecimiento económico. El caso de la República Dominicana*, Geneva: ILO.

——— (1987). *World Labour Report 1987*, Geneva.

——— (1989) *Recuperación Económica y Empleo*, Geneva: ILO

IMF (1988) *IFS Supplement on Trade Statistics*, No. 15.

JEWKES, J., D. SAWERS, and R. STILLERMAN (1958) *The Sources of Invention*, London: Macmillan.

JOHNSON, H. (1954) "Increasing Productivity, Income-price Trends and the Trade Balance" in H. Johnson (1967) *International Trade and Economic Growth*, Cambridge, MA: Harvard University Press.

——— (1965) "Optimal Trade Intervention in the Presence of Domestic Distortions" in Baldwin et al. *Trade, Growth and the Balance of Payments*, Amsterdam: North Holland, and in Ffrench-Davis (1981).

JOINT DEVELOPMENT COMMITTEE (1987) *Protecting the Poor During Periods of Adjustment*, Washington, DC: World Bank and IMF.

JONES, L. and I. SAKONG (1980) *Government, Business, and Entrepreneurship in Economic Development: The Korean Case*, Cambridge, MA: Harvard University Press.

JUNAC (1981) "Orientaciones para la elaboración del arancel externo común en el Grupo Andino" in Ffrench-Davis (1981).

KALDOR, N. (1972) "The Irrelevance of Equilibrium Economics" in *Economic Journal* 82 (December): 1237–1255. Reprinted in N. Kaldor (1978) *Further Essays in Economic Theory*, London: Duckworth.

——— (1975) "What is Wrong With Economic Theory?" in *Quarterly Journal of Economics* 89 (August): 347–357.

——— (1976) "Capitalismo y desarrollo industrial: algunas lecciones de la experiencia británica" in C. Díaz-Alejandro, C. Teitel, and V. Tokman *Política económica en centro y periferia*, Lecturas No. 16, Mexico: Fondo de Cultura Económica.

——— (1979) "Equilibrium Theory and Growth Theory" in M. J. Boskin (ed.) *Economics and Human Welfare: Essays in Honor of Tibor Scitovsky*, New York: Academic Press.

KAMIEN, M. I. and N. L. SCHWARTZ (1982) *Market Structure and Innovation*, Cambridge: Cambridge University Press.

KATZ, J. (1976) *Importación de tecnología, aprendizaje e industrialización dependiente*, Mexico: Fondo de Cultura Económica.

——— (1980) "Domestic Technology Generation in LDC's: A Review of Research Findings," IDB/ECLAC Research Programme on Scientific and Technological Development in Latin America, Working Paper No. 35.

KATZMAN, M. (1975) "The Brazilian Frontier in Comparative Perspective" in *Comparative Studies in Society and History* 17: 266–288.

KAY, C. (1989) *Latin American Theories of Development and Underdevelopment*, London and New York: Routledge Press.

KAY, J. A. (1987) "The State and the Market: The UK Experience of Privatization" in *Group of Thirty, Occasional Papers No. 23*, New York–London, p. 8.

KAY, J. A. and D. J. THOMPSON (1986) "Privatization: A Policy in Search of a Rationale" in *Economic Journal* 96 (March): 18–32.

KIERZKOWSKI, H. (ed.) (1984) *Monopolistic Competition and International Trade*, Oxford: Clarendon Press.

KIGUEL, M. and I. WOOTON (1985) "Tariff Policy and Equilibrium Growth in the World Economy" in *Journal of Development Economics* 19 (September–October): 187–198.

KIGUEL, M. and N. LIVIATAN (1988) "Inflationary Rigidities and Orthodox Stabilization Policies: Lessons from Latin America" in *The World Bank Economic Review* 2 (September): 273–298.

KINDLEBERGER, C. (1978) *Manias, Panics and Crashes*, New York: Basic Books.

KLIKSBERG, B. (1988) "Cómo transformar el Estado: Un enfoque del problema," mimeo, MIDEPLAN, 25th anniversary, San José, Costa Rica.

———— (1989) "¿Cómo formar gerentes sociales? Elementos para el diseño de estrategias" in *Revista Internacional de Ciencias Administrativas* 56 (March): 231–247.

KNEESE, A. et al. (1970) "Economics and the Environment: A Material Balance Approach" in *Resources for the Future*.

KONDRATIEFF, N. D. (1944) "The Long Waves in Economic Life," in *Reading Business Cycle Theory*, The American Economic Association, Philadelphia, The Blakiston Co.

KOOLEN, R. (1986) "La organización institucional del Estado en relación con la incorporación de la dimensión ambiental en la planificación del desarrollo" in CEPAL/ILPES/PNUMA *La dimensión ambiental en la planificación del desarrollo*, Buenos Aires: Grupo Editor Latinamericano.

KOWARICK, L. (1981) "El precio del progreso: crecimiento económico, expoliación urbana y la cuestión del medio ambiente" in Sunkel and Gligo (1981).

KRUEGER, A. (1978) *Foreign Trade Regimes and Economic Development: Liberalization Attempts and Consequences*, Cambridge, MA: Ballinger Press.

———— (1981) "Interactions Between Inflation and Trade Regime Objectives in Stabilization Programs" in W. Cline and S. Weintraub (eds.) *Economic Stabilization in Developing Countries*, Washington, DC: The Brookings Institution.

———— (1984a) "Trade Policies in Developing Countries" in R. W. Jones and P. B. Kenen (eds.) *Handbook of International Economics* 1, Amsterdam: North Holland.

———— (1984b) "Comparative Advantage and Development Policy 20 Years Later" in M. Syrquin, L. Taylor, and L. E. Westphal (eds.) *Economic Structure and Performance: Essays in Honor of Hollis B. Chenery*, San Diego: Academic Press.

KRUGMAN, P. (ed.) (1986) *Strategic Trade Policy and the New International Economics*, Cambridge, MA: MIT Press.

———— (1987) "Is Free Trade Passé?" in *Journal of Economic Perspectives* 1 (Fall): 131–144.

———— (1989) "New trade theory and the less developed countries," in G. Calvo, et al. *Debt, Stabilization and Development*, Oxford: Basil Blackwell Ltd.

KUHN, T. S. (1970) *The Structure of Scientific Revolutions*, Chicago: Chicago University Press.

KUZNETS, S. (1930) *Secular Movements in Production and Prices*, Boston: Houghton-Mifflin.

—— (1940) "Schumpeter's Business Cycles" in *American Economic Review* 3 (June): 257–271.

—— (1955) "Economic Growth and Income Inequality" in *American Economic Review* 45 (March): 1–28.

—— (1957) "Quantitative Apects of the Economic Growth of Nations: II. Industrial Distribution of National Product and Labour Force" in *Economic Development and Cultural Change* 5, Supplement (July): 3–111.

—— (1966) *Modern Economic Growth*, New Haven, CT: Yale University Press.

LAHERA, E. (1986) "Quince años de la Decisión 24. Evaluación y perspectivas" in *Notas Técnicas CIEPLAN*, No. 82.

LAL, D. (1983) *The Poverty of Development Economics*, Hobart Paperback, 16, London: Institute of Economic Affairs.

LALL, S. (1980) *The Multinational Corporation*, London: Macmillan.

LANGONI, C. G. (1973) *Distribuçao da renda e desenvolvimento económico do Brasil*, Rio de Janeiro: Editoria Expressao e Cultura.

LAVADOS, J. (1983) "La evolución de la política científica y tecnológica en América latina" in I. Lavados (ed.) *El Rol del Estado en el Desarrollo Científico y Tecnológico en América Latina*, Serie Documentos de Trabajo, Special issue, Santiago: Corporación de Promoción Universitaria.

LEIBENSTEIN, H. (1966) "Allocative Efficiency Versus X Efficiency" in *American Economic Review* 6 (June): 392–415.

LEIJONHUFVUD, A. (1968) *On Keynesian Economics and the Economics of Keynes*, London: Oxford University Press.

LEWIS, W. A. (1954) "Economic Development with Unlimited Supplies of Labour" in *The Manchester School of Economics and Social Studies* 22 (May): 139–191.

—— (1955) *The Theory of Economic Growth*, London: Allen and Unwin.

—— (1964) "Closing Remarks" in Baer and Kerstenetzky (1964).

—— (1977) *The Evolution of the International Economic Order*, Princeton, NJ: Princeton University Press.

LIPSEY, R. (1991) "Getting There: The Path to an Hemispheric Free Trade Area." Contribution to Overseas Development Council Project: U.S. Latin American Relations in the 1990s, mimeo.

LIPSEY, R. and K. LANCASTER (1957) "The General Theory of the Second Best" in *Review of Economic Studies* 24 (March): 11–32.

LITTLE, I., T. SCITOVSKY, and M. SCOTT (1970) *Industry and Trade in Some Developing Countries: A Comparative Study*, Oxford: Oxford University Press.

LOPES, F. (1984) "Inflaçao inercial, hiperinflaçao e desinflaçao: Nota de conjectura" in *Revista de ANPEC*, No. 9, Rio de Janeiro.

LÓPEZ CORDOVEZ, L. (1985) "Transformaciones, tendencias y perspectivas" in *Pensamiento Iberoamericano: Revista de Economia Política* 8 (July–December): 15–35.

LUSTIG, N. (1981) *Distribución del Ingreso y Crecimiento en México. Un Análisis de las Ideas Estructuralistas*, Mexico: El Colegio de México.

—— (1984) "La desigual distribución del ingreso y la riqueza" in R. Cordera and C. Tello (comps.) *La desigualdad en México*, Mexico: Siglo Veintiuno.

—— (1988a) "Del estructuralismo al neoestructuralismo: La búsqueda de un paradigma heterodoxo" in *Colección Estudios CIEPLAN* 23, Special issue (March): 35–50. Reprinted in English in P. Meller (ed.) (1991) *The Latin American Development Debate: Neostructuralism, Neomonetarism and Adjustment Processes*, Boulder, CO: Westview Press.

—— (1988b) "Crisis económica y nivel de vida" in *Estudios Económicos* 2 (July–December): 227–249, Mexico: El Colegio de México.

—— (1989a) "Políticas de estabilización, nivel de actividad, salarios reales y empleo: Argentina, Brasil, México y Perú en los ochentas," mimeo, Washington, DC: The Brookings Institution.

—— (1989b) "The Impact of the Economic Crisis on Living Standards in Mexico: 1982–1985" in *Brookings Discussion Papers* (July), Washington, DC: The Brookings Institution.

LYDALL, H. (1977) *Income Distribution During the Process of Development,* Income Distribution and Employment Programme, Working Paper 52, Geneva: ILO.

MACEDO, R. (1987) "La infancia en Brasil y la crisis económica: Situación del estado de Sao Paulo" in G. A. Cornia, R. Jolly, and F. Stewart (eds.) *Ajuste con Rostro Humano: Estudio de Países* 2, Madrid: Siglo Veintiuno de España Editores S.A.

MACHADO, A. and J. TORRES (1987) *El sistema agroalimentario. Una visión integral de la cuestión agraria en América Latina,* Bogota: Editorial Siglo Veintiuno.

MACHADO, F. M. (1988) "¿Cómo aumentar la efectividad del desarrollo tecnológico en América Latina: los sistemas nacionales y de cooperación regional de gestión tecnológica," mimeo, San José.

—— (1989) "¿Gestores tecnológicos o emprendedores de origen técnico?: fragmentación y contexto de la gestión tecnológica y su impacto en la formación de recursos humanos." Presented at the Third Latin American Technological Management Seminar, Buenos Aires: ALTEC.

MACHADO, F. M. and E. DORYAN (1989) "La gestión tecnológica como hilo conductor de la reconversión industrial: conceptos básicos y la experiencia de Costa Rica," mimeo, Ministerio de Ciencia y tecnología, San José.

MACHINEA, J. and J. FANELLI (1988) "El Control de la Hiperinflación: El caso del Plan Austral 1985–1987" in Bruno et al. (1988).

MACHLUP, F. (1967) "Theories of the Firm: Marginalist, Behavioral and Managerial" in *American Economic Review* 57 (March): 1–33.

MAIZELS, A. (1987) "Commodities in Crisis: An Overview of the Main Issues" in *World Development* 15 (May): 537–549.

MALLOY, J. (ed.) (1976) *Authoritarianism and Corporatism in Latin America,* Pittsburgh, PA: Pittsburgh University Press.

MANDELBAUM, K. (1945) *The Industrialization of Backward Areas,* Oxford: Basil Blackwell.

MANSFIELD, E. (1968a) *Industrial Research and Technological Innovation,* London: Norton.

—— (1968b) *The Economics of Technological Change,* London: Norton.

MANSFIELD, E., J. RAPOPORT, A. ROMEO, S. WAGNER, and G. BEARDSLEY (1977) "Social and Private Rates of Return from Industrial Innovation" in *Quarterly Journal of Economics* 91 (May): 221–240.

MANSILLA, M. C. F. (1981) "Metas de desarrollo y problemas ecológicos en América Latina" in *Cuadernos de la Sociedad Venezolana de Planificación,* Nos. 150–152, Caracas, Venezuela.

MARCEL, M. (1989) "La Privatización de Empresas Públicas en Chile 1985–1988" in *Notas Técnicas de CIEPLAN,* No. 125 (January).

MARFÁN, M. (1985) "El conflicto entre la recaudación de impuestos y la inversión privada: elementos teóricos para una reforma tributaria" in *Colección Estudios CIEPLAN* 18 (December): 63–93.

MARRIS, S. (1989) *Deficits and the Dollar: The World Economy at Risk,* Washington, DC: Institute for International Economics.

MARTIN, J. M. F. (1988) "Eficiencia Global de la Economía: Interacción de los Sectores Público y Privado" in Encuentro Regional CLAD-ILPES-INAP, *Reestructuración Económica: Perspectivas de la Intervención Estatal y Nuevas Políticas de Empresas Públicas,* Mexico (April).

MARTÍNEZ ALLIER, J. (1987) "Economía y ecología: Cuestiones fundamentales" in *Pensamiento Iberoamericano: Revista de Economía Política* 12 (July–December): 41–60.

MASSAD, C. and R. ZAHLER (eds.) (1988) *Deuda interna y estabilidad financiera,* Buenos Aires: Grupo Editor Latinoamericano.

MCCLOSKEY, D. N. (1986) *The Rhetoric of Economics,* Hemel Hempstead: Harvester Press.

MCKINNON, R. (1973) *Money and Capital in Economic Development,* Washington, DC: The Brookings Institution.

———— (1979a) "Foreign Trade Regimes and Economic Development: A Review Article" in *Journal of International Economics* 9 (August): 429–452.

———— (1979b) "Represión financiera y el problema de la liberalización dentro de los países menos desarrollados" in *Cuadernos de Economía* 47 (April): 3–22. Reprinted in *The Past and Prospects of the World Economic Order,* London: MacMillan Press.

———— (1988) "Financial Liberalization and Economic Development," Occasional Paper No. 6, San Francisco: International Center for Economic Growth.

MEADOWS, D., D. L. MEADOWS, J. RANDERS, and W. BEHRENS (1972) *Los límites del crecimiento. Informe al Club de Roma sobre el predicamento de la humanidad,* Mexico: Fondo de Cultura Económica.

MEIER, G. and D. SEERS (1984) *Pioneers of Economic Development,* Oxford: Oxford University Press.

MELLAFE, R. (1973) "Frontera agraria; el caso del virreinato peruano en el siglo XVI" in *Tierras Nuevas:* 11–42, Mexico: El Colegio de México.

MELLER, P. (1989) "Críticas y sugerencias en torno a la (eventual) doble condicionalidad del FMI y del Banco Mundial" in *Notas Técnicas CIEPLAN,* No. 128.

MELNICK, S. (1981) "Principales escuelas, tendencias y corrientes de pensamiento" in Sunkel and Gligo (1981).

MESAROVIC, M. and E. PESTEL (1975) *Estrategia de la sobrevivencia: crecimiento orgánico,* Mexico: Fondo de Cultura Económica.

MEZZERA, J. (1984) "Medición del empleo urbano" in *Socialismo y Participación* (September), Lima: Ediciones Socialismo y Participación.

MEZZERA, J. and D. CARBONETTO (1983) *Informe final del Proyecto de Empleo en el SIU,* Caracas: Proyecto OIT.

MITCHEL, D. and D. RONALD (1987) "Market Behavior of Grain Exporters" in *The World Bank Research Observer* 2 (January): 3–21.

MODIANO, E. (1987) "El Plan Cruzado: bases teóricas y limitaciones prácticas" in *El Trimestre Económico* 54, Special issue (September): 223–250.

———— (1988) "El primer intento del Cruzado. El Programa brasileño de estabilización de febrero de 1986" in Bruno et al. (1988).

MORALES, J. (1988) "La inflación y la estabilización en Bolivia" in Bruno et al. (1988).

MOVAREC, M. (1982) "Exports of Latin American Manufactures to the Centres: Their Magnitude and Significance" in *CEPAL Review* 17 (August): 47–77.

MUELLER, C. (1983) "El estado y la expansión de la frontera agrícola en la Amazonia" in ECLA/UNEP (1983).

MUÑOZ, O. (1977) "Estado e industrialización en el ciclo de expansión del salitre" in *Estudios CIEPLAN*, No. 6.

—— (ed.) (1979) *Distribución del ingreso en América Latina*, Buenos Aires: El CID Editor, S.A.

—— (1986) *Chile y su industrialización: pasado, crisis y opciones*, Santiago: Ediciones CIEPLAN.

—— (1988) "El estado y los empresarios: Experiencias comparadas y sus implicaciones para Chile" in *Colección Estudios CIEPLAN* 25 (December): 5–53.

MUÑOZ, O. and H. ORTEGA (1988) "La agricultura y la política económica chilena 1974–86" in *Investigación Agraria: Economía* 3, No. 1, (June): 19–34.

MUSGROVE, P. (1978) *Consumer Behavior in Latin America: Income and Spending of Families in Ten Andean Cities*, Washington, DC: The Brookings Institution.

NADAL EGEA, A. and C. SALAS PÁEZ (1988) *Bibliografía sobre el análisis económico del cambio técnico*, Mexico: El Colegio de México.

NAVARRETE, I. (1960) *La distribución del ingreso y el desarrollo económico de México*, Mexico: UNAM.

NELSON, M. (1973) *The Development of Tropical Lands: Policy Issues in Latin America*, Baltimore, MD: Johns Hopkins University Press.

NELSON, R. R. (1971) "Issues and Suggestions for the Study of Industrial Organization in a Regime of Rapid Technical Change," Discussion Paper No. 103, Yale University Economic Growth Center.

—— (1977) *The Moon and the Ghetto: An Essay on Public Policy Analysis*, New York: Norton.

NELSON, R. R. and S. G. WINTER (1974) "Neoclassical and Evolutionary Theories: Critique and Prospectus" in *Economic Journal* 84 (December): 886–905.

—— (1976) "In Search of a Useful Theory of Innovation" in K. Stroetmann (ed.) *Innovation, Economic Change and Technology Policies*, Basel and Stuttgart: Birkhäuser Verlag.

—— (1982) "The Schumpeterian Trade-off Revisited" in *American Economic Review* 72 (March): 114–132.

NORTH, D. (1984) "Three Approaches to the Study of Institutions" in Colander (1984).

NOYOLA, J. (1956) "El desarrollo económico y la inflación en México y en otros países latinoamericanos" in *Investigación Económica* 16 (4th Trimester): 603–648.

NOZICK, R. (1974) *Anarchy, State and Utopia*, New York: Basic Books.

NURKSE, R. (1953a) *Patterns of Trade and Development*, Oxford: Basil Blackwell.

—— (1953b) *Problems of Capital Formation in Underdeveloped Countries*, New York: Oxford University Press.

O'DONNELL, G. (1978) "Reflections on the Patterns of Change in the Bureaucratic-Authoritarian State" in *Latin American Research Review* 13: 3–38.

—— (1982) *El estado burocrático autoritario, 1966–1973. Triunfos, derrotas y crisis*, Buenos Aires: Editorial Belgrano.

OCAMPO, J. A. (1986) "New Developments in Trade Theory and LDC's" in *Journal of Development Economics* 22 (June): 129–170.

—— (1987) "Una evaluación comparativa de cuatro planes antiinflacionarios recientes" in *El Trimestre Económico* 54, Special issue (September): 7–54.

ODUM, E. (1971) *Fundamentals of Ecology*, Philadelphia: Saunders Co.

OECD (1986) "Science, Technology and Competitiveness" in *STI Review*, No. 1 (Autumn): 85–129.

OLIVERA, J. (1972) "Inflación y rezagos fiscales" in *Revista de Ciencias Económicas.*

OLSON, M. (1982) *The Rise and Decline of Nations: Economic Growth, Stagflation and Social Rigidities,* New Haven, CT and London: Yale University Press.

ORTEGA, E. (1985) "La opción campesina en las estrategias agrícolas" in *Pensamiento Iberoamericano: Revista de Economía Política* 8 (July–December): 97–108.

PACK, H. and L. E. WESTPHAL (1986) "Industrial Strategy and Technological Change: Theory Versus Reality" in *Journal of Development Economics* 22 (June): 87–128.

PALMA, G. (1978) "Dependency: A Formal Theory of Underdevelopment or a Methodology for the Analysis of Concrete Situations of Underdevelopment" in *World Development* 6 (July–August): 881–924.

PAPANEK, G. (1981) "Comments" in W. Cline and S. Weintraub (eds.) *Economic Stabilization in Developing Countries,* Washington, DC: The Brookings Institution.

PAPANEK, G. and O. KYN (1986) "The Effect on Income Distribution of Development, the Growth Rate, and Economic Strategy" in *Journal of Development Economics* 23 (September): 55–65.

PAROT, R., M. RODRIGUEZ, and D. SCHYDLOWSKY (1988) "IMF Backed Stabilization and Growth: An Inductive Study Based on the Costa Rican Case," mimeo, Boston University Center for Latin American Development Studies.

PASINETTI, L. L. (1981) *Structural Change and Economic Growth,* Cambridge: Cambridge University Press.

PATINKIN, D. (1956) *Money, Interest and Prices: An Integration of Monetary and Value Theory,* New York: Row Peterson.

PAUL, J. (ed.) (1982) *Reading Nozick: Essays on Anarchy, State and Utopia,* Oxford: Basil Blackwell.

PAZOS, F. (1969) *Medidas para detener la inflación crónica en América Latina,* Mexico: CEMLA.

PECK, M. J. and R. WILSON (1981) "Innovation, Imitation and Comparative Advantage: The Case of the Consumer Electronics Industry" in H. Giersch (ed.) *Proceedings of Conference on Emerging Technology at Kiel Institute of World Economics,* Tubingen: J. C. B. Mohr.

PENSAMIENTO IBEROAMERICANO: REVISTA DE ECONOMIA POLITICA (1986) "Inflación: Aceleración y Contención," No. 9 (January–June), Madrid, Spain.

—— (1987) "Medio ambiente, deterioro y recuperación," No. 12 (July–December).

—— (1988) "Transición y Perspectivas de la Democracia en Iberoamérica," No. 14 (July–December), Madrid, Spain.

PÉREZ, C. (1985) "Microelectronics, Long Waves and World Structural Change: New Perspectives for Developing Countries" in *World Development* 13 (March): 441–463.

—— (1988a) "The Institutional Implications of the Present Wave of Technical Change for Developing Countries," mimeo, World Bank Seminar on Technology and Long Term Economic Growth Prospects, Washington, DC (November).

—— (1988b) "Tendencias de la industria mundial: nuevos elementos de la competitividad." Texto Conferencia en Seminario Estrategia Industrial Proyecto Fomento ONUDI, August 1988, Caracas.

PÉREZ SALGADO, I. and B. KLIKSBERG (1985) "Políticas de gestión Pública:

El Rol del Estado en la Presente Situación de América Latina y el Caribe" in *Revista Internacional de Ciencias Administrativas* 51, No. 3.

PERU, MINISTERIO DE AGRICULTURA (1980) *Comunidades campesinas del Perú*, Lima.

PFEFFERMANN, G. and R. WEBB (1979) "The Distribution of Income in Brazil" in *Working Paper No. 356* (September), Washington, DC: World Bank.

PINSTRUP-ANDERSEN, P. (1987) "Intervenciones en materia de nutrición" in G. A. Cornia, R. Jolly, and F. Stewart (eds.) *Ajuste con Rostro Humano: Protección de los grupos vulnerables y promoción del crecimiento* 1, Madrid: Siglo Veintiuno de España Editores S.A.

PINTO, A. (1961) "El análisis de la inflación, estructuralistas y monetaristas: un recuento" in *Revista de Economía Latinoamericana* 4 (October–December): 71–95, Caracas.

—— (1965) "Concentración del progreso técnico y de sus frutos en el desarrollo latinoamericano" in *El Trimestre Económico* 32 (January–March): 3–69.

—— (1970) "Naturaleza e implicaciones de la heterogeneidad estructural de la América Latina" in *El Trimestre Económico* 37 (January–March): 83–100.

—— (1974) "El modelo de desarrollo reciente en América Latina" in J. Serra (1974) *Desarrollo Latinoamericano: Ensayos Críticos*, Lectura 6, Mexico: Fondo de Cultura Económica.

—— (1987) "La ofensiva contra el Estado-económico en Chile" in *Colección Estudios CIEPLAN* 21 (June): 117–127.

PINTO DE LA PIEDRA, M. (1988) "El componente social del ajuste económico en América Latina," mimeo, UN/ECLAC (May).

PIÑERA, S. (1979) "Se benefician los pobres del crecimiento económico?" in P. Franco (coord.) (1982) *Pobreza, Necesidades Básicas y Desarrollo* (June), ECLAC/ILPES/UNICEF.

PIORE, M. J. and C. SABEL (1984) *The Second Industrial Divide: Possibilities for Prosperity*, New York: Basic Books.

PORTER, R. (1986) "Competition in Global Industries: A Conceptual Framework" in M. Porter (ed.), *Competition in Global Industries*, Boston, MA: Harvard Business School.

PORTES, A. and S. SASSEN-KOOB (1987) "Making it Underground: Comparative Material on the Informal Sector in Western Market Economies" in *American Journal of Sociology* (July).

PREALC (1978) *Sector informal: Funcionamiento y políticas*, Santiago: PREALC/ILO.

—— (1988) *Política Económica y Actores Sociales. La concertación de Ingresos y Empleo*, Santiago: ILO.

PREALC-ILO (1975) *El problema del empleo en América Latina y el Caribe: Situación, perspectivas y políticas*, Santiago: PREALC.

—— (1988a) *Meeting the Social Debt*, Santiago.

—— (1988b) *Uruguay: Los Desafíos del Crecimiento Equitativo*, Documento de Trabajo (November), Montevideo, Uruguay.

PREBISCH, R. (1950a) *The Economic Development of Latin America and its Principal Problems*, New York: United Nations.

—— (1950b) *Theoretical and Practical Problems of Economic Growth*, Mexico: United Nations.

—— (1951) *Interpretación del proceso de desarrollo latinoamericano en 1949*, Santiago: ECLA.

—— (1959) "Commercial Policy in the Underdeveloped Countries" in *American Economic Review* 49 (Papers and proceedings) (May): 251–273.

———— (1961) "Economic Development or Monetary Stability: The False Dilemma" in *Economic Bulletin for Latin America* 6 (March): 1–26.

———— (1962) "The Economic Development of Latin America and its Principal Problems" in *Economic Bulletin for Latin America* 7 (February): 1–22.

———— (1963) *Hacia una dinámica del desarrollo latinoamericano,* Mexico: Fondo de Cultura Económica.

———— (1970) *Change and Development: Latin America's Great Task.* Report submitted to the Inter-American Development Bank, New York: Praeger.

———— (1976) "A Critique of Peripheral Capitalism" in *CEPAL Review* 1 (First Semester): 9–76.

———— (1977) "En torno a las ideas de la CEPAL: problemas de la industrialización en la América Latina" in Ffrench-Davis (1981).

———— (1981) *Capitalismo periférico. Crisis y transformación,* Mexico: Fondo de Cultura Económica.

———— (1982) "Monetarism, Open Economy Policies and the Ideological Crisis" in *CEPAL Review* 17 (August): 135–151.

PRICE, W. J. and L. W. BASS (1969) "Scientific Research and the Innovative Process" in *Science* 164: 802–806.

QUIJANO, A. (1974) "The Marginal Pole of the Economy and the Marginalized Labour Force" in *Economy and Society,* London: Routledge and Kegan.

RAM, R. (1986) "Government Size and Economic Growth: A New Framework and Some Evidence from Cross-Section and Time Series Data" in *The American Economic Review* 76 (March): 191–203.

RAMA, R. (1985) "Presencia y efectos de la inversión extranjera" in *Pensamiento Iberoamericano: Revista de Economía Política* 8 (July–December): 115–133.

RAMOS, J. (1986a) "Políticas de estabilización" in Cortázar (1986).

———— (1986b) *Neoconservative Economics in the Southern Cone of Latin America: 1973–1983,* Baltimore, MD: Johns Hopkins University Press.

———— (1989) "El enfoque neoestructuralista: reflexiones en torno a un seminario," mimeo, Santiago.

RAMSEY, F. P. (1928) "A Mathematical Theory of Saving" in *Economic Journal* 38 (December): 543–559.

RANIS, G. (1983) "Employment and Income Distribution Constraints in Latin America" in V. Urquidi and S. Trejos (comps.) *Human Resources, Employment and Development, vol. 4, Latin America,* London: The Macmillan Press.

REICH, M., D. M. GORDON, and R. EDWARDS (1975) *Labor Market Segmentation,* Lexington, MA: Lexington Books.

REYES-HEROLES, G. J. (1976) "Política fiscal y redistribución del ingreso" in *Tesis de Licenciatura,* Mexico: ITAM.

RODRÍGUEZ, O. (1980) *La Teoría del Subdesarrollo de la CEPAL,* Mexico: Editorial Siglo Veintiuno.

RODRÍGUEZ, E. and P. MORALES (1990) "Selección de actividades para el programa de reconversión industrial" in *Industrialización y dessarrollo tecnológico.* Informe No. 9, Naciones Unides, Division Conjunta CEPAL/ONUDI (August): 7–47.

RODRÍGUEZ, E. and S. WEISLEDER (1989) "Centroamérica y las biotecnologías: ¿oportunidades o amenazas?" in E. Rodríguez (ed.) *De cara al nuevo milenio,* San José: EUNED.

ROMERO, F. (1988) "Fondo Social de Emergencia. Bolivia." Document prepared for the High Level Seminar "Cómo Recuperar el Progreso Social en América Latina," IDE, ILPES, and UNICEF, Santiago.

ROS, J. (1988) "On Models of Inertial Inflation," mimeo (July), Helsinki: World Institute for Development Economics Research.

ROSALES, O. (1988a) "An Assessment of the Structuralist Paradigm for Latin American Development and the Prospect for its Renovation" in *CEPAL Review* 34 (April): 19–36.
———— (1988b) "El neoestructuralismo en América Latina" in *Pensamiento Iberoamericano: Revista de Economía Política* 14 (July–December): 394–406.
ROSENSTEIN-RODAN, P. (1943) "Problems of Industrialization of Eastern and South-Eastern Europe" in *Economic Journal* 53 (June–September): 202–211.
———— (1944) "The International Development of Economically Backward Areas" in *International Affairs* 20, No. 2 (April): 157–165.
———— (1957) *Notes on the Theory of the Big Push*, Cambridge, MA: MIT Center of International Studies.
ROSENTHAL, G. (1989) *Modernization of the State*. Statement presented to the Special Day of Collective Reflections on Latin America and the Caribbean, March 23, 1989, Paris.
RUFF, L. (1970) "The Economic Common Sense of Pollution" in *The Public Interest*, No. 19.
RYBCZYNSKI, T. (1955) "Factor Endowments and Relative Commodity Prices" in *Economica* 22: 336–341.
SAAVEDRA-RIVANO, N. and I. WOOTON (1983) "The Choice Between International Labour and Capital Mobility in a Dynamic Model of North-South Trade" in *Journal of International Economics* 14 (May): 251–261.
SABATINI, F. and R. JORDÁN (1986) *Crisis urbana: Elementos conceptuales para una aproximación ambiental*, CEPAL/LC/L.387.
SÁBATO, J. A. and M. MACKENZIE (1988) *La producción de tecnología*, Mexico: Editorial Nueva Imagen.
SABEL, C. (1982) *Work and Politics: The Division of Labour in Industry*, Cambridge: Cambridge Studies in Modern Political Economies, Cambridge University Press.
SACHAROPOULOS, G. (1989) "Recovering Growth with Equity." Document presented in seminar, "Growth, Equity and External Financing," Mexico, Universidad Autónoma de México.
SACHS, J. (1987) "Trade and Exchange-rate Policies in Growth-oriented Adjustment Programs" in V. Corbo, M. Goldstein, and M. Khan (eds.) *Growth-oriented Adjustment Programs*, Washington, DC: IMF and World Bank.
———— (1989a) "Social Conflict and Populist Policies in Latin America" in *National Bureau of Economic Research*, Working Paper Series No. 2897, Cambridge, MA.
———— (ed.) (1989b) *Developing Country Debt and the World Economy*, Chicago: University of Chicago Press.
SÁEZ, R. E. (1988) "La selectividad en la política industrial: las experiencias de Japón y Francia" in *Colección Estudios CIEPLAN* 25 (December): 55–77.
SALAZAR-XIRINACHS, J. M. (1986) "La visión de libre mercado sobre los incentivos económicos y la estrategia de desarrollo: una crítica teórica" in *Revista de Ciencias Económicas* 6, No. 1, San José, Costa Rica.
———— (1989) "Empresas públicas, privatización y desregulación: la definición de las fronteras entre lo público y lo privado," mimeo, Alternativas de Desarrollo, San José, Costa Rica.
SALAZAR-XIRINACHS, J. M. and E. DORYAN (1989) "La reconversión industrial y el estado concertador en Costa Rica" in *Pensamiento Iberoamericano: Revista de Economía Política* 17 (January–June): 69–90.
SAMANIEGO, N. (1986) "Los efectos de la crisis de 1982–1986 en las condiciones de vida de la población en México." ECLAC Reunión sobre Crisis

Externa: Proceso de Ajuste y su Impacto Inmediato y de Largo Plazo en el Desarrollo Social ¿Qué Hacer? November 25–28, 1986, Lima, Peru.

SAPSFORD, D. (1985) "The Statistical Debate on the Net Barter Terms of Trade Between Primary Commodities and Manufactures: A Comment and Some Additional Evidence" in *Economic Journal* 95 (September): 781–788.

SARGENT, T. (1981) "The End of Four Big Inflations," NBER Conference Paper No. 90 (January).

SARKAR, P. (1986) "The Terms of Trade Experience of Britain Since the Nineteenth Century" in *Journal of Development Studies* 23 (October): 20–39.

SARMIENTO, E. (1985) "The Imperfections of the Capital Market" in *CEPAL Review* 27 (December): 97–116.

SAVAS, E. S. (1987) *Privatization: The Key to Better Government,* Chatham, NJ: Chatham House Publishers.

SCANDIZZO, P. and D. DIAKOSAWAS (1987) "Instability in the Terms of Trade of Primary Commodities, 1900–1982" in *FAO Economic and Social Development Paper* 64, Rome: FAO.

SCHEJTMAN, A. (1985) "Sistemas alimentarios y opciones de estrategia" in *Pensamiento Iberoamericano: Revista de Economía Política* 8 (July–December): 37–68.

SCHERER, F. M. (1980) *Industrial Market Structure and Economic Performance,* Chicago: Rand McNally.

SCHMOOKLER, J. (1966) *Invention and Economic Growth,* Cambridge, MA: Harvard University Press.

SCHUMPETER, J. A. (1928) "The Instability of Capitalism" in *Economic Journal* 38 (September): 361–386.

―――― (1934) *The Theory of Economic Development,* Cambridge, MA: Harvard University Press.

―――― (1939) *Business Cycles: A Theoretical and Historical Analysis of the Capitalist Process,* New York: McGraw-Hill.

―――― (1943) *Capitalism, Socialism and Democracy,* New York: Harper and Row.

SCHYDLOWSKY, D. (1973) *International Trade Policy in the Economic Growth of Latin America,* Discussion Paper Series No. 5, CLADS: Boston University.

SEERS, D. (1964) "Inflation and Growth: The Heart of the Controversy" in Baer and Kerstenetzky (1964).

SELOWSKY, M. (1989) "Preconditions Necessary for the Recovery of Latin America's Growth." Paper presented to the Latin American Meeting of the World Economic Forum, June 22–23, 1989, Geneva.

SEN, A. (1983) "Development: Which Way Now?" in *Economic Journal* 93 (December): 742–764.

SERRA, J. and M. C. TAVARES (1974) "Más allá del estancamiento. Una discusión sobre el estilo del desarrollo reciente en Brasil" in J. Serra (1974) *Desarrollo latinoamericano: Ensayos críticos,* Lectura 6, Mexico: Fondo de Cultura Económica.

SERVAN-SCHREIBER, J. (1965) *The American Challenge,* Harmondsworth, U.K.: Penguin.

SHAW, E. S. (1973) *Financial Deepening in Economic Development,* Oxford: Oxford University Press.

SHEEHAN, J. (1980) "Market-oriented Economic Policies and Political Repression in Latin America" in *Economic Development and Cultural Change* 28 (January): 267–291.

―――― (1989) "Reducing Poverty in Latin America: Markets, Democracy, and Social Choice." Document presented at the meeting of The Latin American Studies Association, December 1989, Puerto Rico.

SIMONSEN, M. H. (1984) "Desindexacao e Reforma Monetaria" in *Conjuntura Económica* 38 (November): 101–105.

—— (1988) "Estabilización de precios y políticas de ingresos: Teoría y estudio de caso de Brasil" in Bruno et al. (1988).

SINGER, H. W. (1949) "Economic Progress in Under-Developed Countries" in *Social Research* 16 (March): 1–11.

—— (1950) "The Distribution of Gains between Investing and Borrowing Countries" in *American Economic Review* 15 (Papers and proceedings) (May): 473–485.

—— (1975) "The Distribution of Gains from Trade and Investment—Revisited" in *Journal of Development Studies* 11 (July): 376–382.

SJAASTAD, L. A. (1983) "Failure of Economic Liberalism in the Cone of Latin America" in *The World Economy* 6, no. 1 (March): 5–26.

SOETE, L. (1979) "Firm Size and Inventive Activity: The Evidence Reconsidered" in *European Economic Review* 12 (October): 319–340.

SOLIMANO, A. (1989), "How Private Investment Reacts to Changing Macroeconomic Adjustment," *World Bank Working Paper* WP 5212.

SOLOW, R. (1957) "Technical Change and the Aggregate Production Function" in *Review of Economics and Statistics* 39 (August): 312–20.

SOUZA, P. R. and V. E. TOKMAN (1978) "Distribución del ingreso, pobreza y empleo en áreas urbanas" in *El Trimestre Económico* 45 (July–September): 737–766.

SPRAOS, J. (1983) *Inequalizing Trade?* Oxford: Clarendon Press.

STANDING, G. (1986) "Labour Flexibility: Cause or Cure for Unemployment," International Institute for Labour Studies, Public Lectures No. 25, Geneva.

—— (1988) "European Unemployment Insecurity and Flexibility: A Social Dividend Solution," Labour Market Analysis and Employment Planning, ILO, Working Paper No. 23, Geneva.

STEGEMANN, K. (1989) "Policy Rivalry Among Industrial States: What Can We Learn from Models of Strategic Trade Policy?" in *International Organization* 43 (Winter): 73–100.

STEPAN, A. (1974) *The Military in Politics: Changing Patterns in Brazil*, Princeton, NJ: Princeton University Press.

—— (1978) *The State and Society: Peru in Comparative Perspective*, Princeton, NJ: Princeton University Press.

STEWART, F. (1982) "Industrialization, Technical Change and the International Division of Labour" in Helleiner (1982).

STIGLER, G. (1975) "The Economists' Traditional Theory of the Economic Functions of the State" in G. Stigler (ed.) *The Citizen and the State, Essays in Regulation*, Chicago.

STIGLITZ, J. E. (1985) "Information and Economic Analysis: A Perspective" in *Economic Journal* 95 (supplement 1985): 21–41.

STIGLITZ, J. E. and G. F. MATHEWSON (eds.) (1986) *New Developments in the Analysis of Market Structure*, Cambridge, MA: MIT Press.

STONEMAN, P. (1983) *The Economic Analysis of Technological Change*, Oxford: Oxford University Press.

SUNKEL, O. (1960) "Inflation in Chile, an Unorthodox Approach" in *International Economic Papers* 10: 107–131.

—— (1969) "National Development Policy and External Dependence in Latin America" in *Journal of Development Studies* 6 (October): 23–48.

—— (1973) "Transnational Capitalism and National Disintegration in Latin America" in *Social and Economic Studies* 22 (March): 132–176, Jamaica, University of West Indies.

—— (1979) "Transnationalization and its National Consequences" in J. J. Villamil (ed.) *Transnational Capitalism and National Development: New Perspectives on Dependence*, Hemel Hempstead: Harvester Press.

—— (1980) "The Interaction Between Styles of Development and the Environment in Latin America" in *CEPAL Review* 12 (December): 15–49.

—— (1981) *La dimensión ambiental en los estilos de desarrollo de América Latina*, E/CEPAL/G.1143, Santiago: ECLA/UNEP.

—— (1984) "Past, Present and Future of the International Economic Crisis" in *CEPAL Review* 22 (April): 81–105.

—— (1985) *América Latina y la crisis económica internacional: Ocho tesis y una propuesta*, Cuadernos del RIAL, Buenos Aires: Grupo Editor Latinoamericano, S.R.L.

—— (1987a) "Las Relaciones Centro-Periferia y la Transnacionalización" in *Pensamiento Iberoamericano: Revista de Economía Política* 11 (January–June): 31–52.

—— (1987b) "Beyond the World Conservation Strategy: Integrating Development and the Environment in Latin America" in P. Jacobs and D. A. Munro (eds.) *Conservation with Equity; Strategies for Sustainable Development*, Cambridge, U.K.: International Union for the Conservation of Nature.

—— (1989) "From Adjustment and Restructuring to Development" in J. Weeks (ed.) *Debt Disaster? Banks, Governments and Multilaterals Confront the Crisis*, New York and London: New York University Press.

—— (1990) "Reflections on Latin American Development" in J. L. Dietz and D. D. James, (eds.) *Progress Toward Development in Latin America*, Boulder, CO and London: Lynne Rienner Publishers.

SUNKEL, O. and N. GLIGO (eds.) (Vol. 1, 1980 and Vol. 2, 1982) *Estilos de desarrollo y medio ambiente en la América Latina*, Serie Lecturas No. 36, 2 vols., Mexico: Fondo de Cultura Económica.

SUNKEL, O. and P. PAZ (1970) *El subdesarrollo latinoamericano y la teoría del desarrollo*, Mexico: Siglo Veintiuno.

SUNKEL, O. and J. LEAL (1985) "Economía y medio ambiente en la perspectiva del desarrollo" in *El Trimestre Económico*, 205 (January–March): 3–35.

SYRQUIN, M. and S. TEITEL (1982) (eds.) *Trade, Stability, Technology and Equity in Latin America*, New York: Academic Press.

TANZI, V. (1977) "Inflation, Lags in Collection and the Real Value of Tax Revenue" in *IMF Staff Papers* 24 (March): 154–167.

TAVARES, M. C. (1973) "Distribuiçao de Renda, Acumulaçao e Padroes de Industrializaçao" in *A controversia sobre Distribuicao de Renda e Desenvolvimento*, Rio de Janeiro: Zahar Editores.

TAVARES, M. C. and J. SERRA (1971) "Más allá del estancamiento: una discusión sobre el estilo de desarrollo reciente en Brasil" in *El Trimestre Económico* 33 (October–December): 905–950.

TAYLOR, L. (1981) "IS/LM in the Tropics: Diagrammatics of the New Structuralist Macro Critique" in W. Cline and S. Weintraub (eds.) *Economic Stabilization in Developing Countries*, Washington, DC: The Brookings Institution.

—— (1983) *Structuralist Macroeconomics: Applicable Models for the Third World*, New York: Basic Books.

—— (1987) "Varieties of Stabilization Experiences—Toward Sensible Macroeconomics in the Third World," mimeo, MIT.

THIRLWALL, A. P. (1983) "Foreign Trade Elasticities in Centre-Periphery Models of Growth and Development" in *Banca Nazionale del Lavoro Quarterly Review* 36: 249–261.

THOMAS, C. Y. (1974) *Dependence and Transformation: The Economics of Transition to Socialism*, New York: Monthly Review Press.

TIRONI, E. (1989) "Mercado de Trabajo y Violencia," PREALC, Documento de trabajo No. 335, Santiago.

TODARO, M. P. (1989) *Economic Development in the Third World*, New York: Longman.

TOKMAN, V. E. (1975) *Distribución del ingreso, tecnología y empleo, Análisis del sector industrial en el Ecuador, Perú y Venezuela*, serie Cuadernos del ILPES, No. 23, Santiago: CEPAL/ILPES.

——— (1978) "An Exploration into the Nature of the Informal-Formal Sector Relationship" in *World Development* 6 (September–October): 1065–1075.

——— (1981) "La influencia del sector informal sobre la desigualdad económica" in *El Trimestre Económico* 48 (October–December): 931–964.

——— (1982) "Unequal Development and the Absorption of Labour: Latin America (1950–1980)" in *CEPAL Review* 17 (August): 121–133.

——— (1984) "Global Monetarism and Destruction of Industry" in *CEPAL Review* 23 (August): 106–121.

——— (1985) "The Process Accumulation and the Weakness of the Protagonists" in *CEPAL Review* 26 (August): 115–126.

——— (1987) "Progreso técnico, empleo y desarticulación social" in *Pensamiento Iberoamericano: Revista de Economía Política* 11 (January–July): 401–418.

——— (1988) "Urban Employment: Research and Policy in Latin America" in *CEPAL Review* 34 (April): 109–126.

TOKMAN, V. E. and N. GARCIA (1981) *Dinámica del Subempleo en América Latina*, Estudios e Informes de la CEPAL No. 10 (August).

TRIVEDI, P. (1988) "Theory and Practice of the French System of Contracts for Improving Public Enterprise Performance: Some Lessons for LDCs" in *Public Enterprise* 8 (January–March): 28–42.

UNCTAD (1986) *Salient Features of Trends and Policies in Trade of Manufactures and Semi-Manufactures*, Geneva: United Nations.

UNIKEL, L. and A. NECOCHEA (1975) "Desarrollo urbano y regional en América Latina," Serie Lecturas No. 15, Mexico: Fondo de Cultura Económica.

UNITED NATIONS (1975) *Yearbook of International Trade Statistics*.

——— (1981) *Yearbook of International Trade Statistics*.

UNIVERSIDAD NACIONAL AGRARIA LA MOLINA and CENTRO DE ESTUDIOS RURALES ANDINO BARTOLOMÉ DE LAS CASAS (1986) *Estrategias para el desarrollo de la sierra*, Cuzco, Peru.

VAITSOS, C. (1979) "Government Policies for Bargaining with Transnational Enterprises in the Acquisition of Technology" in J. Ramesh and C. Weiss (eds.) *Mobilizing Technology for World Development*, New York: Praeger.

VARAS, A. (1988) "Militares y Armas en América Latina" in *Revista Nueva Sociedad* 30 (October): 98–110.

VERGARA, I. and F. PIZARRO (1981) *Manual sobre control de derrames de petróleo*, Santiago: CEPAL.

VERNON, R. (1966) "International Investment and International Trade in the Product Cycle" in *Quarterly Journal of Economics* 80 (May): 190–207.

——— (1971) *Sovereignty at Bay*, London: Longman.

——— (1987) "Economic Aspects of Privatization Programs," World Bank, EDI.

——— (ed.) (1988) *The Promise of Privatization: A Challenge for U.S. Policy*, New York: Council on Foreign Relations.

VIDART, D. (1980) "Amazonia: Los ecosistemas y los hombres" in *Ciencia Tecnología Desarrollo* 4 (January–March): 1–114.

VIETORITZ, T. and B. HARRISON (1973) "Labour Market Segmentation: Positive Feedback and Divergent Development" in *American Economic Review* 63 (Papers and proceedings) (May): 366–376.

VILLARREAL, R. (1984) *La contrarrevolución monetarista*, Mexico: Ediciones Océano.

VINES, D. (1984) "A North-South Growth Model Along Kaldorian Lines," mimeo (July), Permbroke College, Cambridge University.

VUSKOVIC, P. (1974) "Distribución del ingreso y opciones de desarrollo" in Serra and Tavares (1974).

WALSH, V. (1984) "Invention and Innovation in the Chemical Industry: Demand-pull or Discovery-push?" in *Research Policy* 13, no 4 (August): 211–234.

WALSH, V., B. TOWNSEND, B. ACHILLADELIS, and C. FREEMAN (1979) *Trends in Invention and Innovation in the Chemical Industry*, Brighton, U.K.: University of Sussex, mimeo.

WARD, B. and R. DUBOS (1972) *Una sola tierra: El cuidado y conservación de un pequeño planeta*, Mexico: Fondo de Cultura Económica.

WATKINS, M. H. (1963) "A Staple Theory of Economic Growth" in *The Canadian Journal of Economics and Political Science* 29 (May): 141–158.

WEBB, R. (1972) "The Distribution of Income in Peru," Discussion Paper No. 26 (September), Princeton, NJ: Princeton University Press.

——— (1974) *Income and Employment in the Urban Modern and Traditional Sectors of Peru*, Princeton, NJ: Princeton University Press.

WEISSKOPF, R. (1970) "Income Distribution and Economic Growth in Puerto Rico, Argentina, and Mexico" in *Review of Income and Wealth* 16 (December): 303–332.

WERNECK, R. (ed.) (1988) *Ahorro e inversión en Latinoamérica*, CIID/IDRC (November).

WESTPHAL, L. E. (1984) "Fostering Technological Mastery by Means of Selective Infant-Industry Protection" in M. Syrquin and S. Teitel (eds.) *Trade, Stability, Technology and Equity in Latin America*, New York: Academic Press.

WILLIAMSON, J. (ed.) (1981) *The Crawling-peg: Past Performance and Future Prospects*, London: Macmillan.

——— (1983) *The Open Economy and the World Economy*, New York: Basic Books.

WIONCZEK, M. S. (ed.) (1985) *Politics and Economics of External Debt Crisis: The Latin American Experience*, Boulder, CO: Westview Press.

WORLD BANK (1983) *World Development Report 1983*, Washington, DC.

——— (1986) *World Development Report 1986*, Washington, DC.

——— (1988a) "Half-yearly Revision of Commodity Price Forecasts—December 1987," mimeo (January).

——— (1988b) *World Development Report 1988*, chapter 8, "Strengthening of Public Finance Through Reform of State-Owned Enterprises," Washington, DC.

WORLD BANK and IMF (1987) "Market prospects of raw materials," mimeo (January).

WORLD RESOURCES INSTITUTE (1988) *World Resources 1988–1989*, New York: Basic Books.

YARROW, G. (1986) "Privatization in Theory and Practice" in *Public Policy*, No. 3.

YOSHIKAWA, A. (1988) "Technology Transfer and National Science Policy: Biotechnology Policy in Japan" in *Technology Management Publications*, No. 1.

YUSUF, S. and R. K. PETERS (1985) "Capital Accumulation and Economic Growth: The Korean Paradigm" in *World Bank Staff Working Papers*, No. 712, Washington, DC.

ZAHLER, R. (1988) "Estrategias financieras latinoamericanas: la experiencia del Cono Sur" in *Colección Estudios CIEPLAN* 23, Special issue (March): 117–143.

ZUCKERMAN, E. (1989) *Adjustment Programs and Social Welfare*, Washington, DC: World Bank.

About the Contributors

Adolfo Figueroa, a Peruvian economist, holds a Ph.D. from Vanderbilt University. He has served as professor at the Economics Institute of the Pontificia Universidad Católica del Perú since 1970. He also held the post of technical coordinator of the ECIEL Program (Estudios Conjuntos sobre Integración Económica Latinoamericana) for the project on "Productivity and Education in Rural Latin America" and has acted as consultant for the Food and Agriculture Organization of the United Nations and the International Labour Office in projects dealing with problems in agricultural development. Some of his most noted publications include *La economía campesina de la sierra del Perú* and *Capitalist Development and the Peasant Economy in Peru*.

Ricardo Ffrench-Davis, a Chilean economist, holds a Ph.D. from the University of Chicago and is postgraduate professor at Instituto de Estudios Internacionales and the School of Engineering at the Universidad de Chile. He has held the post of director and vice-president of the Corporación de Investigaciones Económicas para Latinoamérica (CIEPLAN) since its creation. He has also worked as a consultant for the United Nations, the Inter-American Development Bank, and the International Labour Office. His publications include *Políticas económicas en Chile, 1952–70* and *Economía internacional: teorías y políticas para el desarrollo*. He was a member of the United Nations Development Committee and director, studies department, Central Bank of Chile. He is currently principal regional adviser, ECLAC.

Winston Fritsch, a Brazilian economist and engineer, holds a Ph.D. from Cambridge University. A former dean of the Social Studies Center and professor in the Economics Department at the Pontificia Universidad Católica de Río de Janeiro, he has worked as a consultant for several agencies of the United Nations, the Organization for Economic Co-Operation and Development, the Latin American Economic System, the Central Bank of Brazil, and the Banco Nacional de Desarrollo Económico y Social. He has written several studies on international economics, trade, and development for both Brazilian and international journals.

Nicolo Gligo, a Chilean agricultural scientist and agricultural economist, taught agricultural development and planning at the School of Agricultural Science, Universidad de Chile, where he headed the Economic and Social Sciences Department. He has also taught agricultural economics at the Universidad Nacional de Buenos Aires. He has written many articles and books, including *Agricultura y medio ambiente en América Latina.* At present, he holds the post of coordinator of the ECLAC/UNEP Joint Unit for Development and the Environment at the United Nations Economic Commission for Latin America and the Caribbean.

Nora Lustig, a Mexican economist, holds a Ph.D. from the University of California at Berkeley and is a professor at the Centro de Estudios Económicos del Colegio de México and a Visiting Fellow at the Brookings Institution. She has worked as an adviser to the Mexican government and an economic and social consultant for the Nicaraguan Ministry of Agriculture. She has also served as a United Nations official at the Mexican and Central American Office of ECLAC. Her publications include *Distribución del ingreso y crecimiento en México. Un análisis de las ideas estructuralistas* and "Economic Crisis Adjustment and Living Standards in Mexico, 1982–85."

Oscar Muñoz Gomá, a Chilean economist, holds a Ph.D. from Yale University. He has taught at the Schools of Economics at the Universidad de Chile and the Universidad Católica and at the Industrial Engineering Department at the Universidad Diego Portales. He has also been a visiting professor at major universities in the United States. Since 1976 he has done research at CIEPLAN, where he was executive director from 1979 until 1981. He has written several articles and books on economic development, industrialization, income distribution, and Chilean economic history. Some of his most recent publications are *Chile y su industrialización: pasado, crisis y opciones* and "Estado, desarrollo y Equidad: algunas preguntas pendientes." At present, he is chairperson of CIEPLAN's board of directors.

José Antonio Ocampo, a Colombian economist, holds a Ph.D. from Yale University. During his significant public career in Colombia, he has held posts such as executive director of Fundación para la Educación Superior y el Desarrollo (1984–1988), national coordinator of the Employment Mission (1985–1986), and adviser to the Colombian government on coffee affairs (1989–1990). He has taught at the Department of Economics, Universidad de Los Andes (1976–1984 and 1988), where he was director of its Center for Development Studies (1980–1982). He has written several articles and books and is co-author and editor of various volumes dealing mainly with international trade and finance, macroeconomics, development, and Colombian economic history. He is currently adviser to the Colombian Foreign Trade Board.

Joseph Ramos, an economist and engineer from the United States, holds a Ph.D. from Columbia University. For over twenty years he has worked as a professor and economic analyst in areas dealing with employment, development, price stabilization, adjustment, and income distribution. He has been adviser to several Latin American governments in the ministries of finance, planning, and labor and in the central banks. He was employed by the International Labour Office in the Regional Employment Program for Latin America and the Caribbean and as a researcher for Facultad Latinoamericana de Ciencias Sociales. He has written four books and numerous articles for international academic journals. Among his most important works is *Neoconservative Economics in the Southern Cone of Latin America: 1973–1983*. He is currently heading the Industry and Technology Division of ECLAC.

Ennio Rodríguez, a Costa Rican economist, holds a Ph.D. from Sussex University and is a professor at the Universidad de Costa Rica. He is a former member of the governing council of the Consejo Nacional de Investigaciones Científicas y Tecnológicas and of the Junta Administradora para el Desarrollo de la Cordillera Central, as well as former program director of the Federación de Entidades Privadas para Centroamérica y Panamá and minister of foreign financing and external debt. Recently appointed coordinator of an ECLAC project to develop a strategy for investment planning for Central America, he has served in several public and private capacities, among them, secretary of plans and programs of the Liberación Nacional Party. He has published widely on economic development topics in several books and journals. His most recent books are *Cross-conditionality, Banking Regulations and Third World Debt, El desafío del desarrollo centroamericano,* and *De cara al nuevo milenio.*

José Manuel Salazar-Xirinachs, a Costa Rican economist, holds a Ph.D. from Cambridge University. He has taught at the Universidad de Costa Rica, the Universidad Nacional, and Cambridge University and worked as a consultant for the World Bank during 1987–1988 in the area of agricultural policy and as adviser to the Costa Rican ministries of planning and agriculture. Some of his major publications include "La visión del libre mercado sobre los incentivos económicos y la estrategia de desarrollo. Una crítica Teórica" and "La reconversión industrial y el Estado concertador en Costa Rica" (with Eduardo Doryan). He was until recently executive president of Corporación Costarricense de Desarrollo.

Osvaldo Sunkel, a Chilean economist, holds a degree in economics and business administration from the Universidad de Chile and was a postgraduate research student at the London School of Economics. He taught at the Faculty of Economics and the Instituto de Estudios Internacionales, Universidad de Chile, from 1955 to 1973, has been visiting professor at several Latin American, US, and European universities and research centers, and was professorial fellow at the Institute of Development Studies, Sussex University between 1975 and 1986. He has held the posts of director, ECLAC office in Brazil (1959–1961), director of the training program (1962–1965) and the research program (1965–1968) of the Latin American Institute for Economic and Social Planning, and coordinator of the ECLAC/UNEP Development and Environment Program (1978–1988). He has written extensively on inflation, development, international relations, economic history, and the environment. His most important works include *El subdesarrollo latinoamericano y la teoría del desarrollo* (the most recent edition, the twenty-second, in collaboration with Pedro Paz) and *Debt and Development Crises in Latin America: The End of an Illusion* (in collaboration with Stephany Griffith-Jones). At present, he holds the posts of special adviser to the executive secretary, ECLAC; director, *Pensamiento Iberoamericano. Revista de Economía Política*; and president, Corporación de Investigaciones para el Desarrollo.

Víctor E. Tokman, an Argentinian economist, holds a Ph.D. from Oxford University. Visiting fellow at Sussex University and Yale University, as well as professor at the Catholic and National universities of Chile and PREALC and ILPES, he has worked in ECLAC (1964–1965), OAS in Washington, D.C. (1967–1979), and ILPES (1970–1973), and between 1973 and 1988 held the post of director at PREALC. He has written several books and articles on subjects dealing with Latin American development, especially in relation to employment, wages, and income distribution. His best-known contribution to analysis of the informal sector is "An Exploration into the Nature of the Informal-Formal Sector Relationship." His most recent books are *Beyond Regulation: The Informal Economy in Latin America* (Rienner, forthcoming) and *Towards Social Adjustment: Labour Market Issues in Structural Adjustment* (in collaboration with G. Standing). He was director of ILO's employment and development department in Geneva from 1988 to August 1991. As of September 1, 1991 he has again taken over the direction of PREALC.

Index

About the Book

Bringing up to date the well-known Latin American structuralist literature of the 1950s and 1960s on economic development, this book offers a neostructuralist alternative to the neoliberal adjustment policies now so widely advocated.

The book covers the main themes of the development problematique in Latin America: the region's historical background, the consequent nature of its development strategy, the use of its resources, the evolution of its key economic sectors (agriculture and industry), the new external economic environment, and—last, but far from least—the changing role of the state.

In addressing each of these topics, the authors review the relevant early structuralist thinking, critically examine the actual development experience of the 1950s through 1970s, analyze the debt crisis of the 1980s and its consequences, and conclude with a neostructuralist response to contemporary national and international conditions.